Public Relations in Global Cultural Contexts

While public relations practice has become increasingly globalized, scholars are still behind in theorizing about the intersections of culture, communication, and power at this level of practice. This volume emphasizes theories and concepts that highlight global interconnectedness through a range of interpretative and critical approaches to understanding the global significance and impacts of public relations.

Providing a critical examination of public relations' contribution to globalization and international power relations, the chapters included here explore alternative paradigms, most notably interpretive and critical perspectives informed by qualitative research. The volume encourages alternative 'ways of knowing' that overcome the shortcomings of positivist epistemologies. The editors include multiple paradigmatic approaches for a more complex understanding of the subject matter, making a valuable contribution toward widening the philosophical scope of public relations scholarship.

This book will serve well as a core text in classes in international public relations, global public relations, and advanced strategic public relations. Students as well as practitioners of public relations will benefit from reading the perspectives included here.

Nilanjana Bardhan is an Associate Professor in the Department of Speech Communication at Southern Illinois University – Carbondale, USA. She teaches and conducts research in the areas of public relations (especially in global contexts) and intercultural/international communication. She has practitioner experience in India and in the US, and her scholarship has appeared in a number of edited book collections and journals such as the *Journal of Public Relations Research, Journal of Communication Management, Communication Education, Mass Communication and Society,* and the *Journal of Health Communication.*

C. Kay Weaver is a Professor in the Department of Management Communication at the University of Waikato, New Zealand. She has taught across the fields of public relations, communication, media, and film studies in the UK and New Zealand. Her research has been published in a number of books and edited collections and in journals such as *Public Relations Review, Journal of Public Relations Research, Journal of Applied Communication Research, Media, Culture & Society, New Media & Society,* and *Feminist Media Studies.*

Communication Series
Jennings Bryant/Dolf Zillmann, General Editors

Selected Titles in Public Relations (James E. Grunig, advisory editor) include:

Strategic Public Relations Management
Planning and Managing Effective Communication Programs, Second Edition
Austin/Pinkleton

Gaining Influence in Public Relations
The Role of Resistance in Practice
Berger/Reber

Public Relations Theory II
Botan/Hazleton

Crisis Communications
A Casebook Approach, Fourth Edition
Fearn-Banks

Crisis Management by Apology
Corporate Response to Allegations of Wrongdoing
Hearit

Applied Public Relations
Cases in Stakeholder Management, Second Edition
McKee/Lamb

Public Relations in Global Cultural Contexts

Multi-Paradigmatic Perspectives

Edited by
Nilanjana Bardhan
C. Kay Weaver

 Routledge
Taylor & Francis Group

NEW YORK AND LONDON

First published 2011
by Routledge
270 Madison Avenue, New York, NY 10016

Simultaneously published in the UK
by Routledge
2 Park Square, Milton Park, Abingdon, Oxon OX14 4RN

Routledge is an imprint of the Taylor & Francis Group, an informa business

Typeset in Sabon and Gill Sans by EvS Communication Networx, Inc.
Printed and bound in the United States of America on acid-free paper by
Walsworth Publishing Co., Marceline, MO.

The right of Nilanjana Bardhan and C. Kay Weaver to be identified as the
authors of the editorial material, and of the authors for their individual
chapters, has been asserted in accordance with sections 77 and 78 of the
Copyright, Designs and Patents Act 1988.

Library of Congress Cataloging in Publication Data
Public relations in global cultural contexts : multi-paradigmatic perspectives /
edited by Nilanjana Bardhan, C. Kay Weaver.
p. cm.
Includes index.
1. Public relations. 2. Public relations—Cross-cultural studies. I. Bardhan,
Nilanjana. II. Weaver, C. Kay, 1964-
HM1221.P7844 2010
659.2—dc22
2010024798

ISBN 13: 978-0-415-87285-0 (hbk)
ISBN 13: 978-0-415-87286-7 (pbk)
ISBN 13: 978-0-203-86615-3 (ebk)

Contents

List of Figures and Tables

Figures

Tables

Preface

This book brings together essays by public relations scholars geographically located across three continents, and with cultural roots and affiliations in more. These scholars answered our call to put together a volume that would focus on two greatly understudied concepts in public relations scholarship—globalization and culture. No two concepts could be more important for our profession today. While practitioners in the industry have been working daily in global cultural contexts and grappling with the complexities of this experience, scholarship still lags behind in interrogating and theorizing the relationship between globalization and culture as it relates to public relations.

Globalization, in its current form, has blurred many boundaries and neat categories of modernist thought. As a result, it has made the messy concept of culture even messier. In order to present a range of research positions on public relations, globalization, and culture, we decided that including perspectives from public relations scholars working out of different paradigmatic positions would be most useful for our readers. Our contributors, as a collective, emphasize theories and concepts that highlight cultural and global interconnectedness through interpretative, critical/cultural, postmodern, and social scientific approaches. In doing so, they help us better understand how public relations is constituted by and constitutive of global flux. Hence, our readers will encounter various epistemological viewpoints, some of which may be conflicting, but all of which carry the potential for dialogue across paradigms about the role of public relations in a global capacity. It is our hope that students, scholars, and practitioners of public relations will benefit from such a wide range of perspectives.

We emphasize that we do not use the term *global* in the title of this book in a monolithic or homogenizing sense. The discourse of globalization (and culture) is far from fixed and it would be hard to argue "global" public relations is a necessarily definable entity. Therefore, our use of the term *global* is more indicative of the domain of practice; that is, a domain that is increasingly spanning the globe. We deliberately shied away from prescribing an interpretation for the term so our contributors could be flexible in how they used and theorized it in their chapters.

We would like to thank Linda Bathgate at Routledge for her enthusiasm for our initial proposal, and for her encouragement and support throughout the writing and preparation process. We would also like to thank Katherine Ghezzi for her editorial assistance. Our thanks also go out to Jennings Bryant, James Grunig, and an anonymous reviewer of our proposal for their valuable feedback which helped us improve upon our vision for this book. And of course, this volume would not have been possible without our contributors and their insights. Nilanjana would like to thank colleagues and mentors, in particular Hugh Culbertson at Ohio University and Tee Ford Ahmed at West Virginia State University, who have been instrumental in her growth as a teacher-scholar in the field. Kay would like to thank her colleagues in the Department of Management Communication at the University of Waikato for a decade of support and engaging discussions about public relations practice and scholarship.

Nilanjana Bardhan and C. Kay Weaver

About the Contributors

John Baldwin is Professor of Communication at Illinois State University. His research and teaching interests include domestic and international diversity (e.g., interethnic and intercultural communication), especially issues of group difference and intolerance. His research includes studies on sexual harassment, ethnic stereotypes and communication, and the communication of racial and national identity in Brazilian rock and roll music. He has several journal articles and book chapters in intercultural communication readers and an entry on Western communication in *The International Encyclopedia of Communication*. He recently coedited a book, *Redefining Culture*, that analyzes the notion of "culture" from several different disciplinary perspectives.

Nilanjana Bardhan is Associate Professor in the Department of Speech Communication at Southern Illinois University—Carbondale. She teaches and conducts research in the areas of public relations (especially in global contexts) and intercultural/international communication. She has practitioner experience in India and in the United States, and her scholarship has appeared in venues such as the *Journal of Public Relations Research, Journal of Communication Management, Communication Education, Mass Communication and Society* and the *Journal of Health Communication*. She has also authored/coauthored several book chapters and has presented several conference papers.

Jensen Chung is Professor at San Francisco State University, where he teaches corporate communication, organizational communication, leadership communication, and group communication. He has also published journal articles in these areas. He was a government spokesperson and has consulting experiences in organizational leadership communication and public relations in the United States and in parts of Asia. The author of two books in Chinese, he has completed his third book (in English) on the *chi* theory of communication he developed.

Jeffrey Courtright, Associate Professor in the School of Communication at Illinois State University, studies public relations using rhetorical theory and criticism. With Peter Smudde, he edited the book *Power and Public Relations* and is coauthor of *Inspiring Cooperation and Celebrating Organizations*. He has published articles in *Corporate Reputation Review, International Journal of Strategic Communication,* and other journals in public relations, communication, and mass media. He has authored several book chapters and has over 75 scholarly papers to his credit.

Mohan Jyoti Dutta is Professor of Communication and Director of Graduate Studies in the Department of Communication at Purdue University. He teaches and conducts research in public relations theory, critical and cultural approaches to public relations, health communication, globalization and social change, resistance in the subaltern sectors, and postcolonial theory. His most recent work on communication for social change is presented in the culture-centered approach, emphasizing the role of transformative politics of participatory communication in creating global spaces of structural transformation. As a practitioner and performer, he engages in activist projects in collaboration with marginalized communities across the globe. He is the author of *Communicating Health: A Culture-Centered Approach,* and coeditor of *Emerging Perspectives In Health Communication: Meaning, Culture, and Power* and *Communicating for Social Impact: Engaging communication theory, research, and Pedagogy.* He has also published approximately 90 articles and book chapters.

Lee Edwards is a Lecturer in Public Relations and Corporate Communications at Manchester Business School, part of the University of Manchester. She holds a PhD focusing on the nature of power in public relations. She adopts a critical approach to public relations and has published in the *Journal of Public Relations Research, Public Relations Review, Management Communication Quarterly,* and the 2010 edition of the *Handbook of Public Relations.* As a practitioner, Edwards specialized in technology public relations and worked with some of the largest global technology brands.

Derina Holtzhausen is Professor and Director of the School of Journalism and Broadcasting at Oklahoma State University. She is a native South African and naturalized U.S. citizen, with 24 years experience as communications practitioner, entrepreneur, and executive, and 14 years as a professor, researcher, and academic administrator. Her practitioner background includes experience in the financial sector, the tourism sector, public relations counseling, and journalism. Holtzhausen often acts as a guest lecturer on communication management, strategic planning, and organizational communication and still consults in the field. She is a founding editor of the *International Journal of Strategic Communication*. She is a recipient of the Pathfinder Award from the U.S. Institute of Public Relations for her original research agenda on postmodern public relations, and has published 18 articles and book chapters and presented more than 30 conference papers. Her recent book is titled *Public Relations as Activism*.

Michael Kent is Associate Professor of Public Relations at the University of Oklahoma's Gaylord College of Journalism and Mass Communication. He received his doctoral degree from Purdue University. Kent studies public relations technology, dialogue, and mediated public relations. He has written more than 40 articles and book chapters on public relations and communication, some of which have been published in the *Public Relations Review, Public Relations Quarterly, Gazette*, and *Critical Studies in Media Communication*. Kent was a Fulbright Scholar to Riga, Latvia, in 2006, and has published a public relations writing textbook.

Mahuya Pal received her PhD from Purdue University and is Assistant Professor in the Department of Communication at the University of South Florida. Specializing in the area of organizational communication, her research focuses on how the neoliberal economy creates conditions of marginality. Pal's research has appeared in the *Journal of Public Relations Research, Journal of Business Communication*, and *Communication Yearbook*.

Maureen Taylor is Professor and Gaylord Family Chair of Strategic Communication in the Gaylord College of Journalism and Mass Communication at the University of Oklahoma. She earned a PhD in public affairs and issues management from Purdue University in 1996. Taylor's research interest is in international public relations, nation building and civil society campaigns, and new communication technologies. She has conducted research in Malaysia, Taiwan, Bosnia, Croatia, Kosovo, Jordan, and Sudan. In 2001, she served as a Fulbright Scholar at the University of Sarajevo, Bosnia-Herzegovina. Taylor's work has appeared in the *Journal of Public Relations Research, Public Relations Review, Communication Monographs, Human Communication Research, Journal of Communication, Management Communication Quarterly, Gazette*, and the *Atlantic Journal of Communication*.

Robert Wakefield is Associate Professor of Communication at Brigham Young University. He received a PhD from the University of Maryland in 1997. He concentrates his research on stakeholder relations and reputation in transnational entities, examining the impacts of globalization, culture, activism, and other factors on these global practices of public relations. Wakefield practiced and consulted on strategic public relations in 25 nations between 1990 and 2005. Some of his recent research has appeared in the *Journal of Communication Management, Journal of Public Relations Research,* and *Public Relations Journal.*

C. Kay Weaver is Professor in the Department of Management Communication at the University of Waikato, New Zealand, and Convenor of Waikato Management School's PhD program. She teaches public relations, communication theory, and advanced research methods papers. She has published in journals such as *Public Relations Review, Journal of Public Relations Research, Media, Culture & Society, New Media & Society,* and *Feminist Media Studies.* She is coauthor of *Cameras in the Commons, Women Viewing Violence,* and *Violence and the Media,* and is coeditor of *Critical Readings: Violence and the Media.*

Rachel Wolfe received her MS in Communication from Illinois State University, focusing on intercultural and international public relations practices. After receiving her degree, she accepted a position as a senior market research analyst at Caterpillar, Inc. She generates directional insights collected from the voices of customer research for Caterpillar's products and services worldwide.

Chapter I

Introduction

Public Relations in Global Cultural Contexts

Nilanjana Bardhan and C. Kay Weaver

> If we are to attempt to understand the world in the new century, we cannot but come to grips with the concept of globalization.
>
> (Appelbaum & Robinson, 2005, p. xi)

> Globalization has not only increased the importance of "global" public relations but has also provided the opportunity for introspection and self-critique about the practice and scholarship.
>
> (Sriramesh, 2009a, p. 9)

We hear it everywhere. It is a prominent refrain in the discourse of public relations practitioners and scholars. Public relations has gone global. But what does "global public relations" mean in the life world of our field, and what are the implications of globalization for public relations scholarship and practice? The last two decades have radically changed the way people, organizations, and systems communicate and operate across national and cultural borders. While old ways of theorizing about the functions and sociocultural role of public relations are inadequate for conceptualizing new globalizing realities, they are not completely erased either. In other words, we are at an in-between point in our thinking about these matters. Questions related to globalization cannot be theorized by simply reusing dated frames of thinking, and yet, partly as a consequence of critical reactions against them, these frames have provided the impetus for the emergence of new questions. This book maneuvers through this in-between space in order to stretch our thinking and scholarship around public relations in global cultural contexts in newly productive directions.

As educators and scholars of public relations, we have noted three major gaps in the public relations body of knowledge. First, the phenomenon of globalization has not been addressed in all its complexity and remains under theorized and unpoliticized in the field. Second, the concept of culture also needs to be theorized in much more complex terms

2 Nilanjana Bardhan and C. Kay Weaver

within public relations scholarship, especially in terms of its intersections with globalization. Within the current conditions of transnational flows and processes, culture has become increasingly deterritorialized and cultural identities have become fragmented (Sison, 2009). The meager theorizing on culture that does exist in our scholarship (Sriramesh, 2007) predominantly conceptualizes culture as static, clearly definable, and synonymous with territory. Additionally, the nation-state is still, problematically, conceptualized as the natural container of culture (Berking, 2003). Third, there has been insufficient focus on the range of possible paradigmatic approaches in the study of public relations. The social scientific (modernist) systems functionalist approach still dominates the field. The applied focus of this approach has been important to the profession in terms of promoting and stimulating debate about how public relations is and should be practiced. However, equally important are other approaches that question dominant models and beliefs and offer alternative ways of understanding the functions and effects of public relations practice. For example, there is a need for further inclusion of critical/cultural, interpretive, and postmodern approaches that theorize public relations as playing a significant role in the social construction of reality, and which interrogate how power permeates the processes of public relations in a global (dis)order where inequality is endemic (Shome & Hedge, 2002). The relationships between culture, communication, context, and power (Martin & Nakayama, 2010) in practice (as well as in scholarship) needs to be a key focus if we are to stay intellectually current (McKie, 2001), keep providing suggestions for how to improve practice, and genuinely engage with questions of ethics and social responsibility in public relations in a rapidly globalizing and interconnected world.

The purpose of this book is to address these three gaps. While some public relations scholarship has started exploring the complexities of globalization, the nature and role of culture, identity, and power in public relations (e.g., Curtin & Gaither, 2007), and is questioning the adequacy of only a social scientific functional approach to the field, no single volume exists that specifically brings these three issues under one umbrella. The aim of this book is to begin the work of filling these lacunae.

In the 1990s, public relations scholarship started engaging in paradigm debates. Very simply, a paradigm is the research worldview that scholars subscribe to in order to produce what they consider valid knowledge (Guba & Lincoln, 2008; Kuhn, 1996; Mittelman, 2004). While we lean toward the critical paradigm in this book, we have opted for a multiparadigmatic and dialectical stance that is open to all perspectives and values each for what it contributes toward strengthening the public relations body of knowledge. All paradigmatic approaches have something useful to contribute toward knowledge production (Martin

& Nakayama, 1999), and even if they are sometimes contradictory to each other, the tensions generated through contradiction can work to stimulate further theoretical debate and reflection (Botan, 1993). It is also important that public relations scholars are able to engage in dialogue that acknowledges the philosophical grounding of the paradigm(s) which they are affiliated to, and the differences and similarities between different paradigms. Simply rejecting out of hand those who hold different philosophical positions is not what we advocate because this can lead to unproductive sparring that simply attempts to prove that one paradigm is better than others. Respecting philosophical differences and identifying the various merits and contributions that different paradigmatic perspectives bring to understanding both the practice and social, cultural, political, and economic significance of public relations in a multicultural world is what we advocate.

In this book, we opt out of the *either*-or approach to the paradigmatic debate and are vested in what we believe is a more fruitful *both*-and perspective that does not privilege any one paradigm as superior to others. The chapters within this volume theorize the complexities of globalization and culture and, along with these, power, as they apply to public relations, from critical/cultural, interpretive, postmodern, and social scientific perspectives. Such multiparadigmatic knowledge is essential for educators, scholars, students, and practitioners engaged in public relations in global cultural contexts to include in their theoretical toolboxes.

This introductory chapter charts out public relations in the context of globalization, notes the dynamic nature of culture and the current deficiencies in how it is theorized in public relations research, foregrounds the range of paradigmatic approaches in public relations scholarship, emphasizes some of the specific concerns of critical approaches, and concludes with a brief overview of the chapters in this volume.

Public Relations in the Climate of Globalization

There is no one theory or definition of globalization that can account for all of its complexities. The study of globalization is interdisciplinary, and the phenomenon has been theorized from cultural, economic, political, critical, postcolonial, and neoliberal (to name a few) perspectives (see Appelbaum & Robinson, 2005; Held & McGrew, 2000). Some scholars argue that globalization in its current form is just the latest phase, albeit a phase distinctly marked by hyper "technological revolution and global restructuring of capital" (Kellner, 2002, p. 287), in a process that is centuries old and started when humans began to cross borders and boundaries for purposes such as trade, spreading of religion, and colonization of other lands (see S. Hall, 1995; Sriramesh, 2009b). In its current form, according to Appelbaum and Robinson (2005),

Global studies views the world as a single interactive system, rather than as an interplay of discrete nation-states. Its focus is on transnational processes, interactions, and flows, rather than international relations, and on new sets of theoretical, historical, epistemological, and even philosophical questions posed by emergent transnational realities. (p. xi)

Appadurai (1996) articulates globalization in the language of *scapes*. He outlines five scapes: *ethnoscapes* or the heightened movement and migration of people (i.e., cultural bodies) across national and regional borders for work, study, leisure, and other purposes; *mediascapes* or the transnational spread of media content, images, and networks; *technoscapes* or the movement of technology/information across borders; *financescapes* or the flows of capital, financial data, and trade; and *ideoscapes* or the transnational movement and morphing of ideas and ideologies that result from the above scapes. These fluid scapes intersect in myriad configurations to produce flows and disjunctures in an environment of disorderly capitalism. Public relations, in its global scope, is caught up in as well as impacts the workings of these scapes.

Views on Globalization

Arguments about the effects of globalization have tended to coalesce around three perspectives: the globalist view, the skeptical view, and the transformational view (Held & McGrew, 2000; Martell, 2007).

- The *globalists* subscribe to a more economistic (i.e., neoliberal) perspective of globalization. They believe that the rapid spread of market capitalism and multinational corporations and growth in economic interdependence in recent decades has significantly decreased the sovereign power of nation-states. They argue that we live in a flatter (Friedman, 2005) world that is postnational in an economic sense. This is the "globalization-from-above" view.
- The *skeptics* argue that globalization is an imperialistic and uneven process. They believe that the already powerful nation-states are gaining economically and politically from the process, and that historically marginalized nation-states are left out of the benefits of globalization. From a cultural perspective, they argue that the power of nation-states is far from eroding, and that resurgent nationalism and antiglobalization movements are natural responses in the face of the threat of corporate globalization and cultural imperialism from above. This is the "globalization-from-below" view.
- The *transformationalists* take a middle ground approach. Straddling the hyperoptimism of the globalists and the critiques of the

skeptics, they note the uncertainties produced by the emergent structures, flows, and experiences of globalization. They do not predict a "flat" world dominated by neoliberal ideology, are aware of the inequities of the globalization process, but are not antiglobalists. They are interested in more dialectical and less one-sided analyses of the complexities, erasures, and new possibilities that are emerging from global flows and disjunctures.

Whatever viewpoint one subscribes to, there is no denying that globalization has resulted in unprecedented compression of time and space (the world having become perceptibly smaller and interaction more immediate as a consequence of innovations, particularly in communication technologies) (Harvey, 1989), heightened interdependence between nation-states, and the "stretching" of social and professional relationships across vast expanses (Giddens, 1990). The difference between the "inside" and the "outside" of nation-states, cultures, and economies, for example, is harder to mark (Urry, 2005) as the local and the global interlock to transform binaristic perceptions about relations between "Us" and "Other," thereby giving rise to hybrid formations, identities, and sensibilities (see Curtin & Gaither, 2007; Pal & Dutta, 2008). Forces of homogenization and heterogeneity are working simultaneously to generate new patterns and structures of inclusion and exclusion that coexist with some of the old.

State of Public Relations Scholarship and Practice in the Context of Globalization

What the above means for the study and practice of public relations in global cultural contexts is that we need to conceptualize client–public relationship building, culture, communication, and the spread of the industry itself in more interdependent, interconnected, and fluid ways since these phenomena are hallmarks of globalizing processes. Simultaneously, questions of power relations and the view that culture is a site of contested meanings cannot be ignored in a world where differences are intersecting at an increasing speed.

The globalization of the public relations industry is widely acknowledged and yet remains underresearched and meagerly theorized. Within the field, it is the comparative "inter-national" approach which was developed in the 1950s in response to the postcolonial growth of new nation-states and the increasing organization of the world around nation-state based systems during that time (Appelbaum & Robinson, 2005) which dominates. Following this logic, and constrained by its limitations, scholars continue to treat nation-states as separate (rather than interconnected) and culturally static units of analysis and focus on how culture, operationalized through variables conceptualized at the macrolevel of the nation-state, impacts the practice of public relations in these units. While such studies provide valuable information at one level, they are not equipped for understanding transnational interconnections and how factors such as time–space compression, global-local dialectics, and the global scapes identified by Appadurai (1996) permeate practice. As Pal and Dutta (2008) note, "The local-global interplay has fundamentally unseated the notion that public relations practices of nations can be captured, compared and evaluated in large-scale studies that seek to articulate master narratives of public relations practice" (p. 164).

Public relations, as a modern communications industry, is a largely Western phenomenon that developed alongside and in support of capitalism (Miller & Dinan, 2000, 2003). With the global surge of market capitalism since the late 1980s, and given the West-centric political economy of the public relations industry, Western-style public relations was quickly taken to other parts of the world. The globalist view described earlier undergirds much thinking about this spread which is propelled by neoliberal ideology. Trade and academic publications focus on the overseas growth of mostly U.S.-based agencies, the formation of agency networks, and best practices for multinational companies (most of which are based in the West). While there is an instrumental interest in understanding how to be effective in different cultural and political systems, the unquestioned assumption seems to be that Western-style public relations sets the norms for excellence that other cultures are measured against and are expected to emulate (Roth, Hunt, Stravropoulos, & Babik, 1996). Additionally, in burgeoning public relations academic programs around the world, the dominance of mostly U.S. public relations textbooks (Sriramesh, 2004), and the assumption of the primacy of U.S. models of public relations prevalent in these textbooks (McKie & Munshi, 2007) could be seen as a form of epistemic imperialism that suppresses local meanings and realities. Simultaneously, mainstream U.S. textbooks and curricula tend to have a U.S.-centric focus that leaves students in the United States largely unaware of the global diversity of the profession, and limited in their ability to understand complex cultural connectivity (see Bardhan, 2003a).

Indeed, as McKie and Munshi (2007) have detailed, it is only very recently that other histories of public relations have emerged which challenge claims that the United States led the development of the public relations profession (e.g., L'Etang, 2004; Toledano, 2005). While non-U.S. histories can and do demonstrate the error of assuming that all public relations follows U.S. models, the global growth of the public relations industry (and academic knowledge) is largely a "West to Rest" (S. Hall, 1996) flow that is steeped in neoliberal ideologies and marked by historical structural inequities. For example, Western "global" agencies have established offices only in those countries that are already economically prosperous or are showing signs of growth. Large parts of Africa, for example, do not make it onto the global map of public relations activity (Curtin & Gaither, 2007). These would be the concerns of the skeptical (critical) view of globalization in public relations, a view that is currently not very visible in academic or trade discourse. The interrogation of how the dominant discourse on the globalization of public relations supports hegemonic agendas of more powerful global actors began when a few scholars working from postcolonial, postmodern, and other critical perspectives gradually started asking these questions (e.g., Holtzhausen, 2000; L'Etang & Pieczka, 1996; Munshi & McKie, 2001).

Curtin and Gaither (2007) have proposed that more critical/cultural models of public relations are needed that account for the interplay of culture, power, identities, and difference in today's transnational landscape. They draw upon the British cultural studies circuit of culture model, which is influenced by Marxist thought and Foucauldian notions of the relation between power and knowledge, and which comprises five overlapping points or moments (representation, production, consumption, regulation, and identity). These five moments "work in concert to provide a shared cultural space in which meaning is created, shaped, modified and recreated" (p. 38). Curtin and Gaither call their model the culture-economic model of public relations, and claim that this model is a non-West-centric, nonlinear model which envisions public relations activity as dynamic, discursive, and polysemic in nature. Their model is a contribution that allows us to examine public relations as a boundary-crossing, meaning-making, and culture-producing enterprise. In addition to the critical/cultural approach, some scholars have started research from transformationalist perspectives which examine how the global–local dialectic can be addressed through glocal strategies (Bardhan & Patwardhan, 2004; Maynard & Tian, 2004; Molleda & Roberts, 2008; Pal & Dutta, 2008), how cross-national conflict shifting occurs when the public relations playing field is transnational in nature (Molleda, Connolly-Ahern, & Quinn, 2005), and how the political economy perspective can shed light on the interconnected impact of political and economic forces on global practice (Duhé & Sriramesh, 2009). Such research brings into focus the interconnectedness and fluidity of public relations activity in the transnational landscape.

It can be said that in public relations, "globalization is both imposed from above and yet can be contested and reconfigured from below" (Kellner, 2002, p. 286). The work of critical/interpretive scholars, postmodernists, and transformationalists is making inroads into addressing issues of global–local enmeshment, the blurring of cultural and identity boundaries, and the play of power (structural and ideological) and hegemony in global public relations currently dominated by West-centric practice and scholarship. However, much still needs to be accomplished. Several chapters in this book are contributions toward further building this repertoire of scholarship.

The Question of Culture

Culture is central to public relations as a communications profession, and to quote Edward Hall's (1959) often cited statement: "Culture is communication and communication is culture" (p. 97). Culture is not something that is exotic or "out there" but is a part of everyday life and social interaction, and a public relations practitioner does not have to be practicing across national borders to encounter cultural difference and diversity (Sha, 2006).

Practitioners communicate with publics that belong to specific cultural groups, especially in multicultural societies and transnational settings (Banks, 1995, 2000; Sha, 2006); they are involved in the production of culture as cultural intermediaries (Curtin & Gaither, 2007; Featherstone, 1995; Hodges, 2006) who mediate between producers of culturally coded messages and consumers who make cultural sense of those messages; the organizations of clients that practitioners represent have cultural identities that espouse certain values that are usually reflective of the larger societies and ideologies they are embedded in (Sriramesh & White, 1992); practitioners have their own cultural identities; and, the profession itself has developed certain dominant cultural values over time (Hodges, 2006). Public relations is, then, cultural activity (Banks, 1995, 2000). Despite this centrality of culture to the field, the concept itself remains woefully under theorized within it (Sriramesh, 2007), with the consequence that the profession is severely limited in conceiving of how to engage ethically and critically with matters of cultural difference in a globalizing and multicultural world.

Although "culture" has been described as "ordinary" (Williams, 1958) and it permeates our everyday lives in a mundane manner, the concept of culture itself is notoriously complex and difficult to pin down. Kroeber and Kluckhohn (1952) compiled and analyzed over 150 definitions of culture over half a century ago, and the meaning of the term continues to proliferate and remain contested. Essays in a more recent edited volume on culture (Baldwin, Faulkner, Hecht, & Lindsley, 2006) explain that the concept comes to us from anthropology, and that early definitions were highly structural and social scientific in approach. Culture, according to such definitions, is objectively observable, systemic, and pattern-oriented and pertains to the values and behaviors that are common to all who are part of a given culture. Yet, to conceptualize culture in this way is to treat it as static, predictive, and as a causal variable—something one possesses due to membership in a particular cultural system. The interpretive turn challenged this social scientific and objective view, and defined culture as dynamic, ritualistic, process-oriented, and socially constructed through symbolic interaction (Carey, 1989; Geertz, 1973). In turn, more critically oriented definitions, many of which are informed by cultural studies, focus on issues of power, ideology, and difference and on how culture is a site of contested meanings. According to the critical view, different groups, through discourse and identity politics, compete to have a say in what counts as culture. For its part, postmodernism views culture and cultural identities as fragmented and fluid, privileges the local, and is against grand definitions (or metanarratives) of culture.

Culture in the Context of Globalization

In the context of globalization, culture takes on some specific features. Benedict Anderson's (1991) notion of the "imagined community" can be instructive here. Anderson, a historian, theorized that the rise of national consciousness and the possibility of eventually organizing in the form of modern nation-states were aided by the rise of print capitalism in Europe around the 1500s. The mass production and dissemination of printed communication in common vernacular languages in Europe enabled people spread across mostly continuous geographic areas and not in face-to-face contact to experience a sense of community and a shared "way of life" (i.e., culture) with each other. This was an early form of time–space compression and stretching of social relations on a smaller scale. In today's climate of global flows, which includes macrolevel movements across discontinuous spaces of people (embodying culture), ideologies and mediated images/information of places and people once imagined as being "far away," the cultural distance between "here" and "there" and between "Self" and "Other" is shrinking (Gupta & Ferguson, 1992). Culture is increasingly becoming deterritorialized, disembedded from place (Giddens, 1990), and taking on spatial dimensions that are capable of spanning the globe. Featherstone (1995) notes that the complex connectivity of globalization familiarizes us "with greater diversity" and with "the extensive range of local cultures" (p. 86). Cultural imagining transcends the local and national and "[i]n the process, not merely different, more complex identity positions, but also different *modes* [emphasis in original] of cultural identification are arising" (Tomlinson, 1999, p. 105). Thus, culture and territory cannot be conceptualized as synonymous any more. Culture travels (Clifford, 1997), hybridizes, defies fixed definition, and is constructed, maintained, and reformed through communication (Carey, 1989) among people within and across socially constructed cultural borders.

In this scenario, those of the globalist view have made the argument that the triumph of capitalism and the spread of democracy herald the move toward a homogenous world culture (see Fukuyama, 1992; Ohmae, 1995). Theorists of cultural imperialism (see Schiller, 1985), though critical of capitalist domination, have also made totalizing predictions of the Americanization or Westernization of world culture. However, greater connectivity and interdependence does not necessarily lead to conditions of cultural homogeneity. In fact, predictions of one-world culture tacitly assume that Western modernity is capable of erasing the centuries-old deep cultural realities of non-Western cultures (Tomlinson, 1999). The skeptical view questions such predictions and focuses on the resurgence of cultural particularism and protectionism as a response to uneven global processes. Transformationalists take a dialectical approach to the issue of homogenizing and heterogeneous cultural forces. While homogenizing forces bring diverse cultures into closer contact, the outcomes of such contact could be assimilation, resistance, or cultural hybridity depending on particular histories, power configurations, and contexts.

Since the escalation of global processes in the early 1990s, the public relations industry has spread across national borders and grown in terms of size ("Good news," 2010; Miller & Dinan, 2000), and cultural issues have become central to practitioners (Frost, 2000). This growth has been in terms of the spread of firms as well as public relations by government and non-state and non-corporate actors (see Molleda, 2009, for an in-depth analysis of the global growth of the profession). Most public relations firms and networks that claim to be global are owned by West-based media conglomerates and have annual earnings that run into billions of dollars (Morley, 2009; Wilcox & Cameron, 2010). Mostly U.S.-based scholars, responding to the need for cultural knowledge that would help practitioners in unfamiliar cultural landscapes (mostly "emerging markets"), began to research and theorize the practice of international public relations during this time. However, this initial approach, one of the first studies of which was the Excellence project (Grunig, 1992), was epistemologically West-centric and based in the nation-state logic where the nation-state was assumed to be the natural unit of analysis for culture. The initial goals were to test how cultural differences caused public relations practice in other countries to be similar or different from practice in the United States (Bardhan, 2003b; Roth et al., 1996). Such an approach to culture "yielded innumerable clues to the worldwide variation of public relations practice, but often ostensibly validate Western theories rather than generate new, globally sensitive, theories" (Gaither & Curtin, 2008, p. 117). This research agenda was in keeping with the "West to Rest" epistemic mindset, and it was only in the late 1990s that scholars started questioning this reductive view of culture (Banks, 1995,

2000; Curtin & Gaither, 2007; Surma & Daymon, 2009) and the lack of more complex approaches and methods of study in this area.

Public relations practitioners working within global flows and at the intersections of cultural differences need to make it a priority to build intercultural client–public relations and develop message strategies that are non-imperialistic, non-coercive, and in keeping with the cultural climate of a given global–local context. They need to avoid cultural essentialism and, without losing sight of power relations, be able to think of the possibility of culture as deterritorialized and hybrid. This perspective has a large bearing on how effectively practitioners set goals and objectives, define significant publics, conduct media relations, develop message strategy, and engage in other relationship building activities. Drawing from all perspectives, they need to understand how the aggregate nation-state based knowledge about culture can be combined with more communicative, social constructionist, and critical views of how culture works. As scholars, it is our responsibility to aid them in such perspective building.

About Paradigms

Public relations scholarship, like the modern profession itself, had its inception in the West (mostly in the United States) in the latter half of the last century. This scholarship emerged in the heyday of social scientific thinking in U.S. academia. Since the early 1990s, a time when several fields within the communication discipline began engaging more with interpretive, critical, and postmodern epistemologies, there has been increasing discussion about paradigms and paradigm shifts within the public relations body of knowledge. Several public relations scholars from outside the United States have made significant contributions to this discussion.

According to Kuhn (1996), a paradigm "stands for the entire constellation of beliefs, values, techniques, and so on shared by the members of a given community" (p. 175). Furthermore, "members of a shared knowledge community not only normalize certain types of questions, but also suppress the ability to raise other kinds of questions" (Mittelman, 2004, p. 25). A mature paradigm subscribes to specific ontological, epistemological, axiological, and methodological assumptions. The dominant paradigm that a field of inquiry adopts or arises out of greatly impacts the kinds of knowledge produced and the types of impact that knowledge has on action (in our case, public relations action) in the world.

Kuhn explains that a new paradigm emerges when anomalies challenging the old paradigm are too great, and the new and the old cannot find comfortable common ground. While Kuhn's work dealt with the natural sciences and has been extended to the social sciences, Mittelman (2004) points out that staying within the scientific mindset is a limitation that "does not give sufficient credence to socially constructed knowledge outside this community" (p. 25). He argues that there is a need to account for conceptualizations of social realities and conditions that lie outside the paradigmatic assumptions of the social sciences (or positivist thinking). He further argues "that even without a paradigm crisis, an ascendant paradigm could emerge" (p. 26). In other words, disparate paradigms can exist in tension with each other, and one does not have to displace the other. The rest of this section briefly charts out how we apply this insight to public relations scholarship and its paradigms, particularly in global cultural contexts.

Paradigmatic Shifts within Public Relations Scholarship

Early public relations theorizing and the dominant Excellence theory grew out of systems theory, based in the social scientific (rational positivist) paradigm. Leading scholars declared in the 1980s, a time of much focus on theory development in the field, that public relations is a social science (Botan & Hazelton, 1989) and a management function (Cutlip, Center, & Broom, 1990; Grunig & Hunt, 1984). The notion of symmetry underlies the Excellence theory. According to Grunig and White (1992), the notion of symmetry implies the use of "research and dialogue to manage conflict, improve understanding, and build relationships with publics. With the symmetrical model, both the organizations and publics can be persuaded; both also may change their behavior" (p. 39).

While acknowledging the contributions of this "foundational" theory and its spirit of dialogue, we must also note its limitations that are generated by its underlying functionalist and positivist assumptions. These do not equip Excellence theory to critically address issues of power and the socially constructed view of knowledge (Mittelman, 2004). Social scientific ontology assumes a subject (researcher) object (knowledge) divide, and according to Yoshitake (2004), "Positivists assume that there is only one reality and that it can be described in words. A web of rationally constructed theories is viewed as a conceptual net that captures the reality, which is induced based on empirical data and through statistical tests" (p. 19).

Rhetorical theory of public relations, which grew alongside the Excellence theory, "concerns itself principally with how individuals, groups, and organizations make meaning, through argument and counter-argument, to create issues, resolve uncertainty, compete to achieve a preferable position, or to build coalitions—to solve problems. Rhetorical scholars believe that symbolic behavior creates and influences relationships between organizations and publics ..." (Toth, 2009, p. 50). This theoretical approach is persuasion-based, interpretive, and social constructionist, and focuses on meaning construction and communication. Within the interpretive paradigm, Banks (1995, 2000) has also developed a social–interpretive theory of multicultural public relations (see Bardhan's chapter in this volume). More recently, there has been a push to move away from management and functionalist thinking toward a cocreational, dialogic, more public-centered, and relationship-oriented approach that "places an implicit value on relationships going beyond the achievement of an organizational goal ... publics are not just a means to an end ... but instead are partners in the meaning-making process" (Botan & Taylor, 2004, p. 652).

Critiques of the excellence and rhetorical theories have pointed out that both ignore issues of power through arguments of pluralism, or the assumption that all interest groups in society have equal access to resources, the same ability or desire to engage in dialogue, and an equal ability to compete in policy making (Coombs, 1993; Creedon, 1993). "Pluralists fail to recognize how power differences translate into access differences. Power is recognized but the unequal power distribution and its resultant inequities are ignored" (Coombs, 1993, p. 113). Questions such as who controls dialogue, who has the option of engaging in dialogue, who benefits from the status quo, structural inequities, and who has the resources to invest in advocacy and persuasion are not addressed adequately (see also Dozier & Lauzen, 2000). Another critique has been that Excellence and rhetorical approaches have been more preoccupied with managing rather than promoting diversity (Cheney & Christensen, 2001). Furthermore, the plausibility of the notion of symmetry has been questioned, and postmodern notions of dissensus (Holtzhausen, 2000) and dissymmetry where "the goal is to value various symmetries, rather than to achieve homeostasis by minimizing differences" (Creedon, 1993, p. 164) have been forwarded.

Such critiques have led to the growth of a critical–postmodern paradigm in public relations which drops the subject–object divide of social science and challenges the taken-for-granted assumptions and shortfalls of the dominant theories in order to "transform those social, political and economic structures which limit human potential ... and debate the strategies of domination that are implicit in such structures" (L'Etang, 2005, pp. 521–522). For example, postcolonial scholarship highlights the Western theoretical, methodological, and cultural domination in the study of public relations as well as the structural biases of the industry at the global level that privilege elite publics over subaltern ones (Dutta-Bergman, 2005; Munshi & McKie, 2001). The critical–postmodern paradigm, with its preoccupation with power, makes possible introspection and challenges the public relations body of knowledge to "critically examine what it is that public relations practitioners do, and the consequences of that practice for society" (Gower, 2006, p. 180).

The social scientific approach to studying public relations in diverse cultures contributes to building universalizing theory about global practice. Such knowledge can be useful at a macrolevel. However, it must be kept in mind that this approach is still based in modernist Western science traditions. The social scientific paradigm, thus, may be seen as a globalization-from-above initiative (i.e., in the world of scholarship) since it engages in top-down etic theorizing. The rhetorical approach may also be seen as such, unless it is more open to issues of power and context in rhetorical activity, and to culturally different approaches to the role of rhetoric and advocacy in public communication.

In a world of multiple realities, the interpretive paradigm aids in studying the socially constructed nature of knowledge and communication in intercultural interaction in global public relations activity. This paradigm facilitates the understanding of public relations as communicative and cocreational rather than simply as a management function. However, the critical–postmodern paradigm goes one step further and calls for the examination of how public relations is implicated in issues of power and hegemony. This is especially relevant in a world marked by vast North–South economic discrepancies, deep digital divides, and neocolonial structural and ideological domination that can perpetuate old power dynamics if not thoroughly questioned. According to Elmer (2007), "By expanding the legitimate area of enquiry both intellectually and geographically we may yet recover valuable cultural practices that have slipped from view. Crucially, the globalized environment requires understandings that are not merely instrumental and economically driven, but which maintain an appropriate engagement with culture and with politics ..." (p. 366).

It is obvious that each of the paradigms in which public relations theory and research is based contribute to our understandings of the roles, functions, and consequences of public relations in society in different ways. As Botan (1993) states about public relations scholarship, a "paradigm struggle does not necessarily mean a negative relationship exists, rather it describes a sometimes comfortable, sometimes uncomfortable process of working through differences in assumptive world views, vocabularies, goals, and, maybe most significantly, loyalties" (p. 108). Some public relations scholars have already noted the need for a multiparadigmatic stance in a rapidly globalizing world (Botan, 1993; Gower, 2006; Ihlen, van Ruler, & Fredriksson, 2009; McKie & Munshi, 2007; Toth, 2009), and we add our voices to theirs in suggesting a dialectical (or transformationalist) approach. Here we draw from intercultural communication scholars Martin and Nakayama (1999) who posit that a dialectical approach to paradigms enables scholars to engage in multiple ways of conducting research, see the possible connections between paradigms, as well as hold contradictory ideas simultaneously (p. 14). Such intellectual flexibility is a skill that is not simply advisable but necessary for scholars, educators, and practitioners of public relations in global cultural contexts.

The Critical Turn

While advocating the value of multi-paradigmatic perspectives in public relations, we do lean toward the critical paradigm in this book because we subscribe to the view that critical theory provides much needed insight into the role that public relations plays in shaping culture in the context of globalization. We are not alone in this view. Gower (2006), for example, has argued that "Globalization, with its emphasis on integration, power, multinational companies, and democracy, demands attention from our critical/cultural theorists" (p. 186). Indeed, in the context of globalization, critical theory places center stage, questions of what the public sphere and democracy looks like in a transnational and deterritorialized polity. Further, it asks: how can we realize the goals of human emancipation and democratic participation in contexts of massive asymmetries of power in relation to social, economic, political, and cultural resources? These questions have always been at the heart of critical theory, though the aims of this paradigm have perhaps been much misunderstood by its detractors within public relations scholarship.

In the public relations field, critical theory seeks to provide alternative ways of examining public relations practice which largely stand in opposition to functionalist systems theory approaches. That is, while functionalist systems theories are promoted as objective, scientific, impartial, and focused on identifying how to perform "effective," "excellent," "best practice" public relations (originating as they do from the positivist paradigm), critical theory has argued that we need to consider how both public relations scholarship and practice serve particular interests—notably those with the resources to institute public relations communication and campaigns, such as corporations and governments. In these terms, critical theorists have been interested in exposing how public relations may support and contribute to systems of oppression, and, additionally how its role in such oppression can be obscured by normative theories of practice. Indeed, critical theorists have decried the systems-based Excellence theory as idealistic, based on a naive "belief that society exists around the equilibrium of consensus" (Pieczka, 2006, p. 356), and failing to consider the unequal nature of power relations between those who have the financial ability to pay for public relations initiatives, and the audiences of those initiatives.

Critical theory originated from the German Frankfurt School in the

1920s and '30s, drew on Marxist sociology and philosophy, and, consequently was centrally focused on critiquing and changing capitalist sociopolitical economic structures for the benefit of the socially disenfranchised. Marx's (1975) own concisely articulated definition of critical theory as "the self-clarification of the struggles and wishes of the age" (p. 209) clearly aligns the concerns of the approach with "those oppositional social movements with which it has a partisan though not uncritical reflection" (Fraser, 1985, p. 97). In its original manifestation it was the working class, or "proletariat," which comprised the focus of critical theory's emancipatory aims, but such a singular focus is less likely in current critical research given that "oppression has many faces and that focusing on any one at the expense of others (e.g., class oppression versus racism) often elides the interconnections among them" (Kincheloe & McLaren, 2008, p. 405).

However, while all critical theorists are concerned with exposing relationships of power and oppression in social, cultural, or political life, critical theory comprises a broad range of theoretical and methodological perspectives, ones which advocate different practice-based approaches to addressing systems of oppression. For example, neo-Marxist informed scholars Millar and Dinan (2007) regard public relations as a linchpin of the "neo-liberal revolution" (p. 302) and corporate power, and actively protest against this through campaigns such as the ALTER-EU campaign for lobbying disclosure in the European Commission. Others, such as McKie and Munshi (2007), work with and within public relations scholarship, education, and practice, bringing critical theories to it with the intent on "creating PR with a conscience" (p. 8). Many critical public relations writers are interested in deconstructing public relations campaigns (e.g., Durham, 2005; Motion & Weaver, 2005; Weaver & Motion, 2002) and core key concepts in the field (e.g., Berger, 2005; Leitch & Neilson, 2001), investigating the intricate and mutually supportive relationships and information flows between public relations, the media, and politics (e.g., Davis, 2007; Moloney, 2000; Palmer 2000), and theoretically and historically invigorating the analysis and understanding of the role of public relations in organizations and in global society (e.g., L'Etang, 2005, 2006; McKie & Munshi, 2007; Sklair, 2007). In these, and many other critical projects, critical theorists have extended the boundaries of knowledge about public relations. The critical project is indeed a very broad one; it does not have a singular unifying focus—aside perhaps from its concern with investigating public relations in the context of power—and it does not propose any one strategy for ethical practice of public relations. But then, as Kincheloe and McLaren (2007) have stated, "Critical theory should not be treated as a universal grammar of revolutionary thought objectified and reduced to discrete formulaic pronouncements or strategies" (p. 404).

A constant refrain of attack against critical theoretical approaches to public relations made by advocates of the functionalist systems Excellence theory is that critical theory fails to make a contribution to public relations practice. For example, Grunig (2001) has proclaimed that "in a professional field such as public relations, I believe scholars must go beyond criticizing theories; they also have the obligation to replace theories with something better—an obligation that many critical scholars do not fulfill" (p. 17). This sentiment was more recently repeated by Tyma (2008) who argued that "Unfortunately ... although critical and postmodern approaches to public relations do an excellent job of identifying and articulating the socio-cultural concerns within and surrounding the public relations profession, these same critiques fall short of providing solutions toward these concerns for those same practitioners" (p. 195). Criticisms such as these are, however, symptomatic of functional academics' paradigmatic mindset that scholarship, research, and theory should necessarily serve the interests of professional practice. To be sure some critical researchers conduct research and campaign as scholars and activists for the regulation and exposure of deceptive public relations— Millar and Dinan being two prominent examples with their founding of Spinwatch, the "independent non-profit making organisation which monitors the role of public relations and spin in contemporary society" (Spinwatch, n.d.).

Yet others argue that,

> Critical public relations should not necessarily feel accountable to applied scholars or to the practice to justify their work. As intellectuals in the field critical scholars should feel free to push back the boundaries of knowledge, explore and define the boundaries of the field, engage with methodological debates, engage with contemporary intellectual thought more broadly with a view to considering the implications for public relations and ... educate publics more broadly about the practice and its role in organizations and society. (L'Etang, 2005, p. 524; see also Dozier & Lauzen, 2000)

It is in these terms that we encourage readers to engage with the critical contents of this book as a lens through which to understand, theorize, and reflect on the significance and impact of public relations in a world marked by severe power inequities.

Brief Overview of the Chapters

This introduction is followed by Lee Edwards's chapter which couples Arjun Appadurai's theory of the work of the imagination with Pierre Bourdieu's theory of symbolic power to explore how public relations participates in the distribution of power in the context of globalization. Edwards's chapter is firmly positioned within a critical theory perspective, and is one which is skeptical of the possibility that public relations is able to serve the interests of groups other than those that employ its services. However, Edwards is careful not to theorize power as a unidirectional force—imposed by the already socially and resource advantaged upon those with less social, cultural, political, or economic power. She significantly complicates arguments about the power that public relations wields in a globalizing world. In contextualizing the public relations profession as "a system, a discourse technology, and a field of professional practice situated in the global environment," Edwards stresses that there is no guarantee that public relations efforts will prove persuasively effective, and that indeed these efforts may be negated or undermined by the specific cultural dynamics of a given locality. Appadurai's concept of scapes provides a route into theorizing these complex dynamics of power as related to the "work of the imagination." As Edward's chapter details, the possibilities of what can be symbolically imagined are influenced in a myriad of ways: by global systems and structures, national and local cultural environments, by different forms and types of organizations such as activist groups, non-government and government agencies, and by public relations practice. She argues that public relations practitioners need to keep in mind the many forces at work which create perceptions of our lived realities, and how these forces may affect responses to public relations communication.

Michael Kent and Maureen Taylor's chapter reviews a range of intercultural communication theories and examines how these can inform public relations in global contexts. They begin by outlining how public relations scholarship initially drew on Geert Hofstede's cultural dimensions that influence communication and relationships in organizational settings. Hofstede's approach has been influential in studies of intercultural communication, but as Kent and Taylor stress, it provides a very limited, and static, understanding of culture. Therefore, Kent and Taylor explore how personal influence, relational, dialogic, and generic approaches can offer greater insights into how to effectively operate in intercultural and globalized contexts. However, practicing public relations in unfamiliar cultures also requires practitioners to understand the many complex expectations around how human relationships are conducted within and across cultures. Kent and Taylor, therefore, outline a range of variables which can assist in understanding how relationships can be created and changed by public relations. They conceptualize public relations as an organic process of evolving relationships, an approach that allows a move away from traditional, managerial approaches to international public relations and a move toward a cocreational understanding of public relations as third culture building.

Nilanjana Bardhan's chapter provides an in-depth examination of the utility of the third culture building model recommended by Kent and Taylor. She specifically explores the shortcomings of the social scientific conceptualization of "culture" and "communication" in current public relations scholarship, especially in the context of global flux. The chapter is anchored in the premise that at the ground level on the global stage, the public relations success of an organization is ultimately dependent on how individual practitioners, representing the client organization, jointly accomplish intercultural communication and relationship building with strategic members of culturally diverse publics. In keeping with this ground-up, interpretative, and socially constructivist approach, Bardhan theorizes how the notion of third culture building can serve as a dynamic as well as dialogic framework for conceptualizing as well as practicing successful client–public relationship building in "transcultural" public relations work.

Jeffrey Courtright, Rachel Wolfe, and John Baldwin's chapter returns to a further examination of Hofstede's cultural dimensions, and explicates how this can assist in understanding public relations practice in the context of globalization. Courtright et al. consider both the strengths and limitations of Hofstede's "scientifically" derived dimensions, the criticisms of the methodology used in their development, and how the dimensions have been conceptualized and applied in the study of different national cultures. Rightly, Courtright et al. outline how the dimensions have been critiqued as portraying all peoples and groups within specific national cultures as essentially culturally the same, as depicting cultures as having one type of value or its opposite (dichotomizing), and as static. However, Courtright et al. do not suggest that Hofstede's framework should be rejected outright. Rather, their concern is to highlight the dangers of applying it in highly simplistic and monolithic ways, and to demonstrate its merits when applied in a carefully nuanced manner. In illustrating how this can be done, the authors use the dimensions of culture to explore how Dove's award winning public relations "Campaign for Real Beauty" targeted audiences in different global contexts in generic and, at times, specific terms. However, Courtright et al.'s discussion also makes the case for bringing in other conceptual approaches, such as rhetorical analysis, to more fully appreciate how global public relations campaigns attempt to create strategic connections with diverse target audiences.

Derina Holtzhausen's chapter focuses on what postmodern theory can contribute to both the theoretical and applied understandings of the role of public relations in processes of globalization. Holtzhausen outlines what are, in her view, the differences between postmodern, critical, and social theory approaches, and how these variously conceptualize language, discourse, and power in relation to public relations.

The chapter examines the role that public relations plays in the process of globalization and in framing this process as "progress." The chapter also offers an exploration of how public relations practitioners working in globalizing contexts are required to navigate a vast array of complex interpersonal, organizational, cultural, and national interests and politics. Holtzhausen proposes that, in the context of globalization, an ethic of postmodern public relations practice would strive to promote not consensus, but dissensus, and activism rather than unquestioning conformity to organizational goals.

Robert Wakefield's chapter specifically focuses on transnational entities, and explores how the generic–specific theory of public relations can contribute to understanding how to effectively practice public relations in a globalizing world. The generic–specific theory explores tensions between using a generic approach to public relations practice, and attending to the specific needs of local societies, communities, and cultures in which organizations operate. Research into the generic–specific theory approach has been with us since the early 1990s and, as Wakefield details, was in part an extension of the Excellence program of theory development. While the Excellence studies—and the two-way symmetrical concept that was so central to the defining of Excellence in public relations practice—advocated the need for organizations to engage in dialogue with stakeholders, trends toward practicing public relations on a global transnational scale clearly complicated questions of how it would be possible to achieve this in local contexts. Wakefield's chapter provides a useful insight into how the generic–specific theory evolved, and how it can be used as a framework to study public relations practices of transnational corporations (TNCs). He also urges TNCs to be aware of their obligations to the communities in which they operate, and to resource public relations practitioners to achieve them. Wakefield uses the generic–specific theory as a base for his arguments to warn of the hostilities that TNCs could well attract if they fail to engage in meaningful, culturally informed, and long-term relationship building practices in local communities.

Mohan Jyoti Dutta and Mahuya Pal's chapter is firmly positioned within a critical theoretical perspective. The chapter provides a detailed explanation of concepts central to postcolonial theory, such as "Orientalism," "modernity," and the notion of the "Third world." They theorize the integral connections between the nation-state, Western flows of neoliberal capitalism, colonization, civil society, and the history of public relations. For Dutta and Pal, public relations is a key tool in the globalization process, and one which contributes to hegemonic systems of inequality and oppression carried out by transnational corporations. Drawing on examples from Exxon Mobil and the U.S. "War on Iraq," Dutta and Pal illustrate how public relations has been used to support the financial interests of corporations and nation-states to the significant neglect of the welfare of the environment and subaltern groups. They conclude their chapter by reflecting on the position of subaltern scholarship, and the potential of its contribution to activist politics in public relations as part of the movement for social justice and change.

Jensen Chung's chapter brings the Eastern philosophy of *I-Ching* to bear upon consideration of how to practice public relations in global cultural contexts. In doing so, Chung's chapter introduces us to a paradigmatic approach to thinking about public relations in the globalizing world very different from any of the other chapters in this book. As is argued earlier in this chapter, public relations scholarship has been criticized for its "West to Rest" approach which assumes the global universal applicability of Western theoretical concepts. More recently, however, "Intercultural researchers, both East Asian and North America, [have been] urged to pay special attention to the deep and complicated interrelations between … religions and their traditional mental cultures in generating new religion-related research paradigms" (Ishii, 2006, p. 17). In explaining the concept of *chi*, which originated from the Chinese philosophies of Taoism and Confucianism, Chung provides valuable insight into how spiritual notions of energy flow and harmony can give rise to *chi-shih* strategies in public relations, and how these contrast with commonly held Western goal-orientated and financially motivated communication values.

The final chapter of the book, by C. Kay Weaver, presents an in-depth examination of the methodologies that inform systems and critical theorizing of public relations, and positions these approaches as "cultures" in their own right. The chapter also identifies the blind spots and weaknesses of both systems "Excellence" and critical approaches. Weaver argues that we need to understand how certain cultural values, biases, and agendas inform all research, and calls for a more explicit articulation of these values within scholarship. In making the case for new methodological initiatives in the study of public relations in global contexts, Weaver draws on *kaupapa* Maori perspectives which argue that "subjects" of research investigations should be reimagined as coresearchers where they have the power to determine research design, questions, methods of analysis, and the dissemination of research "knowledge." Weaver argues that this participatory approach provides a means by which "people" can become the central focus of public relations research and theory agendas in a globalizing world.

Conclusion

In bringing together the work of the contributing authors to this book, we have been mindful of our own subjectivities not only as critical–

interpretive scholars, but also as public relations researchers and educators who believe in the value of examining public relations as a practice, profession, and social phenomenon from a range of approaches. Our aim has been to provide space for different theoretical and methodological perspectives to articulate how public relations is implicated in culture building in a globalizing world. An additional aim has been to encourage public relations scholarship to move beyond the approach that equates country with culture, an approach that has so far dominated most theorizing of public relations in the context of globalization.

From this it is our hope that public relations theory, research, and education can make better sense of public relations as an intercultural communication practice that is deeply impacted by the global flows of power, information, and capital. We offer this volume in the spirit of healthy interrogation, of ourselves as well as of extant scholarship/practice, and hope that students, colleagues, and practitioners will become increasingly comfortable with the idea that it is acceptable, in fact necessary, to not get "frozen" in prescriptive modes of thinking and practice, and to challenge existing structures and practices that are hegemonic or lean toward cultural imperialism. Only through such exercises can public relations become a force for community and relationship building in a culturally complex world.

References

Anderson, B. (1991). *Imagined communities*. London: Verso.

Appadurai, A. (1996). *Modernity at large*. Minneapolis, MN: University of Minnesota Press.

Appelbaum, R., & Robinson, W. (2005). Introduction: Toward a critical globalization studies—Continued debates, new directions, neglected topics. In R. Appelbaum & W. Robinson (Eds.), *Critical globalization studies* (pp. xi-xxxiii). New York: Routledge.

Baldwin, J., Faulkner, S., Hecht, M., & Lindsley, S. (Eds.). (2006). *Redefining culture: Perspectives across the disciplines*. Mahwah, NJ: Erlbaum.

Banks, S. (1995). *Multicultural public relations: A social-interpretive approach*. Thousand Oaks, CA: Sage.

Banks, S. (2000). *Multicultural public relations: A social-interpretive approach* (2nd ed.). Ames, IA: Iowa State University Press.

Bardhan, N. (2003a). Creating spaces for international and multi(intercultural) perspectives in undergraduate public relations education. *Communication Education, 52*(2), 164–172.

Bardhan, N. (2003b). Rupturing public relations metanarratives: The example of India. *Journal of Public Relations Research, 15*(3), 225–248.

Bardhan, N., & Patwardhan, P. (2004). Multinational corporations and public relations in a traditionally resistant host culture. *Journal of Communication Management, 8*(3), 246–263.

Berger, B. (2005). Power over, power with, and power to relations: Critical reflections on public relations, the dominant coalition, and activism. *Journal of Public Relations Research, 17*(1), 5–28.

Berking, H. (2003). "Ethnicity is everywhere": On globalization and the transformation of cultural identity. *Current Sociology, 51*(3–4), 248–264.

Botan, C. (1993). Introduction to the paradigm struggle in public relations. *Public Relations Review, 19*(2), 107–110.

Botan, C., & Hazleton, V. Jr. (Eds.). (1989). *Public relations theory.* Hillsdale, NJ: Erlbaum.

Botan, C., & Taylor, M. (2004). Public relations: State of the field. *Journal of Communication, 54*(4), 645–661.

Carey, J. (1989). *Communication as culture: Essays on media and society.* Boston, MA: Unwin Hyman.

Cheney, G., & Christensen, L. (2001). Public relations as contested terrain: A critical response. In R. Heath (Ed.), *Handbook of public relations* (pp. 167–182). Thousand Oaks, CA: Sage.

Clifford, J. (1997). *Routes: Travel and translation in the late twentieth century.* Cambridge, MA: Harvard University Press.

Coombs, W. T. (1993). Philosophical underpinnings: Ramifications of a pluralist paradigm. *Public Relations Review, 19*(2), 111–119.

Creedon, P. (1993). Acknowledging the infrasystem: A critical feminist analysis of systems theory. *Public Relations Review, 19*(2), 157–166.

Curtin, P., & Gaither, K. T. (2007). *International public relations: Negotiating culture, identity, and power.* Thousand Oaks, CA: Sage.

Cutlip, S., Center, A., & Broom, B. (2000). *Effective public relations* (8th ed.). Upper Saddle River, NJ: Prentice Hall.

Davis, A. (2007). *The mediation of power.* New York: Routledge.

Dozier, D., & Lauzen, M. (2000). Liberating the intellectual domain from the practice: Public relations, activism, and the role of the scholar. *Journal of Public Relations Research, 12*(1), 3–22.

Duhé, S., & Sriramesh, K. (2009). Political economy and public relations. In K. Sriramesh & D. Verčič (Eds.). *The global public relations handbook: Theory, research and practice* (rev. ed., pp. 22–46). New York: Routledge.

Durham, F. (2005). Public relations as structuration: A prescriptive critique of the Starlink global food contamination case. *Journal of Public Relations Research, 17*(1), 29–47.

Dutta-Bergman, M. (2005). Civil society and communication: Not so civil after all. *Journal of Public Relations Research, 17*(3), 267–289.

Elmer, P. (2007). Unmanaging public relations: Reclaiming complex practice in pursuit of global consent. *Public Relations Review, 33*(4), 360–367.

Featherstone, M. (1995). *Undoing culture: Globalization, postmodernism and identity.* London: Sage.

Fraser, N. (1985). What's critical about critical theory? The case of Habermas and gender. *New German Critique, 35*(Spring–Summer), 97–131.

Friedman, T. (2005). *The world is flat: A brief history of the twenty-first century.* New York: Farrar, Straus, & Giroux.

Frost, A. (2000). Negotiating culture in a global environment. *Journal of Communication Management, 4*(4), 369–377.

Fukuyama, F. (1992). *The end of history and the last man.* New York: Avon.

Gaither, T. K., & Curtin, P. (2008). Examining the heuristic value of models of international public relations practice: A case study of the Arla Foods crisis. *Journal of Public Relations Research, 20*(1), 115–137.

Geertz, C. (1973). *The interpretation of cultures.* New York: Basic Books.

Giddens, A. (1990). *The consequences of modernity.* Cambridge, UK: Polity Press.

Good news. (2010, January 14). *The Economist.* Retrieved from http://www.economist.com/business-finance/displaystory.cfm?story_id=15276746

Gower, K. (2006). Public relations research at the crossroads. *Journal of Public Relations Research, 18*(2), 177–190.

Grunig, J. (Ed.). (1992). *Excellence in public relations and communication management.* Hillsdale, NJ: Erlbaum.

Grunig, J. E. (2001). Two-way symmetrical public relations: Past, present, and future. In R. L. Heath (Ed.), *Handbook of public relations* (pp. 11–30). Thousand Oaks, CA: Sage.

Grunig, J., & Hunt, T. (1984). *Managing public relations.* New York: Holt, Rinehart & Winston.

Grunig, J., & White, J. (1992). The effect of worldviews on public relations theory and practice. In J. Grunig (Ed.), *Excellence in public relations and communication management* (pp. 31–64). Hillsdale, NJ: Erlbaum.

Guba, E. G., & Lincoln, Y. S. (2008). Paradigmatic controversies, contradictions, and emerging confluences. In N. K. Denzin & Y. S. Lincoln (Eds.), *The landscape of qualitative research* (3rd ed., pp. 255–286). Thousand Oaks, CA: Sage.

Gupta, A., & Ferguson, J. (1992). Beyond "culture:" Space, identity, and the politics of difference. *Cultural Anthropology, 7*(1), 6–23.

Hall, E. T. (1959). *The silent language.* New York: Doubleday.

Hall, S. (1995). New cultures for old. In D. Massey & P. Jess (Eds.), *A place in the world?* (pp. 175–213). New York: Oxford University Press/Open University Press.

Hall, S. (1996). The west and the rest: Discourse and power. In H. Hall, D. Held, D. Hubert, & K. Thompson (Eds.), *Modernity: An introduction to modern societies* (pp. 184–227). Malden, MA: Blackwell.

Harvey, D. (1989). *The condition of postmodernity.* Oxford, UK: Blackwell.

Held, D., & McGrew, A. (2000). The great globalization debate: An introduction. In D. Held & A. McGrew (Eds.), *The global transformations readers* (pp. 1–45). Cambridge, UK: Polity Press.

Hodges, C. (2006). "PRP culture:" A framework for exploring public relations practitioners as cultural intermediaries. *Journal of Communication Management, 10*(1), 80–93.

Holtzhausen, D. (2000). Postmodern values in public relations. *Journal of Public Relations Research, 12*(1), 93–114.

Ihlen, Ø., van Ruler, B., & Fredriksson, M. (Eds.). (2009). *Public relations as social theory: Key figures and concepts.* New York: Routledge.

Ishii, S. (2006). Complementing contemporary intercultural communication research with East Asian sociocultural perspectives and practices. *China Media research, 2*(1), 13–20.

Kellner, D. (2002). Theorizing globalization. *Sociological Theory, 20*(3), 285–305.

Kincheloe, J. L., & McLaren, P. (2007). Rethinking critical theory and qualitative research. In N. K. Denzin & Y. S. Lincoln (Eds.), *The landscapes of qualitative research* (3rd ed., pp. 403–455). Thousand Oaks, CA: Sage.

Kroeber, A., & Kluckhohn, C. (1952). *Culture: A critical review of concepts and definitions.* Cambridge, MA: Harvard University Press.

Kuhn, T. (1996). *The structure of scientific revolutions* (3rd ed.). Chicago, IL: University of Chicago Press.

Leitch, S., & Neilson, D. (2001). Bringing publics into public relations: New directions for research and practice. *Australian Journal of Communication, 24*(2), 17–32.

L'Etang, J. (2004). *Public relations in Britain: A history of professional practice in the twentieth century.* Mahwah, NJ: Erlbaum.

L'Etang, J. (2005). Critical public relations: Some reflections. *Public Relations Review, 31*(4), 521–526.

L'Etang, J. (2006). Public relations and propaganda: Conceptual issues, methodological problems, and public relations discourse. In J. L'Etang & M. Pieczka (Eds.), *Public relations: Critical debates and contemporary practice* (pp. 23–40). London: Erlbaum.

L'Etang, J., & Pieczka, M. (1996). *Critical perspectives in public relations.* London: International Thomson Business Press.

Martell, L. (2007). The third wave in globalization theory. *International Studies Review, 9*(2), 173–196.

Martin, J., & Nakayama, T. (1999). Thinking dialectically about culture and communication. *Communication Theory, 9*(1), 1–25.

Martin, J., & Nakayama, T. (2010). *Intercultural communication in contexts* (5th ed.). New York: McGraw-Hill.

Marx, K. (1975). A letter to Ruge, September 1843. In R. Livingstone & G. Benton (Trans.), *Karl Marx: Early writings* (pp. 206–209). New York: Vintage Books.

Maynard, M., & Tian, Y. (2004). Between global and local: Content analysis of the Chinese web sites of the 100 top global brands. *Public Relations Review, 30*(3), 285–291.

McKie, D. (2001). Updating public relations: "New science," research paradigms, and uneven developments. In R. Heath (Ed.), *Handbook of public relations* (pp. 75–91). Thousand Oaks, CA: Sage.

McKie, D. (2005). Critical theory. In R. L. Heath (Ed.), *Encyclopedia of public relations* (Vol. 1, pp. 226–228). Thousand Oaks, CA: Sage.

McKie, D., & Munshi, D. (2007). *Reconfiguring public relations: Ecology, equity, and enterprise.* New York: Routledge.

Miller, D., & Dinan, W. (2000). The rise of the PR industry in Britain, 1979–1998. *European Journal of Communication, 15*(1), 5–35.

Miller, D., & Dinan, W. (2003). Global public relations and global capitalism. In D. Demers (Ed.), *Terrorism, globalization and mass communication* (pp. 193–214). Spokane, WA: Marquette Books.

Miller, D., & Dinan, W. (2007). Conclusion: Countering corporate spin. In W.

Dinan & D. Miller (Eds.), *Thinker, faker, spinner, spy* (pp. 295–304). London: Pluto Press.

Mittelman, J. (2004). *Whither globalization? The vortex of knowledge and ideology.* London: Routledge.

Molleda, J-C. (2009). Global public relations. Retrieved from http://www.instituteforpr.org/essential_knowledge/detail/global_public_relations/

Molleda, J-C., Connolly-Ahern, C., & Quinn, C. (2005). Cross-national conflict shifting: Expanding a theory of global public relations management through quantitative content analysis. *Journalism Studies, 6*(1), 87–102.

Molleda, J-C., & Roberts, M. (2008). The value of "authenticity" in "glocal" strategic communication: The new Juan Valdez Campaign. *International Journal of Strategic Communication, 2*(3), 154–174.

Moloney, K. (2000). *Rethinking public relations: The spin and the substance.* London: Routledge.

Morley, M. (2009). How to manage your global reputation. In K. Sriramesh & D. Verčič (Eds.), *The global public relations handbook* (rev. ed., pp. 861–869). New York: Routledge.

Motion, J., & Weaver, C. K. (2005). A discourse model for critical public relations research: The Life Sciences Network and the battle for truth. *Journal of Public Relations Research, 17*(1), 49–67.

Munshi, D., & McKie, D. (2001). Different bodies of knowledge: Diversity and diversification in public relations. *Australian Journal of Communication, 28*(3), 11–22.

Ohmae, K. (1995). *The end of the nation state.* New York: Free Press.

Pal, M., & Dutta, M. (2008). Public relations in a global context: The relevance of critical modernism as a theoretical lens. *Journal of Public Relations Research, 20*(2), 159–179.

Palmer, J. (2000). *Spinning into control: News values and source strategies.* London: Leicester University Press.

Pieczka, M. (2006). Paradigms, systems theory, and public relations. In J. L'Etang & M. Pieczka (Eds.), *Public relations: Critical debates and contemporary practice* (pp. 333–357). London: Erlbaum.

Roth, N., Hunt, T., Stravropoulos, M., & Babik, K. (1996). Can't we all just get along? Cultural variables in codes of ethics. *Public Relations Review, 22*(2), 151–161.

Schiller, H. (1985). Electronic information flows. New basis for global domination? In P. Drummond & R. Paterson (Eds.), *Television in transition* (pp. 11–20). London: BFI.

Sha, B.-L. (2006). Cultural identity in the segmentation of publics: An emerging theory of intercultural public relations. *Journal of Public Relations Research, 18*(1), 45–65.

Shome, R., & Hegde, R. (2002). Culture, communication, and the challenge of globalization. *Critical Studies in Media Communication, 19*(2), 172–189.

Sison, M. (2009). Whose cultural values? Exploring public relations' approaches to understanding audiences. *PRism, 6*(2). Retrieved from www.praxis.massey.ac.nz/prism_on-line_journ.html

Sklair, L. (2007). Achilles has two heels: Crises of capitalist globalization. In W.

Dinan & D. Miller (Eds.) *Thinker, faker, spinner, spy* (pp. 21–32). London: Pluto Press.

Spinwatch (n.d.) What is Spinwatch? Retrieved from http://www.spinwatch. org/about-spinwatch-mainmenu-13/4428-what-is-spinwatch

Sriramesh, K. (2004). Epilogue: The need for multiculturalism in public relations education in Asia. In K. Sriramesh (Ed.), *Public relations in Asia: An anthology* (pp. 321–341). Singapore: Thomson Learning.

Sriramesh, K. (2007). The relationship between culture and public relations. In E. Toth (Ed.), *The future of excellence in public relations and communication management* (pp. 507–526). Mahwah, NJ: Erlbaum.

Sriramesh, K. (2009a). Globalisation and public relations: An overview looking into the future. *PRism, 6*(2). Retrieved from www.praxis.massey.ac.nz/ prism_on-line_journ.html

Sriramesh, K. (2009b). Introduction. In K. Sriramesh & D. Verčič (Eds.), *The global public relations handbook: Theory, research and practice* (rev. ed., pp. xxxiii–xl). New York: Routledge.

Sriramesh, K., & White, J. (1992). Societal culture and public relations. In J. Grunig (Ed.), *Excellence in public relations and communication management* (pp. 597–614). Hillsdale, NJ: Erlbaum.

Surma, A., & Daymon, C. (2009, July). *Critical discourses in the culture-public relations relationship.* Paper presented at the 16th Bledcom International Public Relations Research Symposium, Lake Bled, Slovenia.

Toledano, M. (2005). Public relations in Israel: The evolution of public relations as a profession in Israel's changing political, socio-cultural, and economic environment. (Unpublished doctoral dissertation). Université de Paris, France.

Tomlinson, J. (1999). *Globalization and culture.* Chicago, IL: University of Chicago Press.

Toth, E. (2009). The case for pluralistic studies of public relations. In R. Heath, E. Toth, & D. Waymer (Eds.), *Rhetorical and critical approaches to public relations* (Vol. 2, pp. 48–60). New York: Routledge.

Tyma, A. (2008). Public relations through a new lens; Critical praxis via the "Excellence Theory." *International Journal of Communication, 2,* 193–205.

Urry, J. (2005). The complexities of the global. *Theory, Culture & Society, 22*(5), 235–254.

Weaver, C. K., & Motion, J. (2002). Sabotage and subterfuge: Public relations, democracy and genetic engineering in New Zealand. *Media, Culture & Society, 24*(3), 325–343.

Weaver, C. K., Motion, J., & Roper, J. (2006). From propaganda to discourse (and back again): Truth, power, the public interest and public relations. In J. L'Etang & M. Pieczka (Eds.), *Public relations: Critical debates and contemporary practice* (pp. 7–40). London: Erlbaum.

Wilcox, D., & Cameron, G. (2010). *Public relations strategies and tactics* (9th ed.). Boston, MA: Pearson Education.

Williams, R. (1958). *Culture and society 1780-1950.* New York: Columbia University Press.

Yoshitake, M. (2004). Research paradigm for dialogue among diversities. In G-M. Chen & W. Starosta (Eds.), *International and Intercultural Communication Annual: Vol. 27. Dialogue among diversities* (pp. 16–42). Washington, DC: National Communication Association.

Chapter 2

Critical Perspectives in Global Public Relations

Theorizing Power

Lee Edwards

In this chapter, my aim is to theorize power in public relations by con-textualizing the profession as a system, a discourse technology, and a field of professional practice, situated in a global environment. I com-bine Appadurai's (1996) conceptualization of globalization as "work of the imagination" and his description of global cultural flows as mech-anisms by which global modernity is transmitted and sustained, with Pierre Bourdieu's (1991, 2000) notion of symbolic power, to reveal the substance and direction of the effects of public relations work both as a hegemonic instrument and a tool for resistance. This approach recog-nizes that power is manifested in different ways, forms, and places, and must be addressed from a number of viewpoints if it is to be adequately understood. To this end, rather than using a single theoretical frame-work for the discussion, I adopt Bourdieu's approach to theory as a set of tools chosen on the basis of their appropriateness to the object of study (Bourdieu & Wacquant, 1992, p. 227).

Critical understandings of power underpin the approach I outline, but have limitations in their ability to address the complexity of power in a global context. I begin by outlining some of these limitations to set the scene for the subsequent discussion. I then develop my arguments drawing on Appadurai and Bourdieu, to create a new conceptualization of power in public relations in global cultural contexts. My aim is not to present a definitive understanding of power in this context, but to offer a starting point from which further scholarship may emerge.

The Starting Point: Critical Theory and Public Relations

Critical examinations of public relations activity tend to examine the manner in which public relations practice maintains the hegemony of powerful groups and individuals over those who have fewer opportu-nities, skills, and resources to make themselves heard (Kim & Dutta,

2009; L'Etang, 2005; Pal & Dutta, 2008). This perspective is an important complement to normative scholarship that tends to focus more on the organizational role of public relations and the benefits it offers to organizations and their publics, as a means of building relationships and achieving mutually beneficial outcomes. Regardless of the ideological principles behind the analysis, scholars from both schools would agree that public relations work is designed to favor its employers, even if this bias is not always overt—and may be consciously disguised (Edwards, 2009).

The "discourse of suspicion" adopted by critical communication theorists (Mumby, 1997) is productive because it reveals the often invisible processes by which our lives are framed and our possibilities circumscribed through discourse. However, critical approaches tend to focus on structural dominance perpetuated through cultural and ideological control and neglect the important and often successful efforts of "othered" participants in the communications process to undermine the work of dominant groups (Demetrious, 2006; Munshi & McKie, 2001). In doing so, critical work continues to privilege the voices of dominant groups even as it challenges them. In public relations scholarship, this effect is seen in the continued dominance of empirical work based in commercial or governmental organizations and the relative lack of attention paid to activist groups, community groups, and non-governmental organizations (NGOs) (McKie & Munshi, 2007; Sallot, Lyon, Acosta-Alzuru, & Jones, 2003).

This chapter takes the opportunity presented by globalization theory to complicate the notion of power in critical public relations scholarship. The complexity of a globally connected world introduces a "discourse of vulnerability" (Mumby, 1997) by problematizing the notion of communication as a source of dominance and highlighting times, spaces, and places where the most strenuous efforts to persuade are undermined by the cultural, social, and discursive dynamics in specific localities. In other words, power in global public relations practice is a complex matter. Global public relations work is produced locally, disseminated nationally and globally, and deconstructed locally again, often far removed from its origins. It is contextualized by the interests on behalf of which it works and the outlets, including media systems, through which it is disseminated; more often than not, such interests perpetuate systems of domination that disadvantage marginalized groups and populations. Yet closer examination of local practices and discourses reveals daily challenges to such systems. Global public relations must recognize the power of local practitioners and audiences to reinterpret globally disseminated messages and reject their underlying assumptions. In the process, the historical and current contexts that define the stage for public relations activity should be acknowledged as fundamental to this interaction.

The Work of the Imagination and Symbolic Power

Appadurai (1996) argues that one of the defining characteristics of global modernity is the work of the imagination in the context of globally mediated events and migration flows. He focuses specifically on the cultural dimensions of globalization and argues that this work "is a space of contestation in which individuals and groups seek to annex the global into their own practices of the modern" (Appadurai, 1996, p. 4). In other words, the work of the imagination is part of the process of formulating group and individual identities in the context of a particular time and place, but in light of specific historical dynamics, information flows, and biographical connections that span the globe. It is a social practice, accessible to ordinary people not least through the existence of the mass media, which generates imaginaries that can connect people and create imagined communities (Anderson, 1991) across physical, political, and geographical boundaries. As Appadurai succinctly puts it, "The imagination is now central to all forms of agency, is itself a social fact, and is the key component of the new global order" (1996, p. 31).

Individuals exist in the context of global structures that frame their activities, and Appadurai is careful not to underemphasize the importance of global systems and structures. He notes, for example, that "consumption in the contemporary world is often a form of drudgery, part of the capitalist civilizing process" (Appadurai, 1996, p. 7). Nonetheless, the notion of imagination foregrounds agency and transformation and suggests that globalization is potentially productive rather than always destructive (Tomlinson, 2003). The mass media open up options of enacting normative roles in imaginative ways and make possible a "community of sentiment" (Appadurai, 1996, p. 8) that can transcend traditional geographical, cultural, social, or political boundaries, imagines and feels things together, and is capable of shared collective action.[1] Different media, for example, are used selectively by individuals and their content interpreted in ways that don't necessarily correspond to the intentions of those developing the original communication. This transformative action is not only social and cultural, but is also political and embedded in the articulations of histories understood at local, national, and global levels. As new imaginaries emerge that are shaped by understandings of the past, they simultaneously constitute new histories that form the present and the future.

In this sense, the work of the imagination connects the local with the national and the national with the global, but it makes these connections unpredictable. Information is not uniformly taken up, but interpreted in light of historical, temporal, and spatial specifics of local and national contexts. This dynamic represents a potential rupturing of normative possibilities available to individuals and groups, and is fundamental to the complexity observed in globalization processes (Held & McGrew, 2003).

Appadurai's emphasis on the imagination as "the locus of negotiation between sites of agency and globally defined fields of possibility" (1996, p. 31) implicitly recognizes an ongoing power struggle between individuals and the factors shaping their environment. This aligns with the ideas of sociologist Pierre Bourdieu, who argues that power is best understood as symbolic power, or the power to present a specific version of reality to others in a particular community and have those others adopt that view of reality as their own (Bourdieu, 1991). In particular, imagination is reminiscent of Bourdieu's notion of the "field of the possibles"— the range of social trajectories and positions perceived by individuals as available to them, and defined by their habitus (Bourdieu, 1984, p. 110). Habitus is the set of durable dispositions developed and inculcated over time and shaped by the normative representations of reality that we adopt from those who have symbolic power over us. These dispositions determine the way we comprehend our social environment and our role within it. They are embodied, expressed linguistically, and correspond to our symbolic power relative to others with whom we connect (Bourdieu, 1990, 1991).

The temporal aspect of habitus incorporates history, and indeed Bourdieu discusses history not in terms of political and social events, but in terms of normative understandings of the self and one's place in the world, understandings that have been built up over time and are seen to be "common sense" (Bourdieu, 2000). Moreover, he suggests that habitus can be specific to a particular field of practice,[2] where members compete for power and position themselves relative to others in the field in terms of the norms specified by the habitus (Bourdieu, 1992). The positions available to us in the field, defined not only by others but by our acceptance of their version of reality, are also understood as the limits of our particular field of the possibles, and frame the choices we make (Bourdieu, 1984).

Bourdieu does not grapple with questions of globalization in his work, but a combination of his ideas and Appadurai's framework is productive for understanding the power of public relations in this context. The notion of habitus has been criticized for being both too structural and too static (Crossley, 2003; King, 2000), but if one interprets the possibilities that it produces as one aspect of Appadurai's work of the imagination, agency is integrated into the picture and a degree of unpredictability in the formation and evolution of habitus emerges. Moreover, the global context of imagination work extends Bourdieu's use of fields to incorporate global communities of practice as much as those limited to one particular location. It also highlights their permeability and helps explain how in this particular context, a "field of the possibles" may become more diverse than in Bourdieu's original formulation. In turn, Bourdieu's articulation of symbolic power and its operation through representations of reality more explicitly reveals the dynamics of power that underpin the work of the imagination and explain why Appadurai argues that it is fundamental to the global order. Given that public relations' primary function is to operate in the interests of organizations—even if this includes engaging with external interests on a certain level—this allows us to begin to understand why and how the profession wields the power to influence global environments.

Feeding the Imagination: Global Cultural Flows

The question arises as to where the substance of the work of the imagination comes from. At first sight, Bourdieu's work does not appear helpful in providing an impetus for imagination because of his emphasis on dominance over resistance. He argues that dominant groups decide the bases for the relative positioning of themselves and others in the world, communicate these understandings, and these understandings are accepted because of their normative appearance (Bourdieu, 1991). The emphasis on the symbolic violence of dominant groups in this formulation has been criticized for being at the expense of those who resist such notions and draw on alternative sources for their own imagination work (Couldry, 2005). However, Bourdieu does acknowledge that normative discourses are challenged if there is a distance between practice and discourse—in other words, if lived experience does not correspond to the dominant discourse—and this raises the possibility of "heretical subversion" (Bourdieu, 1991, p. 128): the emergence of alternative representations of the world that have the power to change lived experience (Bourdieu, 2000).

Appadurai's (1996) work adds more depth to our understanding of how change emerges by explicitly moving away from traditional formulations of dominance and, instead, focusing on the new global cultural economy as "a complex, overlapping, disjunctive order that cannot any longer be understood in terms of existing centre-periphery models" (p. 32). Globalization, in other words, is fundamentally about the new forms, growth, and density of networks that span the globe to create "thick" globalism (Keohane & Nye, 2003). Such a world can incorporate the fact that our lives are always characterized by potential, if not always actual reimaginings that hold the possibility of change.

Appadurai argues that global modernity is characterized by five global cultural flows (1996, pp. 31–36). *Ethnoscapes* are the landscapes of moving people and groups prompted by modern global phenomena such as capital flows, technological developments, mass media imaginaries, national and international conflicts. As Appadurai points out, their constantly changing environment means that "these moving groups can never afford to let their imaginations rest too long, even if they wish to" (1996, p. 34). *Technoscapes* are the global configurations and distributions of technology that move rapidly around the world linked to political and economic dynamics and the availability of labor. *Financescapes* refer to the complex configuration and high-speed distribution of global capital flows. *Mediascapes* are defined as the distribution of both the capability of disseminating information around the world via media outlets and the substantive content of that information. They mix the world of commodities, news, and politics in their presentation of images and narratives that blur the line between reality and fiction for media consumers and provide material "out of which scripts can be formed of imagined lives, their own as well as those of others living in other places. These scripts ... help to constitute narratives of the Other and protonarratives of possible lives" (1996, p. 35–36). Finally, *ideoscapes* are the mosaic of images that relate to state ideologies and the counterideologies that are explicitly focused on capturing state power. Each of these flows can both reinforce and disturb the dynamics of the others, and it is the disjunctures between them that shape global cultural economies in a manner that is unique in history.

For the purposes of this discussion, the flows can be understood as sources of material for the work of the imagination outlined above. This material comprises both the substance of the flows—the discourses that emerge to define and justify their topography at any one time—but also the quotidian practical experience of such flows. Discourse and practice inform each other and this dialectic helps shape the imagined worlds, or field of the possibles, that individuals and groups are able to develop. For example, migration from rural to urban areas in search of employment in high-tech industries is imagined because of the narratives represented in mediascapes about the possibility of liberation through financial wealth and consequent access to consumption; the flow of global capital to those urban areas that allow such industries to emerge; and the ideological positionings of particular regions and nations that justify their claim to some of that capital. However, the global division of labor means the lived reality of working in high-tech industries in Bangalore, India, as compared to California in the United States, for example, could not be more different and produces very different scales of access to consumption for communities engaged in it (Giddens, 1990). The narratives of mediascapes and ideoscapes are reimagined very differently in light of this practical reality.

Taking these cultural flows and their dynamics into account helps overcome the limitations of Bourdieu's conditions for the formation of a "field of the possibles" by recognizing the fluid reality of fields that make up today's global cultural economy. A constant feature of globalization is the manner in which the disjunctures between cultural flows generate alternative imaginaries by shaping experience in a particular way and in a particular location. Consequently, fields of practice and the discourses that define them have to be understood as continuously contested rather than static, even if one particular view of the world tends to dominate in a historical moment.

This discussion allows us to incorporate two of the main characteristics of globalization, fluidity and resistance, into standard critical approaches to public relations. The next section describes in more detail how these new insights can be productive in understanding the power inherent in public relations as a global practice.

Public Relations, Imagination, and Power

Perhaps the most obvious understanding of public relations in the context of globalization is as a means of engagement in a discursive struggle at local, national, and global levels, to define the work of the imagination. This is not only a struggle over the present and future, but also over the particular histories that are chosen as the primary frames for imaginative work. In this section, I add to this view by arguing that public relations is implicated in a number of ways as a mechanism through which symbolic power is both sustained and contested through a global discursive struggle. First, public relations can be understood as a producer of the discourses that make up each of the five cultural flows. Second, it is a structural dynamic, part of the systems that help generate and maintain the movement of those flows across time and space and partially reconfigure collective social space in the form of "transworld" connections, unconstrained by traditional territorial borders (Scholte, 2003). Third, it is a contested field in itself, with its own dynamics of self-interest and self-preservation that inevitably shape its effects on the environment.

Public Relations as Global Discourse Production

Public relations as global discourse production is most obviously implicated in Appadurai's mediascapes and ideoscapes. It produces and disseminates information through communication technologies such as online media, television and radio outlets that are part of the mediascapes that straddle the world. Consequently, its discourses always have the potential to reach beyond the local, even if this was not the original intent. Ideologically, public relations works in the interests of those who pay for it, whether that be government, commercial interests, NGOs, or activist groups. It is produced to persuade its audiences of a particular version of reality that will shape their attitudes and behaviors in favor of a specific form of consumption, production, agitation, or citizenship (McKie & Munshi, 2007; Miller & Dinan, 2007; Moloney, 2006; Motion, 2005). In other words, it is one of the tools used by groups and, to a lesser extent, individuals, in the struggle for symbolic power in global cultural contexts.

Much previous research examining public relations work in an international context tends to interpret this power struggle in the context of specific countries or campaigns, executed by or on behalf of individual organizations (Curtin & Gaither, 2007; Moss, 2002; Sriramesh & Verčič, 2009). Similarly, critical work tends to examine the effects of specific campaigns on the relative power of dominant and dominated groups, in relation to one particular issue or context (e.g., Mickey, 2002; Motion & Weaver, 2005). These approaches are important, but it would be a mistake to understand the effects of public relations discourses purely in terms of such specificity, as if it could be isolated from the rest of its environment (Edwards, 2009). Globalization theories remind us that the conditions for the production and the reception of discourse are complex (Held & McGrew, 2003). The cultural flows that Appadurai describes are meshed together such that public relations discourses cannot be interpreted as an element only of mediascapes or ideoscapes. The conditions for their production, distribution, and effects must be sought in these connections rather than in single strands.

The symbolic discourses that frame understandings of localities shape the manner in which other ideologies are accepted and interpreted in that context. At the same time, the insertion of new "raw material" from other global spaces and times, into such localities, generates disjunctures that interact with, and change the uptake of different elements of those symbolic discourses. The effects on our lives are political, social, cultural, and economic. For example, government-led media coverage of political oppression in a distant country may alter Western discourses about asylum-seekers from that country present in ideoscapes, albeit in terms that remain acceptable to local and national political and commercial interests. Elsewhere, citizens living under oppressive regimes may imagine new interpretations of the actions and discourses of local and national demagogues because of access to activist communications from NGOs. These new imaginaries will be formed from the possibilities presented by the NGOs and the particular social and economic circumstances that define the way such possibilities may be realized.

Such interactions constitute a continuous dialectical process, a conversation enacted through the correspondences and disjunctures of various cultural flows at local, national, and global levels. Where cultural flows have a natural "fit," the interaction between their discourses is seamless. Financescapes, for example, are underpinned by particular ideoscapes that promote, through public relations narratives produced on behalf of financial interests, certain topographies of capital distribution and use, most commonly on the basis of neoliberal principles. Because these neatly coincide with the discourses of consumption that circulate in mediascapes, those in the West who have the wealth to consume are likely to barely notice the symbolic power being exerted over them. In contrast, where cultural flows clash, new imaginaries emerge and change is an option. The economic migrations that form part of the substance of ethnoscapes are made possible in part by the imaginaries developed by public relations practitioners on behalf of cultural, financial, political, and economic interests and presented in mediascapes using the distribution mechanisms available in technoscapes. These imaginaries are interpreted as particular possibilities by groups and individuals, some of whom enact them in their own lives. These movements and the new imaginaries they represent, in turn, create new foundations on which existing discourses can be extended or challenged through further public relations work.

In this way, the production of discourses through public relations makes a major contribution to the manner in which these conversations evolve and the symbolic power that one or other viewpoint attracts.

Public Relations and Global Structures

The discourses produced by public relations are only one element in the overall picture of the power that the profession is capable of wielding in a globalizing world. Bourdieu (1999) highlights the importance of objective structures in the generation, maintenance, and reproduction of symbolic power. These need to be taken into account in analyses of public relations in the context of globalization.

Bourdieu argues that systems of relations in particular fields are hierarchical and inherently in conflict: they are structured in oppositional terms, where the fundamental division is between those that dominate and those that are dominated. These symbolic systems offer ways of understanding the world by organizing it into comprehensible systems (structuring structures); ways of knowing the world through shared meanings (structured structures); and ways of political organization, through their integrative role (for dominant groups) and divisive role (between dominant and dominated groups). In short, they play a major role in creating habitus (Bourdieu, 1990; Swartz, 1997) and are, therefore, fundamental to the work of the imagination.

Bourdieu's breakdown of symbolic systems into structuring structures, structured structures, and political organization is helpful when considering the multiple levels on which public relations works. It not only informs our cultural understandings of the world we live in, but structures that world as well, since structures are perpetuated and justified through discourse. His view also fits well with Appadurai's argument that cultural flows do not remain abstract, but generate concrete action through enacted imaginaries, and this action has structural and political as well as subjective consequences (Appadurai, 1996).

For example, campaigns on behalf of political, activist, or commercial interests represent the structures of the world in a particular way. Neoliberal presentations of the market economy suggest that consumption liberates the individual; progress is interpreted as wealth accumulation. These discourses act as structuring structures in that they promote certain systems of production, consumption, and regulation. They validate consumption as a valuable and substantive activity; they prioritize profit over welfare; they position government as a protector of the free market rather than as a manager of its effects. As structured structures, discourses produce shared meanings, circulated via mass media imaginaries, on the basis of which we develop "collective imaginaries"—common understandings of the world, its past and present, our role within it, and the future possibilities it holds.

These structured and structuring effects of public relations discourses are clearly mechanisms of symbolic power. Public relations campaigns on behalf of commercial organizations and (Western) governments reinforce these structures by valorizing neoliberal ideologies in their particular context. As McKie and Munshi (2007) have pointed out, this can have particularly damaging effects on those disempowered by the discourse, marginalizing and penalizing those who do not fit, whether they be organizations that do not use profit as their primary guide for success and consequently attract a lower share price, or individuals who are unable or reluctant to consume, or whose limited access to technology means they cannot engage in systems of political participation and citizenship. This "othering" of groups and individuals continues through the material consequences of enacting a neoliberal ideology. Environmental damage, notably in developing countries, becomes a legitimate consequence of ensuring successful, cost-effective production to maintain a market. Companies may try to minimize their effects, but stopping the damage altogether is rarely an option (McKie & Galloway, 2007; Munshi & Kurian, 2005).

The structural effects of public relations are also evident if it is understood as a system, enmeshed with other systems, including the media, relevant industry sectors, and its sister professions such as marketing and advertising. The professionalization process has generated a desire to separate public relations from its context as part of a wider status project (Pieczka & L'Etang, 2006), and idealistic views of public relations present it as separate and different from marketing, or media, or change management, with its own history and professional identity (Ewen, 1996; Gregory, 2009; L'Etang, 2004; Wilcox & Cameron, 2009). This separation generates status, allows budgets to be defended and jobs to be protected, and creates a rationale for research (Toth, 2002), but cocoons practitioners from recognizing the far-reaching impact of their daily endeavors. A territorial view of public relations has its place (Scholte, 2003), but without a corresponding recognition of the transworld connections the profession creates through its global presence (Sriramesh & Verčič, 2007), public relations is ill-prepared for a world where "thick" globalism means that the imagination of a remote population has a potentially significant effect on apparently localized communications efforts (Elmer, 2007; Keohane & Nye, 2003; McKie & Munshi, 2007).

Appadurai's (1996) work also offers a way of understanding public relations and its infrastructure in terms of its interconnectivity. The notion of cultural flows demonstrates how practitioners are always implicated in the global processes that shape our lives, whether they are members of a Western government information service, a spokesperson for Medécins Sans Frontières working in refugee camps in Pakistan, head of communications for a global enterprise, or the most junior member of an account team in a local agency. This reality is often forgotten.

Technoscapes are a useful starting point. They are part of public relations' infrastructure in the context of globalization, shaping the speed and topography of the dissemination of discourses and determining the possibilities for their uptake. Like public relations tactics and strategies, technoscapes are not neutral or simple channels; they can provide valuable opportunities for previously marginalized groups and individuals to engage in civil society and the political process (see Mathews, 2003). Yet, simultaneously, they produce an ongoing process of "othering" that public relations work perpetuates through its emphasis on technology as a distributive mechanism for information (Warschauer, 2003). The popularity of digital and online technologies as public relations dissemination tactics, and the increasing use of that technology alongside or in preference to print and oral techniques (e.g. Breakenridge, 2008; Duhé, 2007; Tench & Willis, 2009), means that populations in the global South with limited access to technological infrastructure are marginalized from major trade and information flows. Nationally, the dynamic of exclusion persists as populations that have limited technological skills, or fragmented access to technology, such as the elderly, poor, or migrant communities, are excluded from debates that affect their lives. Locally, access to information distributed via digital or online technology defines the haves and have-nots: those who can log on to the Internet on a daily basis via a computer at home are able to keep up with information flows to a much greater extent than those who have to visit the library to use a computer.

The bias toward Western audiences in the distribution mechanisms of technoscapes is also echoed in the fact that certain discourses—usually those generated by dominant groups—are more widely disseminated than others through the mass media, generating shared experiences and imagined communities across time and space (Appadurai, 1996) and perpetuating their dominance on a global level. This is not merely a question of greater access to media, but is also a function of the symbiotic relationship between public relations work and global media structures: the one cannot exist without the other.

Global media is dominated by very few global media conglomerates, most of whom have their headquarters in the United States. The news and information they disseminate reflect the political and commercial ideologies that define their home nation and, more broadly, the developed world, squeezing out local cultural products and ideologies and limiting access to the public sphere for those who voice alternative views (McChesney, 1999, 2000). The global public relations industry is deeply implicated in this process because of its structure. A recent analysis of the top 150 PR consultancies in the United Kingdom was dominated by groups domiciled in North America or Europe but with a global reach (*PR Week*, 2009). Their position in the public relations hierarchy is determined by their market capitalization; the companies they own cover marketing, public relations, and media-related activities. All are active in the financial sector and all benefit from income derived from global campaigns; that is, campaigns that implicitly recognize the power of public relations to influence a globalizing world.

The discourses produced by such companies on behalf of their clients complement rather than challenge the needs of global media conglomerates and generate power that operates in a specific direction: from North to South, West to East, rich to poor. The hand-in-glove relationship between public relations work, media, and corporate interests, means an international campaign to promote a new range of clothing for a global brand has a much wider ideological and material effect than those practitioners might expect or have time to think about. It justifies the production of those clothes by citizens of developing countries, in difficult conditions, and usually with very low pay. It justifies the exploitation and disposal of resources used to make the clothes, such as water, cotton, chemical dyes, and bleach. It justifies consumption in a world where that might not be possible or advisable for everyone in the target audience. And it justifies the disposal of perfectly good clothing in favor of the new trend, increasing the burden of waste we put on the planet and its citizens in remote places.

Yet, such campaigns pass uncontroversially into the mediascape because, ideologically and economically, they "fit" with mass media agendas dominated by Western interests. Moreover, the consistency of the discourses promoted in the global media system means such messages connect with a wide range of campaigns underpinned by similar commercial and political interests, to reinforce the ideology of material consumption and production as structured structures: "natural" moments that constitute us and define our location in the world (Appadurai, 1996; Bourdieu, 1984).

The Importance of the Professional Field

The third aspect of public relations work that shapes the power it exerts is the reality that this work takes place in the context of a professional field that spans local, national, and global environments. Fields are competitive spaces where agents engage in a struggle for symbolic power. This power, Bourdieu argues, is determined by the mix of economic, social, and cultural capital that each agent in the field can lay claim to and transform into symbolic capital; that is, capital that represents more in terms of its symbolic value than its material attributes suggest (Bourdieu, 1997). The criteria by which symbolic value is attributed are determined by dominant agents in the field and invariably correspond to the capital that those agents already possess, thereby maintaining their dominant position and ability to define the locations of others in the field. In public relations, the most symbolically powerful companies—those which, for example, are in the annual "Top 150" lists—measure their success in terms of financial resources, market capitalization, accounts with major global and national brands, and the global footprint of the consultancy's own operations (e.g., Edelman, 2009; WPP, 2009). Organizations struggle to position themselves in relation to other colleagues or groups using these criteria, not least because this helps them compete effectively for a slice of the financial "pie" available to fund public relations work.

While ostensibly associated with the status of individual companies, and indirectly practitioners, this set of criteria also determines the value and prestige associated with different types of public relations work. Public relations in sectors such as the financial, healthcare, pharmaceutical, or technology industries benefit from the mainstream position of their (client) organizations and can attract large budgets; in contrast, practitioners in the not-for-profit sector are likely to have fewer resources to work with and are less widely recognized for their work than their counterparts (e.g., Chartered Institute of Public Relations, 2009). There may be a tradition of taking on pro bono work for a cause-related organization in some consultancies, but these accounts are unlikely to command the same energy or time from practitioners as their commercial counterparts. Thus, the structure of the public relations industry and the importance of financial success for those at the top also produce a bias towards industries that benefit the "developed" world and its dominant interests more than its "developing" counterparts.

Of course, public relations practitioners engage in struggles for symbolic power wherever their skills are deployed, and this may include activist, third sector, NGO, or other organizations that challenge rather than accept the status quo. Practitioners in the same consultancy may be working on campaigns that are diametrically opposed in ideological terms and compete directly for "voice" in mediascapes, in order to generate new imaginaries. In Bourdieu's terms, the representations of reality made through public relations by groups opposing dominant discourses, such as charities or environmental organizations, inject a missing ingredient that demonstrates the ways in which apparently different lives are in fact connected. This allows collective identity, or the "collective imaginary" described by Appadurai, to develop.

> The political labour of representation ... enables agents to discover within themselves common properties that lie beyond the diversity of particular situations which isolate, divide and demobilize, and to construct their social identity on the basis of characteristics or experiences which seemed totally dissimilar so long as the principle of pertinence by virtue of which they could be constituted as indices of membership of the same class was lacking. (Bourdieu, 1991, p. 130)

In reaction to this, public relations work by members of dominant groups produces

> a substitute for everything that is threatened by the very existence of heretical discourse ... they endeavour to impose universally, through a discourse permeated by the simplicity and transparency of common sense, the feeling of obviousness and necessity which this world imposes on them; having an interest in leaving things as they are, they attempt to undermine politics in a depoliticized political discourse, produced through a process of neutralization or, even, better, of negation, which seeks to restore the doxa to its original state of innocence. (Bourdieu, 1991, p. 131)

I have already established that these discursive struggles do not take place on a level playing field, but the structure of the field of public relations itself does nothing to help alleviate this imbalance. The logic of the overarching field of power means that the majority of public relations professionals will seek capital that improves their position in society through jobs that offer good pay and professional status. While some of the larger NGOs and not-for-profit organizations may be able to compete on these terms to attract professionals, smaller charities and activist groups simply cannot. Talent and valuable social capital will tend to migrate away from this sector, leaving it less well-equipped for engaging in and challenging discourses that dominate ideoscapes and mediascapes and "other" the people for whom such groups provide an important voice.

The Potential for Resistance

The context of globalization for public relations work refocuses the lens of critical analysis onto the complexity of power in an overwhelmingly connected environment. The articulation between Appadurai's global cultural flows means that ideoscapes cannot be separated from technoscapes, financescapes, or other cultural flows and supports postcolonial interpretations of communication as one of the main tactical and ideological tools through which the world is divided (Munshi & Kurian, 2005; Shome & Hedge, 2002). Correspondingly, the power exerted by public relations work does not inhere solely in the messages it creates and disseminates, but in the distribution mechanisms that it uses, the economic resources it structures and legitimates, and the relative value it accords some people over others.

And yet the complexity of our globalizing world reminds us that it would be incorrect to suppose that this dynamic goes unchallenged. Even if symbolic power seems most often to lie with dominant groups, postcolonial theorists remind us that these groups cannot exist without the "other" (Said, 1978/1995). To combat the tendency to overemphasize the role of dominant groups and individuals, agency and subjectivity must be reintroduced into the analysis, and in this chapter I have demonstrated how Appadurai's (1996) conception of the work of the imagination is useful here.

Imagination is an important locus of resistance to symbolic power and can lead to material changes in global cultural flows that have a tangible effect on the global order as it affects particular places at particular times. Of course, the work of the imagination, in Appadurai's terms, uses the raw materials of global cultural flows in a specific and relevant way and is not the sole province of groups and individuals that critical theorists might traditionally view as subordinated. Moreover, because cultural flows are characterized by coherence more often than clashes, one might argue that the imaginaries of dominant groups are more deeply embedded in the global order. However, because these imaginaries are characterized by common sense understandings of the world, they do not generate the same impetus to action as the disjunctures between the flows that prompt the development of alternative views of reality. The articulation of disjunctures through discourse "exploits the possibility of changing the social world by changing the representation of this world which contributes to its reality ..." (Bourdieu, 1991, p. 128). This is a political act, particularly in the form of collective imaginaries prompted by mass media that influence individual and collective identity, and can have positive and negative consequences (Appadurai, 1996). Still, the dynamic is ultimately productive and "contributes practically to the reality of what it announces by the fact of ... making it conceivable and above all credible and thus creating the collective representation which will contribute to its production" (Bourdieu, 1991, p. 128).

Henderson (2005) illustrates the possibilities such resistance can offer at a local and national level with her analysis of the public relations activities of the GE Free Coalition, set up in New Zealand to counter the dominant voices of scientific and industry groups during a government consultation process on genetic modification (GM) policy. Science and industry bodies defined New Zealand's future competitiveness in terms of its acceptance of GM as a means of competitive advantage in global research and commodity markets. In contrast, the GE Free Coalition comprised a number of interest groups whose aim was to ensure that public concerns about GM were taken into account by the government. They employed the gamut of public relations tactics, including lobbying, media relations work, Web-based campaigns, media stunts, and grassroots initiatives, to successfully reposition the discourse (Roper, 2002) around GM, emphasizing the scientific and economic value of a pure, natural environment, during the consultation period. Their efforts "bought time, ensured that there would be continuing debate about the regulatory environment, and effectively contested the dominant discourses about genetic engineering" (Henderson, 2005, p. 133).

On a global scale, Roper (2002) and Juris (2005) illustrate the many ways in which antiglobalization movements counter government and corporate communication by using the technologies and media available to them to generate alternative discourses about the political, social, and economic world order. Their work gives rise to new imaginaries as it circulates through the technoscapes and mediascapes that characterize Appadurai's modernity. Juris (2005) describes the rapid spread of Indymedia centers, communication hubs located across the globe and used by activist groups to bypass traditional media outlets and directly communicate "grassroots, non-corporate coverage," not only from major global events such as the anti-WTO protests, but also in response to local and national economic and political conditions (Independent Media Center, 2009). These stories weave together an alternative narrative of dominant global systems and generate local, national, and global resistance. Their efforts have been so challenging to dominant groups that Indymedia Centers in a range of countries have been raided and their technology and files destroyed (Juris, 2005). Roper (2002) emphasizes the importance of taking such efforts seriously; in presenting an alternative, they generate new public expectations of corporate and government conduct that are rooted in powerful alternative and collective imaginaries of the world order. Politicians and corporate bodies that ignore them will face increasing challenges to their legitimacy, and will need to respond in order to survive.

Conclusion

This chapter has drawn on the notion of imagination work and cultural flows to reflect on the power of public relations in a globalizing world. The possibilities produced by the work of the imagination, and the connectedness of global modernity through the cultural flows described in this chapter, remind us that to examine *only* normative practicalities of global public relations, or *only* the resistance of activist discourses, produces an incomplete representation of the effects of public relations in global contexts. Recognizing the power of public relations discourses to produce new imaginaries, or fields of the possible, in the context of cultural flows, reveals the multifaceted nature of the power exercised by global public relations practices, regardless of who initiates them.

In public relations research and education, more nuanced explorations of this power are called for, explorations that reflect on the social, political, cultural, and economic landscapes that public relations practitioners shape through their work. The inextricable links between global cultural flows and public relations' role in maintaining or disrupting those connections, should form part of the context for understanding the profession. Practitioners themselves must recognize the fact that their work generates "cascades," or sequences of action that migrate and evolve across space and time, local, national, and global contexts (Rosenau, 1990). In doing so, they may become more reflexive about their own work, less judgmental of others' right to be heard, and more cognizant of the possible reactions to their activities. Even widely disseminated imagined worlds produced through public relations work must engage with alternative perceptions of reality and be prepared for change.

Discussion Questions

1. Think about where you see yourself in 2, 5, or 10 years' time. What possibilities are available to you? How are these (the work of your imagination) shaped by Appadurai's cultural flows?
2. How does the discourse of the Fairtrade Movement (www.fairtrade.org.uk) contrast with "Western," or neoliberal assumptions about consumption and production? How is a "Fairtrade world" imagined?

3. Choose an issue of a national newspaper in your country. What overall themes do the stories relate to (e.g., business, celebrity, politics, sports)? What kinds of ideologies underpin the themes? What is *not* written about? Try rewriting a story from the paper using a different set of assumptions to generate a different "imaginary."

4. Visit www.indymedia.org and read four or five stories on the front page that interest you. How do they change your view of the countries and people featured? What do you have in common with them? How does this help you develop a collective imaginary that means you relate to their particular situation?

5. Visit the Web page of a global public relations company (e.g., Weber Shandwick/Edelman/Hill & Knowlton) and find a case study of an international public relations campaign. How is the success of such campaigns measured? In light of Appadurai's cultural flows, what effects are ignored? Why do you think this is?

Notes

1. The community of Michael Jackson fans around the world, which became particularly visible after his death in June 2009 because of the scale of their grief, is a good example of such a community.

2. A field may be a particular community or a professional body or another group whose members identify themselves relative to each other.

References

Anderson, B. (1991). *Imagined communities*. London: Verso.

Appadurai, A. (1996). *Modernity at large: Cultural dimensions of globalization*. Minneapolis, MN: University of Minnesota Press.

Bourdieu, P. (1984). *Distinction: A social critique of the judgement of taste*. London: Routledge & Kegan Paul.

Bourdieu, P. (1990). *The logic of practice*. Cambridge, UK: Polity Press.

Bourdieu, P. (1991). *Language and symbolic power* (G. Raymond & M. Adamson, Trans.). Cambridge, UK: Polity Press.

Bourdieu, P. (1992). *The field of cultural production: Essays in art and literature*. Cambridge, UK: Polity Press.

Bourdieu, P. (1997). The forms of capital. In A. H. Halsey, H. Lauder, P. Brown, & A. Stuart Wells (Eds.), *Education, culture, economy, society* (pp. 46–59). Oxford, UK: Oxford University Press.

Bourdieu, P. (1999). *The weight of the world: Social suffering in contemporary society*. Cambridge, UK: Polity Press.

Bourdieu, P. (2000). *Pascalian meditations*. Stanford, CA: Stanford University Press/Polity Press.

Bourdieu, P., & Wacquant, L. (1992). *An invitation to reflexive sociology*. Chicago, IL: Polity Press.

Breakenridge, D. (2008). *PR 2.0: New media, new tools, new audiences*. Upper Saddle River, NJ: FT Press.

Chartered Institute of Public Relations. (2009). CIPR Excellence Awards 2009. Retrieved from http://www.cipr.co.uk/news/index.htm

Couldry, N. (2005). The individual point of view: Learning from Bourdieu's "The Weight of the World." *Cultural Studies <=> Critical Methodologies, 5*(3), 354–372.

Crossley, N. (2003). From reproduction to transformation: Social movement fields and the radical habitus. *Theory, Culture and Society, 20*(6), 43–68.

Curtin, P. A., & Gaither, T. K. (2007). *International public relations: Negotiating culture, identity and power*. Thousand Oaks, CA: Sage.

Demetrious, K. (2006). Active voices. In J. L'Etang & M. Pieczka (Eds.), *Public relations: Critical debates and contemporary practice* (pp. 93–107). Mahwah, NJ: Erlbaum.

Duhé, S. (Ed.). (2007). *New media and public relations*. New York: Lang.

Edelman. (2009). Edelman Corporate Brochure. Retrieved from http://www.nxtbook.com

Edwards, L. (2009). Symbolic power and public relations practice: Locating individual practitioners in their social context. *Journal of Public Relations Research, 21*(3), 251–272.

Elmer, P. (2007). Unmanaging public relations: Reclaiming complex practice in pursuit of global consent. *Public Relations Review, 33*(4), 360–367.

Ewen, S. (1996). *PR! A social history of spin*. New York: Basic Books.

Giddens, A. (1990). *The consequences of modernity*. Cambridge, UK: Polity Press.

Gregory, A. (2009). Public relations as planned communication. In R. Tench & L. Yeomans (Eds.), *Exploring public relations* (2nd ed., pp. 174–197). Harlow, UK: Pearson.

Held, D., & McGrew, A. (2003). The great globalization debate: An introduction. In D. Held & A. McGrew (Eds.), *The global transformation reader* (pp. 1–50). Cambridge, UK: Polity Press.

Henderson, A. (2005). Activism in "Paradise": Identity management in a public relations campaign against genetic engineering. *Journal of Public Relations Research, 17*(2), 117–137.

Independent Media Center. (2009). Independent Media Center. Retrieved from http://www.indymedia.org/en/

Juris, J. S. (2005). The new digital media and activist networking within anti-corporate globalization movements. *The Annals of the American Academy of Political and Social Science, 597*, 189–208.

Keohane, R. O., & Nye, J. S. (2003). Globalization: What's new? What's not? (And so what?). In D. Held & A. McGrew (Eds.), *The global transformations reader* (pp. 75–83). Cambridge, UK: Polity Press.

Kim, I., & Dutta, M. J. (2009). Studying crisis communication from the subaltern studies framework: Grassroots activism in the wake of Hurricane Katrina. *Journal of Public Relations Research, 21*(2), 142–164.

King, A. (2000). Thinking with Bourdieu against Bourdieu: A "practical" critique of the habitus. *Sociological Theory, 18*(3), 417–433.

L'Etang, J. (2004). *Public relations in Britain: A history of professional practice in the 20th century.* Mahwah, NJ: Erlbaum.

L'Etang, J. (2005). Critical public relations: Some reflections. *Public Relations Review, 31*(4), 521–526.

Mathews, J. (2003). Power shift. In D. Held & A. McGrew (Eds.), *The global transformations reader* (pp. 204–212). Cambridge, UK: Polity Press.

McChesney, R. W. (1999). *Rich media, poor democracy: Communication politics in dubious times.* Chicago, IL: University of Illinois Press.

McChesney, R. W. (2000). The political economy of communication and the future of the field. *Media, Culture & Society, 22*(1), 109–116.

McKie, D., & Galloway, C. (2007). Climate change after denial: Global reach, global responsibilities and public relations. *Public Relations Review, 33*(4), 368–376.

McKie, D., & Munshi, D. (2007). *Reconfiguring public relations: Ecology, equity and enterprise.* Abingdon, UK: Routledge.

Mickey, T. J. (2002). *Deconstructing public relations: Public relations criticism.* Mahwah, NJ: Erlbaum.

Miller, D., & Dinan, W. (2007). *Thinker, faker, spinner, spy: Corporate PR and the assault on democracy.* London: Pluto Press.

Moloney, K. (2006). *Rethinking public relations: PR propaganda and democracy* (2nd ed.). Abingdon, UK: Routledge.

Moss, D. (2002). *Public relations cases: International perspectives.* London: Routledge.

Motion, J. (2005). Participative public relations: Power to the people or legitimacy for government discourse? *Public Relations Review, 31*(4), 505–512.

Motion, J., & Weaver, C. K. (2005). A discourse perspective for critical public relations research: Life Sciences Network and the battle for truth. *Journal of Public Relations Research, 17*(1), 49–67.

Mumby, D. K. (1997). Modernism, postmodernism and communication studies: A rereading of an ongoing debate. *Communication Theory, 7*(1), 1–28.

Munshi, D., & Kurian, P. (2005). Imperializing spin cycles: A postcolonial look at public relations, greenwashing, and the separation of publics. *Public Relations Review, 31*(4), 513–520.

Munshi, D., & McKie, D. (2001). Different bodies of knowledge: Diversity and diversification in Public Relations. *Australian Journal of Communication, 28*(3), 11–22.

Pal, M., & Dutta, M. J. (2008). Public relations in a global context: The relevance of critical modernism as a theoretical lens. *Journal of Public Relations Research, 20*(2), 159–179.

Pieczka, M., & L'Etang, J. (2006). Public relations and the question of professionalism. In J. L'Etang & M. Pieczka (Eds.), *Public relations: Critical debates and contemporary practice* (pp. 265–278). Mahwah, NJ: Erlbaum.

PR Week. (2009). *PR Week* top 150 consultancies 2009. London: Haymarket.

Roper, J. (2002). Government, corporate or social power? The Internet as a tool in the struggle for dominance in public policy. *Journal of Public Affairs, 2*(3), 113–124.

Rosenau, J. (1990). *Turbulence in world politics: A theory of change and continuity.* Princeton, NJ: Princeton University Press.

Said, E. (1995). *Orientalism* (2nd ed.). Harmondsworth, UK: Penguin. (Original work published 1978)

Sallot, L. M., Lyon, L. J., Acosta-Alzuru, C., & Jones, K. O. (2003). From aardvark to zebra: A new millennium analysis of theory development in public relations academic journals. *Journal of Public Relations Research, 15*(1), 27–90.

Scholte, J. (2003). What is "global" about globalization? In D. Held & A. McGrew (Eds.), *The global transformations reader* (pp. 84–91). Cambridge, UK: Polity Press.

Shome, R., & Hegde, R. (2002). Postcolonial approaches to communication: Charting the terrain, engaging the inheritance. *Communication Theory, 12*(3), 249–270.

Sriramesh, K., & Verčič, D. (2007). Introduction to this special section: The impact of globalization on public relations. *Public Relations Review, 33*(3), 355–359.

Sriramesh, K., & Verčič, D. (2009). *The global public relations handbook: Theory, research and practice* (rev. ed.). New York: Routledge.

Swartz, D. (1997). *Culture and power: The sociology of Pierre Bourdieu.* Chicago, IL: University of Chicago Press.

Tench, R., & Willis, P. (2009). Creativity, deception or ethical malpractice: A critique of the Trumanisation of marketing public relations through guerrilla campaigns. *Ethical Space, 6*(2), 47–55.

Tomlinson, J. (2003). Globalization and cultural identity. In D. Held & A. McGrew (Eds.), *The global transformations reader* (pp. 269–277). Cambridge, UK: Polity Press.

Toth, E. (2002). Postmodernism for modern public relations: The cash value and application of critical research in public relations. *Public Relations Review, 28*(3), 243–250.

Warschauer, M. (2003). *Technology and social inclusion: Rethinking the digital divide.* Cambridge, MA: MIT Press.

Wilcox, D. L., & Cameron, G. T. (2009). *Public relations: Strategies and tactics* (9th ed.). Boston, MA: Pearson/Allyn & Bacon.

WPP. (2009). 2008 WPP Annual Report. Retrieved from http://www.hilland knowlton.com/about/annualreport

Suggested Readings

Appadurai, A. (2001). Deep democracy: Urban governmentality and the horizon of politics. *Environment and Urbanization, 13(2)*, 23–43.

Giddens, A. (2002). *Runaway world: How globalization is reshaping our lives.* London: Profile Books.

Juris, J. (2008). *Networking futures: The movements against corporate globalization.* London: Duke University Press.

Said, E. (1993). *Culture and imperialism.* London: Vintage.

Swartz, D. (1997). *Culture and power: The sociology of Pierre Bourdieu.* Chicago, IL: University of Chicago Press.

Chapter 3

How Intercultural Communication Theory Informs Public Relations Practice in Global Settings

Michael Kent and Maureen Taylor

Culture is a multifaceted concept that has often been used to refer to a group of people who share similar views and interpretations of their world. These interpretations might include national identity, race, religion, geographic location, interpersonal relationships, and a host of other factors. Speaking of "a culture," however, is misleading. People identify with many cultures (often called cocultures) simultaneously, and not every member of a particular culture shares all of the same cultural beliefs (Martin & Nakayama, 1999). From a communication perspective, culture consists of shared experiences and negotiated meaning and provides a way to deal with ambiguity and uncertainty (Samovar & Porter, 2001).

As globalization and new communication technologies bring the world closer together, there is a greater need for public relations practitioners to help organizations navigate cultural terrains. Communication in the 21st century will be marked by efforts to reduce ambiguity and uncertainty in an ever smaller, yet more tightly networked world. It is this ambiguity and uncertainty that has allowed the practice of public relations to emerge as a valuable organizational communication function.

A central part of many public relations professionals' jobs is to communicate with multiple stakeholders and stakeseekers. Communicating with diverse publics is a difficult enough task in a nation or region when the public relations practitioner shares the same overarching cultural background with the public. Communication becomes an even more complex task when organizations seek to engage in relationships with global publics that live and work across many real and perceived boundaries. Many public relations practitioners are being called upon to build relationships in complex cultural environments. Are they up to the challenge?

This chapter reflects on different intercultural communication theories that have been used in both the communication and public relations literatures. By having a wider range of theories and ideas to draw upon, scholars and professionals are better equipped to understand the complexities of intercultural public relations. In intercultural communication readers and textbooks, a number of issues are consistently highlighted as important topics of analysis and discussion. These include, but are not limited to: national identity, cultural identity, and cultural identification, nonverbal communication, perceptual differences (time, status, trust), gender identification (masculinity/femininity), experiences of discrimination, individualism vs. collectivism, a sense of "otherness" when interacting in unfamiliar cultures, religious and ideological differences, negotiation of friendship and kinship, ethical questions, linguistic differences, code switching, and others (see Martin, Nakayama, & Flores, 2002; Samovar & Porter, 2003). For a person interested in culture in general, any of these issues (or a combination of them) might provide a valuable lens through which to understand the cultural norms and values of those from another region, country, or cultural group. However, from the standpoint of a professional communicator tasked with creating messages for multiple publics and negotiating relationships among diverse stakeholders, it might be best to take a generic approach (outlined below) to understanding public relations situations in global environments.

Globalization and new communication technologies have brought individuals, groups, and organizations closer together. What happens in one country now can have immediate effects on people, organizations, and relationships in many other countries. Indeed, given the complexity of culture, no single person or organization could learn about every cultural practice or communication pattern in every culture. What is actually more useful than trying to understand every aspect of every nation's culture is to consider intercultural communication and public relations from a relational and generic perspective.

Martin and Nakayama (1999) provided a useful framework for intercultural communication that emphasizes relational rather than culture-specific approaches guiding intercultural interactions. In intercultural communication research, the dialectical perspective is based on a holistic approach that places the "relationship" at the center of the communication (Martin & Nakayama, 1999, p. 14).

Relationships are a central goal of public relations communication, and many factors influence an organization's relationships with its publics. Organization–public relationships are influenced by organizational actions, existing and evolving reputations, media coverage, recent crises, leadership, activism, the economy, and even new communication technologies such as blogs and YouTube postings. Public relations professionals also need to consider that culture, as a fluid phenomenon, influences how organizations enact relationships with domestic and international publics.

Central to intercultural competence is understanding that, like interpersonal relationships with our friends and family, effective intercultural communication is based on shared patterns of experience and interaction as well as a general and a specific understanding of individual cultures. In the past, some public relations scholars have argued that a single theory (such as Excellence theory) might be able to account for understanding international practices of public relations (J. Grunig, 1992; Verčič, L. Grunig, & J. Grunig, 1996). Just as our relationships with our friends, family, coworkers, teachers, mentors, and even public institutions are different, cultures are also different. Clearly, given the complexity of meaning making and relationships, the one-theory-fits-all approach to intercultural communication is impossible in global contexts.

A better approach to understanding intercultural public relations is to understand that a practitioner should start by learning the answer to certain "generic" cultural questions (Kent & Taylor, 2007). Just as laying the foundation for an interpersonal relationship requires that one learn a number of general and specific facts about the other person, laying the foundation for intercultural interactions requires both specific and general knowledge.

Relational approaches to intercultural communication provide a framework for understanding relationships that are created by and changed by public relations. When we conceptualize public relations within "an organic framework of evolving relationships" (Pal & Dutta, 2008, p. 168), we can move past the traditional, managerial approaches to international public relations that focus on national boundaries and instead move toward understanding relationships wherever they form and in whatever forms they take (Pal & Dutta, 2008).

Our discussion is premised on the idea that people from different cultures come together when an exigency (a problem or opportunity) emerges that requires communication (Bitzer, 1968). This communication is intercultural and involves an imperative for shared meaning that seeks to build understanding and relationships. Thus, intercultural public relations is an interpretative communication activity that requires multiple, often simultaneous, frameworks for creating and changing relationships. This chapter is organized as follows: first, we review the principles of the generic theory as they relate to intercultural communication research. A generic approach focuses on practitioners asking questions that consider the general *context* of an intercultural communication situation. Genre theory provides a roadmap for these considerations. Then we reflect on different theories that explain how meaning is constructed in intercultural contexts. The final section provides an overarching framework, known as third culture building, as a way through which public relations practitioners can reflect on the theories mentioned in the first parts of the chapter, and use these theories to enact mutually beneficial relationships with publics at home and abroad.

Understanding the Big Picture: A Generic Approach to Intercultural Public Relations

Intercultural communication is an interpretative activity. Over the years, public relations scholars have drawn upon only a limited number of cultural theories and concepts (cultural variability, high/low context, face, *guanxi*, etc.) and have constructed even fewer intercultural public relations theories. When one thinks about culture and public relations, the work of Geert Hofstede (1997) often comes to mind. Hofstede's values work has been used as a foundation in business, communication, intercultural, interpersonal, and public relations research (see also the chapter by Courtright, Wolfe, and Baldwin in this volume). His work has been compelling for a variety of reasons, which include the business focus, the breadth of countries surveyed in his research, and the ease of applying his principles to international settings. Hofstede identified five cultural variables that influence communication and relationships in organizational settings: power distance, uncertainty avoidance, masculinity/femininity, individualism/collectivism, and Confucianism, or "long-term orientation" (LTO).

Hofstede's work has been considered a good start for understanding the dynamics of international and organizational communication, and public relations. His work emerged as a heuristic for international communication during a time when the field of public relations sought to align its practice with management theories and activities. Top scholars such as those involved in the Excellence research argued that public relations was a "management process" and that once public relations practitioners gained access to the dominant coalition, the public relations function would be valued and respected (see Grunig, 1992). Hofstede's managerial focus is understandable given the nature of his research that surveyed professionals at international branches of IBM. Turning to Hofstede's work to help explain international public relations was natural for public relations scholars.

Research Traditions in International Public Relations

The field of public relations was introduced to Hofstede in the 1992 Excellence study (Grunig, 1992). A chapter written by Sriramesh and White (1992) explained how understanding organizational and national culture could be a part of Excellent public relations. Sriramesh applied Hofstede's theory to public relations relationships in South Indian organizations (1992). Culbertson and Chen's 1996 edited book, *International Public Relations*, contained several chapters that included a discussion or application of Hofstede's dimensions of culture to national practices of public relations. Over the last decade, scholars have applied Hofstede to studying public relations in nations that included Western Europe during the 1999 Coca Cola tainting crisis (Taylor, 2000) Taiwan (Wu & Taylor, 2003), and Slovenia (Verčič et al., 1996). These were useful case studies, but as Martin and Nakayama (1999) and others have claimed, Hofstede's research embodies a static understanding of culture. What authors in the late 1990s and early 2000s found may need to be revisited in order to better describe culture and public relations within the dynamic conditions of globalization.

Other cultural models, such as Sriramesh's personal influence model and Kent and Taylor's (2002) research on dialogic communication, may help show the dynamic nature of culture as it influences public relations theory and practice.

Personal Influence

The personal influence model of public relations (Sriramesh, 1992) provides a valuable framework for understanding how culture may influence the development of public relations in a nation (or culture). The model is common in countries and organizations that are hierarchical, tightly controlled by the government, or subject to cronyism. Personal influence is often exercised behind the scenes by local business professionals, organizational and government leaders, and by local politicians or party members to achieve organizational or individual success.

Research shows that personal influence is common to India, other parts of Asia, Africa, and other nations. In "low-context" (see below) nations like the United States, having access to, or exercising personal influence is not a requirement for organizational or personal success, but it often helps. Some types of occupations and institutions rely more heavily on personal influence for success. In "high-context" cultures, like South Korea, however, personal influence is crucial and members of in-groups and those with connections are often more successful at achieving organizational and personal goals; for example, party members in communist or socialist states, members of in-groups, royalty, individuals with higher social status, people from higher castes, businesspeople, and individuals with more resources (Taylor & Kent, 1999).

The personal influence model reminds public relations theorists and practitioners that relationships are key. But, in this model, the relationship is not with a general public such as a community or regional group, but rather relationships of value are with people in positions of influence who can help the public relations practitioner accomplish his or her job. Another framework, dialogic communication, may be better able to enhance relationships with publics.

Dialogic Communication

The dialogic model of public relations (Pearson, 1989) strives to maintain equality and equity among stakeholders. The goal of dialogic organizations is not simply to enact managerial goals but also to serve the needs of stakeholders and stakeseekers. Dialogic communicators mediate between the interests of the organization and its key publics and seek mutual understanding rather than influence or adherence (Kent & Taylor, 1998, 2002).

Dialogue, as the word implies, refers to conversation or talk. Dialogic public relations refers to a kind of interpersonal interaction that acknowledges the individual self-worth and value of others and tries to create long-lasting, stable relationships with other people. As a professional practice, dialogue includes the ability to listen (with an open mind), empathize with others, admit when one is wrong, and be changed or altered by the experience of communicating with others. Ultimately, dialogue is a collection of interpersonal and intercultural communication skills and an orientation toward other people rather than a set of rules. Dialogic communicators do not ignore people because they can. They try to understand the needs of others and *actually* value their opinions (Anderson, Baxter, & Cissna, 2003; Anderson, Cissna, & Arnett, 1994; Buber, 1970; Christians, 1990). One way to implement the dialogic model is through an understanding of a generic approach to intercultural public relations.

The Profession Moves Toward a Generic Approach

As communication professionals, public relations practitioners understand that the first thing that one has to do before communicating about anything is to conduct research. The "R" in the RACE formula (Research, Action, Communication, Evaluation) applies when creating any message, whether the message is created for an internal group of employee stakeholders, or is designed for an external group of stakeseekers such as activists or consumers.

In some cases, research about key publics is obtained through environmental scanning and monitoring. This may include macrolevel areas of consideration including political systems, economic development, media ownership, or other societal factors. In other situations, however, communication professionals need to conduct some formal research (interviews, surveys, reviewing primary and secondary sources) in order to understand key publics. The importance to the creation of effective messages of conducting research is not a new concept, every public relations student learns it. Indeed, the ancient Greeks and Romans wrote about the process of "invention" or the finding and gathering of information useful to constructing arguments and compelling messages.

In the modern era of public communication research, rhetorical scholars developed a targeted process of background research designed to understand specific communication situations, called "genres." A communication situation involves understanding the background and assumptions of audience members, their cultural beliefs, and their expectations as audience members. Genre theory goes back more than 50 years to scholars who include Frye (1957) and Black (1965) (see also Kent, 1997; Kent & Taylor, 2007).

A genre refers to "a class of messages having important structural and content similarities, which, as a class, create special expectations in listeners. Inaugural addresses, then, constitute a genre, because they share textual features and are delivered in similar circumstances every four years" (Hart, 1990, p. 183; see also Hart & Daughton, 2004). As Martin (1976) explains: "A rhetorical genre is produced by a recurrent, distinctive relationship among three elements, (1) occasion, (2) audience and (3) speaker-role, from which springs discourse necessarily displaying recurrent similarities in theme, style, tactics, and perhaps presentational elements" (p. 247). In essence, genre-specific messages are based on research about target publics, occasions, and other situational factors, including culture.

The generic (or genre) approach to international public relations has been proposed as a model for preparing for international or intercultural public relations situations because it emphasizes genuine understanding of other cultures and communication, rather than simply convincing stakeholders to do what we want. According to Kent and Taylor (2007), a public relations professional who is interested in communicating with international or intercultural publics should engage in six activities:

(1) Identify features of the situation
(2) Identify the intended audience effects
(3) Clarify the motivational intent of the organization and publics
(4) Examine how meaning is created
(5) Examine strategic considerations
(6) Use communication principles and theory to understand how culture influences organizations and communication. (p. 11)

First, the practitioner needs to identify the *features of the situation*. The public relations practitioner needs to take a broad approach to understanding the rhetorical situation before him or her. Questions such as these need to be answered: "What are the expectations of the public for our communication?" and "Which specific norms and values will guide our publics' interpretation of our messages?" The first principle is where the practitioner should make an attempt to understand the general context of what factors might shape how publics might create or respond to communication from the organization.

Effective and ethical intercultural communication depends upon understanding *how a public is likely to respond to a message* (i.e., passively, because the group feels powerless or because the government does not allow dissent; actively, because the group believes that it has a vested interest or feels empowered to take action). Additionally, public relations communication needs to consider *where compelling messages should come from in a culture* (what media outlets, which spokespeople), and other demographics. For instance, in some cultures, religious figures have great public influence, whereas, in other cultures, athletes and celebrities have the ability to shape how people understand situations and issues.

The second issue within a generic approach to intercultural communication and public relations is to *identify the intended audience effects*. Once we understand the situation, then we need to reflect on the goals of the organization's actual communication. To be ethical, we need to ask if our communication efforts are intent on honest persuasion, propaganda, or marketing. If our goals are propaganda or marketing, then we need to consider goals based on relationship building. The second generic principle calls for understanding the goals of the communication efforts. Having clear goals lies at the heart of all effective public relations, however, when dealing with global audiences there is a tendency toward ethnocentrism. *Ethnocentrism* refers to the tendency to judge other cultures in comparison to our own, and to believe that our own culture is superior to other cultures. All cultures tend to make sense of the world based on their own experiences, and take for granted that others see the world in the same way.

Burke (1984) called our tendency to judge things based on our own experiences "occupational psychosis" (pp. 37–48). Other scholars have referred to this as "frame conflict" (Reddy, 1993), or the inability to see things beyond our own frames of experience. Whether we call the tendency to judge the world based on our own experiences ethnocentrism, occupational psychosis, or frame conflict, does not really matter; what matters is that we appreciate the importance of understanding other cultures and *not* judging them by our own cultural standards. Every culture and coculture (groups within larger cultures) is different. Whether one culture is "better" than another should never be a pressing question.

As Reddy (1993) argues, to communicate effectively with intercultural publics requires effort and there is no recipe for success, except for hard work. For organizations that wish to engage global publics, talking louder does not make the message any clearer. Effective intercultural communication requires research, cultural experience, sensitivity, and empathy.

The third step of a generic approach is for the public relations practitioner to *clarify the motivational intent of both the organization and publics*. The goal is to find where the interests of both the organization and the public intersect. Identifying shared cultural values is where the organization has the greatest chance of building a relationship with the public. Different kinds of knowledge are needed for effective interpersonal interactions (as compared to print, broadcast, or electronic messages). Interpersonal contact requires an understanding of issues like face, non-verbal communication, and time (discussed in some detail below). Creating print and electronic messages requires an understanding of cultural symbols and icons, colors, music, and cultural values that are unique to a nation or culture.

The fourth step of a generic approach ensures that the organization's messages make sense within the culture. This fourth generic principle suggests that professionals should *examine the archetypal or symbolic nature of language and communication in that culture*. Every nation/ culture defines itself by both what it is, and what it is not (Burke, 1973), in relation to its neighbors, and in relation to the people and governments considered heroes and villains. Identification by *unawareness* refers to the kind of implicit identification people feel as a result of being part of an organization, group, cause, or activity, and the implicit otherness/ enmity people feel toward those who are a part of groups, causes, or activities, that compete with their organization's cultural views (Burke, 1973, pp. 263–275). We make sense of the world metaphorically.

By learning about cultural archetypes, heroes, villains, and social and political leaders, public relations professionals will be better prepared to succeed in global and intercultural contexts. For example, one just needs to take a look at maps of the world in other countries when one travels. Many countries have maps that show their part of the world as the dominant, central location by which all other nations are positioned. Nationalistic and geographic identification by unawareness exists in every nation, and understanding how people see themselves in relation to others is essential to communicative success (Taylor & Kent, 2000).

A fifth step within a generic approach is to *examine the strategic considerations* that communicators can draw upon to further make their message culturally appropriate. Strategic considerations include issues such as respect for elders, the role of the government, religious and social features, trust, and perceptions of time. Understanding culture involves understanding the role that various public and private institutions play in people's lives, as well as how people see themselves fitting into society. Religion is, of course, only one cultural value. It is equally important to understand the nature of the media system in the nation or culture that a practitioner intends to communicate with. For example, the idea of a free press takes many forms. In Britain, citizens pay a television tax/license for every television set that they have in their homes to help fund an independent medium (BBC). In Korea, the media often share unfavorable information with businesses and influential citizens before publishing critical news reports. Korean editors allow organizations a chance to provide a response *before* a damning story is published. In Malaysia (and many other countries), the government is often informed of a crisis first, before the news is shared with the general public (Taylor & Kent, 1999).

A sixth and final step calls upon the practitioner *to use communication principles and theory to understand the culture being examined* and how cultures influence organizations and communication. Kent and Taylor (2007) argue that the sixth generic principle is actually the most important principle.

It is a mistake to think that communication is easy, that communication does not take work, or that any time two people speak the same language they are communicating effectively. We know from research into rhetoric and persuasion that people who understand their publics, who understand what motivates an audience, and who know how to structure an effective public speech, tend to give better speeches. Similarly, in fields like human communication, mass communication, political science, psychology, and sociology, we know that understanding theory, how people think and understand ideas, *and the process of meaning making*, is essential to effective communication. Effective intercultural communication is no different. Thousands of scholars and professionals have studied aspects of intercultural communication. And, as suggested, there are many theories and theoretical concepts developed with the aim of understanding how to effectively communicate with people from different nations and cultural backgrounds.

We devote the rest of the chapter to sharing some of these principles and theories. As suggested above, the generic principles are intended to identify elements of occasion, audience, and situational goals. The generic approach fits perfectly with professional research into international and intercultural communication situations since the heart of the generic approach is understanding relationships and how to use cultural knowledge to build those relationships. Effective practitioners should understand fundamental intercultural communication theories and be able to use that knowledge to improve their own intercultural communication. Discussion of several key theories comprises the next section of this chapter.

Theories that Facilitate Cocreation of Meaning in Intercultural Public Relations

The field of public relations has been moving from a functional approach, which has viewed publics as a means to accomplish organizational goals, to a cocreational approach. The cocreational approach posits that public relations creates shared meanings, interpretations, and goals. This perspective is long-term in its orientation, and focuses on relationships among publics and organizations (Botan & Taylor, 2004, p. 652). The cocreational approach argues that public relations is best understood as a meaning making process that brings both the organization and publics together.

Public relations professionals engage in intercultural communication for a variety of reasons, but all of these reasons involve meaning making. Practitioners might interview or survey members of a coculture in order to learn about their beliefs, values, and attitudes. If a professional works in a global organization, she or he might collaborate with colleagues in another nation or region as part of a communication campaign or marketing initiative. Even if a practitioner never leaves his or her own country, she or he might be asked to develop prosocial messages aimed at diverse cultural groups as part of a public health or governmental services initiative within his or her own nation.

Ultimately, understanding how individuals and groups from other nations, regions, or cultures see the world (their paradigm) is essential to effective intercultural communication. According to Kuhn (1970), a *paradigm*, or worldview, shapes how people see their world. A paradigm is similar to an ideology except that paradigms are more personal and represent models, assumptions, beliefs, and values that constitute how individuals and groups view reality. Paradigms may also vary by region, social class, race, ethnicity, and gender. Thus, ideologies describe the social world and the actors in it (which *groups* can be trusted, who runs things), while paradigms describe the world itself for the community that shares them (what counts as "good" and "bad," which *individuals* can be trusted). Our ideologies and paradigms influence our mental images of the world. If, for example, we believe that the world is a "mean" place, then we are likely to support calls for enhanced penalties for criminals. Conversely, someone who sees the world optimistically might call for enhanced educational and rehabilitation programs for criminals. Public relations professionals, to be able to build relationships with culturally diverse individuals and publics, need to understand different worldviews and understand why people act as they do.

Indeed, correctly interpreting the actions of others is key to reducing ambiguity and uncertainty in intercultural communication. In the

1950s, Talcott Parsons, a Harvard sociologist, argued that one of the ways to understand human relations is to understand how people make sense of the world around them. Parsons suggested that dichotomous pairs could describe the actions of individuals and cultural groups.

Parsons' Pattern Variables

A pattern variable is described as "a dichotomy, one side of which must be chosen by an actor before the meaning of a situation is determinate for him/her, and thus before s/he can act with respect to that situation" (Parsons & Shils, 1951, p. 77). In general, actors do not really think about their choices so much as they act on shared paradigms that shape how they make sense of the world. According to Parsons, acts involve "the relationship of an actor to a situation ... and it is conceived as a choice ... among alternative ways of defining the situation. The ... act, however, does not occur independently but as one unit in the context of a wider system of actor–situation relationships" (1960, p. 467).

Parsons identified five variables that he claimed were universal: affectivity, ascription, collectivism, diffuseness, and particularism. Other scholars have subsequently examined many of the relational variables identified by Parsons (Dubin, 1960; Lipset, 1963). When Parsons proposed his variables more than 60 years ago, he argued that many of the variables associated with collectivist societies were premodern; that is, status, relationships, collectivism.[1] We now know with 60 years of hindsight that cultures are more complex than the pejorative modern/premodern framework might suggest. Nevertheless, Parsons's pattern variables are a precursor to many other cultural theories, and because of this they are worth understanding as a starting point toward a dialogic/generic approach to global public relations.

Affectivity/Instrumentalism Affectivity has two dimensions: affectivity (love, trust, nurturing) and instrumentalism (situational, transitory, selfishness). Affectivity refers to the role that relationships play in shaping people's actions. Affectivity correlates closely with collectivism in the sense that decisions are made based on one's familial and cultural bonds rather than what one might obtain now. Affectivity is also similar to Hofstede's (1997) notion of Confucian dynamism or long-term orientation (LTO) and Hall's (2000a) idea of high and low context. Affectivity is an important concept because so many of the decisions that people make are guided by cultural beliefs tied to family and relationships. Indeed, Phau and Wan (2006) have shown how both public relations and advertising draw upon this concept in persuasive communication.

Ascription/Achievement   Ascription/achievement has to do with how people treat other people based on their status or performance. Like Hofstede's (1997) notion of power distance, which helps to explain how people relate to other people based on their *perceived* status, ascription/ achievement tries to explain how an individual would treat an object or another individual because of who she or he is, what it is, what it does, or what response it produces. In other words, ascription suggests that an individual would give priority to certain *attributes* that object/ individual possess over any specific *performance* or actions of objects/ individuals; that is, Bill Gates is important simply because he is wealthy and not because he has lived his life well. Being wealthy, famous, and powerful is enough. Achievement suggests that individuals should be given priority because of their specific past performances. Achievement is actually a very useful concept for organizations that seek to enhance their reputation with publics across the world. Organizations that are achievement-oriented are motivated to innovate (like Apple computers), rather than work to undermine fair competition and fair trade (like Microsoft) (Kent, 2008). Since relationships are built on trust and shared experiences, achievement focused organizations are seen as more trustworthy and honest and more deserving of stakeholder support.

Universalism/Particularism   In a universalistic orientation, people, or objects are categorized in terms of some universal or general frame of reference. Particularism comes closest to what the cocreational theories of public relations take as a guiding assumption: that the existence of a relationship alters how we treat others and how they treat us (Kent & Taylor, 1998, 2002). Ironically, both universalism and particularism can exist in the same individual or culture. Indeed, the existence of a relationship is what, in many cultures, allows individuals and members of other groups to be seen as "friends" ("He's a good guy, he's not like the others ..."). When another individual or group can be thought of as a special case, she, he, or they can be granted special (or equal) privileges, while the larger group can still be treated unfairly.

Specificity/Diffuseness   Specificity/diffuseness refers to how we respond to people or objects. When only particular aspects of a person or object are responded to (position, education, age, gender, sex, etc.), a specificity orientation prevails (a characteristic of individualistic cultures). When a person or an object is treated in a holistic manner (father/mother, group member, friend), a diffuseness orientation is displayed (a characteristic of collectivist cultures).

Diffuse cultures are harder to join and harder to build strong relationships with when one is an outsider. In diffuse cultures, people have multiple, overlapping, social ties. Diffuse cultures also present special persuasion-related obstacles. Messages of actuation need to focus on familiar concepts and social ties rather than on individual gain. Additionally, negotiations cannot be framed as "mutually beneficial" so much as beneficial to the community or group of which one is a part. Diffuse cultures do not think in terms of "I" but instead consider the "we."

Specificity poses its own challenges for global public relations. In highly specific cultures, relationships are equally difficult to negotiate since "professionalism" should be maintained in business dealings. Similarly, when individuals from specific cultures interact with members of diffuse cultures, both groups will have difficulty seeing eye-to-eye on relationships, and what constitutes good business.

Intercultural public relations professionals can benefit from Parsons's theory but must also understand its limitations. Parsons's pattern variables are a good starting point because they help us to understand orientations as suggested by the dialogic and generic approaches. They are, however, only a starting place. The framework reflects the intellectual times in which it was proposed. The most important aspect missing from Parsons's variables is recognition of the social construction of meaning and culture. No culture is either specific or diffuse. Shades of gray (and negotiated meaning) always exist when talking about communication and culture. Parsons's pattern variables schema was originally developed to explain variations across national cultural boundaries. Parsons's work has some "baggage," but like all intercultural concepts, his schema is useful when combined with several other cultural descriptors. Culture is too complex for any single schema to account for everything, but when paired with the work of Kluckhohn and Strodtbeck, intercultural relationship building can be enhanced.

Kluckhohn and Strodtbeck's Value Orientations

Kluckhohn and Strodtbeck (1961) argued that cultures find solutions to common human problems like the nature of being, the nature of action, and the nature of relationships (p. 4). They posit five problems for which all cultures must find solutions (see Gudykunst & Ting-Toomey, 1988, p. 50; Zaharna, 2001).

The first question to be answered is: "What is the character of innate human nature: good, evil, a combination of good and evil, or neutral?" The human nature orientation assumes that human nature is either changeable (mutable), or unchangeable (immutable). A nation's/culture's views regarding the basic human nature of other groups will influence decisions to make war, allocate scarce resources, provide access to social services, and shape how the police and legal system work. Views of good and evil also influence the level of trust that individuals and groups have in others. Indeed, organizations are often ascribed human characteristics and thought of as good or evil. This question about good and evil is valuable for understanding and practicing public relations in global contexts. In many situations, public relations will be called upon to build or rebuild trust between the organization and its publics.

A second question that Kluckhohn and Strodtbeck attempt to answer is this: "What is the relation of humanity to nature and the supernatural?" The human–nature (or environment) orientation hints at the relation between humans and nature and is subcategorized into: mastery-over-nature (all forces of nature can and should be overcome or put to use by humans), harmony-with-nature (human life, nature, and the supernatural are all extensions of each other), and subjugation-to-nature (nothing can be done to control nature—fate must be accepted). Cultures that believe in mastery over nature, like the mainstream U.S. culture, will build levees or sea walls to keep out rising tides, while cultural groups that believe in harmony with nature tend to build less permanent structures, live farther inland, or simply build their dwellings on stilts to let rising tides flow past. A group's cultural orientation toward nature is instructive of the lifestyle that the nation/culture values: permanence vs. change, mastery over nature vs. harmony with it. A public relations practitioner should know this orientation in advance of any communication or relationship building efforts.

A third question posed by Kluckhohn and Strodtbeck (1961) inquired: "What is the temporal (time) focus of human life?" The temporal feature of human life concerns: past (cultures that highly value traditions and their ancestors), present (cultures that have no traditions or believe in fate), and future (where change is valued highly, new is better than old). Long before Hofstede (1997) explored Confucian dynamism or the long-term orientation value, scholars like Kluckhohn and Strodtbeck (1961), and Hall (1983) were aware of the fact that cultural groups had different perceptions of time. The issue of cultural orientations toward time is important in intercultural and international public relations settings.

Not all cultures place the same value on time or see it the same way. For example, in the United States, one is raised hearing the expression "time is money." However, in other nations, entire sectors may shut down on weekdays between noon and 2 p.m. for siesta/lunch break. In many nations, no one works on Fridays (Muslim nations) or Sundays (Christian nations) with the exception of a few family-run restaurant owners. In the United States, there are 24-hour shopping, banking, and gas stations. Yet, in many nations, weekends are for families and many people will not conduct business during this time.

Kluckhohn and Strodtbeck's temporal orientation is on the past, present, and future, much like Hofstede's long-term orientation. Hall identified two orientations toward time that can help to make sense of the behaviors and actions of various cultures: monochronic and polychronic time; also called "M-time" and "P-time."

Time as a Cultural Orientation

Monochronic time involves the North European system of doing things sequentially, one thing at a time; polychronic time, on the other hand, "stresses involvement of people and completion of transactions rather than adherence to preset schedules" (Hall, 2000b, p. 280). Polychronic time places an emphasis on "doing" rather than "accomplishing." We often hear of people from the United States "multitasking" or doing more than one thing at a time. Multitasking is similar to the polychronic orientation except that polychronic cultures do not do several things at the same time as a way to be more productive. Rather, as Hall explains:

> P-time stresses involvement of people and completion of transactions rather than adherence to preset schedules. Appointments are not taken as seriously and, as a consequence, are frequently broken. P-time is treated as less tangible than M-time. For polychronic people, time is seldom experienced as "wasted," and is apt to be considered a point rather than a ribbon or a road, but that point is often sacred. (2000b, pp. 280–281)

Like orientations toward nature, a group's perception and valuation of time significantly influences decision making. Perceptions of time also influence individuals' and groups' perceptions of the importance of patience vs. quick action, as well as responsiveness via technology like the Internet and e-mail. Understanding a culture's temporal focus is a very important feature of message design and effective intercultural communication and relationship building. Indeed, consider that crisis communication is one of the fastest growing areas of public relations practice and research. Temporal orientation will influence how organizations and publics interpret crisis responses. When a crisis response does not meet a culture's temporal expectations, an organization's reputation may be damaged.

The Concept of Face in Intercultural Communication

Organizations, no matter where they are from or their motive for existence, seek to project an image or reputation that is positive. The public relations function helps organizations to communicate this constructed image. Every communication tactic in a public relations program or campaign seeks to create or reinforce a certain image. For instance, a consumer products company from Japan seeks to communicate an image showing that it is innovative and high tech. A U.S. car company seeks to communicate an image of quality and dependability. A company from China wants to project an image of safety in light of the recent quality control issues in pet food, baby milk, and children's toys. A nongovernmental organization (NGO) in any nation seeks a public image that recognizes it as a positive, contributing force in society.

Images are created via Web pages, brochures, news releases, annual reports, and other communication tactics. These tactics make every effort possible to project a positive image of the company or organization. An organization's public image is known as "face" in the intercultural communication literature, and it has clear applications for public relations.

The concept of face is a metaphor that refers to such entities as politeness, respect, pride, dignity, honor, and shame (Ting-Toomey et al., 1991; Wiseman, 2002). When we speak of "face," we often talk about someone "losing face" (being embarrassed or insulted) or "maintaining face" (not being criticized publicly, not being shamed, or not being put on the spot). Everyone has a sense of face (pride, dignity) although in many cultures, like the United States, face is not something that most people consciously think about in public situations. Instead, many organizations focus on their reputation. Yet, face is a powerful concept throughout the world.

Face always functions along three dimensions and involves efforts to maintain one's own face, help others to maintain their own face, and avoid challenging someone else's face. To help another person to maintain face is actually more valued than retaining one's own face in many cultures. When we prevent another person from being embarrassed or ridiculed this both allows the person being put on the spot to maintain face, as well as helping the person who challenged the other's face to maintain her or his own face by not appearing unkind.

"Face management," and face needs vary in different cultures. Thus, in some cultures (like the mainstream United States), being perceived as clever for making a witty comment in a public situation, thereby embarrassing someone else or making him or her look foolish, is sometimes seen as being socially acceptable. In high face cultures, however, embarrassing someone else with a snide comment both makes the recipient of the comment look bad, and the person who made the comment look worse.

In global contexts, public relations would benefit from understanding the complexities of face for a myriad of stakeholders. For instance, in a crisis, the media often seek to attribute blame. Organizations may be tempted to identify individuals, groups, institutions, or even national leaders as reasons for a crisis. This short-term strategy, while perhaps an easy way to deal with the immediate attention of the crisis, may have serious repercussions for an organization's long-term relationships with its stakeholders. Indeed, long-term attention to face could enhance reputation. Another factor that influences global public relations is context.

Context

Context may be best understood as situation, and it is a key tenet of the generic approach to global public relations mentioned earlier in this chapter. Context provides meaning and behavioral cues that guide people in how to act and react in intercultural encounters (Taylor, 2001). Hall's (2000a) work suggests that the context in which a conversation takes place will significantly influence the interpersonal/intercultural interaction. Hall identified two types of context: high and low.

High context cultures are characterized by communication that is influenced by both the situation and the relationship of the parties involved. In high context situations, much of what the participants communicate is unspoken or relationally based: people in high context cultures tend to know how to behave because of the nature of the relational roles that they play. Employees "know" what their supervisors want, partners and friends "know" or try to guess the needs of the other rather than asking them—and when they guess wrong, politeness (or face) prevents a friend, partner, or guest from telling the host. Relationships in high context societies tend to be very structured.

In low context cultures, communication is driven by what is actually spoken or written. Participants from low context cultures "say what they mean," and rely on written documents and formal agreements. When a person from a low context culture is uncertain about what someone wants, they ask. From a public relations standpoint, professionals need to understand that in high context communication settings (e.g., Asia, South America, the Middle East), indirectness and subtlety are highly regarded while in low context communication settings (e.g., North America, Australasia, Northern Europe), directness and candor are preferred.

The type of context prevalent in a culture will influence how much and what type of information is included in public relations tactics. For instance, when organizational leaders in low context cultures make mistakes, there is often pressure on them to apologize or find someone to blame. Apologies are enacted differently in each culture. For example, in 2001, a U.S. nuclear submarine, the U.S.S. Greenville, collided with a Japanese trawler. This accident occurred near Hawaii's Pearl Harbor and nine Japanese fishermen were killed. In U.S. mainstream culture, probably due to the litigious legal system, apologizing often means accepting responsibility for a wrongdoing. American companies and organizations avoid apologizing for fear that accepting responsibility will mean a lawsuit. In Japan, however, apologizing is usually an honorable way for both the offended and the offender to gracefully deal with an unfortunate situation. The U.S. Navy formally apologized to the Japanese government and the families of the fishermen. Yet, as Lazare (2004) noted, the apology was too late, not perceived to be sincere, and came from a third party (not the captain of the submarine). The Japanese families did not feel that the Navy genuinely empathized with their loss. This example shows that multiple cultural lenses (apology, status, time) are used when people attempt to make sense of the actions and motives of those from another culture.

Empathy

The concept of empathy is familiar to interpersonal and intercultural communication scholars but is probably not as well understood by public relations professionals. The U.S.S. Greenville example above suggests that it is a key factor in relationship building, especially after a crisis. Empathy refers to the ability of a person to put him- or herself into the shoes of another, to see the world as the other does. Empathy, in contradistinction to sympathy, has nothing at all to do with feeling sorry for another person. Empathy and sympathy, however, often go hand-in-hand.

The ability to empathize is related to one's ability to transcend ethnocentrism. Indeed, one of the reasons that intercultural communication campaigns often fail is because of the inability of campaign planners to see the world from the perspective of the audience (Taylor, 2000). Reddy (1993) calls this "frame conflict" (mentioned earlier), and argues that our language itself is often what tricks us into thinking that everyone sees the world the same way. Public relations practitioners need to put themselves in the place of others as they engage stakeholders.

As Reddy suggests, our language and our culture actually trick us into thinking that everyone thinks about the world the same way that we do. In order to transcend our culturally programmed worldviews a new metaphor is required. Reddy argues that we need to move beyond what he calls the "conduit metaphor," the idea that language has tangible substance and fixed meaning that can be transferred to others, and embrace the "toolmakers' paradigm," or the idea that communication takes work on the part of all parties involved. When communication misunderstandings occur, many people implicitly blame the listener (as attribution theory suggests, people often ascribe internal motives to others and external motives to themselves), rather than accepting responsibility for misunderstandings or acknowledging that communication is a two-way street.

In reality, intercultural communication (indeed all communication), requires feedback. No speaker is to blame because they have an accent any more than a listener is to blame for not speaking a particular language. Getting beyond our individual cultural baggage and assumptions and being able to see the world from the standpoint of the other (empathy) is a central component of relationship building.

Empathy does not require us to abandon our own beliefs and resort to radical relativism, pretending that all cultural practices are inherently good (see Holtzhausen's chapter in this volume). Every culture, even our own, has flaws. But being able to see the world from the standpoint of the public is a powerful communication skill and a prerequisite to effective intercultural communication and relationships. The final part of this chapter calls for a third culture building approach to enacting public relations and relationship building in global settings (see also Bardhan's chapter in this volume).

Public Relations in Global Settings: An Orientation Toward Third Culture Building

Public relations is about building, changing, and maintaining relationships. Building a relationship is not an easy task, and it is even more complicated when the public and the organization have different cultural frameworks that guide their understanding of the situation. The concept of third culture building may help us to develop a relational and dialogic approach to intercultural public relations.

Third culture was initially conceptualized in regard to children who grow up overseas (Chao, Nagano, Solidon, Luna, & Geist, 2003; Pollock & Van Reken, 2001; Useem, Donoghue, & Useem, 1963). Sociologists noted that third culture children were able to walk in two worlds, and reflect both on their own culture as well as on the culture of the country in which they had spent much of their life. These children had the potential to serve as bridges between cultures. In communication, third culture has been offered as a way of understanding how members of different groups *coconstruct* meaning. Based on a Weickian (1995) perspective of enactment, individuals and organizations impact their environment just as the environment in turns impacts the individual and the organization.[2] Third culture building argues that intercultural communication is not about variables and outcomes but rather intercultural communication should be thought of as interactions and processes that enable *shared* meaning construction in chaotic, unpredictable environments. Third culture takes the variable-driven frameworks of Parsons, Kluckhohn and Strodtbeck, Hall, Hofstede, and others, and then asks: "What can I pull from all of these theories (and others) to make sense of interactions and communication? How can I engage others relationally and dialogically?"

The concept of third culture, first introduced by Casmir (1978) in communication research, was explicated in 1993 in a series of articles published in *Communication Yearbook* (Belay, 1993; Casmir, 1993; Shuter, 1993) and then later extended both methodologically and theoretically by Casmir (1999). Casmir proposed third culture building as a way of moving beyond the static, etic approach to understanding intercultural communication. Casmir (1999) noted:

> My own concern with developing an adequate conceptual model responsive to the challenges and processes which were identified above is based on the acceptance of communication as an ongoing negotiation of meaning. My emphasis results in seeing the dialogic nature of human communication as necessary to electively deal with chaotic systems and environments. That is the case because dialogue and negotiation deal with the study of those things we do together to make sense of any given setting. (p. 98)

Third culture building is premised on a dialogic orientation and shared meaning. Botan and Taylor (2004) have noted that public relations is moving toward such a paradigm as well. Third culture building helps to take out the manipulation of communication, and instead focuses on shared meaning construction and shared outcome. As public relations takes a turn toward cocreation of meaning in its general theory building, third culture provides a roadmap for engaging in ethical relationships with publics at home and abroad.

We believe that third culture orientation of public relations in global contexts is an appropriate synthesis of the theories and frameworks noted in this chapter. There are many cultural frameworks that are useful for helping public relations practitioners to communicate with global publics. In isolation, each framework can only provide one piece of the complex intercultural puzzle. Yet, when taken together, issues such as orientation directed toward the world, empathy, face, and context provide the background for communicators to build dialogic relationships. The frameworks and theories provided in the early part of this chapter are valuable for helping organizations communicate with diverse publics. They are most valuable when they are part of an orientation toward the needs and expectations of others. In other words, if this chapter could be summed up in one concept then this concept would be a *dialogic orientation*. Global public relations and intercultural communication in general are best achieved when the public relations practitioner takes an empathic orientation to the "other" and seeks to understand his or her motivation, values, and expectations.

Conclusion

At the heart of competence in intercultural communication is a relational and dialogic approach that moves away from traditional, managerial, top-down approaches to public relations in global cultural contexts, and moves toward understanding relationships and cultural diversity in whatever form they take. This move reflects a broader trend in public relations whereby the field is moving away from a functional view of publics and communication and, instead, is embracing a cocreational perspective in its theorizing and practice.

Students, public relations professionals, and educators, indeed, all communication professionals would benefit from first-hand experience in a number of cultures. Although most of us will never be able to gain expertise about every country and every culture, all of us can enact a dialogic orientation that will allow us to understand those cultures. However, it is equally important to understand how diverse stakeholders and publics view the world, the range of such beliefs, and how our own beliefs and ethnocentrisms lead us to see the world in incomplete ways.

The future of intercultural communication is not in knowing where a nation or culture falls on a social science dimension or scale. Rather, the future of intercultural communication competency is in the ability of practitioners to ask: "What do different theories of intercultural communication provide that will help me to make sense of interactions and communication? How can I engage others relationally and dialogically?" It is our sincere belief that a dialogic orientation is the future of international/intercultural public relations in global contexts.

Discussion Questions

1. Many people mistakenly assume that "face" is an Eastern concept and that people from more direct (low context) cultures are largely unaware of or unconcerned about face. In what ways might having a more complex understanding of face allow you to be a more effective communicator within your own culture?

2. How much does context influence how we communicate with others? For example, does the context of being "friends" versus simply "acquaintances" alter your communication? How about "student and teacher," "parent and child," "grandchild and grandparent" and "employer and employee?" What influence do such contexts have on your communication? Now explain what role context plays in public relations practice.

3. How is "talk" different from "dialogue?" When you talk with your friends, or in class, certain people often tend to dominate the conversation—maybe sometimes you are the one who dominates

a conversation. How would a dialogic conversation be different? What difference would being dialogic with your friends make, and how would it influence your conversations? Now apply this to public relations: How would the profession be different if dialogue was the prime focus of communication?

4. What is your position toward the world in light of Kluckhohn and Strodtbeck's (1961) value orientations: "the relation of humanity to nature" and "the temporal focus of human life"? For example, how might that influence your decision to build a golf course rather than a community garden?

5. How much does your orientation toward time (monochronic vs. polychronic) influence how you do things? What would happen if the emphasis in your classes was not on "grades" and "accomplishments" (monochronic orientation) but on doing "interaction"/"process" (or polychromic orientation)? How would the learning environment be different?

6. What are the characteristics of a public relations professional who can enact third culture building? Be specific. Identify and describe these characteristics.

Notes

1. See www.sociology.org.uk/pathway1.htm?p1pmp5b.htm for an excellent overview
2. Weick's (1995) concept of enactment is valuable for understanding how individuals and organizations create meaning through interactions and then are influenced by these interactions.

References

Anderson, R., Baxter, L. A., & Cissna, K. N. (2003). *Dialogue: Theorizing difference in communication studies.* Thousand Oaks, CA: Sage.

Anderson, R., Cissna, K. N., & Arnett, R. C. (1994). *The reach of dialogue: Confirmation, voice, and community.* Cresskill, NJ: Hampton Press.

Belay, G. (1993). Toward a paradigm shift for intercultural and international communication. *Communication Yearbook, 16,* 437–557.

Bitzer, L. F. (1968). The rhetorical situation. *Philosophy & Rhetoric 1*(1), 1–14.

Black, E. (1965). *Rhetorical criticism: A study in method.* Madison, WI: University of Wisconsin Press.

Botan, C. H., & Taylor, M. (2004). Public relations: The state of the field. *Journal of Communication, 54*(4), 645–661.

Buber, M. (1970). *I and thou* (W. Kaufmann, Trans.). New York: Scribner.

Burke, K. (1984). *Permanence and change: An anatomy of purpose* (3rd ed.). Los Angeles, CA: University of California Press.

Burke, K. (1973). The rhetorical situation. In L. Thayer (Ed.), *Communication: Ethical and moral issues* (pp. 263–275). London: Gordon & Breach.

Casmir, F. (1978). A multicultural perspective on human communication. In F. Casmir (Ed.), *Intercultural and international communication* (pp. 241–257). Washington, DC: University Press of America.

Casmir, F. L. (1993). Third-culture building: A paradigm shift for international and intercultural communication. *Communication Yearbook, 16,* 407–428.

Casmir, F. L. (1999). Foundations for the study of intercultural communication based on a third culture-building model. *International Journal of Intercultural Relations, 23*(1), 91–116.

Chao, I-L., Nagano, N., Solidon, B., Luna, L., & Geist, P. (2003). Voicing identities somewhere in the midst of two worlds. In L. A. Samovar & R. E. Porter (Eds.), *Intercultural communication: A reader* (10th ed., pp. 189–204). Belmont, CA: Thompson/Wadsworth.

Christians, C. G. (1990). Social responsibility: Ethics and new technologies. In R. L. Johannesen (Ed.), *Ethics in human communication* (pp. 265–278). Prospect Heights, IL: Waveland.

Culbertson, H., & Chen, N. (Eds.). (1996). *International public relations: A comparative analysis.* Mahwah, NJ: Erlbaum.

Dubin, R. (1960). Parsons' actor: Continuities in social theory. *American Sociological Review, 25*(4), 457–466.

Frye, N. (1957). *Anatomy of criticism: Four essays.* Princeton, NJ: Princeton University Press.

Grunig, J. E. (Ed.). (1992). *Excellence in public relations and communication management.* Hillsdale, NJ: Erlbaum.

Grunig, J. E. (2006). Furnishing the edifice: Ongoing research on public relations as a strategic management function. *Journal of Public Relations Research, 18*(2), 151–176.

Gudykunst, W. B., & Ting-Toomey, S. (1988). *Culture and interpersonal communication.* Newbury Park, CA: Sage.

Hall, E. T. (1983). *The dance of life: The other dimension of time.* New York: Doubleday.

Hall, E. T. (2000a). Context and meaning. In L. A. Samovar, & R. E. Porter (Eds.), *Intercultural communication: A reader* (9th ed., pp. 34–42). Belmont, CA: Wadsworth.

Hall, E. T. (2000b). Monochronic and polychronic time. In L. A. Samovar & R. E. Porter (Eds.), *Intercultural communication: A reader* (9th ed., pp. 380–386). Belmont, CA: Wadsworth.

Hart, R. P. (1990). *Modern rhetorical criticism.* Glenview, IL: Scott, Foresman/Little, Brown, Higher Education.

Hart, R. P., & Daughton, S. M. (2004). *Modern rhetorical criticism* (3rd ed.). Boston, MA: Allyn & Bacon.

Hofstede, G. (1997). *Cultures and organizations: Software of the mind.* New York: McGraw-Hill.

Kent, M. L. (1997). *The rhetoric of eulogy: A generic critique of classic and contemporary funeral oratory* (Unpublished doctoral dissertation). Purdue University, West Lafayette, IN.

Kent, M. L., (2008). Critical analysis of blogging in public relations. *Public Relations Review, 34*(1), 32–40.

Kent, M. L., & Taylor, M. (1998). Building dialogic relationships through the World Wide Web. *Public Relations Review, 24*(3), 321–334.

Kent, M. L., & Taylor, M. (2002). Toward a dialogic theory of public relations. *Public Relations Review, 28*(1), 21–37.

Kent, M. L., & Taylor, M. (2007). Beyond "excellence" in international public relations research: An examination of generic theory in Bosnian public relations. *Public Relations Review, 33*(3), 10–20.

Kluckhohn, F. R., & Strodtbeck, F. L. (1961). *Variations in value orientations.* Evanston, IL: Row, Peterson.

Kuhn, T. S. (1970). *The structure of scientific revolutions.* Chicago, IL: University of Chicago Press.

Lazare, A. (2004). *On apologies.* New York: Oxford University Press.

Lipset, S. M. (1963). The value patterns of democracy: A case study in comparative analysis. *American Sociological Review, 28*(4), 515–531.

Martin, H. H. (1976). A generic exploration: Staged withdrawal, the rhetoric of resignation. *Central States Speech Journal, 27*(4), 247–257.

Martin, J. N., & Nakayama, T. K. (1999). Thinking dialectically about culture and communication. *Communication Theory, 9*(1), 1–25.

Martin, J. N., Nakayama, T. K., & Flores L. A. (Eds.). (2002). *Readings in intercultural communication: Experiences and contexts* (2nd ed.). Boston, MA: McGraw Hill.

Pal, M., & Dutta, M. J. (2008). Public relations in a global context: The relevance of critical modernism as a theoretical lens. *Journal of Public Relations Research, 20*(2), 159–179.

Parsons, T. (1960). Pattern variables revisited: A response to Robert Dubin. *American Sociological Review, 25*(4), 467–483.

Parsons, T., & Shils, E. A. (1951). *Toward a general theory of action.* Cambridge, MA: Harvard University Press.

Pearson, R. (1989). *A theory of public relations ethics* (Unpublished doctoral dissertation). Ohio University, Athens.

Phau, M., & Wan, H. H. (2006). Persuasion: An intrinsic function of public relations. In C. H. Botan & V. Hazleton (Eds.), *Public relations theory* (Vol. 2, pp. 101–136). Mahwah, NJ: Erlbaum.

Pollock, D., & Van Reken, R. (2001). *Third culture kids.* Yarmouth, ME: Intercultural Press.

Reddy, M. (1993). The conduit metaphor: A case of frame conflict in our language about language. In A. Ortony (Ed.), *Metaphor and thought* (2nd ed., pp. 164–201). Cambridge, UK: Cambridge University Press.

Rhee, Y. (2002). Global public relations: A cross-cultural study of the excellence theory in South Korea. *Journal of Public Relations Research, 14*(3), 159–184

Samovar, L. A., & Porter, R. E. (2001). *Communication between cultures* (4th ed.). Belmont, CA: Wadsworth.

Samovar, L. A., & Porter, R. E. (Eds.). (2003). *Intercultural communication: A reader* (10th ed.). Belmont, CA: Thompson/Wadsworth.

Shuter, R. (1993). On third-culture building. *Communication Yearbook, 16*, 429–436.

Sriramesh, K. (1992). Societal culture and public relations: Ethnographic evidence from India. *Public Relations Review, 18*(2), 201–211.

Sriramesh, K., & White, J. (1992). Societal culture and public relations. In J. E. Grunig (Ed.), *Excellence in public relations and communication management* (pp. 597–614). Hillsdale, NJ: Erlbaum.

Taylor, M. (2000). Cultural variance as a challenge to global public relations: A case study of the Coca-Cola tainting scare in Western Europe. *Public Relations Review, 26*(3), 277–293.

Taylor, M. (2001). International public relations: Opportunities and challenges for the next century. In R. L. Heath (Ed.), *Handbook of public relations* (pp. 629–637). Thousand Oaks, CA: Sage.

Taylor, M., & Kent, M. L. (1999). Challenging assumptions of international public relations: When government is the most important public. *Public Relations Review, 25*(2), 131–144.

Taylor, M., & Kent, M. L. (2000). Media transitions in Bosnia: From propagandistic past to uncertain future. *Gazette, 65*(5), 355–371.

Ting-Toomey, S., Gao, G., Trubisky, P., Yang, Z., Kim, H. S., Lin, S., & Nishida, T. (1991). Culture, face maintenance, and styles of handling interpersonal conflict: A study in five cultures. *International Journal of Conflict Management, 2*(4), 275–296.

Useem, J., Donoghue, J., & Useem, R., (1963). Men in the middle of the third culture. *Human Organization, 22*(33), 129–144.

Verčič, D., Grunig, L. A., & Grunig, J. E. (1996). Global and specific principles of public relations: Evidence from Slovenia. In H. M. Culbertson & N. Chen (Eds.), *International public relations: A comparative analysis* (pp. 31–66). Mahwah, NJ: Erlbaum.

Weick, K. E. (1995). *Sensemaking in organizations.* Thousand Oaks, CA: Sage.

Wiseman, R. L. (2002). Intercultural communication competence. In W. B. Gudykunst & B. Mody (Eds.), *Handbook of international and intercultural communication* (2nd ed., pp. 207–224). Thousand Oaks, CA: Sage.

Wu, M. Y., & Taylor, M. (2003). Public relations in Taiwan: Roles, professionalism, and relationship to marketing. *Public Relations Review, 29*(4), 473–483.

Zaharna, R. S. (2001). "In-awareness" approach to international public relations. *Public Relations Review, 27*(2), 135–148.

Suggested Readings

Berkowitz, D., & Lee, J. (2004). Media relations in Korea: *Cheong* between journalist and public relations practitioner. *Public Relations Review, 30*(4), 431–437.

Granovetter, M. S. (1973). The strength of weak ties. *American Journal of Sociology, 78*(6), 1360–1380.

Hatzios, A., & Lariscy, R. W. (2008). Perceptions of utility and importance of international public relations education among educators and practitioners. *Journalism & Mass Communication Educator, 63*(3), 241–258.

Huang, Y.-H. (2000). The personal influence model and *Gao Guanxi* in Taiwan Chinese public relations. *Public Relations Review, 26*(2), 219–236.

Lim, S., Goh, J., & Sriramesh, K. (2005). Applicability of the generic principles of excellent public relations in a different cultural context: The case study of Singapore. *Journal of Public Relations Research, 17*(4), 315–340.

Kruckeberg, D., & Tsetsura, K. (2008). The Chicago school in global community: Concept explication for communication theories and practices. *Asian Communication Research, 5*(1), 9–30.

Morrison, T., & Conway, W. A. (2006). *Kiss, bow, or shake hands: The best selling guide to doing business in more than 60 countries* (2nd ed.). Adams, MA: Adams Media.

Robinson, J. H. (2003). Communication in Korea: Playing things by the eye. In L. A. Samovar & R. E. Porter (Eds.), *Intercultural communication: A reader* (10th ed., pp. 57–64). Belmont, CA: Thompson/Wadsworth.

Romano, A., & Mwangi, S. (2008). *International journalism and democracy: Civic engagement models from around the world.* New York: Routledge.

Tampere, K. (2008). Stakeholder thinking and a pedagogical approach in public relations processes: Experience from transition societies. *Journal of Public Relations Research, 20*(1), 71–93.

Taylor, M. (2009). Protocol journalism as a framework for understanding public relations-media relationships in Kosovo. *Public Relations Review, 35*(1), 23–30.

Wu, M., & Baah-Boakye, K. (2009). Public relations in Ghana: Work-related cultural values and public relations models. *Public Relations Review, 35*(1), 83–85.

Chapter 4

Culture, Communication, and Third Culture Building in Public Relations within Global Flux

Nilanjana Bardhan

The public relations profession, like most other professions, is caught up in the simultaneously converging and diverging forces of globalization. Appadurai (1996) writes that global compression and flux have unleashed a state of affairs that "has to be seen as a complex, overlapping, disjunctive order" (p. 32). Neat categories are hard to apply in spaces touched by the postmodern world of disorderly capitalism, new media communication technologies, and escalating cultural border crossings. Space and time are taking on less bounded meanings, and are experienced in more continuous, compressed, overlapping, and disjunctive manners. The global and the local are hybridizing into glocal realities and practices, and in a spatial, temporal, and cultural sense, the distance between "here" and "there" can no longer be understood just in terms of physical distance. Rupturing the more static ways of understanding these issues, however, also brings with it the epistemological and ontological challenges of "understanding social change and cultural transformation as situated within interconnected spaces" (Gupta & Ferguson, 1992, p. 8).

In this climate of global flux and connectivity, public relations is practiced by a range of different entities with different priorities, agendas, and ideological orientations. A list would include multinational corporations, firms servicing such corporations, national governments, regional alliances such as the European Union and NATO, international organizations such as the United Nations, various non-state and non-corporate transnational actors such as non-governmental organizations (NGOs) and activist groups, international media, international labor groups, think tanks, and so on (Culbertson, 1996). The list is not exhaustive but proliferating. Depending on their nature and mission, these different types of organizations, corporations, and alliances may value culture differently, but they are all, nonetheless, embedded in and constitutive of a world where cultural differences are rapidly interfacing and reconfiguring through the heightened interactions of people and practices.

How should public relations scholars and practitioners think about culture and communication in a climate of fluidity and multidirectional tensions? What kinds of theories and models can help practitioners work with global cultural complexities? Scant in current scholarship are theories and models that are equipped to address the shifting, and often contradictory and unpredictable nature of culture and communication in the context of complex connectivity (Tomlinson, 1999). But the future for such work looks bright. Over the last decade, public relations scholarship in the United States has included more cocreational and relational approaches that are less instrumental and mechanistic than the bulk of previous positivist theorizing. Scholars are focusing more on "communication as a meaning making process" (Botan & Taylor, 2004, p. 652; also see Kent and Taylor's chapter in this volume). There has also been a prominent rhetorical focus all along. Simultaneously, scholars in Europe, Australia, and New Zealand have been working through critical, sociological, and constructivist lenses (see Ihlen & van Ruler, 2007; L'Etang, 2005). However, there still remains a clear need to theorize culture in less positivist ways, and develop more dynamic conceptualizations of culture and communication than are currently available—conceptualizations that are inspired by social constructionist, interpretive, postmodern, and critical/cultural approaches to communicative interaction, dialogue, and relationship building (Bardhan, 2007; Pal & Dutta, 2008).

In this chapter, I work through a social constructionist and interpretive lens. I first outline the dominant conceptualizations of culture and communication in much of "international" public relations scholarship. I argue that current conceptualizations are not equipped to address global flux which is characterized by complex global–local dialectical tensions, time–space compression, and heightened flows of people, technology, capital, media, and attendant ideologies (Appadurai, 1996; Pal & Dutta, 2008). By drawing upon Fred Casmir's notion of third culture building, I demonstrate that an emergent coconstitutive approach to culture and communication that can address the dynamic nature of culture in a climate of global flux is necessary for public relations scholars and practitioners to adopt. I position the *transcultural practitioner* as a third culture, or third realm builder, and explain the theoretical, ethical, as well as practical utilities of this positionality. Overall, the chapter highlights the importance of microlevel human interactions in transcultural public relations. It also establishes a conceptual link between the micro- and macrolevels of communicative relationship building, and concludes with what scholars, students, educators, and especially practitioners of public relations can gain from embracing the interpretive and social constructionist model of third culture building.

Public Relations as Transcultural and Glocal

Since organizations, corporations, and alliances are increasingly multinational in nature, an increasing amount of public relations activity is transpiring in transcultural spaces. At this point, I should differentiate between the terms *multinational* and *transcultural* as used in this chapter. I deliberately use the term *transcultural* and not *multinational* in order to move away from the "country as culture" logic that is predominant in current conceptualizations of culture in international public relations scholarship. Such a conceptualization is static from a global flux perspective (Gaither & Curtin, 2008; Pal & Dutta, 2008). As Gupta and Ferguson (1992) note, "It is so taken for granted that each country embodies its own distinctive culture and society that the terms 'society' and 'culture' are routinely simply appended to the names of nation-states … national naturalisms present associations of people and place as solid, commonsensical, and agreed-upon, when they are in fact contested, uncertain, and in flux" (pp. 6–7, 12).

A country is first and foremost a political and geographic category and not always synonymous with or the only measure of culture/cultural identities. Furthermore, national cultures are socially constructed (i.e., they are not fixed), and their boundaries and meanings change over time (Moon, 1996). While people may identify with national cultures, they also simultaneously identify with other cultural positionalities, sometimes in-between positionalities, based on ethnicity, religion, race, gender, region, diasporic status, sexual orientation, and so on (Curtin & Gaither, 2007; Pal & Dutta, 2008). These other varying cultural positionalities do not necessarily follow the territorial scale of the nation-state (Gupta & Ferguson, 1992; Moon, 1996). Sha's (2006) study on the relationship between the cultural identities of publics and the situational theory of public relations demonstrates that, "Intranational public relations still may be intercultural in nature" (p. 48). Additionally, heightened migration and travel propelled by global forces makes culture a dynamic and traveling variable. Culture works over, under, and in-between national boundaries, and is far from static. This dynamism makes impossible neat correlations between country and culture. Macnamara (2004), a transcultural public relations practitioner, emphasizes that the old fixed ways of thinking about culture and cultural identity are archaic in current times. Public relations scholarship needs to rupture the grand narrative of "national culture."

To return to the distinction between the terms *multinational* and *transcultural*, a corporation or organization is structurally multinational when it has significant operations, and therefore significant publics, in more than one country (Wakefield, 2001). Public relations becomes transcultural when public relations action and communication occur at the junctures (spaces) of global forces and the cultural realities of a locality. These junctures may be conceptualized as transcultural spaces of communication and interaction, spaces where cultural differences intersect. Here I borrow from de Certeau's (1984, p. 117) differentiation between "place" and "space." While place is a geographically fixed location, space is dynamic and produced as an effect of the people that constitute that place and their meaning making practices. Transcultural space is located in physical place but is *not* reducible to just that place and is characterized by the active practices of complex connectivity. Tomlinson defines complex connectivity as "the rapidly developing and ever-densening network of interconnections and interdependencies" that characterize globalization (Tomlinson, 1999, p. 2). The interactions and communication in transcultural spaces are impacted by forces beyond that physical space; that is, by more global forces such as those of capital, dominant cultures, economic and political ideologies, and new communication technologies (Roudometof, 2005). Hence, it would be accurate to say that multinational organizations and corporations engage in transcultural public relations practices that are more spatially oriented than place bound.

When it comes to building communicative relationships with diverse publics in transcultural spaces, the need is usually glocal (Robertson, 1992). The term *glocal* is derived from the Japanese concept of *dochakuka,* which means to adapt the global to local conditions. Robertson (1995) writes, "There is a widespread tendency to regard this [global–local] problematic as straightforwardly involving a polarity, which assumes its most acute form in the claim that we live in a world of local assertions *against* [emphasis in original] globalizing trends, a world in which the very idea of locality is sometimes cast as a form of opposition or resistance to the hegemonically global ..." (p. 29). He holds that what is local is actually contained within the global, and that due to the increasing global interconnections between commerce, people, and media, no local spaces, practices, and ideologies in the world today can remain divorced from the globality in which they are ultimately embedded. Tomlinson (1999) also argues against artificial binaries, and theorizes the global-local dialectic in terms of complex connectivity rather than grappling with the dichotomous conception of them as separate fixed realities. Tsing (2000) agrees that current conditions of globalization are imploding sedimented binaries (such as global/local, Self's culture/Other's culture, center/periphery). Such implosions are resulting in dynamic interstitial realities, alliances, and projects (such as transcultural campaigns) that are best studied by focusing on how multiple (cultural) realities and positionalities are "differentially and dialogically negotiated, refused or erased" (p. 345).

In a similar vein, public relations practitioner and scholar Wakefield (2001) states: "What public relations needs is a 'paradigm shift' to reflect its emerging globalization.... The new paradigm ought to account for a more comprehensive approach that creates thinking and acting at both the local and global levels of the organization" (p. 641; also see Wakefield's chapter in this volume). Some scholars have already started studying how the glocal manifests itself in public relations practice. For example, in a study of the Chinese Web sites of 100 top global brands, Maynard and Tian (2004) found that these brands successfully followed a glocal strategy which involved working closely with local communities, local governments, and incorporating local entertainment trends. Bardhan and Patwardhan (2004) studied Unilever's and Suzuki's public relations approach in India and found the use of similar glocal strategies. Molleda and Roberts's (2008) study demonstrates the successful glocal communication strategies that were deployed to make possible a smooth transition between the older actor who played Juan Valdez, the domestically as well as globally known brand character for Colombian coffee, and a new actor who was scheduled to replace the aging Juan Valdez actor. These studies are much needed contributions that investigate the glocal nuances of public relations strategies in transcultural spaces; however, a gap is still detectable when it comes to theorizing the dynamics of (microlevel) dialogic communication and relationship building that occurs in such spaces.

One possible reason for this gap could be the overwhelming focus on mass communication rather than interpersonal communication in extant public relations scholarship as well as practice (Jahansoozi, 2006). This is an unfortunate gap since effective public relations requires a combination of human (interpersonal) communication and mass communication efforts. Furthermore, research in more collectivist cultures around the world that are less media-centric shows the vital role (inter)personal relations play in accomplishing public relations objectives (J. Grunig, L. Grunig, Sriramesh, Huang, & Lyra, 1995). Therefore, while the macrolevel study of the glocal is under way in public relations scholarship, the microlevel of communication and relationship building needs more attention. This is where third culture building can be useful as a communication model.

While the specifics of third culture building will be elaborated on a little later in this chapter, at this point I would like to briefly introduce this model to demonstrate its good fit for conceptualizing the dynamic nature of culture and communication in global flux. The model is social constructionist and interpretive in nature. An interpretive approach subscribes to the view that reality (and thereby culture) is socially constructed through communicative interaction (Berger & Luckmann, 1966; Pearce & Cronen, 1980). First proposed by Fred Casmir in 1978, the third culture building model is equipped to collapse the social science-driven category gap between culture and communication evident in positivist international public relations scholarship (Gaither & Curtin, 2008). According to this model, *culture and communication are not considered to be two separate categories.* Instead, "participants engage in an active, coordinated, mutually beneficial process of *building* [emphasis in original] a relationship.... The forms, the ends, the values, the interactional rules emerge only as the process develops over time, similar to what we observe in the gradual development of cultures—thus the concept 'third-culture building'" (Casmir, 1993, p. 419). Once two individuals from different cultures meet and interact, they go through an intersubjective process of seeking information about each other, questioning their own attitudes and culturally specific values, revising some, replacing some, integrating changes into "existing constellations," and reconfiguring the relationship based on these mutual negotiations (Casmir, 1993, p. 422; see also Starosta, 1991). The third culture they cocreate is not literally a fixed third culture or an end state, but an emergent open-ended third realm of cultural understanding that results from mutual ongoing inter-action (Casmir, 1978). *Mutuality and the willingness to change are necessary criteria for third culture building.*

Casmir suggested the need to move away from the more static and binaristic dominance–submission models of communication and rhetoric which, according to him, are popular with Western scholars, models which are "based on persuasion, logic, and the exertion of influence over listeners by well-trained skilled speakers and writers" (Casmir, 1993, p. 407). Such models are instrumental in nature wherein the communicator attempts to seek mastery during communication interaction (Botan, 1993), an orientation which, in the context of public relations, would be one defined by control and not in keeping with the spirit of mutual negotiation between organizations and their various publics. In transcultural contexts, instrumental approaches to communication increase the chances of practices of cultural imperialism. Obvious examples would include Nestlé's aggressive marketing of infant formula in "third world" locations in opposition to World Health Organization codes and local cultural and social practices supportive of breastfeeding (Williams & Murphy, 1990), and Disney's cultural arrogance in assuming that U.S. cultural norms and entertainment practices would work just as well in its new theme park in France (Packman & Casmir, 1999).

"Culture" and "Communication" in Public Relations Scholarship

In a world of global flux, multicultural societies, and heightened intercultural contact and connectivity, it is vital to pay attention to how we conceptualize culture, how cultural differences impact public relations practice, and how practitioners can successfully negotiate cultural differences through effective and ethical intercultural communication. Despite this need, the concept of culture remains woefully under theorized in public relations scholarship. Sriramesh, one of the first public relations scholars to study the relationship between culture and the profession (see Sriramesh & White, 1992), wrote: "Sadly, culture has yet to be integrated into the public relations body of knowledge. It appears that culture's time has not yet come after all for our field" (Sriramesh, 2007, p. 507). In a globally interconnected world, no communication profession can afford to put the analysis of culture on the backburner. The concept of culture needs to be treated in all its complexity and viewed through diverse paradigmatic lenses.

Every research paradigm has its ontological, epistemological, and axiological assumptions, strengths, and weaknesses. Martin and Nakayama (1999) note that all paradigms have something useful to offer. They state that unless we can think dialectically about various paradigms, our scholarship will remain reductive and incapable of producing multidimensional knowledge about complex concepts. Currently, certain ontological and epistemological assumptions about culture and communication are central in much of the extant scholarship in public relations. These assumptions need to be decentered in order to make space for other understandings.

The social scientific or functionalist approach to conceptualizing culture and communication is currently dominant in public relations scholarship. Public relations research in this vein has primarily followed a systems theory-oriented communication management perspective: communication is mechanistically conceptualized as transfer (one-way and two-way) between the organization and its publics; the instrumental and functional management focus is predominant; and culture is objectively conceptualized as acquired, transferred across generations, and usually fixed at the nation-state level. Martin and Nakayama (2010) note that, "Social science researchers focus not on culture per se but on the *influence* [emphasis in original] of culture on communication" (p. 86). Thus culture and communication are treated as two separate categories or variables; it is assumed that they can be precisely (i.e., quantitatively) measured; and they are usually studied for statistically significant and predictive relationships.

Over the last decade and a half, public relations scholars have mainly applied social scientific intercultural communication theory to the field of public relations as well as developed some theoretical frameworks of their own. Although a detailed analysis of all the major studies that have been conducted or the theoretical pieces that have been published is beyond the scope of this chapter, some broad brush strokes are possible.

Geert Hofstede's (1984, 2001) dimensions of national culture— individualism/collectivism, power distance, masculinity/femininity, uncertainty avoidance—has become a popular typology for studying public relations cultures in various countries (e.g., Cooper-Chen & Tanaka, 2008; Ihator, 2000; Rhee, 2002; Sriramesh, 1996; Sriramesh & Verčič, 2001; Sriramesh & White, 1992; Wu, Taylor, & Chen, 2001; see also chapters by Kent and Taylor, and by Courtright, Wolfe, & Baldwin in this volume). Other works include Zaharna's (2001) research on cultural "in-awareness." Drawing from the work of pioneer intercultural communication scholar Edward Hall, Zaharna stresses that adopting an "in-awareness" approach can help practitioners become conscious of taken-for-granted (i.e., invisible to Self) cultural assumptions that come into play during public relations interactions in cross-cultural settings (Zaharna, 2001). Guided by the works of Edward Hall, Florence Kluckhohn, and Dorothy Lee, Zaharna further suggests that practitioners must also take into consideration the following factors: whether a culture is high context or low context, its orientation to time (monochronic or polychronic), whether it stresses doing or being, whether it has a future or past tense orientation, and whether it is conceptualized as linear or nonlinear. Banks's (1995, 2000) social-interpretive theory of multicultural public relations is another significant contribution. In addition to Banks, Botan (1992) and Sriramesh and Verčič (2001) have developed useful frameworks for studying public relations in country contexts.

Verčič, L. Grunig, and J. Grunig (1996) proposed the generic–specific theory of international public relations (see Wakefield's chapter in this volume for an in-depth analysis of this theory). Drawing upon Brinkerhoff and Ingle's theory of structured flexibility, which has been applied to management literature, Verčič et al. (1996) developed "a middle-ground theory between cultural relativism and ethnocentrism" (p. 33). Drawing from the first phase of the study on Excellence in public relations which collected data from 326 organizations in the United States, Canada, and the United Kingdom, they proposed nine characteristics of Excellent public relations, which they suggested should be considered the generic principles of excellent public relations at the global level. They further suggested that the generic principles should be strategically adjusted to work with the (specific) cultural and political system of the country in question (Verčič et al., 1996).

As is evident from the above, the bulk of the research in international–intercultural public relations has been social scientific in nature. While acknowledging the worthwhile contributions made by this line of research, it is necessary to broaden the repertoire to include other ways of conceptualizing culture and communication and the relationship between them (Gaither & Curtin, 2008). The "inter-national" approach equates country with culture and is comparative in nature. While country comparisons can provide useful aggregate information at a macro level, they are not adequate for investigating how communication across cultures is or can be *jointly* accomplished during micro human interactions between people involved in transcultural public relations. They are also not equipped to address the postmodern complexities of culture outlined earlier (see Pal & Dutta, 2008; also see chapter by Holtzhausen in this volume). One way to theorize the interpersonal dimension would be to subscribe to the more cocreative, dialogic, interpretive, and intersubjective perspective that culture is not a static and geographically determined "out there" phenomenon but is continuously constructed, maintained, repaired, and transformed by people jointly and dynamically engaging in communication (Carey, 1989, p. 23). Interpretivists assume "that human experience, including communication, is subjective, and that human behavior is neither predetermined nor easily predicted" (Martin & Nakayama, 2010, p. 59). According to the interpretive paradigm, culture and communication are coconstitutive, processual and symbolic in nature (Martin & Nakayama, 2010).

The Microlevel of Human Communication

Hannerz (1997) notes that "The connection between cultural process and territory, we should remind ourselves, is only contingent. As socially organized meaning, culture is primarily a phenomenon of interaction, and only if interactions are tied to particular spaces is culture likewise so" (pp. 116–117). If the meaning of culture is primarily tied to the interactions of people rather than just to location, then it becomes vital to study the human and micro-transcultural communication aspects of public relations. As Zaharna (2000) notes, "Practitioners can also enhance their effectiveness by a general awareness of how culture affects the interpersonal aspects of various public relations activities" (p. 94). Sriramesh (2007) adds that "the body of knowledge in public relations has yet to study the linkage among culture, interpersonal trust, and public relations" (p. 519).

Let's take a look at this example. In 1992, Disney Corporation decided to open a theme park in the Paris area. Despite great optimism on the part of Disney, the operation at its start was losing over U.S. $1 million a day, and the perception and press coverage of the new theme park was far from complimentary. In short, Disneyland Paris was a public relations debacle. Cultural arrogance, a confrontational attitude, and predetermined procedures were Disney's biggest problems. Most of these unfortunate interactions played out in the realm of human communication and interaction. Disney personnel from the United States did not behave like good guests in another culture, and fiercely held onto their own U.S.-centric cultural practices. For example, upper management did not show respect for French labor laws and insisted on an ultra-strict Disney uniform and cleanliness codes. French culinary practices and cultural norms were grossly neglected when Disney would not allow the selling of wine in the theme park, provided no options for sit-down meals, and included ice in soft drinks. Disney management's unwillingness to mutually share power and work toward a third culture at the relational level soon gave rise to descriptors and metaphors for the theme park such as "cultural Chernobyl" and "cancerous growth." Disney had to make several changes to redeem itself and salvage its reputation. Some of the changes occurred through personnel restructuring and local employee empowerment. The U.S. CEO of Euro Disney was replaced by a French CEO well versed in both cultures, and employees from over 92 countries were hired. Closer attention was paid to contextual cultural values and micro level communication in order to achieve a jointly constructed sense of third culture (example drawn from Packman & Casmir, 1999).

The above example demonstrates that inattention to mutuality in transcultural relationship building at the micro level, and thinking of culture in fixed and binaristic ways (My culture vs. Your culture) when the need is glocal, can result in unwanted perceptions of cultural imperialism. It also demonstrates that effective interpersonal level communication and dialogue lie at the heart of building successful organization–public relationships in glocal contexts. Almost 10 years ago, Coombs (2001) wrote: "As public relations moves into the 21st century, interpersonal communication theory will provide important insights into the analysis and practice of public relations and will shape how we define the field" (p. 114). The call to include interpersonal theory has been sporadic over the research trajectory of public relations (Ferguson, 1984; J. Grunig, 1990; Heath, 2000; Thomlison, 2000; Toth, 2000, 1989; Toth & Heath, 1992). However, inspired by Ferguson's (1984) call to make relationships the central focus of study in public relations, there has been a more systematic push in the United States over the last decade or so to develop theory on organization–public relations (see Broom, Casey, & Ritchey, 1997; Ledingham, 2006; Ledingham & Bruning, 2000). This push has led to an increased exploration of what interpersonal communication theory has to offer (Rhee, 2007). Some of this work has been conducted in different countries such as China and Taiwan (Huang, 2001; Hung, 2005; Ni, 2009). This body of work has also been predominantly social scientific in how it conceptualizes culture and communication, and it focuses mainly on the attributes, antecedents, and outcomes of organization–public relationships.

Jahansoozi (2006) makes a good observation that in addition to these relational elements, it is also important to study mutuality since "mutual influence is the cornerstone of interpersonal communication," and that the study of interpersonal communication in public relations cannot ignore this aspect of relationship building (p. 75). Mutuality in interpersonal communication can be studied well through interpretive and social constructivist approaches that focus on intersubjectivity, dialogue, and the coconstruction of meaning through communicative interaction. Borrowing from sociologist Erving Goffman's work on social interactionism, Johansson (2007) stresses the importance of mutuality in interpersonal communication, and notes that "[i]n interpersonal communication, interactants are coconstructing the definitions of the situation. However passive the role of an audience or listener may seem to be, every person will define the situation by virtue of the response to the individual, and the communicated impression" (pp. 276–277).

Dialogue is a central characteristic of interpersonal (as well as intercultural) communication. Pearson (1989) was perhaps the first scholar to advocate for dialogue in public relations communication. He wrote that dialogue "is intimately connected with the attitude of a speaker toward self, audience, topic and situation" (pp. 124–125). He noted that values such as "honesty, concern for the other person, genuineness, open-mindedness, mutual respect, empathy, lack of pretense, non-manipulative intent, and encouragement of free expression" (p. 125) are central for the dialogic process to be successful. Building further upon Pearson's work, Botan (1993) differentiates between monologic and dialogic communication in public relations. A practitioner who subscribes to a monologic view believes in gaining "instrumental mastery of a situation" (p. 76), or what Casmir has called the dominance–submission approach to communication. Botan, like Pearson, questions the ethics of such an approach, and argues that practitioners, especially those practicing in transcultural contexts which are infused with heightened perceptions of power differentials and cultural disparities, should communicate in the spirit of dialogue. Such an approach would "assume that the real goal is not reducing publics to the service of the client through instrumental mastery, but joining with the publics in the process of uncovering new interpretations of the world, some of which may benefit the client, but some of which may benefit the public" (Botan, 1993, p. 76). Woodward (2000) has similarly noted that a transactional philosophy that honors dialogue and context and believes in mutual transformation through communicative interaction is needed for public relations practice, especially in transcultural contexts.

The study of interpersonal/intercultural and dialogic communication is also important because of the connections between micro and macro levels of social construction of reality. Toth (2000) has emphasized that it is necessary to understand how relationships are communicatively built by public relations practitioners at the micro level, a level that sets the tone for relationships at the more meso and macro levels. Casmir (1993) has similarly posited, in proposing the model of third culture building, that "all institutions initially, and always, are the results of the efforts of individual human beings" (p. 408). Drawing upon Anthony Giddens's structuration theory, Falkheimer (2007) explains that "social structures are reproduced or transformed through repetition (on a macro-level) of individual acts" (p. 288). Similarly, also using structuration theory, Durham (2005) notes that practitioners, clients, and publics are all "bound to each other within a common social context" (p. 35), and that practitioners should realize that, through how they communicate at the micro levels, they can become creative agents of change at more macro levels. Despite this important micro/macro relationship, research on the micro interpretive level of communication is scant in transcultural public relations research (Banks, 1995, 2000).

The third culture building model is conceptualized at the interpersonal level of human communication, and holds promise for theory building at the micro level of transcultural public relations. Micro level theorizing, in turn, could contribute to theory building at the organization–public level. The model is interpretive in nature and well suited for addressing the understudied aspect of mutuality, as well as the dynamic nature of culture and communication.

Toward Third Culture Building

A few scholars have already stressed the importance of and paved the way for interpersonal level research in transcultural public relations (Banks, 1995, 2000; Burk, 1994; J. Grunig et al., 1995; Lyra, 1991). I build on their work as I position third culture building as a model that public relations scholars and practitioners might find useful for theorizing and practicing socially responsible transcultural public relations.

Lyra's (1991) research on public relations in Greece was an early conceptual step toward the notion of third culture building. In a meta-research that combined her thesis findings with two other country studies (India and Taiwan), J. Grunig et al. (1995) forwarded the cultural interpreter or translator model or role. They found that multinational companies often hire local public relations practitioners to play the role of cultural brokers, and that "the cultural interpreter model, therefore, seems to exist in organizations that do business in another country, where it needs someone who understands the language, culture, customs and political system of the host country" (p. 182; see Holtzhausen's chapter for a power-related critique of this model). Wu et al. (2001) developed a scale for the model within a larger study, tested it in the public relations culture of Taiwan, and found it to be culturally significant. J. Grunig et al. (1995) further stated that the cultural interpreter model "also may be found in an organization in a single country that must work in an environment with diverse groups" (p. 183).

While he did not draw upon third culture building per se, it should be noted that Banks (1995, 2000) has also forwarded a notion similar to third culture building. He was one of the first public relations scholars to employ a social–interpretive approach to building a theory of multicultural public relations. Borrowing from Collier and Thomas's (1988) interpretive view of cultural identity interaction, he states that the social–interpretive approach has a bias toward face-to-face communication, and that effective multicultural public relations is *"the successful negotiation of mutual meanings that result in positive outcomes* [emphasis in original] in any communication activity" (Banks, 2000, p. 38,). He further proposes that the successful intercultural–interpersonal public relations encounter is marked by communication that "affirms participants' cultural identities," "embraces the constitutive nature of communication," "accepts the diversity of interpretations," and "remains open to reinterpretation" (p. 38).

The third culture building model provides the needed shift from the more social scientific cultural interpreter–translator model to Banks's interpretive approach, and helps us move toward a more dialogic model for interpersonal communication in transcultural public relations, as well as toward a cultural role for the practitioner. I will expand on how it does so a little later in this chapter, but at this point, a valid question might be: Why third culture building and not some other model or theory of intercultural communication? There are at least two good reasons for this. First, unlike the majority of intercultural communication theories and models that focus on the individual and how individuals adapt or get acculturated to cultural differences (usually in host cultures), third culture building actually focuses on the process of people from different cultural backgrounds communicating *together* to negotiate their differences (Casmir, 1999). In this respect, it is a truly intersubjective and cocreative model (Botan & Taylor, 2004), which emphasizes the mutuality, dialogue, and transformation necessary for transcultural communication. Second, this model provides a vantage point for discussing issues of power differentials in transcultural public relations contexts. Power is never static. It is dynamic as well as contested (Holtzhausen, 2000; Weaver, Motion, & Roper, 2006). The manners in which power dynamics play out in communication depend upon macro as well as micro contextual factors. While the macro structural contexts of power get focused on predominantly (Curtin & Gaither, 2007), lesser attention is paid to the micro interactional contexts, which are equally relevant and a part of how power plays out at other levels (see related notion of micro practices of power in Holtzhausen's chapter). Third culture building, as a model, is well equipped to explore how the micro dynamics of power are negotiated through communicative action. The issue of power is also discussed in more detail later.

Third Culture Building Model

Casmir first proposed the third culture building model for intercultural and international communication in 1978 (see also Useem, Donohue, & Useem, 1963). Taking a more interpretive and interpersonal approach to culture and communication than was common at that time, and stating that he perceived "problems with any approach which sees the 'use' of communication primarily as an attempt to influence others," he offered "a model which focuses on the situational, interactional communication *processes* [emphasis in original] between individuals from various nations, or cultures" (Casmir, 1978, pp. 248, 249). He added, "I view this process as the conscious establishment of a *third* or *alternate realm* [emphasis in original] ..." (1978, pp. 249–250). About a decade later, he and his colleague wrote, "A third culture is a situational subculture wherein temporary behavioral adjustments can be made by the interacting persons as they attempt to reach a mutually agreed upon goal(s).... A third culture can develop only through interaction. It develops by necessity when culturally dissimilar persons combine to carry out a mutually agreed-upon task" (Casmir & Asuncion-Lande, 1989, p. 294).

Casmir has conceptually fleshed out the model's domain since he first proposed it. In one of his later writings, he emphasizes how third culture building as a model entails an intense ethical responsibility toward the cultural Other (Casmir, 1997), and that "it is ultimately centered on enabling all those who engage in the building of third cultures.... Such enablement would produce the foundation for making individuals both resolute and open, both able to take a stand and to listen, while keeping in mind the need for being part of the future together" (p. 93). The model attempts to celebrate and fuse with the cultural Other, it is open-ended and emergent in that no cultural end state is predicted, and it attempts to move away from an individualistic and Cartesian notion of an autonomous, unitary Self.

Casmir emphasizes that dialogic communication is a central factor in third culture building, and that culture must be understood as a phenomenon that is always in flux since "culture is in people, not merely in some vague contact with an environment existing around them" (Casmir, 1997, p. 111). He adds that people are creators of culture and the authors of cultural change, and that "no amount of cultural information will automatically or significantly contribute to our understanding of how human beings *build* relationships *together* and *negotiate* meanings together [emphasis in original]. That requires emic involvement in such processes" (Casmir, 1997, p. 105). Casmir, however, is realistic about the model and writes that the third culture building model may not work in every situation, and may end at any time due to a variety of unfavorable intervening factors. Despite this caveat, he stresses that it is worthwhile to continue developing it because of the promise it holds for building mutual relations across cultural differences.

From the above it is obvious that Casmir's model is normative; that is, it is more advisory than explanatory. He advocates for an orientation that requires a genuine willingness on one's part to adjust and even transform one's cultural beliefs and values along with understanding the cultural Other. He conceptualizes third culture building as an intersubjective process wherein communication is conceptualized as symbolic interaction and not just as transfer. Third culture building requires an attitude that is different from the stance that one should simply try and understand the cultural Other (which has been the well intentioned but limited stance in most of the social scientific scholarship in international public relations). The latter stance does not require the kind of mutuality, personal commitment, and openness to change that Casmir stresses so much. Furthermore, it increases the risk of cultural imperialism since the conceptual dichotomy between "Self's culture" and "Other's culture" is still maintained. According to Casmir and Asuncion-Lande (1989), "What is *not* intercultural communication is any attempt to enable representatives of one culture to learn, understand, *and adopt* [emphasis in original] the patterns of the [self's] culture" (p. 289). In fact, this could be seen as an ethnocentric attitude that ultimately values the Self's culture over the Other's, the Disneyland Paris debacle outlined earlier being the perfect case in point. Casmir and Asuncion-Lande (1989) further remark: "The ability of human beings to think the seemingly 'unthinkable,' to do the 'undoable,' and to believe the 'unbelievable' has brought about human developments because we were able, through interaction, to transcend that which we had found limiting in our own cultures" (p. 293). Thus, third culture building is a model that promises shared cultural growth over cultural imperialism.

Mutual cultural transformation takes time. Casmir (1999) states that time is an essential factor in the building of meaningful and mutually satisfactory third cultures. Here it is necessary to note the difference between the building of a third *culture* and third *realm*. The former suggests greater relational depth and a greater degree of mutual cultural transformation. A third culture would be more desirable when the goal is to build a lasting long-term relationship. The notion of third realm is more applicable when the goal is to accomplish a short-term negotiation. Since public relations practitioners engage in long and short-term relationship building efforts, both these notions are relevant.

The Transcultural Practitioner as a Third Culture/ Realm Builder

The number of public relations practitioners working transculturally across the globe is on the rise. At the interpersonal level, these practitioners have to strategically locate, and communicate and build relationships with, for example, key representatives of local governments, local media, civic groups, local opinion leaders, consumers or members, perhaps local practitioners, maybe celebrities, and any other person who is a representative of a significant public, a stakeholder, or is involved in campaign development. However, as Verčič (2009) has written, "There continues to be little information on the profile of the model global corporate public relations practitioner. Are they to be natives in a country in which they are serving or are they to be professional expatriates committed only to their corporations? Are they building lasting relationships with their stakeholders or moving from country to country (as professional diplomats do) so often that this is not possible?" (p. 804). Verčič's observation need not be restricted to just the corporate practitioner. Irrespective of the type of organization or firm they work for, there is an obvious need to develop a profile or a role for practitioners working transculturally, a role that involves culture and highlights the types of intercultural communication and relationship building skills such practitioners need to cultivate (Burk, 1994).

In the area of role research, four hierarchical practitioner roles have been developed over the last two decades that correspond to the cultural, political, and economic context of the public relations industry in the United States (Broom, 1982; Broom & Dozier, 1986; Broom & Smith, 1978; Dozier, 1984, 1992). Dozier (1992) describes these four roles that are typically assumed by Western public relations practitioners working in democratic and capitalist economic settings. The highest role is that of the *expert prescriber* while the lowest role is that of the *communication technician*. In the middle lie the roles of *communication facilitator* and *problem-solving facilitator*. Dozier (1992) further posits that the first three roles are collapsible into the category of *communication manager* while the last role remains that of *communication technician*. Practitioners in the former role are more involved in strategy, planning, and liaison maintenance, and they work closely with the organization's dominant coalition (management). Those in the latter role mostly produce the communication tools necessary to achieve public relations goals and objectives. Although these roles have been quantitatively tested in various countries, the domain of the roles themselves does not involve culture. While some work has been done on the gender dynamics of the above roles in the United States (e.g., Aldoory, 2007; Hon, L. Grunig & Dozier, 1992; Toth, Serini, Wright, & Emig, 1998), more research is needed on how culture is a central aspect of practitioner roles in the climate of global flux (see Curtin & Gaither, 2007; Hodges, 2006).

The third culture building model carries potential for further advancing a culture-oriented role for the public relations practitioner working in dynamic transcultural spaces. The cultural translator–interpreter model focuses on the importance of recruiting local practitioners to help multinational companies understand local cultures. Its limitation, however, is that it puts the onus of building bridges across cultural differences on the cultural Other, but stops short of exploring the possibility of the production of an intersubjectively and mutually accomplished third culture. In other words, the *perceived* Self/Other cultural binary is maintained since the goal here is to understand the Other. Banks's (1995, 2000) social–interpretive theory is based on the dialogic coconstructive approach to reaching intercultural understanding, and does make a move toward collapsing the binary. When third culture building is added to the picture, we can start envisioning all interpersonal level communication in transcultural public relations as aspiring toward cocreating a third culture wherein the Self/Other cultural binary can be communicatively collapsed. Such a collapse can be a good thing if power equations can be revised in favor of the less powerful.

Hence, I propose that attempts to collapse the perceived Self/Other cultural binary can increase the chances of successful negotiations in transcultural public relations and decrease the chances of cultural imperialism. In the interpersonal context, the collapsing of the Self/Other cultural binary can occur through mutual decentering of the perceived culture of the Self. Such decentering could be accomplished by assuming equal responsibility, by being willing to change, and by shifting attention to the work of mutual transformation and third culture building that could give rise to creative third dimension (and–both) solutions for seemingly irreconcilable (either–or) cultural differences.

I also propose that whatever cultural background she or he may be from, a transcultural practitioner should attempt to be a third culture–realm builder. This, at first, may seem like a minor point, but I argue that this shift in how practitioners *think* of their cultural positionality could make a significant difference in how they *practice* transcultural public relations. A practitioner who, instead of seeing (cultural) difference as something "distant" or as the onus of the Other sees that difference as becoming a part of the Self through interaction, is in a position to work with people from disparate cultures *creatively* (as opposed to defensively) and not see difference as a *problem* to be overcome.

For a public relations practitioner to be adept at third culture building, she or he has to assume a dynamic cultural identity. This practitioner needs to be a kind of cosmopolitan person who is comfortable navigating the glocal (Tomlinson, 1999), a cultural being-in-progress who does not primarily judge various cultural values and practices but is capable of working and growing with and within them as necessary. According to Featherstone (1995), a category of professionals (cultural intermediaries) such as lawyers, management consultants, advertisers, and media experts have become prominent in the global landscape (we could easily add public relations professionals to this list). They are people who have "become familiar with a number of national cultures as well as developing, and in some cases living in, third cultures" (Featherstone, 1995, p. 91). Some scholars have fruitfully borrowed this concept of cultural intermediaries from cultural studies and applied it to what public relations practitioners do (Curtin & Gaither, 2007; Hodges, 2006). Cultural intermediaries are producers of culture since they are involved in meaning production at the junctures of production and consumption (Nixon & du Gay, 2002). When we perceive practitioners as producers of culture it moves us toward a more dynamic conceptualization of culture as it plays out in practice. Hodges (2006) posits that the kinds of relationship building and communication practices public relations practitioners as cultural intermediaries engage in depends on their lifeworld or "the way in which practitioners live, create and relate to the world of public relations work" (p. 85). To this useful conceptualization I would add that the transcultural practitioner's lifeworld needs to include a very particular orientation toward culture and relationship building—a third culture orientation.

Some Notes on Power, and a Caveat

While the third culture building model has been acknowledged for its noble intentions, some scholars have critiqued it for not being rigorous enough in incorporating issues of power and irreconcilable differences (Belay, 1993; Shuter, 1993). This matter is very pertinent, especially since the word in critical public relations scholarship is that there is not enough research on how power plays out in public relations practice (Edwards, 2006; Gower, 2006; L'Etang, 2005; Weaver et al., 2006). I agree with this viewpoint. By analyzing power, we can move toward more socially responsible models and theories of transcultural public relations. Thus, the question now becomes: To what extent is the third culture building model equipped to address issues of power discrepancies in transcultural public relations?

All interpersonal interactions, especially intercultural ones, are inevitably marked by power differentials. As Martin and Nakayama (2010) observe, "We are not equal in our intercultural encounters, nor can we ever be equal. Long histories of imperialism, colonialism, exploitation, wars, genocide, and more leave cultural groups out of balance when they communicate" (p. 133). In a similar vein, Belay (1993) offers a power-related critique of third culture building by noting that the model is not equipped to address power differentials and focuses, perhaps too optimistically, on fusion and transformation. In its place, he offers what he calls the "interactive multiculture building" model. This model "projects tolerance for differences and mutual respect among cultures" (Belay,

1993, p. 451), and simultaneously affirms the possibility of transformation. In other words, it acknowledges that power and difference play a significant role in determining whether or not the possibility for mutual transformation exists.

While Belay's critique is pertinent, Casmir *does* take the matter of power differentials into consideration, and is not naïvely focused on uncomplicated fusion. He makes a cogent point when he states that third culture building is a "mutually beneficial creative process that does not necessarily depend on 'equal' contributions from the involved partners. Rather, the process finds its meaning in contributions determined by and *valued* [emphasis in original] because of mutually agreed-upon needs. That is the case regardless of what percentage of the total each contribution represents" (Casmir, 1993, pp. 419–420). Casmir accepts that it is inevitable that power differences, whether material or symbolic, will exist. However, despite that inevitability, he argues that it is still possible to reach a level of mutuality and intercultural understanding that is acceptable to all parties involved. This argument is akin to the notion of control mutuality in interpersonal communication (Stafford & Canary, 1991) which describes how unequal partners engaged in communication mutually decide where and mostly with whom power lies in a given relational context (Hon & J. Grunig, 1999). Jahansoozi (2006, citing L'Etang, 1996), notes that "Openly recognizing where the power lies in the relationship facilitates achieving the desired relational outcome" (p. 76). In-depth micro level qualitative studies that examine how practitioners discursively engage in successful third culture building could shed more light on how control mutuality is accomplished during this process.

An argument in favor of Casmir's model and its relation to power is that the model attempts to dislodge rather than maintain the Self/Other binary during the third culture building process. It allows us to focus on how power works at the interpersonal level of intercultural interaction. Binaries, and the hierarchies binaries tend to produce, often form the basis of power discrepancies. One of the conceptual goals of the model is to collapse, through transformation, the hierarchies and power differentials constructed through binaristic thought and modes of communication. This is a move away from an "either–or" logic where the first term (Self) in the binary (Self/Cultural Other) is considered to be superior (Sarup, 1996, p. 57). So, while "equality" in a larger macro sense might not be possible, micro negotiations between interactants with the goal of reaching an acceptable solution which is *mutually generated in context* becomes a distinct possibility. As already mentioned, the micro level dynamics of power can change the dynamics at the macro level, perhaps in favor of the less powerful. With that point made, we can now move toward a more Foucauldian notion of power (Holtzhausen, 2000).

Power, like culture, is not a static "thing," and need not always be conceptualized in a grand top-down deterministic fashion (Berger 2005; Curtin & Gaither, 2007; Weaver et al., 2006). While nobody or no entity is beyond power plays, power is not a fixed phenomenon (Foucault, 1980) and we cannot assume that the larger entity with more resources (such as the multinational corporation) will *always* have more power in every situation. For example, Curtin and Gaither (2007) point out that despite all its power, Coca-Cola could not get consumers to accept New Coke®. Power does not unconditionally reside in structures, but is enacted through people who constitute and discursively give meanings to those structures.

Foucault (1980), in writing about micropractices of power, argues that power is always open to renegotiation since it is primarily based in the practices of people interacting, and that it is not some abstract thing that any one entity possesses (Holtzhausen, 2000; Holtzhausen & Voto, 2002). As Holtzhausen (2000), also using Foucault, has pointed out, power operates at various levels and can be ascending as well as descending in nature. In fact, power is multi-modal, multi-scalar, and multi-directional. A focus on micro practices can help us understand how the meanings, tensions, and directional realities of power can change at the individual level of human interaction, and that the context of interaction matters. An individual who is more powerful in one context can be less so in another. Martin and Nakayama (1999) have labeled this phenomenon the "privilege-disadvantage dialectic," stating that "individuals may be simultaneously privileged and disadvantaged, or privileged in some contexts and disadvantaged in others" (p. 18). For example, a female practitioner may represent a large multinational company and be powerful in that macro sense, and yet she may not be in a position of power in the transcultural moment of interaction and cultural negotiation with a male representative of a civic group in a more patriarchal local host culture. Power is always contextual and contested, and much of the contestation occurs through symbolic, cultural, and interactive communication. A third culture building focus allows us to focus on the complexities and the micropolitics (Holzhausen, 2000) of power in transcultural public relations.

Now for the caveat: Some may perceive the normative role of the transcultural practitioner as a third culture/realm builder as too idealistic or even unrealistic. Shuter (1993) offers a pragmatic critique of Casmir's model. He notes that motive is the crucial missing element in intercultural communication models advocating relational synergy and interdependence (see also Starosta & Olorunnisola, 1995). Why should two individuals from different cultural backgrounds be inspired to build a third culture? What incentives and motives would create the condition of willingness to engage in "a renegotiation and synthesis of the most integral part of the human cultural experience—attitudes, values, and mores" (Shuter, 1993, p. 431)? Shuter has a good point, and he offers the notion of "culturalism" instead, which gives a pragmatist's twist to Casmir's third culture building model. The assumption behind culturalism is that enlightened self-interest and task-centered motives could be incentives for cooperation and interdependence for mutual gain (p. 434). Shuter does not believe, however, that cultural participants will permanently adjust their cultural values for such ends. In other words, cultural adjustments would only be temporarily made for particular mutual gains.

Shuter makes a good point. Even though the practitioner may be interested in third culture/realm building, the other interactants belonging to external public groups may not have sufficient incentive or desire to be involved in this process. For example, a non-local, non-governmental organization (NGO) trying to reduce deaths and injuries caused during unsafe abortions in a culture that is patriarchal with a majority Roman Catholic population (Curtin & Gaither, 2007) could face a good amount of resistance. So could an NGO working to enroll working children in school in a culture where due to extreme poverty, parents over generations have believed that children are more useful when they are earning than when they are in school. Or, a multinational company could simply face nationalistic resistance from members of a postcolonial culture who expect practices of cultural/economic imperialism from that company (Bardhan & Patwardhan, 2004). Third culture building requires everyone involved to be open to change, and that means being willing to disrupt one's cultural comfort zone and perhaps ideological beliefs. Not everybody welcomes change, especially if the change involves adjusting long-held beliefs that have deep cultural roots, or giving up power advantages. Third culture building may not always be a possibility, especially when vast differences or polarized perceptions preexist. Perhaps, in such situations, the transcultural practitioner could try and locate members of significant publics (preferably opinion leaders) who are willing to engage in dialogue and reach a mutually acceptable course of action that is non-coercive. Negotiations from that point onwards could change overall perceptions. As Holtzhausen (2002) notes, power differentials are inevitable from a postmodern perspective, and postmodern practitioners need to see conflict as normal and not seek forced consensus. Shuter also posits that it is more possible to build a third realm rather than a more enduring third culture. However, it could be argued that this depends on the situation. If the relationship is perceived by all involved to be a long-term one that could be mutually beneficial, then more change and transformation is a good possibility.

Change is inevitable in our world, and it can occur through coercive communication or through dialogue and mutual negotiation. In the case of transcultural public relations, change through third culture building is a good possibility when there is a perception of enlightened self- interest on the part of the organization and the publics in question. Casmir recognizes that for third culture building to be successful, all cultural interactants need to be willing to change and value the benefits of engaging in non-coercive third culture building. All parties involved, despite power differentials, need to feel that they are gaining from the process.

Closing Thoughts

The story of McDonald's in Moscow, Russia, provides a good example of third culture building. The company opened its first outlet in Moscow in 1990, and today it has over 75 outlets all over the country. Muscovites have domesticated McDonald's and made it into a culinary phenomenon that is perceived to be part of the larger cultural landscape of Russia. Food culture in Russia is communal in nature, and food grown locally is preferred over supplies flown in from some anonymous place. McDonald's uses local supplies, clearly communicates its local thrust in its advertising and public relations efforts, and focuses on building public acceptance. Furthermore, space is also used in a communal sense; that is, McDonald's outlets are not perceived as private spaces with private rules, McDonald's lets the community in. For example, patrons are allowed to bring their own food and beverages to add to the menu, those celebrating birthdays for their children are welcome to bring their own decorations, there is no limit on how much time one can spend at McDonald's, people conduct meetings and business at McDonald's, and street children find it to be a safe haven. The company conducts market surveys on a regular basis to keep itself informed of public opinion, and it focuses on community relations projects, social network building, and collective responsibility in its everyday practices and policies. McDonald's has embedded itself into the cultural landscape through intentional and focused micro level, and consequently macro level third culture building policies and public relations practices. It is still McDonald's, but in a Russian way (example drawn from Caldwell, 2004).

The above example demonstrates that success stories of third culture building in transcultural public relations practice do exist. For public relations scholars, this means that there is a need to empirically study, using appropriate methods, the communication practices of practitioners already engaged in third culture building efforts in order to better understand how they are accomplished as well as what challenges they face. Such studies could help develop third culture theory that is particular to transcultural public relations (a proposition also encouraged by Kent and Taylor in this volume). Beyond demonstrating this need, this chapter makes a few other contributions to public relations scholarship. First, by explicating how the third culture building model can help us conceptualize communication and culture in the context of global flux, it highlights the limitations of the static country=culture logic. Second, since third culture building is a dialogic and intersubjective model, the arguments in this chapter contribute to the dialogic perspective, for which there is a need and an increasing interest in public relations scholarship. Kent and Taylor (2002) note that the increasing focus on dialogue indicates a "theoretical shift—from public relations reflecting an emphasis on managing communication to an emphasis on communication as a tool for negotiating relationships" (p. 23). Finally, this chapter contributes to the growing line of theorizing in public relations scholarship that focuses on the coconstitutive nature of micro and macro levels of communication and relationship building (e.g., Durham, 2005; Falkheimer, 2007).

From a pedagogical perspective, this chapter highlights to public relations students the need to think in more complex ways about how culture works in global flux, what that means for public relations praxis, and how they need to prepare themselves to work successfully in transcultural spaces. It is hoped that it demonstrates to them the value of subscribing to a third culture attitude by taking more courses in (inter) cultural communication, taking advantage of study abroad opportunities, being interested in rather than feeling frustrated by cultural difference, and traveling whenever possible. For educators, this means that they need to encourage students to take courses in intercultural communication in addition to those in international/global public relations that are already offered, and help students see the connections between culture, the public relations industry, and the practitioner's lifeworld (Hodges, 2006).

Practitioners may use the third culture building model to make better theoretical sense of their practice and their own cultural identity positions, and to be more self-reflexive while working in transcultural spaces. If they understand the value of third culture building it could also encourage them to be more engaged in training opportunities (see Burk, 1994) that teach them to develop transcultural mindsets. Perhaps they could proactively start such initiatives in their places of work. Overall, third culture building holds value for teaching practitioners how to become more culturally competent, less ethnocentric, and generally more cosmopolitan in their attitude toward the cultural differences they experience while working in transcultural spaces.

By proposing third culture building as a model through which to theorize and practice transcultural public relations, I have demonstrated in this chapter the suitability of interpretive and social constructionist approaches for conceptualizing the dynamic relationship between culture and communication in transcultural public relations. To wrap up in the words of Tomlinson (1999), "Globalization disturbs the way we conceptualize 'culture.' For culture has long had connotations tying it to the idea of a fixed locality" (p. 26). Global flux has deterritorialized culture, and public relations scholarship needs to catch up with the ground reality that "culture" can no longer be conceptualized with a capital "C" (Tsing, 2000). Culture takes on many forms, not just that of the nation-state, and is produced and negotiated through people interacting with each other in increasingly transcultural spaces. This dynamic perception of culture makes third culture building in public relations work imaginable.

Discussion Questions

1. How would you describe global flux? Can you think of particular ways in which the phenomenon of global flux has changed our perceptions of "culture" and "public" in public relations?
2. In this chapter, the term *transcultural* is selected over the term *multinational* to discuss public relations in relation to global flux. Is this is good choice? If yes, why? If no, can you think of a more accurate term? Provide a clear rationale for your term.
3. Explain the differences between the social scientific and interpretive definition/description of culture and communication and the relationship between them.
4. How can the micro level of relationship building be related to the macro level of relationship building in transcultural public relations? Explain with an example.
5. How does the third culture building model redefine the relationship between cultural Self and cultural Other? What promise does this redefinition hold for transcultural public relations?
6. Is the third culture building model adequately equipped to address issues of power inequalities between organizations and publics? Explain your view on this with clear rationales and references to particular theories of power (e.g., Foucault's notion of the micropolitics of power).
7. Describe at least two strengths and two weaknesses of the third culture building model as applied to transcultural public relations.

References

Aldoory, L. (2007). Reconceiving gender for an "Excellent" future in public relations scholarship. In E. Toth (Ed.), *The future of excellence in public relations and communication management* (pp. 399–411). Mahwah, NJ: Erlbaum.

Appadurai, A. (1996). *Modernity at large*. Minneapolis, MN: University of Minnesota Press.

Banks, S. (1995). *Multicultural public relations: A social-interpretive approach.* Thousand Oaks, CA: Sage.

Banks, S. (2000). *Multicultural public relations: A social-interpretive approach* (2nd ed.). Ames, IA: Iowa State University Press.

Bardhan, N. (2007, November). *What's global and what's local? Shortfalls of current conceptualizations in transnational public relations.* Paper presented at the annual convention of the National Communication Association, Chicago, IL.

Bardhan, N., & Patwardhan, P. (2004). Multinational corporations and public relations in a traditionally resistant host culture. *Journal of Communication Management, 8*(3), 246–263.

Belay, G. (1993). Toward a paradigm shift for intercultural and international communication: New research directions. *Communication Yearbook, 16,* 437–457.

Berger, B. (2005). Power over, power with, and power to relations: Critical reflections on public relations, the dominant coalition, and activism. *Journal of Public Relations Research, 17*(1), 5–28.

Berger, P., & Luckmann, T. (1966). *The social construction of reality.* Garden City, NY: Doubleday.

Botan, C. (1992). International public relations: Critique and reformulation. *Public Relations Review, 18*(2), 149–159.

Botan, C. (1993). A human nature approach to image and ethics in international public relations. *Journal of Public Relations Research, 5*(2), 71–81.

Botan, C., & Taylor, M. (2004). Public relations: State of the field. *Journal of Communication, 54*(4), 645–661.

Broom, G. (1982). A comparison of sex roles in public relations. *Public Relations Review, 8*(1), 17–22.

Broom, G., Casey, S., & Ritchey, J. (1997). Toward a concept and theory of organization-public relationships. *Journal of Public Relations Research, 9*(2), 83–98.

Broom, G., & Dozier, D. (1986). Advancement for public relations role models. *Public Relations Review, 12*(1), 37–56.

Broom, G., & Smith, G. (1978, August). *Toward an understanding of public relations roles: An empirical test of five role models' impact on clients.* Paper presented at the annual meeting of the Association for Education in Journalism, Seattle, WA.

Burk, J. (1994). Training MNC employees as culturally sensitive boundary spanners. *Public Relations Quarterly, 39*(2), 40–44.

Caldwell, M. (2004). Domesticating the French fry: McDonald's and consumerism in Moscow. *Journal of Consumer Culture, 4*(1), 5–26.

Carey, J. (1989). *Communication as culture: Essays on media and society.* Boston, MA: Unwin Hyman.

Casmir, F. (1978). A multicultural perspective on human communication. In F. Casmir (Ed.), *Intercultural and international communication* (pp. 241–257). Washington, DC: University Press of America.

Casmir, F. (1993). Third-culture building: A paradigm shift for international and intercultural communication. *Communication Yearbook, 16,* 407–428.

Casmir, F. (1997). Ethics, culture and communication: An application of the third-culture building model to international and intercultural communication. In F. Casmir (Ed.), *Ethics in intercultural and international communication* (pp. 89–118). Mahwah, NJ: Erlbaum.

Casmir, F. (1999). Foundations for the study of intercultural communication based on a third-culture building model. *International Journal of Intercultural Relations, 23*(1), 91–116

Casmir, F., & Asuncion-Lande, N. C. (1989). Intercultural communication revisited: Conceptualization, paradigm building, and methodological approaches. *Communication Yearbook 12,* 278–309.

Collier, M. J., & Thomas, M. (1988). Cultural identity: An interpretive perspective. In Y. Y. Kim & W. B. Gugykunst (Eds.), *Theories in intercultural communication* (pp. 94–120). Newbury Park, CA: Sage.

Coombs, W. T. (2001). Interpersonal communication and public relations. In R. Heath (Ed.), *Handbook of public relations* (pp. 105–114). Thousand Oaks, CA: Sage.

Cooper-Chen, A., & Tanaka, M. (2008). Public relations in Japan: The cultural roots of Kouhou. *Journal of Public Relations Research, 20*(1), 94–114.

Culbertson, H. (1996). Introduction. In H. Culbertson & N. Chen (Eds.), *International public relations: A comparative analysis* (pp. 1–13). Mahwah, NJ: Erlbaum.

Curtin, P., & Gaither, T. (2005). Privileging identity, difference, and power: The circuit of culture as a basis for public relations theory. *Journal of Public Relations Research, 17*(2), 91–115.

Curtin, P., & Gaither, K. T. (2007). *International public relations: Negotiating culture, identity, and power.* Thousand Oaks, CA: Sage.

de Certeau, M. (1984). *The practice of everyday life.* Berkeley, CA: University of California Press.

Dozier, D. (1984). Program evaluation and roles of practitioners. *Public Relations Review, 10*(2), 13–21.

Dozier, D. (1992). The organizational roles of communications and public relations practitioners. In J. Grunig (Ed.), *Excellence in public relations and communication management* (pp. 327–355). Hillsdale, NJ: Erlbaum.

Durham, F. (2005). Public relations as structuration: A prescriptive critique of the StarLink global food contamination case. *Journal of Public Relations Research, 17*(1), 29–47.

Edwards, L. (2006). Rethinking power in public relations. *Public Relations Review, 32*(3), 229–231.

Falkheimer, J. (2007). Anthony Giddens and public relations: A third way perspective. *Public Relations Review, 33*(3), 287–293.

Featherstone, M. (1995). *Undoing culture: Globalization, postmodernism and identity.* London: Sage.

Ferguson, M. (1984, August). *Building theory in public relations: Interorganizational relationships.* Paper presented at the convention of the Association for Education in Journalism and Mass Communication, Gainesville, FL.

Foucault, M. (1980). *The history of sexuality.* New York: Vintage Books.

Gaither, T. K., & Curtin, P. (2008). Examining the heuristic value of models of international public relations practice: A case study of the Arla Foods crisis. *Journal of Public Relations Research, 20*(1), 115–137.

Gower, K. (2006). Public relations research at the crossroads. *Journal of Public Relations Research, 18*(2), 177–190.

Grunig, J. (1990). Theory and practice of interactive media relations. *Public Relations Quarterly, 35*(3), 18–23.

Grunig, J., Grunig, L., Sriramesh, K., Huang, Y., & Lyra, A. (1995). Models of public relations in an international setting. *Journal of Public Relations Research, 7*(3), 163–186.

Gupta, A., & Ferguson, J. (1992). Beyond "culture": Space, identity, and the politics of difference. *Cultural Anthropology, 7*(1), 6–23.

Hannerz, U. (1997). Scenarios for peripheral cultures. In A. King (Ed.), *Culture, globalization and the world-system* (pp. 107–128). Minneapolis, MN: University of Minnesota Press.

Heath, R. (2000). A rhetorical perspective on the values of public relations: Crossroads and pathways toward concurrence. *Journal of Public Relations Research, 12*(1), 69–91.

Hodges, C. (2006). "PRP culture": A framework for exploring public relations practitioners as cultural intermediaries. *Journal of Communication Management, 10*(1), 80–93.

Hofstede, G. (1984). *Culture's consequences: International differences in work related issues.* Beverly Hills, CA: Sage.

Hofstede, G. (2001). *Culture's consequences: International differences in work related issues* (2nd ed.). Thousand Oaks, CA: Sage.

Holtzhausen, D. (2000). Postmodern values in public relations. *Journal of Public Relations Research, 12*(1), 93–114.

Holtzhausen, D., & Voto, R. (2002). Resistance from the margins: The postmodern public relations practitioner as organizational activist. *Journal of Public Relations Research, 14*(1), 57–84.

Hon, L. C., & Grunig, J. (1999). *Measuring relationships in public relations.* Gainesville, FL: Institute for Public Relations.

Hon, L. C., Grunig, L., & Dozier, D. (1992). Women in public relations: Problems and opportunities. In J. Grunig (Ed.), *Excellence in public relations and communication management* (pp. 419–438). Hillsdale, NJ: Erlbaum.

Huang, Y. (2001). OPRA: A cross-cultural, multiple-item scale for measuring organization-public relationships. *Journal of Public Relations Research, 13*(1), 61–90.

Hung, C. J. F. (2005). Exploring types of organization-public relationships and their implication for relationship management in public relations. *Journal of Public Relations Research, 17*(4), 393–426.

Ihator, A. (2000). Understanding the cultural patterns of the world—An imperative in implementing strategic international PR programs. *Public Relations Quarterly, 45*(4), 38–44.

Ihlen, Ø., & van Ruler, B. (2007). How public relations works: Theoretical roots and public relations perspectives. *Public Relations Review, 33*(3), 243–248.

Jahansoozi, J. (2006). Relationships, transparency, and evaluation: The implications for public relations. In J. L'Etang & M. Pieczka (Eds.), *Public relations: Critical debates and contemporary practice* (pp. 61–91). London: Erlbaum.

Johansson, C. (2007). Goffman's sociology: An inspiring resource for developing public relations theory. *Public Relations Review, 33*(3), 275–280.

Kent, M., & Taylor, M. (2002). Toward a dialogic theory of public relations. *Public Relations Review, 28*(1), 21–37.

Ledingham, J. (2006). Relationship management: A general theory of public relations. In C. Botan & V. Hazleton (Eds.), *Public relations theory* (Vol.2, pp. 465–483). Mahwah, NJ: Erlbaum.

Ledingham, J., & Bruning, S. (2000). *Public relations as relationship management: A relational approach to the study and practice of public relations.* Mahwah, NJ: Erlbaum.

L'Etang, J. (2005). Critical public relations: Some reflections. *Public Relations Review, 31*(4), 521–526.

L'Etang, J. (2006). Public relations and rhetoric. In J. L'Etang & M. Pieczka (Eds.), *Critical perspective in public relations* (pp. 106–123). London: International Thomson Business Press.

Lyra, A. (1991). *Public relations in Greece: Models, role and gender* (Unpublished master's thesis). University of Maryland, College Park.

Macnamara, J. (2004). The crucial role of research in multicultural and cross-cultural communication. *Journal of Communication Management, 8*(3), 322–334.

Martin, J., & Nakayama, T. (1999). Thinking dialectically about culture and communication. *Communication Theory, (9)*1, 1–25.

Martin, J., & Nakayama, T. (2010). *Intercultural communication in contexts* (5th ed.). New York: McGraw-Hill.

Maynard, M., & Tian, Y. (2004). Between global and local: Content analysis of the Chinese web sites of the 100 top global brands. *Public Relations Review, 30*(3), 285–291.

Molleda, J-C., & Roberts, M. (2008). The value of "authenticity" in "glocal" strategic communication: The new Juan Valdez campaign. *International Journal of Strategic Communication, 2(3)*, 154–174.

Moon, D. (1996). Concepts of "culture": Implications for intercultural communication research. *Communication Quarterly, 44*(1), 70–84.

Ni, L. (2009). Strategic role of relationship building: Perceived links between employee-organization relationships and globalization strategies. *Journal of Public Relations Research, 21*(1), 100–120.

Nixon, S., & du Gay, P. (2002). Who needs cultural intermediaries? *Cultural Studies, 16*(4), 495–500.

Packman, H., & Casmir, F. (1999). Learning from the Euro Disney experience. *Gazette, 61*(6), 473–489.

Pal, M., & Dutta, M. (2008). Public relations in a global context: The relevance of critical modernism as a theoretical lens. *Journal of Public Relations Research, 20*(2), 159–179.

Pearce, W., & Cronen, V. (1980). *Communication action and meaning: The creation of social realities.* New York: Praeger.

Pearson, R. (1989). Business ethics as communication ethics: Public relations practice and the idea of dialogue. In C. Botan & V. Hazleton, Jr. (Eds.), *Public relations theory* (pp. 111–131). Hillsdale, NJ: Erlbaum.

Rhee, Y. (2002). Global public relations: A cross-cultural study of the Excellence theory in South Korea. *Journal of Public Relations Research, 14*(3), 159–184.

Rhee, Y. (2007). Interpersonal communication as an element of symmetrical public relations: A case study. In E. Toth (Ed.), *The future of excellence in public relations and communication management* (pp. 103–117). Mahwah, NJ: Erlbaum.

Robertson, R. (1992). *Social theory and global culture.* London: Sage.

Robertson, R. (1995). Glocalization: Time-space and homogeneity-heterogeneity. In M. Featherstone, S. Lash, & R. Robertson (Eds.), *Global modernities* (pp. 25–44). London: Sage.

Roudometof, V. (2005). Transnationalism, cosmopolitanism, and glocalization. *Current Sociology, 53*(1), 113–135.

Sarup, M. (1996). *Identity, culture and the postmodern world.* Edinburgh, Scotland: Edinburgh University Press.

Sha, B.-L. (2006). Cultural identity in the segmentation of publics: An emerging theory of intercultural public relations. *Journal of Public Relations Research, 18*(1), 45–65.

Shuter, R. (1993). On third-culture building. *Communication Yearbook, 16,* 429–436.

Sriramesh, K. (1996). Power distance and public relations: An ethnographic study of Southern Indian organizations. In H. Culbertson & N. Chen (Eds.), *International public relations: A comparative analysis* (pp. 171–190). Mahwah, NJ: Erlbaum.

Sriramesh, K. (2007). The relationship between culture and public relations. In E. Toth (Ed.), *The future of excellence in public relations and communication management* (pp. 507–526). Mahwah, NJ: Erlbaum.

Sriramesh, K., & Verčič, D. (2001). International public relations: A framework for future research. *Journal of Communication Management, 6*(2), 103–117.

Sriramesh, K., & White, J. (1992). Societal culture and public relations. In J. Grunig (Ed.), *Excellence in public relations and communication management* (pp. 597–614). Hillsdale, NJ: Erlbaum.

Stafford, L., & Canary, D. (1991). Maintenance strategies and romantic relationship type, gender and relational characteristics. *Journal of Social and Personal Relationships, 8*(2), 217–242.

Starosta, W. (1991, May). *Third culture building: Chronological development and the role of third parties.* Paper presented at the annual meeting of the International Communication Association, Chicago, IL.

Starosta, W., & Olorunnisola, A. (1995, April). *A meta-model for third culture development.* Paper presented at the annual convention of the Eastern Communication Association, Pittsburgh, PA.

Thomlison, T. (2000). An interpersonal primer with implications for public relations. In J. Ledingham & S. Bruning (Eds.), *Public relations as relationship management* (pp. 177–203). Mahwah, NJ: Erlbaum.

Tomlinson, J. (1999). *Globalization and culture.* Chicago, IL: University of Chicago Press.

Toth, E. (1989, November). *The crisis: When interpersonal communication the-*

ory explains public relations behavior. Paper presented at the annual meeting of the Speech Communication Association, San Francisco, CA.

Toth, E. (2000). From personal influence to interpersonal influence: A model for relationship management. In J. Ledingham & S. Bruning (Eds.), *Public relations as relationship management* (pp. 205–219). Mahwah, NJ: Erlbaum.

Toth, E., & Heath, R. (1992). *Rhetorical and critical approaches to public relations.* Hillsdale, NJ: Erlbaum.

Toth, E., Serini, S., Wright, D., & Emig, A. (1998). Trends in public relations roles: 1990–1995. *Public Relations Review, 24*(2), 145–163.

Tsing, A. (2000). The global situation. *Cultural Anthropology, 15*(3), 327–360.

Useem, J., Donoghue, J, & Useem, R. (1963). Men in the middle of the third culture. *Human Organization, 22*(33), 129–144.

Verčič, D. (2009). Public relations of movers and shakers: Transnational corporations. In K. Sriramesh & D. Verčič (Eds.), *The global public relations handbook: Theory, research and practice* (rev. ed., pp. 795–806). New York: Routledge.

Verčič, D., Grunig, L., & Grunig, J. (1996). Global and specific principles of public relations. In H. Culbertson & N. Chen (Eds.), *International public relations: A comparative analysis* (pp. 31–65). Mahwah, NJ: Erlbaum.

Wakefield, R. (2001). Effective public relations in the multinational organization. In R. Heath & G. Vasquez (Eds.), *Handbook of public relations* (pp. 625–647). Thousand Oaks, CA: Sage Publications.

Weaver, C. K., Motion, J., & Roper, J. (2006). From propaganda to discourse (and back again): Truth, power, the public interest and public relations. In J. L'Etang & M. Pieczka (Eds.), *Public relations: Critical debates and contemporary practice* (pp. 7–21). London: Erlbaum.

Williams, O., & Murphy, P. (1990). The ethics of virtue: A moral theory for marketing. *Journal of Macromarketing, 10*(1), 19–29.

Woodward, W. (2000). Transactional philosophy as a basis for dialogue in public relations. *Journal of Public Relations Research, 12*(3), 255–275.

Wu, M. Y., Taylor, M., & Chen, M. J. (2001). Cultural and societal influences on Taiwanese public relations. *Public Relations Review, 27*(3), 317–336.

Zaharna, R. (2000). Intercultural communication and international public relations: Exploring parallels. *Communication Quarterly, 48*(1), 85–100.

Zaharna, R. (2001). "In-awareness" approach to international public relations. *Public Relations Review, 27*(2), 135–148.

Suggested Readings

Chen, G-M., & Starosta, W. (2004). Communication among cultural diversities. In G-M. Chen & W. Starosta (Eds.), *International and intercultural communication annual: Vol. 27. Dialogue among diversities* (pp. 3–15). Washington, DC: National Communication Association.

Frost, A. (2000). Negotiating culture in a global environment. *Journal of Communication Management, 4*(4), 369–377.

Giddens, A. (1984). *The constitution of society: Outline of the theory of structuration.* Berkeley, CA: University of California Press.

Hannerz, U. (1997). *Transnational connections: Culture, people, places.* London: Routledge.

Hutchison, L., & Pauly, J. (2003). Think local, act local: The fate of community relations in an age of global public relations. In D. Demers (Ed.), *Terrorism, globalization and mass communication* (pp. 233–248). Spokane, WA: Marquette Books.

Lee, S. (2006). Somewhere in the middle: The measurement of third culture. *Journal of Intercultural Communication Research, 35*(3), 253–264.

L'Etang, J., & Pieczka, M. (Eds.). (2006). *Public Relations: Critical debates and contemporary practice.* Mahwah, NJ: Erlbaum.

Macmanus, T. (2000). Public relations: The cultural dimension. In D. Moss, D. Verčič, & G. Warnaby (Eds.), *Perspectives on public relations research* (pp. 159–178). London: Routledge.

Mckie, D., & Munshi, D. (2007). *Reconfiguring public relations: Ecology, equity and enterprise.* London: Routledge.

Rosenau, J. (2003). *Distant proximities: Dynamics beyond globalization.* Princeton, NJ: Princeton University Press.

Spicer, C. (1997). Communication from a collaborative frame. In C. Spicer (Ed.), *Organizational public relations: A political perspective* (pp. 202–221). Mahwah, NJ: Erlbaum.

Urry, J. (2003). *Global complexity.* Cambridge, UK: Polity Press.

White, J. (1987, August). *Public relations in the social construction of reality: Theoretical and practical implications of Berger and Luckmann's view of the social construction of reality.* Paper presented at the annual meeting of the Association for Education in Journalism and Mass Communication, San Antonio, TX.

Yoshitake, M. (2004). Research paradigm for dialogue among diversities. In G-M. Chen & W. Starosta (Eds.), *International and intercultural communication annual: Vol. 27. Dialogue among diversities* (pp. 16–42). Washington, DC: National Communication Association.

Chapter 5

Intercultural Typologies and Public Relations Research

A Critique of Hofstede's Dimensions

Jeffrey Courtright, Rachel Wolfe, and John Baldwin

One of the major ongoing areas of work among intercultural and international communication scholars is the development of frameworks and approaches to understand and compare cultures. One of the frameworks that has received the most attention in the social scientific paradigm in the intercultural communication field is that provided by Dutch organizational psychologist Geert Hofstede (1984, 1986, 1997). In 1980, he published a book describing his research in 40 national cultures, in which he analyzed organizational values, placing them on a set of four contrasting dimensions—individualism/collectivism, power distance, uncertainty avoidance, and masculinity/femininity. The dimensions are well-developed, and built on an incredible wealth of research. They have clear application to education and management (Hofstede, 1986), and Hofstede has published several books and has developed a very useful Web site (1987–2009) to explain the dimensions and show their value in explaining differences between national cultures in both everyday communication and business practices.

Indeed, in the area of intercultural communication, researchers and theorists have perhaps used Hofstede's set of dimensions, in part or whole, more than any other framework, and international/intercultural public relations researchers seem to be following suit (see also Kent and Taylor's chapter in this volume). In this chapter, we present Hofstede's dimensions as commonly understood, with a discussion of both their strengths and limitations. We then apply the dimensions specifically to a global public relations phenomenon, Dove's "Campaign for Real Beauty." Finally, noting some of the limitations of the framework, we offer public relations students and researchers alternative tools for cultural understanding.

Hofstede's Dimensions

Hofstede developed his original findings based on a longitudinal study conducted from 1967 to 1973, which was based on data from over

50,000 respondents in 53 countries (Hofstede, 1984). He conducted his original study within the framework of a specific multinational organization—IBM—in the attempt to identify national cultural differences specifically as opposed to other differences (e.g., occupation, education, income level) that could predict communication and organizational behavior. Hofstede used the data from his survey research to construct his original dimensions.

Hofstede's Original Four Dimensions

The first dimension, *power distance*, refers to "the extent to which the less powerful members of institutions and organizations within a country expect and accept that power is distributed unequally" (Hofstede, 1997, p. 28). Hofstede (1984) concluded that the surrounding social and cultural environment supports a view of equality or inequality present in organizations, and, in his 1997 book, *Cultures and Organizations, Software of the Mind*, he outlines how one can see this dimension play out in organizations and schools as well as in political and economic societal structures. Nations (treated as separate cultures) range in score from a very low power distance index (PDI), in which organizations may be consultative and subordinates might participate in decision making or call superiors (e.g., teachers) even by their first name, to countries with a high PDI, in which one would expect different rules to apply to those of high status, and the people see such differential treatment as just and right.

The second dimension, *uncertainty avoidance*, is "the extent to which the members of a culture feel threatened by uncertain or unknown situations" (Hofstede, 1997, p. 113). The uncertainty avoidance index (UAI) determines the reactions of people within a society to unpredictable situations. Strong uncertainty avoidance is characterized by viewing uncertainty as a threat. National cultures with high UAI value rules as necessary and desired for social order (Hofstede, 1980, 1997): people tend to see difference in a negative light. In cultures with weak UAI, people are more likely to accept ambiguity as a normal feature of life and enact rules only if there is strict necessity. In cultures characterized by low UAI, people might embrace change or ambiguity; rules might be more lax in some ways, with unclear or weaker punishment for violation; and strangers might find a warmer welcome.

A third dimension suggests that cultures, just like people, subscribe to particular gender roles that govern social practices. The *masculinity/femininity* dimension extends supposed biological trends of males and females to a cultural framework. Unfortunately, the dimension has two (sometimes competing) definitions. First, in a so-called masculine culture, both men and women will value "masculine" traits such as strength and measurable achievement and material success and progress, over relationship building and collaboration, the latter being the mark of a "feminine" society (Hofstede, 1980, 1998). In this regard, feminine society would privilege caring for others and relationship preservation, through face-saving behaviors, for example. Another definition suggests that masculine cultures, following a traditional social structure, keep gender roles distinct: Men do "men" things and women do "women" things, while feminine culture allows or even encourages more fluid gender roles; thus, men might change diapers and cook, and women might work construction and ride motorcycles.

Hofstede's fourth original dimension is *individualism/collectivism*.

He (1997) explains:

> Individualism pertains to societies in which the ties between individuals are loose: Everyone is expected to look after himself or herself and his or her immediate family. Collectivism as its opposite pertains to societies in which people from birth onwards are integrated into strong, cohesive ingroups, which throughout people's lifetime continue to protect them in exchange for unquestioning loyalty. (p. 51)

Individualistic cultures base identity on the individual: "I" thinking and improving self-worth are central tenets (Hofstede 1984, 1997). Such cultures emphasize tasks over relationships. They also tend to use low-context styles of communication (Hofstede, 1997); that is, where meaning is in the "explicit code" or actual words (Hall, 1959).

Collectivist cultures, on the other hand, are "high context," in which meaning resides within the communicators, understood based on role position and situational context (Hall, 1959). This allows speakers either to use more silence, to rely more on non-verbal communication and verbal nuance, or to use verbal communication for other purposes, such as "ornamentation" and "exaggeration," rather than to convey explicit meanings. By definition, collectivist cultures emphasize the group: "we" thinking and group membership are primary considerations. People value relationships over tasks and practice high context communication (Hofstede, 1997). This dimension has received much attention from other scholars, such as cross-cultural psychologist Harry Triandis and his colleagues (Kim, Triandis, Kâğitçibaşi, Choi, & Yoon, 1994; Triandis, 1995), who, for example, differentiate between two types of individualism and collectivism (horizontal and vertical), based on whether cultures accept and honor status difference. However, many intercultural communication scholars rely more on Hofstede's conceptualization.

Hofstede's dimensions have become a prominent framework for theorizing of intercultural communication within the social scientific paradigm. They appear in many introductory texts, and constitute one of the pillars of intercultural communication; for example, Gudykunst and Lee (2002), discussing the construction of intercultural communication theory, set as criteria for evaluating such theory that it "incorporate more than one dimension of cultural variability" and "directly link the dimensions of cultural variability being used to specific cultural norms and rules that influence the communication behavior being explained" (p. 44). They present explicitly Hofstede's (1980) dimensions and high and low context communication (Hall, 1959), with special attention to individualism/collectivism, which has a prominent place in their model of intercultural communication. So also, many other intercultural communication scholars have used Hofstede's dimensions, especially individualism/collectivism (e.g., Kim, 1993, 2005; Ting-Toomey, 1988), and, more recently, power distance (Ting-Toomey, 2005; Ting-Toomey & Kurogi, 1998), uncertainty avoidance (Gudkyunst, 2005), and others. Specific research applications also abound. Kale (2006) uses Hofstede's dimensions to measure the cultural implications of the design of Internet gaming sites. Vadi and Meri (2005) utilize Hofstede's dimensions to evaluate Estonian culture as it is experienced in the hotel industry. Kalliny, Cruthirds, and Minor (2006) use Hofstede's dimensions as a theoretical framework for examining differences in the uses of humor between Arabs and Americans and the impacts they have on business management styles.

In creating his dimensions, Hofstede developed a benchmark that serves as a guideline for much of current cross-cultural research and theory. His dimensions appear in both academic research and international and global business applications. The dimensionality of cultures—especially individualism/collectivism—has become an everyday way to describe and evaluate cultural differences. However, the wide adoption, adaptation, and application of Hofstede's dimensions have also led to a growing critique of this framework.

A Critique of the Original Dimensions

From our view, the dimensions have several qualities that are worthy of recommendation, and, for this reason, we continue to use them in some ways in our own teaching and research. The dimensions were systematically developed, based on an incredibly large sample of 50,000 participants (Hofstede, 1984), with participants well beyond Hofstede's original IBM sample. It includes more cultures (measured in terms of countries) than any other study of which we are aware, with now over 70 countries and regions available for comparison (Hofstede, 1987–2009); and, as participants in all cultures have taken an equivalent version of the scales, this does allow for some cultural comparison. The dimensions provide a common language with which to discuss how, for example, Mexico and Indonesia might be similar or different. They have garnered much attention from scholars: psychologists and organizational researchers have linked individualism, especially (though not necessarily Hofstede's version), to a wide array of both personality traits and behaviors (Bond & Smith, 1996; Triandis & Suh, 2002). Further, the dimensions provide us with a useful way of thinking about cross-cultural differences. For example, Kohls's (2001) discussion of South Korea, along with our own experience, suggests that concepts such as collectivism explain the *soju* (rice-wine) ritual of filling only the other person's glass or the practice of gift-giving; and power distance helps us make sense of introductions, bows, and much body language. Finally, the wide use of the dimensions provides a common language, across disciplines, with which to understand national cultures.

That being said, the dimensions have received increasing criticism, especially but not exclusively from within the field of intercultural communication. These criticisms seem to revolve around methodological, conceptual, and application issues.

Methodological Issues   Some of the greatest criticisms of the dimensions, from a social scientific perspective, are based upon the original creation of the scores. Writers such as Hui and Triandis (1985) and Cai (1998) suggest a variety of concerns for cross-cultural scale validation, noting that it is difficult to get a scale that has all aspects of conceptual validity even across two cultures, requiring back-translation (a process of having one person translate a scale into a second language and an independent person translate it back for comparison) and even the creation of survey items from each culture included; thus, the measures could have translational and equivalency issues. In addition, the original sample, taken from IBM employees, may have produced results that are *not generalizable* to entire cultures: McSweeney (2002) and Smith (2002) argue that Hofstede's use of the IBM databank has limitations that researchers frequently overlook. McSweeney (2002) maintains that the data collection method within the IBM organization and later primarily within marketing-to-sales occupations, greatly restricts our ability to make predictions of wider audiences (i.e., the "generalizability") of the original scores. McSweeney also contends that Hofstede's claim to control for organizational and occupational differences is not addressed. In response to critiques, Hofstede (2002) has made minor changes to his approach, as well as offered explicit rejoinders. He has also extended the sample to include a variety of other populations, though these samples are still mostly comprised of students and professionals (Hofstede,

1987–2009). It is possible that, within a culture, the values prevalent in academic and business contexts will not extend, for example, to working class individuals or those with little formal education. While no one expects the values to apply to all members of a given national culture (e.g., to "countercultures") there may, in fact, be large pockets of individuals within a culture that do not ascribe to a professional value system.

Critiques by McSweeney and others elicited lengthy debates in leading journals such as *Human Relations* and *Psychological Bulletin*. In sum, McSweeney (2002) argues that "on a few occasions he [Hofstede] has added to his model, but he has never acknowledged any significant errors or weaknesses in that research" (p. 90). Smith (2002) notes that Hofstede "prefers to revise the way that he computes his measures rather than to revise his concepts" (p. 125). However, the fact that Hofstede's work is heuristic, that is, it leads to new research and discussion, cannot be denied.

Conceptual Issues   Hofstede's dimensions raise numerous conceptual questions. The first is: Could there be other dimensions? In 1987, the Chinese Cultural Connection, a research group, posited that the four supposedly universal dimensions were insufficient for capturing Chinese social reality. Thus, they developed a fifth dimension, Confucian work dynamism, to refer to a cultural value on pragmatism and hard work and thrift, with a long-term vision for rewards. Appropriately, Chinese respondents scored quite high on this pragmatic value, while U.S. respondents scored low. Hofstede now incorporates this dimension into his Web site under the term "long-term orientation." However, a problem with using the same four (or even five) dimensions in a cookie-cutter approach to culture is that it could exclude from our vision other viable cultural dimensions.

The conceptualization of the dimensions, themselves, warrants more consideration. We saw above the difficulty of the dual meaning of masculinity/femininity. It may be, however, that even the notion of dimensions as dichotomous needs revisiting. Treating the dimensions as continua, in which we think of one culture as having a *higher* individualism score than another, has more theoretical power and face validity—that is, it makes more sense—than treating cultures on a dichotomy by saying that a culture is *either* individualist *or* collectivist. The two dimensions could exist within a single culture (or subculture). Most scholars, in fact, echo the idea that both ends of a continuum exist in all cultures, but that cultures have value preferences that put them at a particular place on a continuum.

But the very notion of a continuum suggests that values like individualism and collectivism could not both exist at a higher level within the same culture. Scholars who study self-construal, the individual-level (psychological) component of individualism/collectivism, suggest that independent and interdependent self-construal are not mirror images of one another, but exist independently. Some scholars (e.g., Martin & Nakayama, 1999; Pudlinski, 1994) argue for a dialectical approach to intercultural communication and to culture, suggesting a shifting, relational, and dialectical tension between seemingly opposite values such as change and stability, rather than a specific, dichotomous, and static cultural preference. Such tensions might also be experienced in specific cultures on a single Hofstedian dimension. For example, F. Johnson (2000) identifies two of the main values of African American culture as individual expression *and* community. These two values, representing a form of individualism and a form of collectivism, exist side by side within the culture, rather than on a continuum. Also for example, Fitch's work (1998) suggests that concepts of both *hierarchia* (hierarchy, status) and *confianza* (trust, a sense of interpersonal connectedness) undergird most social relations in Colombia.

Finally, in terms of conceptualization, it is possible that even nations that score similarly in the same area of a single dimension may not communicate or experience the value in the same ways. For example, Guatemala and the Philippines might have very similar power distance scores, but the nuances of status (how it is shown, to whom) could differ in important, even if subtle ways. That is, traditional measures of these cultural dimensions may merely tap *how members respond to the researcher's notions, and not reflect the specific culture's definitions, constructs, or social realities.* Thus, it may be that concepts such as individualism contain more than one dimension, a critique leveled by Kâğitçibaşi and Berry (1989), or that a culture might prefer one point of a continuum (e.g., higher power distance) in one context, such as an organization, and another point in the continuum (e.g., more egalitarianism) in another context, such as a religious situation. Miller (2002) states that subtle cultural differences in meanings, as well as contextual specificity within cultures, pose a fundamental challenge to the traditional notion of individualism and collectivism.

Application Issues Some of the concerns with the Hofstedian framework relate not to the construction of the dimensions themselves nor to Hofstede's work, but with the way scholars and trainers commonly apply them. Two primary application concerns are essentialization (applying the dimensions to all individuals and groups within a national culture) and dichotomization (treating the dimensions as "either–or" explanations, rather than on a continuum). It is difficult to determine the degree to which these are problems in the conceptualization or problems in the application of the concepts by researchers.

Martin and Nakayama (1999) point out in their dialectical approach to intercultural communication that, "people are both [cultural] group members and individuals and intercultural interaction is characterized by both" (p. 15). Hofstede has rigorously defended his dimensions as culture-level predictors that should not be applied to individuals; yet the temptation to do so by researchers is not easily resisted. Smith (2002) notes: "What is the use of characterizing cultures as a whole, if we cannot then start to use our characterizations to gain a more fine-grained understanding of what goes on within them?" (p. 122). To this end, the current trend in intercultural research is *not* to rely merely on Hofstede, but to include both cultural-level predictors (such as Hofstede's dimensions) along with individual-level predictors, such as psychological variables. Thus, Gudykunst and Y. Y. Kim (2003), M. S. Kim (2005), and others clearly differentiate between concepts such as self-construal and individualism, or uncertainty avoidance (a description of a culture) and tolerance for ambiguity (a psychological trait), noting that culture will influence the individual-level variables (Gudykunst & Lee, 2002; M. S. Kim, 1995).

However, the idea of essentialization goes beyond the danger of ignoring personal differences. Many current intercultural communication scholars working within post-positivist paradigms have moved away from treating nations as cultures (e.g., Bardhan's chapter in this volume), something inherent in the original Hofstede work. McSweeney (2002) addresses the notion that Hofstede's dimensions may not be the best measure for determining cultural differences, suggesting that evidence of a "national culture," as such, does not exist. He suggests that Hofstede's claim that a national culture is present in all individuals of that nation and thus determines behavioral differences is an incorrect assumption. The charge of essentialization is that much intercultural communication research treats a single culture, such as Thai culture, as monolithic in two senses: first, it ignores the differences of many cocultures (or subcultures) within the dominant culture—cultures based on class, sex/gender, ethnicity, age cohort, and many other factors. Even organizations might differ within a culture. As an example, we could give New Zealand a particular score on the different dimensions, but this would obscure vast cultural differences between the Maori natives (more collectivist) and the European-descended Whites (more individualistic), as well as class, educational, sex, age cohort, and other differences among each group, or social differences, such as among the Maori who have more or less adopted a more urbanized or industrialized culture. In addition, multiple organizational and occupational cultures are likely to exist in any given country (McSweeney, 2002), further confounding the notion that differences among respondents are ultimately rooted in national cultural differences.

Second, the dimensions run the risk of making readers think that cultures do not change; that is, they obscure the dynamic aspect of culture. This is demonstrated in Hofstede's own Web site (1987–2009), which reflects roughly, if not exactly, the same scores for the different nations on the various dimensions as the original 1980 work. Smith (2002) notes that though Hofstede has written new versions of his original study, no new data has been collected and that Hofstede relies on his 20-year-old data as the basis for his claims of the existence of cultural dimensions. The world has changed a lot since 1980, and Smith (2002) argues that some countries' culture index scores may have changed to a point now that Hofstede's original work no longer has any predictive validity. Smith points out that Hofstede finds "significant change in I/C [individualism/collectivism] in most nations over the modest time interval of five years," even though, at the same time, he asserts that national culture is slow to change (p. 125). Certainly, the growing interdependence of media systems, urbanization, industrialization, and globalization are changing and blurring cultures to make any simple placement on a Hofstedian score problematic.

The final practical limitation does not derive from Hofstede himself, but from those who apply the concept. Hofstede originally developed each dimension as a continuum, with the notion that a culture can be very high on a given dimension, such as individualism, very low, or somewhere in the middle. As a continuum, it is understood that the *less* individualistic a culture is, the *more* collectivist it is. That is, the two ends of any given dimension are understood to be bipolar opposites. Although we have highlighted some problems with the notion of continua, we admit that these are still conceptually stronger than dichotomies. In dichotomous thinking, one divides cultures into one of two groups on each continuum. To continue with our example, a culture is *either* "individualist" *or* "collectivist." Unfortunately, it is common in practice, research, and even theory, for scholars to reduce the more theoretically rich continua into dichotomy. That is, researchers make predictions of "individualist" and "collectivist" cultures, rather than discussing cultures that might be, say, "*more* individualistic." As an example, scholars often compare Japan and the United States as countries with high and low power distance, respectively (e.g., Haruta & Hallahan, 2003; Oetzel & Ting-Toomey, 2003). However, a comparison on Hofstede's measures shows that their scores are relatively close. And while Japan scored at about the mean (in 1980) in terms of individualism/collectivism, it is usually referred to simply as a "collectivist" culture. Related either to this closeness of scores, or to the changeability of cultures noted above, in a meta-analysis of many studies that invoke individualism/collectivism to explain cultural and psychological traits, Oyserman, Koon, and Kemmelmeier (2002) found European Americans to be no more individualistic than Latino/as, nor less collectivist than the Japanese. In sum, as critical examinations of Hofstede's dimensions continue to appear, we encourage a general "proceed with caution" approach to applying the dimensions in cross-cultural public relations research in the context of globalization. Hofstede's cultural dimensions may provide insight into some cross-cultural differences and may even provide a framework through which these differences are assessed, but ultimately these dimensions cannot be assumed as the ultimate analysis of cultural differences, especially in a world marked by increasing cultural fluidity and change.

Hofstede's Dimensions as Applied to Public Relations Research

As noted earlier, intercultural communication scholarship has begun to treat individualism/collectivism and other Hofstedian concepts more complexly. However, an overview of many studies from public relations that utilize Hofstede's dimensions finds that, similar to earlier intercultural communication research, more often than not, the dimensions are invoked in terms of national difference as an attempt to explain different public relations practices. For instance, Coombs, Holladay, Hasenauer, and Signitzer (1994) use Hofstede's dimensions to explain cultural differences in professionalization in three countries: Austria, Norway, and the United States. Most often, the dimensions explain differences between Eastern and Western cultures (e.g., Haruta & Hallahan, 2003; Kang & Mastin, 2008; Sriramesh, Kim, & Takasaki, 1999). These investigations, then, seek to explain individuals' behaviors, such as policy writing in South America (Thatcher, 2000). And, as with most studies, public relations research tends to treat nations *as* cultures, rather than look for cultural differences *within* nations (e.g., Gould, Gupta, & Grabner-Kräuter, 2000; Haruta & Hallahan, 2003). Studies of single countries tend to rely, like studies in intercultural communication, more on specific dimensions, such as Confucian work dynamism, uncertainty avoidance, and especially individualism/collectivism (e.g., Cooper-Chen & Kaneshige, 1996; Freitag, 2002).

As researchers in this area often use Hofstede's (1980) definition of culture as a "collective programming of the mind," it is sensible that his dimensions have some overarching influence on the behaviors of individuals. From a communication standpoint, however, the behaviors of individuals are what dictate methods and channels of communication, and it is on these individual behaviors (and their variations) that more research should be focused. Generally, public relations scholars regard Hofstede's dimensions as the accepted constructs on which entire national cultures vary. However, little consideration is given to the actual influence that these dimensions have on individuals' behaviors; it is assumed that they do affect behavior, but they fail to examine how strong that influence really is. In some cases, in fact, the dimensions do not accurately predict behavior. For example, Thomas (1998) noted that her observations in South Korea did not produce the variation of cultural differences that she had originally perceived based on Hofstede's dimensions.

Using Hofstede's dimensions as a framework for measuring cultural differences in individuals' behaviors is then a better application in international/intercultural public relations. In the international public relations literature, researchers often conclude that cultural differences vary greatly and that public relations models and practices should be culture-specific, and that historical public relations models are Western-focused and may be ineffective in other cultures (Sriramesh, 2009). Similarly, Hofstede's dimensions are frequently applied as a theoretical framework to identify cultural differences; however, researchers do not challenge the notion that these dimensions may not be exhaustive and that other indicators of "national culture" that exist may be overlooked. By using the dimensions as a theoretical framework and as the *only* indicators of cultural differences, international/intercultural public relations researchers may be missing critical cultural nuances that are not explained in Hofstede's model, nuances which can provoke unwanted results in public relations applications.

However, some public relations researchers do apply the notion of national culture with caution and consideration (Freitag, 2002; Holtzhausen, Petersen, & Tindall, 2003; Synnott & McKie, 1997; Wu, 2002). Some seek to understand how individuals are similar to and differentiate from the "national culture" dimension of individualism (e.g., Freitag, 2000). Others look at group differences within a culture. For example, Wu (2002) notes that the perception of an overarching Chinese culture by Westerners is not accurate due to the varied regional differences among the Chinese. Holtzhausen, Petersen, and Tindall (2003) consider how cocultures in South Africa are influenced by the national culture and generalized public relations models.

In review, we see that Hofstede's dimensions, especially individualism/collectivism, have strong support in many fields, including intercultural communication generally speaking and international/intercultural public relations specifically. The dimensions, however, require a number of cautions, nuances, and considerations often lacking in the research literature. While intercultural communication scholars are continuing to complicate the dimensions, public relations researchers are just beginning to provide studies and theorization that revise or qualify the dimensions, allowing them to use the positive aspects while avoiding the excesses. One of the main arguments underlying this volume is that, in a globally interconnected world, the nation-state cannot be seen as the only measure of culture; that culture is dynamic rather than static; and that culture and cultural differences and similarities must be studied and theorized in ways that account for supra- and sub-national forces of culture. Hofstede's dimensions thus must be applied by public relations scholars in ways that are cognizant of these complexities. In the next section, we consider the dimensions' usefulness in a specific case study that involves a campaign that is global in its scope.

Dove's "Campaign for Real Beauty"

Dove's "Campaign for Real Beauty" captured special recognition as the top campaign for 2006, winning the Public Relations Society of America's Silver Anvil Award. The campaign's award summary, provided by Unilever (the Dutch company behind the Dove brand) and Edelman Public Relations Worldwide (the agency of record), focused primarily on the campaign's success in the United States:

> Fueled by global research ... Edelman's media relations efforts generated unprecedented awareness for the brand, from segments on "The Today Show" and "Oprah" to the cover of *People* magazine; catapulted Dove into popular culture; and sparked a nationwide dialogue about beauty and how it is portrayed in marketing and advertising. (Public Relations Society of America [PRSA], 2006, ¶4)

Indeed, the campaign's pilot launch in Germany and its U.S. launch, accompanied by a new Dove product line, Dove Firming, used "no television advertising, and billboard/print ads featured minimal copy" (¶5).

This campaign actually is global in scope. Dove has hosted "Campaign for Real Beauty" Web sites in over 30 countries. Begun in 2004, the campaign, especially through efforts such as the Self-Esteem Fund, continues to generate monies to support research regarding obesity and health-related issues such as eating disorders and links to disease in later life (e.g., heart disease, breast cancer). Therefore, although the campaign might appear at first to be a marketing strategy, its thrust is issue oriented, with multiple public relations discourse conventions represented across the various Web sites (e.g., news releases, bios, and case histories) as well as social media links, interactive games and activities, and other tactics designed to build relationships between young women, older women, and the campaign.

The stated purpose of the Dove campaign is to "expand the definition of beauty" beyond the stereotypes perpetuated through Hollywood and Madison Avenue's emphasis on being slim and good looking. Indeed, the campaign does not feature traditional fashion models (Unilever, 2009a). The campaign's communication efforts continue to focus on everyday women, particularly young girls, larger women, and older women, who are susceptible to loss of self-esteem due to the mass media's emphasis on so-called perfection. Unilever has established a Dove Self-Esteem Fund to support its cause and to help women around the world. We might expect some differences in approach for the campaign in particular countries (e.g., it should be safe to assume that the campaign's Brazilian Web site appeals to women in ways different from Dove's campaign site in the United States or Great Britain). Let's first think about how Hofstede's cultural dimensions might inform such assumptions and then look at Dove's various campaign Web sites to see how well Hofstede's work applies.

One way in which Hofstede's dimensions of culture might be used would be to develop a set of expectations that we can apply to any global public relations campaign. Recognizing the pitfalls in application mentioned earlier, we can anticipate how Dove's Campaign for Real Beauty might target different audiences in culture-specific ways. First, campaigns directed at cultures (nations) with high power distance would feature appeals to authority, possibly to hierarchy within the family or group, such as familial authority. Appeals to low PDI likely would entail more egalitarian relationships. Such campaigns might create messages in which all opinions are valued, not privileging experts over laypersons; or they might emphasize familial approaches that treat parents and children as friends or confidants. With regard to the issues found in the Dove campaign, appeals to high PD would employ health and beauty experts. Appeals to low PDI might emphasize relationships between mothers, grandmothers, and daughters, without reference to status distinctions.

Public relations campaigns often address the uncertainties of life and help audiences to find solutions to everyday problems. Hofstede's second dimension, uncertainty avoidance, deals with how much ambiguity people in different cultures are willing to tolerate. We could anticipate that campaigns directed at cultures high in uncertainty avoidance would take a directive approach, giving publics specific steps to perform to solve problems. Uncertainty itself could be an appeal used to lead to predictability. For low UAI cultures, campaigns would offer more latitude for possible solutions (which obviously would work better for image rather than product-oriented campaigns). For the Dove campaign, appeals to uncertainty reduction would include recommendations for specific actions to lose weight, avoid or recover from anorexia or bulimia, or provide support for self-esteem. Appeals to cultures in which uncertainty is more accepted would promote autonomy for audiences in dealing with these issues.

Hofstede's masculinity/femininity dimension should raise issues for campaigns such as Dove's because it is aimed at women in particular, and this dimension relates specifically to role differentiation and to a focus on modesty and caring as opposed to competition. If anything, the global campaign promotes a singular, yet paradoxical view of women that is assertive, urging women to accept themselves for who they are, yet still caters to traditional notions of beauty (i.e., through the selling of skin toners and other products and through use of models with a limited range of "beauty"). The remaining concepts within the dimension suggest that appeals to more "masculine" cultures should emphasize measurable outcomes. Appeals to "feminine" cultures would emphasize relational issues such as saving face. Similar to collectivism, this end of the continuum is other-oriented, concerned with preservation of the dignity of the other. Notably, conventional wisdom argues that even within the United States, women are socialized to take more of this approach to life; a relational approach would make sense as an appeal to women generally. For the Dove campaign, a masculine orientation would focus on weight loss results, numbers of women who suffer from health-related and self-esteem issues, and so on. A more feminine approach should lead rather to qualitative outcomes: feelings of self-worth, higher self-esteem, and overall health. Thus, the campaign as a whole promotes a feminine approach. At the same time, the campaign still offers links to toning gels, thereby reinforcing a continued focus on physical beauty, and portrays women in underwear or naked, contradicting traditionally feminine notions of modesty. Finally, in some cultures (e.g., U.S.) there are links to discussions of how young women can be "powerful and influential, yet still womanly" (Unilever, 2009a) and look to others for inspiration but also look within themselves to set the standard for "real beauty" and what it means to be successful (Unilever, 2009b).

The last two of Hofstede's dimensions are relatively uncomplicated. For the individualism/collectivism dimension, we could expect campaign appeals to individualistic cultures to focus on the formation of one's own opinions and attitudes and doing things for personal benefit; in this case, creating one's own notion of beauty. Campaigns directed toward collectivist cultures should highlight how connections to family, extended family, and friends generate meaning. For the Dove campaign, a collectivist approach to beauty would define beauty in terms of how the relevant group sees it. As for the Chinese-derived dimension of long- versus short-term orientation, campaign appeals to the latter would feature appeals with immediate results. Clearly, we see these types of appeals in communications from the diet and beauty industries in general. Appeals to a long-term orientation would include, in particular for Dove, developing a lifestyle that is health-oriented. Since this orientation focuses on virtue, a respect for tradition, and fulfilling social obligations, education, therefore, would be part of such efforts.

As we turn to an application of Hofstede's cultural dimensions to the Dove Campaign, we should note that we did not analyze all of its Web sites, only the ones which the first two authors, both of whom are mul-tilingual, could translate when needed. In the following subsections, we first note how Hofstede's work might account for the differences found in the different countries' Web sites devoted to the Dove campaign and then argue, with minor reservations, that the campaign provides a rea-sonable approach to negotiating culture in global public relations.

Different Approaches, Cultural Differences?

In some ways, the Dove campaign is right on target in adapting to the various countries that Unilever has chosen to address. Hofstede's dimen-sions and the research figures his research has yielded for these coun-tries (see Table 5.1) might account for the success of the campaign (as well as its failure in at least one country, China). There are, however, ways in which the campaign's approach to certain countries depends upon the dialectical tensions within Hofstede's dimensions. The follow-ing brief analysis highlights these tensions, demonstrates the typology's shortcomings, and suggests the need to turn to other approaches when examining public relations campaigns that are global in scope.

As shown in Table 5.1, each of Hofstede's dimensions are rated out of 100 points, thus providing comparative data between different cultures (assuming country = culture). For example, Australia (IDV = 90) rates very high on individualism when compared to China (IDV = 20). This suggests that China's culture is much more collectivist in orientation. For each dimension, then, zero and 100 represent the opposite ends of a continuum, the labeling of each continuum in the chart corresponding to particular tendencies. The comparison between Australia and Canada illustrates how IDV stands for individualism but a low score for that item implies the collectivist side of the dimension we discussed earlier. A high score for PDI, power distance, therefore, indicates a greater respect for hierarchy and the acceptance of status differences as the norm; a low score indicates a more egalitarian culture. A high score for MAS, masculinity, therefore, contrasts with low scores on that measure, thus pointing to femininity, and so on.

Take, for example, the dimension of power distance. The Dove cam-paign, with its emphasis on empowering women young and old to define beauty more broadly, reflects elements that would appeal to cultures at both ends of the continuum. The use of experts (e.g., doctors and noted makeup/beauty specialists) would be logical choices to appeal to cul-tures with higher power distance. France, however, is the only country whose campaign Web site features a medical expert—on the homepage, no less—which would be consistent with its moderately high rating of PDI (68; see Figure 5.1). In comparison, the German Web site could be expected to not feature such authority figures (Germany's PDI is 35).

Table 5.1   Hofstede's Dimension Scores by Certain Nations from Dove's "Campaign for Real Beauty"

Country	Hofstede Scores				
	PDI	IDV	MAS	UAI	LTO
Australia	36	90	61	51	31
Austria	11	55	79	70	
Belgium	65	75	54	94	
Brazil	69	38	49	76	65
Canada	39	80	52	48	23
Chile	63	23	28	86	
China	80	20	66	30	118
France	68	71	43	86	
Germany	35	67	66	65	31
Italy	50	76	70	75	
Mexico	81	30	69	82	
Netherlands	38	80	14	53	44
Portugal	63	27	31	104	
United Kingdom	35	89	66	35	25
United States	40	91	62	46	29

Key: PDI, power distance; IDV, individualism/collectivism; MAS, masculinity/femininity; UAI, uncertainty avoidance; and LTO, long-term orientation.
Source: Hofstede (1987-2009); lack of LTO scores reflects missing data in the original data.

However, its Web site is the only one to feature a salon professional, just as France's is the only one that employs a doctor as a spokesperson. Although all of the campaign's Web sites feature women on their board of directors, the idea that audiences should give deference to their opinions as leaders is unclear. The fact that the boards are almost entirely comprised of women suggests more of a leveling of hierarchy, of equals speaking to equals.

What Hofstede's PDI ratings may not account for, then, is the success of the campaign in higher PDI countries (e.g., Belgium, Brazil, Chile, Mexico, Portugal). China's high rating of 80, however, may explain why Unilever has abandoned its Real Beauty efforts there and shifted to a partnership in the development of a Chinese-produced television show similar to *Ugly Betty* (Fowler, 2008). In general, however, the dialectical tension between respect for authority and equality among all women (i.e., all women are beautiful) reinforces Hofstede's original intent that the dimensions serve as continua rather than as bipolar oppositions.

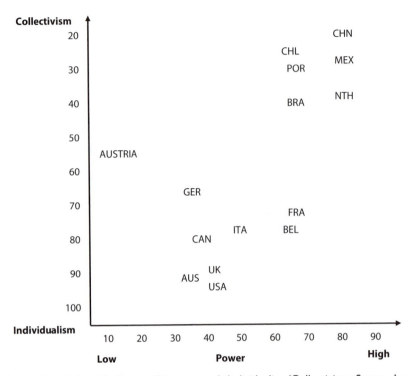

Figure 5.1 Hofstede's Power Distance and Individualism/Collectivism Scores by Certain Nations from Dove's "Campaign for Real Beauty"

This tension cannot alleviate the self-judgment that some women and girls feel.

Likewise, the Dove campaign presents a dialectical tension with regard to uncertainty avoidance (UAI). The campaign seeks to allay self-doubt and, therefore, reduces ambiguity, thereby appealing to cultures with higher UAI (e.g., Portugal, France, and Chile). On the other hand, the variety of solutions offered to women and girls promotes choice and, therefore, capitalizes on ambiguity, which might be more appealing to cultures in which English is considered the primary language, as these cultures tend to be lower in uncertainty avoidance (see Figure 5.2). However, although the campaign privileges discussion of self-image and women's health concerns, such issues necessarily are expressed through emotion rather than cold, hard facts and statistics. This emphasis favors cultures tolerant of ambiguity—but implicitly the campaign offers preferred solutions and a clear sense of what is "normal" and what is not.

How this ambiguity plays out in the different Web sites' links to particular programs is not consistent with the expectations that Hofstede's findings would lead us to. Australia's use of "Body Think" as a more structured approach to self-esteem workshops stands in stark contrast to the United States site's links to do-it-yourself workshops. Both countries fall in the middle of the continuum (see Table 5.1). It should be noted that the United Kingdom site's lack of a link to such programs coincides with a high tolerance for ambiguity, however. Indeed, with all of them providing links to expert opinion and other factual information, there are few differences across the Web sites in their approach to levels of ambiguity.

Application of Hofstede's remaining dimensions reveals no substantial differences across Web sites. The campaign's emphasis on women and caring approaches to problem solving, openness to self-expression, and building relationships naturally leans toward the masculinity/femininity (MAS) dimension's femininity side. However, based on Figure 5.2, such a focus would run into problems in few countries. In contrast, there remains a dialectical tension between individualism and collectivism (IDV). The campaign simultaneously encourages women and girls to improve personal esteem and to recognize that they can still use other women as referent points, albeit not slim, svelte models. As for

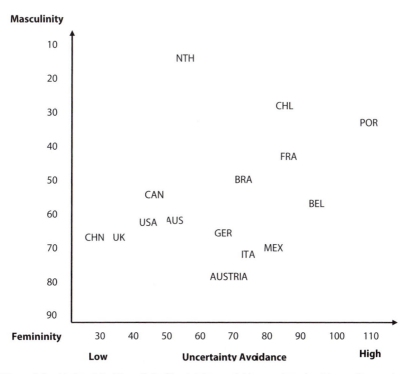

Figure 5.2 Hofstede's Masculinity/Femininity and Uncertainty Avoidance Scores by Certain Nations from Dove's "Campaign for Real Beauty"

long-term orientation (LTO), the Web sites tend toward developing a healthy lifestyle.

In short, the campaign is much more uniform than might be recommended by the cultural differences Hofstede's findings would have Unilever address in its Dove Campaign for Real Beauty. His findings only highlight the dialectical tensions we found in applying the dimensions of power distance, uncertainty avoidance, individualism/collectivism, and long-term orientation. The emphasis on a more feminine worldview should not appeal to so-called masculine cultures. Yet the campaign has generated multiple news stories around the globe each year since 2004 and has linked the Dove brand to the issue of female body image (e.g., Austen, 2006; "Dove Helps Us Define," 2007; Postrel, 2007). What then makes the Dove campaign so successful?

The Campaign as Global Appeal

Beyond the limited individual differences, what distinguishes this global campaign is the homogeneity across cultures. One might be tempted to think, as anticipated above, that the campaign in collectivist cultures, like Mexico, would focus more on family—especially extended family. The opening appeal might be through familial ties, such as through the campaign video, *Onslaught,* found on the campaign's Web sites for several different countries, which urges parents (probably mothers) to teach their daughters about beauty before society does. Even if communication professionals are not familiar with Hofstede, specifically, it seems cultural research would lead to differently oriented campaigns. For example, Friday's (2006) interview study of German and U.S. managers found German managers to value credibility in interactions, whereas U.S. managers sought to be liked—contrary, interestingly, to Hofstede's lower power distance index for Germany. Friday's research would suggest that a German advertisement might privilege a focus on the opinions of experts that lend the campaign credibility. And research on Latino values list respect and family as core values to the culture, suggesting an opening bid that links self-esteem to one's connection to the stability found in one's family (Lindsley, 2000). In reality, the opening bid on the Mexican Web site is the video *Evolution,* which focuses on the transformations to a model before she becomes a billboard icon. The video begins immediately from a black video box, with the following text to the side:

> For years, we have been *deslumbrados* [dazzled] by "perfect" models. They have made us feel like we *should* be like them in order to be considered beautiful ... when their image is, in reality, *an illusion.*

This video denounces the changes to which models and their photos are submitted before arriving before our eyes.

The same video begins the German and Austrian Web pages, though with an opening link that features a picture of the (Caucasian, possibly Germanic) looking woman in the video with a simple invitation box to view the video. This same invitation is issued on the Brazilian and Italian Web sites, though there, the invitation is to the more expected film for more collective cultures, *Onslaught* (Portuguese: *Sob Pressão*, or "under pressure"; Italian, *L'Attacco*, "the attack"). There are subtle differences in the links and in how one moves from page to page, but one can eventually find most elements on most pages. *Onslaught* is available on the German sites (*Angriff*, through the film link); audiences can find the same multinational panel of experts with their credibility-invoking biographies on the Mexican site. Sites from most cultures have links that include mother/daughter resources; links to specific studies (especially the 10-nation study on perceptions of beauty); a variety of interactive sites such as blogs or discussion boards; and several links "just for girls," such as quizzes (trying to determine the image that has been photo-edited), a diary for thoughts on self-esteem, and an interactive image that allows the viewer to stretch an average figure to Barbie-doll proportions. Some countries have contests and some do not, and some pages have more links or more complexity, and others do not.

On initial consideration, Dove's Web sites on beauty seem to invoke simultaneously both niche cultural marketing and universal brand appeal. The universal appeal at first seems to be an approach across all Web sites that incorporate elements that would appeal to both sides of particular Hofstedian dimensions. For example, there are voices of experts and scientific studies (all sponsored by Dove) to appeal to those who value status and expertise (high power distance), but chances for people to share ideas in forums in which all ideas are treated as equal, as well as a collegial approach that suggests egalitarianism. The Web sites are admittedly more complex in some nations, with the United States having notably more links and complexity than most other countries. This could, contrary to Hofstede's lower score for the United States, reflect higher power distance (Kang & Mastin, 2008), or it might be an artifact of the fact that the campaign began in the United States and that more of the materials currently exist in English. The sites incorporate use of subtle flash software (masculine), but are also somewhat feminine in their approach to giving dignity to multiple voices (i.e., in the forums that offer no critique of diverse opinions) and are relational in nature (mother/daughter focus), reflecting femininity (Kang & Mastin, 2008). The Web sites utilize a relatively simple Web design, reflecting high uncertainty avoidance (Kang & Mastin, 2008), but offer very few concrete solutions, focusing rather more on awareness with a vague direction of better skin and health care (low uncertainty avoidance). There are seemingly collective connections to others ("invite a friend," a chance to interact with others to build a sort of community, and links for mother/daughter talks and workshops), as well as to highlight one's own individual perspective (private journals, "share your opinion," contests/games).

A universal appeal that crosses any specific set of Hofstede's values clearly attests to the wisdom of the campaign—a campaign that has retained a sense of branding homogeneity yet has garnered appeal across many cultural contexts. At the same, perhaps the appeal is not as universal as it seems. The power distance elements are, indeed, balanced, but in all the Web sites studied, the experts and studies are sublimated to back pages, sometimes requiring two or three links to locate. The texts are predominantly feminine in focus—interactive and relational—but this may be quite appropriate because even in so-called masculine cultures, women tend to be socialized to be more relational than men (Hofstede, 1987–2009). Linked to this aspect of femininity, of showing respect for others, is a certain open-endedness of the texts that is more tolerant than avoidant of uncertainty. The feminine and open-ended aspects of the sites relate to a sense of connectivity to others. Most tellingly, perhaps, these signs of connectivity—blogs, bulletin boards, mother–daughter connections—really do not evidence a collective culture. The trademark of collective cultures is connection to the *in-group*. Both friendships (invite a friend) and mother–daughter relationships are present in all cultures; even individualistic cultures prize highly the nuclear family and friendship, though the definition of what constitutes a friend might differ. In sum, even in collectivist nations like Mexico, the sites are predominantly individualistic, urging consumers to "express their opinion" and "be themselves." Still, links to area- or nation-specific organizations focusing on women's health may link women's identities to a larger collective within each nation.

Although the sites are relatively homogeneous, there are also subtle differences that we have noted above that suggest cultural distinctiveness, although these are not fully explainable by Hofstede's dimensions. At the core of these is the very notion of beauty. The videos *Onslaught* and *Evolution* are clearly appropriate for Western audiences, including most of Europe—anywhere strongly influenced by the modern (Western) fashion industry. However, advertising specialists have noted how Dove's campaign was not successful in China, largely based on different cultural concepts of beauty to which the campaign simply did not appeal (Fowler, 2008). The traditional notion of beauty urges round rather than sharp-featured faces, small noses, and chubby cheeks (Xu & Finer,

2007), and is likely linked to Confucian propriety and to one's role in society as a woman (i.e., as worker, wife, mother) based on traditionalist Confucian notions (Chinese Culture Connection, 1987). Other research, however, suggests that the "beauty economy" in China is growing so fast that the Chinese needed to invent a new word, *meinü jingji*, to describe it (Xu & Finer, 2007). Chinese women are quickly adopting a Western notion of beauty, seeking to "refashion themselves in terms of Western beauty standards represents a transformation of the communist ideal of woman as producer into the neoliberal image of woman as consumer that epitomizes Western affluent society" (p. 310). Recent promotions of beauty contests in China that, due to requirements that models be both light *and* tall, are having "direct and immediately damaging effects on Chinese women's bodies" (p. 316), and are leading Chinese women to privilege Whiteness in beauty, to the extent that, in one recent study, Chinese women found U.S. models—both men and women, to be more attractive than Chinese models (Jankowiak, Gray, & Hattman, 2008). In this sense, the Dove campaign may have failed *not* because it promoted non-Chinese standards of beauty, but because it *challenged* the mainstream Western value on beauty at a time when it seems as though Chinese women are seeking to adopt this very standard.

In some cases, other frameworks might give us insight into both the Dove campaign and public relations related advertising in general. Scholars in many fields, but especially communication and business, have flocked to Hofstede's value framework. However, other scholars have provided different frameworks. For example, Schwartz (1992) locates 11 values that he feels are present in all cultures in some way, with research showing differences sometimes by age cohort rather than culture. These include self-direction, stimulation, hedonism, achievement, power, security, conformity, tradition, spirituality, benevolence, and universalism. These could serve as a useful lens both for analyzing the (Western) fashion industry (hedonism, stimulation, power, conformity) and Dove's (Unilever, 2009b) response (security in who one is—a security that the fashion industry strives to disrupt; self-direction, universalism, and benevolence, such as that seen in the girl's page link to "How do you impact other's self-esteem?").

Talcott Parsons (1951), a famous sociologist, offered a totally different framework that some have applied to understand cultural diversity (e.g., Gudykunst & Kim, 2003). This framework, which Parsons labeled "pattern variables," referred to a series of dichotomous values that guide a person's (or in this case, a culture's) behavior, such as affect (emotion) versus affect neutrality (reason), instrumentality (goal-orientation) versus expressiveness (enjoying interaction for its own sake), and so on (see also Kent and Taylor's chapter in this volume). Some of his dimensions may also explain some of the specificities. For example, the sites in general focus on affectivity (journals about feelings of self-esteem) but also on knowledge (quizzes, reports, studies); they tend to be more "universalistic" in that anyone can share her or his opinions. And there is more of an expressive orientation, especially on the discussion boards (though perhaps the sites as a whole have the instrumental goals of both informing girls and women about skin and beauty health—and promoting Dove products to improve those health aspects). Studies and biographies of experts present on sites in different cultures might reflect achievement of status over ascription of status (in terms of listing the credentials of the experts), and a certain "particular" view of status, by which more status is granted to some than to others, based on their credentials. But the tucking away of the experts and studies in several of the Web sites foregrounds the more "universal" aspect of status in which everyone shares ideas equally.

Anthropologists Kluckhohn and Strodtbeck (1961) also provide value orientations, though these are, perhaps, better seen as differences in worldview, with some dimensions applying here (for a fuller summary of the perspectives, see Gudykunst & Kim, 2003; Neuliep, 2006; also see chapter by Kent and Taylor in this volume). These include orienta- tions such as human nature (good/evil/good mixed with evil), person- nature (humans as subject to, in harmony with, or seeking to subjugate nature), time (past, present, future), activity (doing, being, or "being-in- becoming"—that is, engaging in activity for metaphysical or spiritual goals), and relational orientation (individualism or collectivism as defined either through lineal or collateral groups). The primary dimension that applies here would be the person–nature orientation. The beauty indus- try is clearly focused on women "controlling" nature, changing their shape and looks through makeup, surgery, diet, and (excessive) exercise (seen especially in the *Onslaught* video). The Dove campaign ostensibly works against that focus with an emphasis on being oneself, and finding one's own beauty. At the same time, the sites offer wrinkle creams and skin-smoothing products, and they still promote the notion that women and girls take control of their own beauty destiny. Thus, the sites, in a way both different from and similar to the beauty industry they oppose, emphasize a more Western notion of control over nature. There is a some- what relational orientation on the Web sites, with focus on connecting to mothers, friends, and anonymous others. The latter, especially, would hardly fall within Kluckhohn and Strodtbeck's 1961 rubric, which could not have imagined Internet chats, social networking sites, or online bul- letin boards. As noted above, the sharing on such networks, especially since this is a largely anonymous and short-term form of sharing of ideas, is individualistic. One might say that the sites are focused on allowing women and girls simply to "be"—to enjoy themselves for who they are, rather than to "become" something "measurable" in some way through prescribed beauty standards. But how activity orientation (doing/being/being-in-becoming) or other Kluckhohn and Strodtbeck value orientations apply here remains to be seen.

Perhaps a more fruitful avenue of inquiry for the analysis of beauty culture and advertisements that address it lies not in any of these frameworks, but in culturally specific notions of beauty and values. Because the sites are mostly similar, it is hard to locate such differences within the Dove campaign. However, it might be notable that the Mexican site, more than others, includes several contests, as opposed to just quizzes one takes with the Internet site as guide. The contests are not with known others (collective), nor do they clearly reflect any other Hofstedian value. Thus, there might be something else within Mexican culture by which people enjoy contests of different sorts. Perhaps the greatest application of culturally specific research, such as an ethnographic approach (Philipsen, Cuoto, & Covarrubias, 2005), would be for researchers to analyze consumers' comments on the discussion boards within each country. Since the site content and layout seem to be largely influenced by international but homogenous branding goals, we may learn the most about cultural responses to beauty by examining perspectives from within separate cultures; that is, an *emic* perspective (Gudykunst & Nishida, 1989).

In sum, the Dove "Campaign for Real Beauty" seems to be a wise global campaign, perhaps what garnered it the Silver Anvil Award in 2006. Part of the cultural, or rather, cross-cultural merit of the campaign is the inclusion of elements that would appeal to various Hofstedian dimensions. Not only does this campaign use the dimensions, but it reflects (perhaps intentionally) the notion of intercultural communication scholars that all dimensions exist, at least to some degree, in every culture. This avoids some of the practical limitations of the dimensions, such as dichotomization (in this case, treating the advertisements from either end of a single continuum; that is, making them purely individualistic or collectivist). This claim, however, has three caveats: first, the Web sites follow a limited view of culture that treats nation-states as being equal to culture. This, of course, obscures great cultural differences within countries. For example, in the entire Brazilian Web site, there are few women of color, despite the fact that nearly 50% of Brazil is Afro-Brazilian or mixed-race. So also, the strong focus on self-esteem, aimed at a higher level of Maslow's Hierarchy of Needs, assumes that more basic needs of security, sustenance, and housing are addressed; thus, the campaign misses the poor or subaltern populations (see Dutta and Pal's chapter in this volume) of the nations to which it is addressed. In this regard, niche marketing, even within nations, could be more productive. Still, the fact that the campaign has met widespread success speaks to the perennial and cross-cultural value of beauty, despite localized definitions of what this beauty is. Second, by not building a stronger diversity among the Web sites, the campaign runs the risk of augmenting top-down homogenizing forces of globalization that are already beginning to erase local cultures. Many critics of globalization, such as those in Latin America (e.g., Ortiz, 2003) accuse globalization of imprinting Western values on the nations that are becoming more globalized. Globalization always comes at the cost of local cultures, especially the local cultures of the economically weaker nations. Thus, as major companies export their products and technology, they are also, inherently, exporting their culture (McPhail, 2002). Finally, both globalization and the Dove campaign obscure subtle ideological biases that favor some cultural standards (individual opinion, a certain notion of beauty—even if simpler and more realistic than the exaggerated notion of Madison Avenue and Hollywood) over others. For this reason, tools of rhetoric may provide another useful framework for analyzing the campaign. This approach is briefly explicated in order to provide a heuristic "footnote" before our conclusion.

Based on the work of Kenneth Burke, rhetoric works in public relations as "the measured and ethical use of language and symbols to inspire cooperation between and organization and its publics" (Courtright & Smudde, 2007, p. 4). Burke's view of symbol use, both discursive and visual, may account for the Dove campaign's flexibility to appeal to multiple cultures with roughly the same messages. In particular, we can apply two Burkean principles: *perspective by incongruity* and *identification*.

Perspective by incongruity (Burke, 1935/1984) best explains the dialectical tensions we found in our application of Hofstede's dimensions. Perspective by incongruity occurs when a person uses two seemingly opposite ideas in tandem; that is, "collective individualism." We could use collective individualism as a phrase to suggest the Dove campaign's simultaneous appeal to individual self-esteem through building relationships with other women. The beauty of such appeals (no pun intended) is that people can *choose* to emphasize one term or the other. For individualist cultures, we could argue that the campaign focuses on individual improvement. For cultures in which identity is defined by the group, the campaign's appeal to listen to and bond with others could be seen as the campaign's main point. To reconcile Hofstede's other dialectical tensions we could likewise argue that the campaign offers "preferred options" for real beauty, through strategies that feature "hierarchical equality," and "long-term pragmatism."

The flexibility of perspective by incongruity is the potential for more audiences to *identify* with ideas they most agree with. *Identification* (Burke, 1950/1969) occurs when a person perceives her or his values, beliefs, or ideas to be similar to those communicated by the speaker. In this case, the Dove campaign resonates with women through self-expression, sharing, and common concerns. Identification, therefore, explains how the campaign could be successful in cultures that score higher in masculinity (MAS) when using Hofstede. More important, the campaign's ability to invite identification regardless of where a culture falls on Hofstede's rating scales for the remaining dimensions makes for a strategic plus. This is particularly striking when criticisms of the campaign's images (e.g., that the models still do not represent the full variety of feminine facial and body characteristics, and the campaign ignores evidence that some standards of beauty may be ingrained in us from birth; see Postrel, 2007) or the fact that other Unilever product promotions—such as the messages for Axe—contradict the "Real Beauty" message (M. K. Johnson, 2008).

Conclusion

In this chapter, then, we have argued for alternatives to the Hofstedian typology. Intercultural communication studies offer other typologies such as value orientations (e.g., Kluckhohn & Strodtbeck, 1961; Parsons, 1951; Schwartz, 1992), as well as approaches that look at each culture's values uniquely (that is, by using an *emic* approach). Taking our cue from rhetorical approaches to public relations, we also briefly applied principles from the work of Kenneth Burke to reinterpret our Hofstedian findings in analyzing the Dove "Campaign for Real Beauty." It is an exciting perspective to think how much more fruitful it could be to apply these alternatives to the creation of global public relations campaigns and to analyze publics and relate with them more strategically.

We, therefore, hope that this chapter has provided a better understanding of one of the most used typologies of culture in the literature today. After reading this chapter, public relations scholars and practitioners should be more aware of the pitfalls related to the application of Hofstede's dimensions and conduct research in ways that respect their strengths and limitations. Teachers of public relations, among other things, may expand upon various issues associated with particular dimensions (e.g., what do "masculine" and "feminine" cultures really mean and is this a helpful distinction?). We also hope that students may appreciate even more the importance of understanding culture through various lenses. For all readers, this chapter should serve as an important step in enhancing understanding and appreciation of the importance of culture in public relations in a rapidly globalizing world, and the intricacies of understanding it.

Discussion Questions

1. What are the strengths and limitations of using a framework like Hofstede's to understand cultural differences in public relations?

What are the strengths and limitations of looking at each culture uniquely, with an in-depth approach such as ethnography?

2. Within your own country, describe some different "cocultures"—cultures within the larger culture. How might these differ from your dominant national culture in terms of Hofstede's values?

3. Think of your own national culture or one you have visited. Look it up on Hofstede's (1987–2009) Web site, if it is there. Do you agree with the value placements on the Web site? Why or why not? What additional values beyond Hofstede's do you think characterize your culture?

4. Imagine yourself 10 to 15 years from now, conducting public relations on behalf of a multinational corporation such as Ikea or Unilever. First, to what extent do you think the culture of these companies' home countries should influence how they conduct public relations? Why? (Look up either company on the Internet to find out where they are based, and then look at Hofstede's Web site.) If you're planning a campaign directed at countries in the European Union, to what extent would you use Hofstede's cultural dimension figures to target different countries? Why?

5. Assume again that you're planning a campaign for Ikea or Unilever directed toward the European Union. Which of the alternative approaches to Hofstede's dimensions, presented at the end of the chapter, would be helpful to you in crafting a campaign? Explain how.

References

Austen, A. (2006, June 23). *The beauty backlash.* BBC News. Retrieved from http://news.bbc.co.uk/2/hi/5074642.stm

Bond, M. H., & Smith, P. B. (1996). Cross-cultural social and organizational psychology. *Annual Review of Psychology, 47,* 205–235.

Burke, K. (1969). *A rhetoric of motives.* Berkeley, CA: University of California Press. (Original work published 1950)

Burke, K. (1984). *Permanence and change: An anatomy of purpose* (3rd ed.). Berkeley: University of California Press. (Original work published 1935)

Cai, D. (1998). Issues in conducting cross-cultural research. In J. N. Martin, T. K. Nakayama, & L. A. Flores (Eds.), *Readings in cultural contexts* (pp. 29–38). Mountain View, CA: Mayfield.

Chinese Culture Connection. (1987). Chinese values and the search for culture-free dimensions of culture. *Journal of Cross-Cultural Psychology, 18*(2), 143–164.

Coombs, W. T., Holladay, S., Hasenauer, G., & Signitzer, B. (1994). A comparative analysis of international public relations: Identification and interpretation of similarities and differences between professionalization in Austria,

Norway, and the United States. *Journal of Public Relations Research, 6*(1), 23–39.

Cooper-Chen, A., & Kaneshige, M. (1996). Public relations practice in Japan: Beginning again for the first time. In H. M. Culbertson & N. Chen (Eds.), *International public relations: A comparative analysis* (pp. 223–237). Mahwah, NJ: Erlbaum.

Courtright, J. L., & Smudde, P. M. (Eds.). (2007). *Power and public relations.* Cresskill, NJ: Hampton Press.

Dove helps us define real beauty. (2007, October 12). *Charlotte* (NC) *Observer,* p. 1E. Retrieved from NewsLibrary database.

Fitch, K. (1998). *Speaking relationally: Culture, communication, and interpersonal connection.* New York: Guilford.

Fowler, G. A. (2008, December 29). Unilever gives "Ugly Betty" a product-plug makeover in China. *Wall Street Journal* (Eastern ed.), p. B1.

Freitag, A. R. (2002). Ascending cultural competence potential: An assessment and profile of U.S. public relations practitioners' preparation for international assignments. *Journal of Public Relations Research, 14*(3), 207–227.

Friday, R. A. (2006). Contrast in discussion behaviors of German and American managers. In L. A. Samovar, R. E. Porter, & E. R. McDaniel (Eds.), *Intercultural communication: A reader* (11th ed., pp. 298–308). Belmont, CA: Wadsworth.

Gould, S. J., Gupta, P. B., & Grabner-Kräuter, S. (2000). Product placements in movies: A cross-cultural analysis of Austrian, French and American consumers' attitudes toward this emerging, international promotional medium. *Journal of Advertising, 29*(4), 41–58.

Gudykunst, W. B. (2005). An anxiety/uncertainty management (AUM) theory of effective communication. In W. B. Gudykunst (Ed.), *Theorizing about intercultural communication* (pp. 281–322). Thousand Oaks, CA: Sage.

Gudykunst, W. B., & Kim, Y. Y. (2003). *Communicating with strangers: An approach to intercultural communication* (4th ed.). Boston, MA: McGraw-Hill.

Gudykunst, W. B., & Lee, C. M. (2002). Cross-cultural communication theories. In W. B. Gudykunst & B. Mody (Eds.), *Handbook of international and intercultural communication* (2nd ed., pp. 25–50). Thousand Oaks, CA: Sage.

Gudykunst, W. B., & Nishida, T. (1989). Theoretical perspectives for studying intercultural communication. In M. K. Asante & W. B. Gudykunst (Eds.), *Handbook of international and intercultural communication* (pp. 17–46). Newbury Park, CA: Sage.

Hall, E. T. (1959). *The silent language.* Garden City, NY: Doubleday.

Haruta, A., & Hallahan, K. (2003). Cultural issues in airline crisis communications: A Japan-U.S. comparative study. *Asian Journal of Communication, 13*(2), 122–150.

Hofstede, G. H. (1980). *Culture's consequences: International differences in work-related values.* Beverly Hills, CA: Sage.

Hofstede, G. H. (1984). *Culture's consequences: International differences in work-related values* (abridged ed.). Beverly Hills, CA: Sage.

Hofstede, G. H. (1986). Cultural differences in teaching and learning. *International Journal of Intercultural Relations, 10*(3), 301–320.

Hofstede, G. H. (1997). *Cultures and organizations, software of the mind: Intercultural cooperation and its importance for survival.* New York: McGraw-Hill.

Hofstede, G. H. (1998). *Masculinity and femininity: The taboo dimension of national cultures.* Thousand Oaks, CA: Sage.

Hofstede, G. H. (2002). Dimensions do not exist: A reply to Brendan McSweeney. *Human Relations, 55*(11), 1355–1361.

Hofstede, G. H. (1987–2009). *Geert Hofstede cultural dimensions.* Retrieved from http://www.geert-hofstede.com/

Holtzhausen, D. R., Petersen, B. K., & Tindall, N. T. J. (2003). Exploding the myth of the symmetrical/asymmetrical dichotomy: Public relations models in the new South Africa. *Journal of Public Relations Research, 15*(4), 305–341.

Hui, C. H., & Triandis, H. C. (1985). Measurement in cross-cultural psychology: A review and comparison of strategies. *Journal of Cross-Cultural Psychology, 16*(2), 131–152.

Jankowiak, W., Gray, P. B., & Hattman, K. (2008). Globalizing evolution: Female choice, nationality, and perception of sexual beauty in China. *Cross-Cultural Research, 42*(3), 248–269.

Johnson, F. (2000). *Speaking culturally: Language diversity in the United States.* Thousand Oaks, CA: Sage.

Johnson, M. K. (2008, February 15). Is Naomi Wolf pulling punches for Dove's Real Beauty campaign? *Lucire.* Retrieved from http://lucire.com/insider/20080215/is-naomi-wolf-pulling-punches-for-doves-real-beauty-campaign/

Johnson, V., & Peppas, S. C. (2003). Crisis management in Belgium: The case of Coca-Cola. *Corporate Communications: An International Journal, 8*(1), 18–22.

Kagitçibasi, C., & Berry, J. W. (1989). Cross-cultural psychology: Current research and trends. *Annual Review of Psychology , 40,* 493–531.

Kale, S. H. (2006). Designing culturally compatible Internet gaming sites. *UNLV Gaming Research & Review Journal, 10*(1), 41–50.

Kalliny, M., Cruthirds, K. W., & Minor, M. S. (2006). Differences between American, Egyptian and Lebanese humor styles. *International Journal of Cross Cultural Management, 6*(1), 121–134.

Kang, D. S., & Mastin, T. (2008). How cultural difference affects international tourism public relations Web sites: A comparative analysis using Hofstede's cultural dimensions. *Public Relations Review, 34*(1), 54–56.

Kapoor, S., Hughes, P. C., Baldwin, J. R., & Blue, J. (2003). The relationship of individualism-collectivism and self-construals to communication styles in India and the United States. *International Journal of Intercultural Relations, 27*(6), 683–700.

Kim, M. S. (1993). Culture-based conversational constraints in explaining cross-cultural strategic competence. In R. L. Wiseman & J. Koester (Eds.), *Intercultural communication competence* (pp. 132–150). Newbury Park, CA: Sage.

Kim, M. S. (1995). Toward a theory of conversational constraints. In R. L. Wiseman (Ed.), *Intercultural communication theory* (pp. 148–169). Thousand Oaks, CA: Sage.

Kim, M. S. (2005). Culture-based conversational constraints theory: Individual- and culture-level analyses. In W. B. Gudykunst (Ed.), *Theorizing about intercultural communication* (pp. 93–117). Thousand Oaks, CA: Sage.

Kim, U., Triandis, H. C., Kâğitçibaşi, C., Choi, S.-C., & Yoon, G. (Eds.). (1994). *Individualism and collectivism: Theory, method, and applications.* Thousand Oaks, CA: Sage.

Kluckhohn, C., & Strodtbeck, F. (1961). *Variations in value orientations.* New York: Row, Peterson.

Kohls, L. R. (2001). *Learning to think Korean: A guide to living and working in Korea.* Yarmouth, ME: Intercultural Press.

Lindsley, S. (2000). U.S. Americans and Mexicans working together: Five core Mexican concepts. In L. A. Samovar & R. E. Porter (Eds.), *Intercultural communication: A reader* (9th ed., pp. 335–341). Belmont, CA: Wadsworth.

Martin, J. N., & Nakayama, T. K. (1999). Thinking dialectically about culture and communication. *Communication Theory, 9,* 1–25.

McPhail, T. L. (2002). *Global communication: Theories, stakeholders, and trends.* Boston, MA: Allyn & Bacon.

McSweeney, B. (2002). Hofstede's model of national cultural differences and their consequences: A triumph of faith—A failure of analysis. *Human Relations, 55*(1), 89–118.

Miller, J. G. (2002). Bringing culture to basic psychological theory—beyond individualism and collectivism: Comment on Oyserman et al. (2002). *Psychological Bulletin, 128*(1), 97–109.

Neuliep, J. W. (2006). *Intercultural communication: A contextual approach* (3rd ed.). Newbury Park, CA: Sage.

Oetzel, J. G., & Ting-Toomey, S. (2003). Face concerns in interpersonal conflict: A cross-cultural empirical test of the face negotiation theory. *Communication Research, 30*(6), 599–624.

Ortiz, R. (2003). Revisitando la noción de imperialism cultural [Revisiting the notion of cultural imperialism]. In R. Ortiz et al. (Eds.), *Comunicación, cultura, y globalización* [Communication, culture, and globalization] (pp. 46–62). Bogotá, Colombia: Pontifica Universidad Javeriana.

Oyserman, D., Koon, H. M., & Kemmelmeier, M. (2002). Rethinking individualism and collectivism: Evaluation of theoretical assumptions and meta-analyses. *Psychological Bulletin, 128*(1), 3–72.

Parsons, T. (1951). *The social system.* Glencoe, IL: Free Press.

Philipsen, G., Cuoto, L. M., & Covarrubias, P. (2005). Speech codes theory: Restatement, revisions, and response to criticisms. In W. B. Gudykunst (Ed.), *Theorizing about intercultural communication* (pp. 55–68). Thousand Oaks, CA: Sage.

Postrel, V. (2007). The truth about beauty. *Atlantic Monthly, 299*(2), 125–127.

Public Relations Society of America. (2006). *Dove campaign for real beauty.* [Inventory No. 6BW-0607D07]. Retrieved from http://www.prsa.org/Intelligence/

Pudlinksi, C. (1994, November). *A theoretical exploration of dialectic approaches in intercultural communication.* Paper presented at the annual convention of the Speech Communication Association, New Orleans, LA.

Schwartz, S. (1992). Universals in the content and structure of values: Theoretical advances and empirical tests in 20 countries. In M. P. Zanna (Ed.), *Advances in experimental social psychology* (Vol. 25, pp. 1–66). San Diego, CA: Academic Press.

Smith, P. B. (2002). "Culture's consequences:" Something old and something new. *Human Relations, 55*(1), 119–135.

Sriramesh, K. (2009). The relationship between culture and public relations. In K. Sriramesh & D. Verčič (Eds.), *The global public relations handbook: Theory, research, and practice* (rev. ed., pp. 47–61). New York: Routledge.

Sriramesh, K., Kim, Y., & Takasaki, M. (1999). Public relations in three Asian cultures: An analysis. *Journal of Public Relations Research, 11*(4), 271–292.

Synnott, G., & McKie, D. (1997). International issues in PR: Researching research and prioritizing priorities. *Journal of Public Relations Research, 9*(4), 259–282.

Thatcher, B. L. (2000). Writing policies and procedures in a U.S./South American context. *Technical Communication Quarterly, 9*(4), 365–399.

Thomas, J. (1998). Contexting Koreans: Does the high/low model work? *Business Communication Quarterly, 61*(4), 9–22.

Ting-Toomey, S. (1988). Intercultural conflict styles: A face-negotiation theory. In Y. Y. Kim & W. B. Gudykunst (Eds.), *Theories in intercultural communication* (pp. 213–235). Newbury Park, CA: Sage.

Ting-Toomey, S. (2005). The matrix of face: An updated face-negotiation theory. In W. B. Gudykunst (Ed.), *Theorizing about intercultural communication* (pp. 71–92). Thousand Oaks, CA: Sage.

Ting-Toomey, S., & Kurogi, A. (1998). Facework competence in intercultural conflict: An updated face-negotiation theory. *International Journal of Intercultural Relations, 22*(2), 187–225.

Triandis, H. C. (1995). *Individualism and collectivism: New directions in social psychology.* Boulder, CO: Westview Press.

Triandis, H. C., & Suh, E. M. (2002). Cultural influences on personality. *Annual Review of Psychology, 53*, 133–160.

Unilever. (2009a). *Campaign for real beauty mission.* Retrieved from http://www.dove.us/#/CFRB/arti_CFRB.aspx[cp-documentid=7049726]/

Unilever. (2009b). *Dove: Girls only: How do you impact others?* Retrieved from http://www.dove.us/#/cfrb/girlsonly/impact_others.aspx/

Vadi, M., & Meri, R. (2005). Estonian culture in the framework of Hofstede's model (case of hotel industry). *Trames, 9*(3), 268–284.

Wu, X. (2002). Doing PR in China: A 2001 version—Concepts, practices and some misperceptions. *Public Relations Quarterly, 47*(2), 10–18.

Xu, G., & Feiner, S. (2007). *Meinü Jinji* / China's beauty economy: Buying looks, shifting value, and changing place. *Feminist Economics, 13*(3), 307–323.

Suggested Readings

Harris, P. T., & Moran, R. T. (2000). *Managing cultural differences: Leadership strategies for a new world of business.* Houston, TX: Gulf.

Kim, M.-S. (2007). Our culture, their culture, and beyond: Further thoughts on ethnocentrism in Hofstede's discourse. *Journal of Multicultural Discourses, 2*(1), 26–31.

McKie, D. (2005). Review essay: Globalizing public relations: Old wine, new bottles, and good years. *Public Relations Review, 31*(1), 149–152.

Ming-Yi, W., Taylor, M., & Mong-Ju, C. (2001). Exploring societal and cultural influences on Taiwanese public relations. *Public Relations Review, 27*(3), 317–336.

Moran, R. T., Braaten, D. O., & Walsh, J. E., Jr. (Eds.). (1994). *International business case studies for the multicultural marketplace.* Houston, TX: Gulf.

Nakata, C. (Ed.). (2009). *Beyond Hofstede: Culture frameworks for global marketing and management.* Basingstoke, UK: Palgrave Macmillan.

Taylor, M. (2000). Cultural variance as a challenge to global public relations: A case study of the Coca-Cola scare in Europe. *Public Relations Review, 26*(3), 277–293.

Vasquez, G. M., & Taylor, M. (1999). What cultural values influence American public relations practitioners? *Public Relations Review, 25*(4), 433–449.

Wu, M.-Y., & Baah-Boakye, K. (2009). Public relations in Ghana: Work-related cultural values and public relations models. *Public Relations Review, 35*(1), 83–85.

Chapter 6

The Need for a Postmodern Turn in Global Public Relations

Derina Holtzhausen

There is no single way to practice public relations. Critical theorists argue that our worldview (the basic assumptions we hold about society and how it functions) play an important role in how we conduct ourselves in any given situation.[1] This also is true for the practice of public relations (J. E. Grunig, 1994). Thus, public relations practitioners who hold a postmodern view of the world will practice it differently from those who do not. Even if one does not label oneself as postmodern, there might be certain tenets of postmodernism that practitioners might support and unconsciously adhere to, particularly because postmodern thought already has entered cultural practices in many ways.

This chapter elaborates on postmodern public relations practice and explains why an analysis of postmodern theory led me to the notion of activism in practice. I do this by first explaining the differences between postmodernism and critical theory and global and international public relations, as seen from a postmodern perspective. The chapter provides a postmodern critique of global and international public relations, respectively, and in each instance elaborates on the pitfalls practitioners can face in these kinds of practice. The chapter concludes with an in-depth discussion of a definition of public relations as activism, as previously proposed by Holtzhausen and Voto (2002).

Postmodern Thought

Postmodernism brings a slightly different paradigm to global public relations than that offered by critical theory. There is some debate on what constitutes these two paradigms, and perspectives often overlap. For instance, while I have argued that postmodernists analyze the intersections between power, politics, and knowledge, Pal and Dutta (2008) argue these issues belong to critical modernism. At the core of this debate lies the argument whether postmodernism represents a rupture with modernism, or whether postmodernism is a continuation of modernism.

The concept of rupture comes from the notion that postmodern society is so different from modern society that any continuation of theory and philosophical thought is impossible. Others argue that postmodernism is merely a continuation of modernism. I prefer Lyotard's (1992) argument, namely, that postmodernism is a condition that precedes modernism: "A work can become modern only if it is first postmodern" (p. 147). He rejects the notion of a rupture with modernity as "a way of forgetting or repressing the past ... repeating it and not surpassing it" (Lyotard, 1993, p. 48). The implication of this viewpoint is that all existing practice and theory need to be criticized for fear that they might become a metanarrative, or dominant paradigm.

I prefer to focus on the basic assumptions of the type of critique to determine whether it is postmodern or not. Perhaps the most significant difference is that critical theory mainly focuses on how power is shaped by critiquing capitalist production and social systems from a Marxist perspective. Postmodernists focus on how power is *discursively constituted* through political and knowledge production processes, and view Marxism as merely another debate on capitalism. Marxism focuses on "economic activity ... [and] on the degree to which the economic **base** determines the nature and structure of the rest of society [bold in original]" (Edgar & Sedgwick, 2002, p. 221). Postmodernism focuses on the use of language and meaning creation in establishing systems of power in society. However, Edgar and Sedgwick (2002) argue that critical theory in the 1980s morphed into "an approach to textual criticism which draws upon the writings of thinkers linked with structuralism, post-structuralism and postmodernism" (p. 91), such as Foucault, Derrida, and Lyotard who have always been linked to postmodern thought.

Thus, it is clearly difficult to draw a sharp distinction between critical theory, social theory, and postmodernism; these differences are not very apparent and, one might perhaps argue, not that important. Postmodern scholars would argue that the desire to create strict differences between critical discourses and postmodernism is a symptom of the desire to categorize and differentiate between intellectual discourses to establish dominance of one over the other, which is exactly what postmodernism objects to. In fact, this "dedifferentiation" of intellectual spheres (Connor, 1989, p. 202) is one of the important distinctions of postmodernism. It is exactly the desire to resist dominant theoretical discourses that sets postmodernism apart from critical and social theory. Postmodernists argue for complexity, which speaks against the neat packaging of ideas and thoughts into distinct categories and segments of thought. In fact, postmodernists view themselves as intellectual nomads, who roam across different theoretical approaches and paradigms in search of narratives that can explain power imbalances in society (Deleuze & Guattari, 1983).

There are, nonetheless, some basic philosophical differences between critical, social, and postmodern theory that are difficult to bridge (Best & Kellner, 1991, p. 298). Perhaps the most significant is the postmodern notion that all theory and practice are local and immediate. One of the most important tenets of postmodern theory is the rejection of metanarratives or normative and totalizing discourses; that is, meaning systems that are prescriptive and are assumed to represent the best possible or only solution. In public relations one such example is the Excellence theory (L. A. Grunig, J. E. Grunig, & Dozier, 2002). Similarly, Ihlen, van Ruler, and Fredriksson (2009) argue that public relations belongs to the sphere of social theories. Although both these approaches offer valuable perspectives on the field, it is important to understand that each brings its own theoretical lens to the analysis that does not represent all available perspectives. A postmodern perspective strongly argues against approaches that aim to establish single, hegemonic discourses in any field of study because they close possibilities for other theoretical interpretations and so stymie philosophical thought and the growth of knowledge. The major endeavors of postmodern scholars are to always investigate their own theories and positions through a process of reflexivity with the aim of dislodging previously held positions. Privileging one theoretical discourse over another is, therefore, thoroughly un-postmodern.

This is the very reason why Seidman (1997) anticipates the end of sociological theory in favor of social theory, which he positions as postmodern in approach. Seidman's position emanates from his critique of sociological theory as social science, which "derived [its] legitimacy from the twin claims of being true and contributing to human advancement" (p. 4), and which champions social change at the macro level of society. Sociologists, therefore, argue change is possible by addressing it at a policy and political level. Social theory approaches, on the other hand, "abandon absolute standards, universal categories, and grand theories; they favor local, historically contextualized, and pragmatic types of social inquiry" (p. 5). This focuses social change on the micro level, that is, at the level of everyday life and social interaction. In contrast to the "millennial social hopes that have been at the center of modernist sociological theory" (p. 119), Seidman promotes social theory as "giv[ing] up the modernist idol of human emancipation in favor of deconstructing false closure, prying open present and future social possibilities ... where hegemonic discourses posit closure and a frozen order" (p. 120). While Best and Kellner (1991) still hold out hope for both macro and micro level theorizing, Seidman (1997) argues for a postmodern approach that gets involved in the immediate events and local struggles for justice. He equates sociology with an approach that focuses on macro level theorizing and social theory with micro level theorizing. This argument also is central to the role of postmodern public relations practice in terms of both global and international practice (as I explain below).

Another important attribute of postmodern theory that sets it apart from other theoretical perspectives is how it approaches discourse. Two approaches to discourse exist in postmodernism, articulated by Foucault and Lyotard respectively (Edgar & Sedgwick, 2002). As Edgar and Sedgwick point out, discourse does not have a single meaning and in its technical sense it can merely refer to how people speak to or about each other. In critical theory, this often is the unit of analysis. The postmodern approach focuses on narrative discourse analysis always and how, through representation and story-telling (for example in historical texts) meaning is formed and systems of privilege and power are constituted through the use of language, of which Foucault (1972) is the major proponent. Lyotard (1988), develops the concept of a "genre of discourse" (p. 29). Building on some basic tenets of poststructuralism, Lyotard argues that systems of language give validity to the discourses developed within the particular genres of discourse.

Discourse is not only embedded in written or spoken language, but also in signs and symbols. The concept of discourse emanated from new ways of looking at how meaning is formed. Discourse is shaped by society and its institutions. Discourses differ "with the kinds of institutions and social practices in which they took shape, and with the positions of those who speak and those whom they address" (Macdonnell, 1986, p. 1). A discourse takes effect indirectly or directly through its relation to another discourse because language does not reflect an external reality that exists outside of those involved in the discourse. Crucial to the argument of discourse is that meanings are to be found only in the concrete forms of differing social and institutional practices, and that there can be no meaning in language per se. The argument that discourse is formed and meaning is created through institutional practice, particularly through the use of language and signs in institutional context, situates public relations practice squarely in the postmodern debate. Public relations practitioners often are the agents charged with shaping discourses on behalf of institutions and powerful communicative entities in society, thus masking the powerful interests behind those discourses (Holtzhausen, 2002).

Like critical theorists, the process postmodernists use to expose underlying power structures in language is called deconstruction, which entails a method of discourse analysis. The method of discourse analysis deconstructs how language is used to entrench existing power relations to the detriment of those who are less powerful or marginalized in society, particularly because their discourses are drowned out by the discourse of those in power (see also Dutta and Pal's and Edwards's chapters in this volume). The powerful can do this because they use people such as public relations practitioners to present their ideas as rational and truthful. One of the strategies powerful entities use is binary opposites to indicate where power is situated; that is, man/woman, White/Black, white collar/blue collar, civilization/nature, straight/gay, capitalist/socialist, high culture/low culture, and, for example, journalism/public relations. In each of these examples of binary oppositions, it is clear which term represents the preferred norm for society. Deconstruction, like discourse, follows from poststructuralism and particularly from the work of Derrida, who is generally viewed as one of the earliest postmodernists. However, postmodernism departs from structuralism in the sense that it argues against the possibility of language to offer rational and truthful statements. Language can never accurately or neutrally describe any thought or situation and the person who used the language immediately loses control over the meaning of the utterance. Language is, therefore, unstable and always open to alternative interpretations. Postmodernists also argue that it is possible to gain power by resisting dominant discourses and exposing their underlying ideologies, thus creating strategies for resistance to dominating power through the use of discourse. However, postmodernists particularly focus on resistance in everyday practice in the immediate environment rather than at a larger societal level (Lyotard, 1984; West, 1997). This also is the aim of this chapter; that is, to make practitioners aware of strategies they can use to resist becoming part of dominant power structures. Because discourse, and therefore power, is diffused and unstable, it is also possible to resist power at many different stages of language dissemination.

Postmodern approaches clearly have important implications for developing an appreciation of what could constitute postmodern public relations practice. But before the role of the postmodern practitioner in global and international public relations can be explicated, it is important to address globalization from a postmodern perspective, and apply key postmodern theoretical perspectives to this phenomenon. First, however, it is important to address how the concept of globalization is applied in public relations theory and how it might differ from international public relations.

Global Public Relations versus International Public Relations

Two approaches compete for theoretical dominance in the field of international public relations. One holds that this practice should be called global public relations and is an approach that resulted from the Excellence study (Sriramesh & Verčič, 2003; Verčič, L. A. Grunig, & J. E. Grunig, 1996). This approach holds that the best public relations for global practice is generic across national borders and is based on the principles of Excellence, then adapted at the local level based on local cultural and other practices (see Wakefield's chapter in this volume). The argument goes that the same principles that apply to the Excellence theory also are true in global public relations, despite different practices at the local level. The other approach argues that local culture affects public relations practices in profound and unique ways because of the differences in social, political, legal, cultural, media, and education systems in each country. Practitioners should be aware of what Zaharna (2001) calls the *in-awareness* approach to *international* public relations and should familiarize themselves with conditions in every aspect of the country before entering into practice there. Generic public relations practices, therefore, do not apply since all practice is local, even if there are aspects of Excellent practice involved. From a postmodern perspective, *global* public relations and *international* public relations are two very different forms of practice, each with its own set of challenges for the postmodern practitioner.

The distinction between global and international is important because both experience unique challenges and are deconstructed differently in postmodernism. Also, the type of venture in which the practitioner is involved will determine how they practice public relations. Public relations practitioners generally operate in four kinds of foreign endeavors: international, multinational, transnational, and global (Sylvie, Wicks, Hollifield, Lacy, & Broadrick Sohn, 2008). In *international* ventures, public relations practitioners work for organizations that create products or services for the local market and then adapt those products or services for other countries. Multinational organizations will have their headquarters in one country but will create subsidiaries in foreign markets that have a great deal of autonomy in product development and will focus on product development for that specific environment. Global ventures produce products that will be distributed globally, such as, Hollywood movies, computer and other technological products, or sports equipment, to mention a few. Sylvie et al. (2008) add to global ventures the transnational organization, which they state "is a network approach to global expansion" (p. 91) and relies on foreign subsidiaries to not only adopt and adapt ideas from headquarters for local markets, but also expect foreign subsidiaries to develop products for their own markets while passing on the best ideas to headquarters for global distribution. They go on to state: "The transnational model is based on a fluid exchange of ideas, knowledge, and products across the company's subsidiaries and markets" (p. 91).

One might argue that international ventures have been around since countries started trading with each other. From a public relations perspective, the international and multinational models would apply when a parent company enters one or more countries on a selective basis, is very aware of the cultural and local practices of that country, and has a closer relationship with host cultures than a global organization. The focus of global and transnational organizations, however, is on global expansion, which provides for a different set of circumstances for public relations practice. A postmodern approach offers different analyses of these two types of practices.

The Postmodern Critique of Globalization

Although Adam Smith and Karl Marx already anticipated the negative consequences of globalization, it is truly only with the advent of new communication technologies that their predictions have come true. Smith and Marx anticipated that globalization would lead to the destruction of local communities because of the continuous need of capitalism to create new markets. Best and Kellner argue that "[A] networked society mediated by computer and communication technologies" has facilitated the restructuring of capitalism "grounded in sophisticated technoscience; a rapidly expanding world telecommunication system; a multimedia and interactive technoculture; … and novel forms of information technology, consumption, and politics" (2001, pp. 205–206). What this means is that globalization cannot be separated from capitalism. To survive, capitalist institutions have to accumulate wealth. To do that, capitalism depends on the creation of markets in those areas where markets do not exist. To create new buyers, the nature of traditional life first has to be changed: "This means that the non-capitalist ways of gaining livelihood must be sapped and replaced by the capitalist ones" (Bauman, 1993, p. 210). To enable globalization, traditional capitalism first has to be restructured. To reflect this restructuring, the era of globalism also is called the *postindustrial phase* of Western industrial development, which followed the factory system and subsequently the more technically complex system organized along bureaucratic principles (Bell, 1973; Burns, 1962). "[P]ost-industrial society is organized around the creation of knowledge and the uses of information … post-industrial society is shaped by its methods of acquiring, processing, and distributing information, all of which have been revolutionized by the computer" (Hatch & Cunliffe, 2006, p. 92). This leads to the commodification of knowledge and information, which is a prominent feature of postindustrial society.

Public relations facilitates globalization in the postindustrial era through its practice of *technoscience* and its ability to create and disseminate messages (L'Etang, 2004). Technoscience refers to science, particularly social sciences, in the service of *technocapitalism* (Best & Kellner, 2001) and is used for the sole purpose of improving production and measuring yield. Technocapitalism, in turn, refers to "the synthesis of capital and technology in the present organization of society" (p. 213) and emerges in the form of more power to markets and transnational and global companies and less power to nation-states (see the notion of *transnational hegemony* in Dutta and Pal's chapter in this volume). Public relations is no stranger to the processes of technoscience, most notably in the form of Management by Objectives (MBO) and by identifying itself as a social *science*, which focuses on the measurable outcomes of communication practices. As social science, public relations is marked by its use of quantifiable measures to categorize people and their communication processes in order to control these processes for the benefit of the organizations they work for. Technoscience also promotes hegemonic discourses. Roper (2005) argues that the Excellence theory creates a hegemonic discourse for public relations practice that facilitates the growth and proliferation of globalization. By gaining knowledge of symmetrical and asymmetrical communication as posited in the Excellence theory, Roper argues that public relations practitioners help their organizations gain influence over nation-states by compromising just enough to get what they want. She states: "[T]hese compromises, in the long term, favor the corporations much more than their critical stakeholders in civil society and can serve to dilute the negotiation power of those stakeholders" (p. 84). One can thus see how global practice differs from international public relations, and also can understand why the Excellence theory would more likely be a tool for global organizations. Many of these organizations originated in Western countries and their practitioners were educated at institutions where they were exposed to the Excellence theory. Contrarily, international public relations is more likely to take place on a country-to-country basis and will be less likely to involve practitioners academically trained in Excellent public relations. In South Africa, for instance, many communication practitioners were never educated in public relations, despite the country's strong system of public relations education (Holtzhausen & Tindall, 2009). It might well be, as Roper (2005) suggested, that it is the practitioners who have formal public relations education, and therefore, are knowledgeable about Excellence theory, who make globalization possible because of their knowledge.

Postmodernists argue that the use of language facilitates globalization, particularly through a discourse of *progress* that creates the desire for goods and services by creating feelings of inferiority in communities that do not have modern material possessions or modern manufacturing and farming processes (Bauman, 1993). This leads to the fragmentation of societies that allows for their reconstitution into *developing* societies. Public relations practitioners not only shape the content that creates these messages of progress but also those of desire for new goods and services. Thus global public relations practices facilitate the ability of global capitalism to destroy traditional societies that in the past have been able to sustain themselves in harmony with their environment. Furthermore, global public relations often is one of the tools through which the messages are created that make people believe their traditional lifestyles are unworthy and uncivilized. As a result, they strive for those consumer goods that are at the basis of much environmental destruction. Global public relations practice thus shapes the ability of organizations to create a metanarrative (Lyotard, 1992) of progress, despite the harm this brings to local communities and the threats to the autonomy of nation-states to determine their own destiny. Metanarratives are discourses that go unchallenged because they are deemed true and irreversible. The aim of metanarratives is to dominate through single central ideologies and theories, which are presented as rational, objective, and truthful. Post-modernists argue that metanarratives and the truth they profess to present are merely the viewpoints of some dominant groups in society who wish to maintain their power. From this it is clear why postmodernists would view *progress* as such a metanarrative.

The above postmodern critique of globalization should not be viewed as a state of hopelessness for the global practitioner. The aim of such criticism is to make practitioners aware of the harm their practices can cause and to encourage them to understand, gain knowledge of, and acknowledge these issues in order to adapt their practices consistent with activism. The first step in this process is to acknowledge the complexity and chaos inherent in the situations they deal with through the process of reflexivity. In the postmodern context, reflexivity means thinking through and consciously rejecting preconceived ideas, stereotypes, and interpretations. Being reflexive in the global practice can be very difficult. Because so much knowledge comes to public relations practitioners through survey research, information presented in the form of graphics, representations by experts and coworkers, the media, or in the form of power from above, it might be difficult to analyze and identify underlying ideologies. Most information about communities and people is never garnered through direct contact with those communities that our practices affect. This kind of "unconnected" and etic knowledge is presented as rational and objective, which makes it very difficult to keep the emotional links to the people affected by our practices. It glibly removes the complexity and ambiguity inherent in all situations and desensitizes and dehumanizes us, as Bauman (1993) so powerfully argues.

An example of the inherent complexity in public relations practice is the consistent appearance of *aporiae*[2] in practice. In fact, it might well be one of the most contradictory professional practices today. One example of an aporia in public relations is the continuous struggle between serving the interests of the organization while also serving those of local communities as part of practitioners' service to stakeholders. Often these tensions cannot be overcome and practitioners have to muddle through difficult and chaotic situations. Being aware of aporiae and acknowledging the complexity inherent in practice is part of the consciousness of the postmodern practitioner.

Global practices can have unintended consequences that are not necessarily negative. One cannot deny that modern technology and medicine in many parts of the world have brought relief from disease and radically improved the quality of life for millions of people. For instance, birth control medication has given women who have access to it more control over their lives in many parts of the world where sex is a taboo subject. Taboo subjects often are taboo because not allowing discussion of the topic entrenches one party's power, or because society has labeled it shameful. These silences often keep dehumanizing practices in place, such as female circumcision. In many African cultures, for instance, sex is not talked about, which prevents women from exposing the high levels of sexual abuse they suffer (this may also be true in many pockets of Western cultures). In South Africa, it was a major development when President Nelson Mandela spoke about HIV/AIDS at the 13th International AIDS Conference held in Durban, South Africa, in 2000 (Brown, 2000) because sex is such a taboo topic in that country. But sometimes the desire for profits motivates organizations to break taboos. One such example is the demystification of menstruation, which was a taboo subject in every society at some stage and often still is. When Kotex wanted to increase sales of their sanitary napkins they started to promote the product by displaying it prominently in pharmacies (Heinrich & Batchelor, 2004). As a result, a topic that was even a taboo between mothers and daughters and a subject of shame for women in some societies, because of the original desire for profit has now become a natural phenomenon that is viewed as a necessary function of a healthy woman's body.

Similarly, the desire for global or multinational media companies to make a profit had the unintentional outcome of promoting concepts of democracy and political participation in many countries where people were not previously allowed to participate in these practices. Kraidy (2009) describes how media ownership within the Saudi royal family has allowed for the screening of the program *Star Academy*, which is based on the *Big Brother* concept. The program was produced in Lebanon and transmitted to many Middle Eastern countries, among others Saudi Arabia. This is an example of how capitalist interests can sometimes trump certain local cultural values that are actually oppressive for the population or for marginalized groups within it. Religious criticism of the show was tempered by the financial interests of the royal family. The program generated a lot of discussion and controversy in that country because women and men lived in the house together, which seriously challenged

Saudi religious beliefs about the role of women in society. Furthermore, viewers could vote for their favorite cast member, which exposed Saudis to basic voting procedures. This is an example of how hybrid media texts, in this case a reality television format taken from the West and translated into a Middle Eastern idiom based on Lebanese social practices and norms, can "crystallize broader social and political struggles" (p. 345). Another example of how modern technology facilitates free speech and democracy was the use of Twitter in the highly contested 2009 Iranian election to let the world know what was happening on the streets of Teheran (Grossman, 2009). Some even call it the "Twitter revolution" (Morozov, 2009, p. 11).

As these examples demonstrate, while global media and technological practices pose threats to traditional societies, they "should also be looked at dialectically in terms of the openings they may provide for change and social reconstruction, the conflicts they are already generating, and the possibilities they offer for greater democratization" (Best & Kellner, 2001, p. 214). It is, therefore, important that postmodern public relations practitioners who practice globally should look for dialectical opportunities to stimulate discussion and debates.

Structural Possibilities for Global Practice

An avenue for practice that is increasingly available to public relations practitioners is network organizations, a phenomenon of the network society (Castells, 1996), which is a phenomenon of postmodern society in an era of globalization. Network society has five attributes (Barney, 2004):

- a shift in capitalist economies from an industrial to an informational base;
- the organization of capitalist economic activity globally, on the network model;
- reorientation of the temporal and spatial organization of human activity, in response to technologies that enable real-time communication across vast distances;
- distribution of power based on access to networks and control over flows; and
- tension between localized human identity and placeless networks. (p. 177)

Network organizations have similar attributes; that is, they allow independent public relations practitioners and those in smaller agencies to bid against big firms by developing networks that bring together the different strengths of members (Holtzhausen, 2007). New communication technologies facilitate networks, which allow practitioners to work across space and time and become globally competitive. These networks are by definition temporary, and practitioners can simultaneously be part of many different such networks, spreading their risk and making them globally marketable. Networking with other practitioners is fundamental to the creation of network organizations. In a recent survey, Holtzhausen and Werder (2008) found that the network structure was the most prevalent organizational structure in U.S. practice, with a mean of 5.05 on a 7-point scale. Network structures also appear to be the most egalitarian organizational structure, with no statistically significant differences found in gender, organizational type, or job level in terms of those working in this kind of organization.

The temporary nature of network structures fits with the postmodern notion of the "temporary contract [which] is in practice supplanting permanent institutions in the professional, emotional, sexual, cultural, family, and international domains, as well as in political affairs" (Lyotard, 1984, p. 66). The preference for temporary structures reflects the postmodern resistance to dominant and hegemonic structures that have the potential to result in "terror" (p. 67). Through network organizations, practitioners become part of global information networks, which have huge emancipatory potential if all information is made freely accessible. Information that is controlled and regulated to promote the market will commoditize knowledge itself and will be governed by its ability to perform. Thus, knowledge that does not have measurable profit outcomes will become redundant; that is, information as *technoknowledge*. The activist practitioner will ensure that global stakeholders will be supplied "with the information they usually lack for making knowledgeable decisions ... [by giving] the public free access to the memory and data banks" (p. 67). Lyotard calls this language games of perfect information because it will exclude the possibility of closure in any argument, which would promote a postmodern form of politics that "would respect both the desire for justice and the desire for the unknown" (p. 67).

One of the problems of information and knowledge networks is that they rely on technology and thus exclude those nations and peoples who do not have access. Although ubiquitous in the United States, Europe, and many Asian countries, technology in many developing countries is only accessible to the educated middle and upper classes. This further promotes a digital divide between developed and developing regions and separates the world into two classes of people. The one class easily navigates knowledge across time and space and is comfortable with knowledge and cultural artifacts generated in environments other than its own. This class of people is comfortable with its own identity and does not necessarily feel threatened by foreign ideas, particularly because these are generated within a single *genre of discourse* of internationalism

(Lyotard, 1988, p. 29). The unconnected class is not exposed to other ways of thinking and doing and often remains captured in vacuums of knowledge, thus becoming the victims of powerful local entities and discriminatory cultural practices. Although it is not inherently wrong to live without technology, that will keep these communities from sharing in a global economy, if they so wish. Also, if people are unaware of how social practices change in other regions, they often are unable to challenge their own social circumstances. As a result, people in this class often feel threatened by new knowledge and tend to close ranks, falling back on nationalist and ethnic identities (West, 1997). The politics of identity is a very important part of the postmodern struggle because it is important to people to understand that there is no single dominant or desired identity, particularly as articulated in dominant and dominating discourses generated particularly through Western mass media. However, it also is important for all people to challenge whether their identity is uniquely cultural or rather ethnic chauvinism. It is when global practice meets local identity that the differences between global and international public relations disappear and the two practices merge; that is, at some stage, whether it is global or international practice, practitioners will come in contact with local social and cultural practices that will affect their practice.

Postmodernism and International Public Relations

Globalization processes would be impossible without facilitation by local nodes. Postmodernists have consistently argued that all practice should be local (Eribon, 1991; Lyotard, 1984) and, as seen above, are critical of any general theories of global public relations that would promote hegemonic practice, thus entrenching powerful global interests even further, particularly at local levels.

However, the argument against global public relations and for the adoption of local culture in the practice of public relations also raises questions from a postmodern perspective. The liberal assumption about culture is that it is benign and should be recognized as such. Therefore, culture cannot be challenged. This argument holds that colonial powers have destroyed cultural societies and should now assist with their reconstruction. People have the right to live their lives as they think fit and should not need the permission of colonial powers. This is indeed a valid argument; however, it fails to recognize that what often is called culture is sometimes nothing but political power in disguise. In many countries in the world, colonial power was replaced with "ethnic chauvinism" (West, 1997, p. 81); a kind of macabre dance of irony in which one evil was replaced with another. For instance, in many countries in Africa, despots ruled for years after colonial powers left, which often led to genocide and ethnic cleansing. Furthermore, liberal and ethnic expressions of culture often only express the dominant male viewpoint of what culture represents and are invariably homogenous articulations that deliberately suppress the diversity and heterogeneity of the societies they claim to represent. In this way, the very concept of *culture* is used to hide the political nature of what is called culture. Culture is often used as an argument against challenges on issues of equality, individuality, and democracy. In many countries patriarchy goes unchallenged because it is called culture, despite the abusive practices that accompany it.

It is, however, highly questionable if these practices are in fact culture, and even if they are, whether these abusive and suppressive cultural practices should be respected and tolerated. Liberal public relations practice, when assuming all practice is culture, leads to public relations being used to build relationships with local power holders who do not necessarily pursue or support principles of equality and democracy or look out for the interests of subaltern groups. Often it is the dominant language and sign systems in local environments that ensure their power, while the media systems that promote these dominant language systems are owned and operated by the powers they benefit and promote. Bauman (1993) quite rightly observes:

> The most ruthless and murderous suppression of individual autonomy happens to be perpetuated in the name of "human rights" ... collectivized as "rights of a minority" (but always a minority desiring to be the majority, or at least desiring the right to behave like one). (pp. 46–47)

Not only do global companies often further entrench these "systems of power" (Best & Kellner, 2001), but international practitioners often ingratiate themselves with these powerful networks and so help sustain them. Invariably these power holders are sustained through the financial benefits they gain from partnerships with powerful international and global organizations because their power allows these organizations to operate without resistance.

Two international public relations models of practice show how local nodes assist in perpetuating systems of domination. One is the personal influence model (Sriramesh & White, 1992), which is used when public relations practitioners are expected to develop contacts with important people. The other is the cultural interpreter model, which applies when local practitioners interpret local cultural practices for multinational companies (J. E. Grunig, L. A. Grunig, Sriramesh, Huang, & Lyra, 1995). At face value the cultural interpreter model appears benign. What can be wrong with a practice that helps others to better understand local culture? The problem is that it is often only the cultural practices of the ruling elites in the local environment that are interpreted and then presented as homogenous articulations of culture.

A personal example comes to mind of such a homogenous interpretation of culture. When I was head of corporate communication of the South African Tourism Board during the first half of the 1990s, one of my tasks was to receive the groups of visiting journalists from the more than 20 countries where South Africa had tourism offices. On one occasion a group of Japanese journalists visited the country. I was informed of their visit only after their departure and told that a meeting with me was not included in their schedule because Japanese journalists form tight-knit press clubs that do not welcome women, either as journalists or public relations practitioners. This happened despite the fact that South Africa at that time had already moved to a democratic society with a newly elected Black government. In this instance, the male-centric perspective of women as cultural artifacts dominated the organization's decision to exclude me, while I experienced this as a deeply political and gendered act.

Local public relations practices can be discriminatory and naïve, particularly when practitioners are not educated in the practice. Practitioners representing global and transnational interests should be careful that female practitioners are not subjected to humiliating situations in the course of their duties. On a visit to South Africa a few years ago a young Black female practitioner told me she was instructed to launch a health campaign in a rural area still governed by ethnic rulers. The South African constitution provides for traditional governance in ethnic environments. This practitioner, a thoroughly modern urbanite, had to ensure that she covered herself and had to take a man with her who had to speak on her behalf and ask the chieftain's permission for her to address him. Once granted, she had to ask the chieftain's permission to speak to his people. Although she said she did not mind if it was necessary to get the job done, this carried a certain level of humiliation. This reminded me of the day a client asked me to arrange an event for him in an exclusive club in downtown Johannesburg. Unbeknown to either of us the club was an elite male establishment in the British tradition of gentleman's clubs, which excluded the physical presence of women under all circumstances. I walked into the building in awe of the cut glass windows, the smell of leather, and the life size painting of Queen Elizabeth II on the landing of the exquisitely carved spiral staircase, only to be guided out by a Black man to the sidewalk where I was made to wait for the manager to come and speak to me. The irony that a White female was thrown out of a club by a Black man in racist South Africa was not lost on me. The fact that White women sometimes were lower on the rung than Black males would have been totally lost on most cultural interpreters if they were not part of the South African English establishment.

One problem is that cultural interpreters become the objective and "disinterested third party" who see others in their society as "categorical stereotypes" (Bauman, 1993, pp. 114–115). The cultural interpreter's responsibility is now to the group and not to the individual human being. Thus the cultural interpreter helps to socialize the enterprise in the new environment, which is a management process based on the "classification and differentiation of socially assigned rights and duties" (p. 120). The aim of socialization is to discipline, normalize, control, segregate, and supervise.

The personal influence model speaks for itself. It is clearly a role that aligns itself with dominant power systems in an effort to garner influence. In the United States this is typically the role of lobbyists who, despite different forms of legislation, nonetheless manage to use the deep pockets of their sponsors to seek political influence.

While a postmodern critique might sound severe, postmodernism also offers opportunities for dialectical interventions that could enable public relations practitioners working in international or global contexts to navigate and preserve the inherent complexity in the global environment while simultaneously resisting discriminatory and anti-democratic practices. Certain conditions are necessary for practitioners to make use of these dialectical interventions and enact the role of the public relations activist.

The Activist Practitioner

Rosina Voto and I previously started the project of clarifying the role of the activist public relations practitioner:

> The practitioner as organizational activist will serve as *a* [emphasis added] conscience in the organization by resisting dominant power structures, particularly when these structures are not inclusive; will preference employees' and external publics' discourse over that of management; will make the most humane decision in a particular situation; and will promote new ways of thinking and problem solving through dissensus and conflict. These actions will contribute to a culture of emancipation and liberation in the organization. (Holtzhausen & Voto, 2002, p. 64)

To understand how public relations practitioners can become activists, it is appropriate to provide a more detailed analysis of this definition.

Resistance Strategies

One of the philosophical problems with postmodern theory is that many scholars argue it denies the ability to be an activist because standing up for a principle also involves the attempt to start a hegemonic discourse. For instance, if one stands up for democracy and emancipation, the question immediately becomes who determines what is democracy and who determines who is in need of emancipation? It is, therefore, important to make sure that these terms are not used to hide discriminatory practices. This is the reason why postmodernists argue that all involvement in democratizing and emancipatory processes must be local and at the request of local people (Eribon, 1991; Lyotard, 1984; West, 1997). It is not for the practitioner to decide who is deserving of support or not. However, the practitioner will not be able to get involved at all if there is no involvement with grassroots activities at local nodes. Practitioners involved in global and transnational organizations cannot, therefore, stand back and let cultural interpreters decide for them who is deserving of their support. Once they understand how the organization they represent can affect and harm local stakeholders, they can actively become involved with those stakeholders and help them state their case. Thus knowledge and understanding of local issues and processes are important. It is equally important for practitioners to understand how their practice often perpetuates injustice. Even practitioners who do not anticipate working in the international sphere will most likely at some stage in their careers be challenged to deal with people with cultural perspectives different from their own. Understanding what the possible effects of their practices and those of their organizations, even countries, might have on people different from themselves is one of the aims of a postmodern approach to public relations practice.

Resistance is impossible without a critical stance, and workers who acquire and apply such a stance have been described as "critical worker researchers" (Kincheloe & McLaren, 1994, p. 147) or "cultural workers" (West, 1997, p. 74). These workers are "talented (and usually privileged) contributors to culture who desire to align themselves with demoralized, demobilized, depoliticized and disorganized people in order to empower and enable social action and, if possible, to enlist collective insurgency for the expansion of freedom, democracy and individuality" (p. 66). In his analysis, West lays out the foundation for what might be the project of the postmodern activist practitioner: empowerment, enabling of social action, and expansion of freedom, democracy, and individuality. Practitioners can do this by lessening the organization's negative impact. For instance, by centralizing organizational power and resources and promoting a culture of consumption that "view people as mere spectatorial consumers and passive citizens" (p. 78), the public relations practitioner will not be able to be an activist in the postmodern sense. As I have previously argued (Holtzhausen, 2002), a decentralized communication system that is situated in local and regional offices offers better opportunities for participative communication practices than a centralized structure.

Public relations activists as critical cultural workers must aspire to preserve the ability of those resisting the organization to stand up for themselves, speak out and insist on having their voices heard. This is not easy for activist public relations practitioners. As West (1997) says of all critical workers, while practitioners feel impelled to reveal the power structures within their immediate work environment they remain financially dependent on the very structures they are critiquing, making their criticism "simultaneously progressive *and* co-opted [emphasis in original]" (p. 66). But he also stresses that no change can happen without pressure on the system. Thus even co-opted pressure is better than none. This tension is an excellent example of an aporia, namely, the desire for change cannot be reconciled with the need to survive, yet both of these must be realized. Although this might sound idealistic to many, practitioners act as activists every day (see examples of activist practice in Holtzhausen, 2000; Holtzhausen & Voto, 2002). It is also important to remember that resistance does not require grand gestures or overt rebellion. Speaking up at meetings, creating inclusionary strategies, being conscious of possible harm, and making others aware of potential discriminatory practices all are immediate strategies activist practitioners can use on a daily basis. Living consciously in daily micropractice is the first step to activism.

To West's call to action in terms of freedom, democracy, and individuality, Best and Kellner (2001) add to the emancipatory project "reverence for nature, respect for all life, sustainability, and ecological balance" (p. 11). They too mention the importance of understanding through analysis, which "should engage both negative and positive developments, criticizing forms of oppression, domination, and exploitation, while valorizing positive possibilities for moral and technical evolution" (p. 15). This will lay bare the complex nature of society, which is the only way of preserving the chaos and ensuring the prominence of aporiae brought about by the cultural politics of difference. One way of doing this is to bring as many different perspectives to the analysis as possible. Public relations practitioners in their role as environmental scanners and authors of position papers are uniquely positioned to provide these kinds of analyses.

It is equally important for practitioners to understand how their practice often perpetuates injustice. Even practitioners who do not anticipate working in the international sphere will most likely at some stage in their careers be challenged to deal with people with cultural perspectives different from their own. Understanding what the possible effects of their practices and those of their organizations, even countries, might have on people different from themselves is one of the aims of a postmodern approach to public relations practice. Postmodernists call this involvement in the immediate and local event *micropolitics*, whereas *macropolitics* focuses on the overall state of society and power struggles at the institutional level.

Giving Preference to Stakeholders' Voices

If public relations practitioners view their practice as inherently democratic rather than economic, that is, political rather than financial, they will also view their role differently, namely, that they represent the interests of stakeholders to the organization in much the same way they represent the interests of the organization to its stakeholders. South African practitioners reported that in an effort to help their organizations survive in very turbulent environments, they have to give preference to previously marginalized publics over the viewpoints of the organization (Holtzhausen, 2005). This might sound foreign to most practitioners, who get their monthly pay checks from organizations. Much of this argument has to do with a critical analysis of agency theory (Hatch, 1997; Pfeffer, 1997; Wright, Mukherjib, & Kroll, 2001), an economic theory that argues that when an organization becomes too large for the single owner (the principal) to manage, agents are appointed to manage on behalf of principals. In typical organizations, managers would be agents. But increasingly the survival of organizations is facilitated by day-to-day government interventions in the form of tax breaks, concessions, and other forms of positive legislation—not even including recent events such as the U.S. bailout of huge financial organizations—that indirectly give taxpayers a much larger share in these organizations than they ever had before. I would argue that taxpayers and the communities in which these organizations operate have in fact become principals in these organizations together with shareholders, even though shareholding will not reflect that. Furthermore, employee share schemes would make many employees principals as well, which means that the public relations practitioners' responsibility also lies with them, beyond their normal employee stakeholder status.

From this perspective, stakeholders become more important than the organization itself. Without stakeholder relations organizations will be unsustainable because an organization that does not adhere to the value system of its environment will be shut down, as neoinstitutional theory suggests (Sandhu, 2009) and as reported above (Holtzhausen, 2005). If an organization is accountable to all its stakeholders, those stakeholders would include taxpayers and communities. There are already indications that democracy brings more accountability for stakeholders and relates to their preferences. In a study on the impact of democracy on public relations practice in the South African context, practitioners reported that they privileged their organizations' stakeholders over management and viewed it as part of activist public relations practice (Holtzhausen, 2005; Holtzhausen, Petersen, & Tindall, 2003). For them, activist behavior meant challenging the dominant management paradigm when they found that to be discriminatory and unjust. Thus, an open communication climate is vital to the democratic institution.

The provision of information is as important as open communication. It will be the duty of the public relations activist to make sure that stakeholders have all the information they need to make informed decisions, which, according to Lyotard (1984), is a precondition for language games "of perfect information" (p. 67). Accessibility to information ensures that no party is privileged in a debate, which "would respect both the desire for justice and the desire for the unknown" (p. 67). The accessibility to information should not lead to a universal consensus, as Habermas proposes (p. 65), but to dissensus, which will prevent metanarratives and metaprescriptives. Lyotard argues that recognition of the heterogeneity of discourses and the insistence that all "language games" must be local and "agreed on by its local players" (p. 66) are important to the concept of dissensus.

Promoting New Ways of Thinking through Dissensus

The use of *dissensus* is a resistance strategy that focuses on the use of language. Lyotard (1992) proposes a practice that promotes dissensus rather than consensus, and activism rather than obedience, which is the only way in which public relations practitioners can practice public relations that is consistent with postmodern ethics. The issue of postmodern public relations as a form of activism that exposes inequalities in society, particularly in those organizations these practitioners work for, is an important one for practitioners. It also is important for educators to understand the effects of the theories on their students when they teach them in an uncritical manner. Theories and perspectives that are not criticized soon become hegemonic discourses.

Continuous change is no longer questioned as being essential for survival. However, how that change is brought about through discursive strategies is where postmodernists diverge from other critical perspectives. Much modern critical thought is based on an analysis of the public sphere and the issue of consensus (Habermas, 1984). Habermas argues that it is possible to reach the truth through "the central experience of the unconstrained, unifying, consensus-building force of argumentative speech" (p. 10). Argumentative speech is made possible through dialogue in the public sphere. He argues that this is made difficult due to the intervention of people, such as mass communication workers, who strategically manipulate communication and make unconstrained argumentative speech difficult.

Postmodernists argue that power distorts all communicative situations and that power determines the direction of consensus; that is, consensus would privilege those who have the most power in the discussion. To counter the role of power in debate, Lyotard (1992) champions dissensus. He argues that consensus co-opts the least powerful in an effort to maintain the status quo to the benefit of the most powerful. One of the problems Lyotard (1988) identified is that the terms of a discussion can take place in the idiom of one party, while the understanding of the other party is not represented or recognized. He calls this a *differend*. Lyotard's (1988) concept of the differend refers to a discussion taking place in the frame of reference of only one party: "A case of differend takes place when the 'regulation' of the conflict that opposes them is done in the idiom of one of the parties while the wrong suffered by the other is not signified by the other in that idiom" (p. 9). An example of a differend is where I was excluded from the meeting with Japanese journalists. A differend exists when participants in a discussion used different "genre[s] of discourse" (p. 29). In the case of the Japanese journalists, I used a genre of political discourse while my male colleagues used a genre of cultural discourse. Lyotard would view these two genres of discourse as incommensurable because it is impossible to do justice to both. I believed I suffered an injustice because my discourse was not recognized as political. If I would have reached agreement with my colleagues it would have been an artificial consensus because it would not have recognized the depth of the differences between us. Also, if I did reach consensus with them, I would not have made any changes in future similar behavior possible and would not have facilitated any change. By stating the nature of the irreconcilable difference, which Lyotard calls a "tensor," I at least raised awareness of the issue.

Lyotard (1992) associates consensus with the end of thinking, and argues that change is only possible when dissensus initiates new ways of thinking and extends thought processes. To deal with these conflicts, both sides in the conflict must be made aware of the conflict and understand why it exists. Resolution of the conflict should never be forced, even if that conflict can never be resolved. To ensure equality and democracy it is important to expose these "tensors" (Lyotard, 1993, p. 54). Public relations practitioners should, therefore, not strive for consensus but should first make the parties involved aware of the tensors and promote dissensus through open discussion, even if it involves conflict. From this discussion it is again evident that postmodernists are intensely aware of the complexity of modern day life and the importance of exposing the many tensions people face in moral and ethical decision making, rather than glossing these over in favor of those who wield the most power. It is the responsibility of the public relations activist to create possibilities for change through creating opportunities for dissent, for opening up debate, without forcing consensus. This is particularly important in global practice, where cultural environments are highly complex and easily subject to misinterpretation, particularly because it is one's natural instinct to understand any given cultural situation from one's own perspective. As I have previously argued (Holtzhausen, 2000), "the postmodern public relations practitioner wants to set the disorder of discourse free from the tight web of constraints that inhibits it" (p. 105). That is the role of the postmodern, activist public relations practitioner in today's globalizing climate.

Conclusion

Striving to be an activist practitioner, as suggested in this chapter, is not easy. I know from personal experience how hard it is to speak up against the norm and to be the only voice raised in defense of those publics who were not considered in a debate. However, through the years I have learned that it is possible, particularly if the words come with conviction and without judgment, anger, or hatred. One also cannot assume that one is always right. It is important to understand that postmodernism (and all other "-isms" for that matter) is a lens through which one chooses to view the world. Other people have other lenses and oftentimes those underlying assumptions cannot be aligned with one's own.

Although I believe it is necessary to respect the viewpoints of others, I also believe it is important to make others aware of the differences one has with them. South Africa would not have changed if people did not speak up about apartheid and discrimination. The change to a democratic society in that country did not happen overnight but was a process of argumentation and debate that took place as much in organizations as it did around dinner tables, in political rallies, and private conversations. Postmodernism does not mean "anything goes" because the "Other" has a powerful voice that when calling out for justice, cannot be ignored.

With the ubiquity of new technology, public relations practitioners will become ever more influential. It is becoming increasingly possible to marginalize the mainstream media and speak directly to our publics. This places a bigger onus on us to be moral and responsible world citizens. Furthermore, it does not require the practitioner to make the big gesture, although that might sometimes be necessary. One recent example would be that of Wendell Potter who left his position as vice president of corporate communications at the health insurance company Cigna because he objected to the misleading and misrepresenting messages the company distributed to stop health care reform (Potter, 2009).

A threat to realizing the potential for postmodern public relations activism is if, as a notion, it becomes cast off as idealistic. I believe framing activism in this way is a disservice to students because it suggests to them that this kind of practice is impractical and that the path of least resistance is preferable. This becomes a self-fulfilling perspective because students assume activist practice is unattainable. There are many examples of how practitioners, through their day-to-day practice, change organizational environments and help improve the lives of others while contributing to the sustainability of their organizations.

Finally, while postmodernism argues for respect of difference, it is important to understand and acknowledge when cultural practices are repressive. Somehow, critiquing culture has become one of the communication taboos I mentioned earlier. The numerous texts arguing for the protection of culture in practice attest to that. I support Bauman's (1993) move in making sure that culture is not a pseudonym for discriminatory practices and that in practice, adherence to group norms does not come between our own moral convictions and the plight of the Other.

Discussion Questions

1. How would the practice of postmodern public relations be different from other forms of public relations practice?
2. What challenges do you think would be faced by practitioners subscribing to postmodern principles in global public relations practice?
3. How realistic do you think it is to be a public relations activist in global practice?
4. Discuss whether you think public relations practitioners have the right to speak out about discriminatory cultural practices in countries other than their own.
5. Discuss whether there indeed are differences between global and international public relations practice, and how that might affect your role as a public relations activist.

Notes

1. For a comprehensive discussion of the influence of worldview see Laudan (1977), Suppe (1979), Kearney (1984), and Littlejohn (1989). For a specific discussion of this topic in public relations see J. Grunig (1989), who based his concepts of symmetrical and asymmetrical communication on the concept of worldview.
2. Bauman (1993) describes an aporia as "a contradiction that cannot be overcome, one that results in a conflict that cannot be resolved" (p. 8).

References

Barney, D. (2004). *The network society*. Malden, MA: Polity Press.

Bauman, Z. (1993). *Postmodern ethics*. Cambridge, MA: Blackwell.

Bell, D. (1973). *The coming of post-industrial society*. New York: Basic Books.

Best, S., & Kellner, D. (1991). *Postmodern theory: Critical interrogations*. New York: Guilford Press.

Best, S., & Kellner, D. (2001). *The postmodern adventure: Science, technology, and cultural studies at the third millennium*. New York: Guilford.

Brown, D. (2000, July 15). Mandela urges united AIDS fight: Drop rhetoric, take action, ex-president says. *The Ottawa Citizen*, World Section, p. B4.

Burns, T. (1962). The sociology of industry. In A. T. Walford, M. Argyle, D. V. Glass, & J. J. Morris (Eds.), *Society: Problems and methods of study* (pp. 185–215). London: Routledge, Kegan & Paul.

Castells, M. (1996). *The rise of the network society*. Oxford, UK: Blackwell.

Connor, S. (1989). *Postmodernist culture: An introduction to theories of the contemporary*. Cambridge, MA: Blackwell.

Deleuze, G., & Guattari, F. (1983). *Anti-Oedipus*. Minneapolis, MN: University of Minnesota Press.

Edgar, A., & Sedgwick, P. (Eds.). (2002). *Cultural theory: The key concepts*. New York: Routledge.

Eribon, D. (1991). *Michel Foucault*. Cambridge, MA: Harvard University Press.

Foucault, M. (1972). *The archaeology of knowledge*. New York: Pantheon Books.

Grossman, L. (2009, June 17). Iran protests: Twitter, the medium of the movement. *Time* (New York ed.), p. 174.

Grunig, J. E. (1989). Symmetrical presuppositions as a framework for public relations theory. In C. H. Botan & J. Vincent Hazleton (Eds.), *Public relations theory* (pp. 17–44). Hillsdale, NJ: Erlbaum.

Grunig, J. E. (1994). World view, ethics, and the two-way symmetrical model of public relations. In W. Armbrecht & U. Zabel (Eds.), *Normative aspekte der public relations* [Normative aspects of public relations] (pp. 69–89). Opladen, Germany: Westdeutscher Verlag.

Grunig, J. E., Grunig, L. A., Sriramesh, K., Huang, Y.-H., & Lyra, A. (1995). Models of public relations in an international setting. *Journal of Public Relations Research, 7*(3), 163–186.

Grunig, L. A., Grunig, J. E., & Dozier, D. M. (2002). *Excellent public relations and effective organizations: A study of communication management in three countries*. Mahwah, NJ: Erlbaum.

Habermas, J. (1984). *The theory of communicative action* (Vol. 1). Boston, MA: Beacon.

Hatch, M. J. (1997). *Organization theory: Modern, symbolic, and postmodern perspectives*. Oxford, UK: Oxford University Press.

Hatch, M. J., & Cunliffe, A. L. (2006). *Organization theory: Modern, symbolic, and postmodern perspectives*. New York: Oxford University Press.

Heinrich, T., & Batchelor, B. (2004). *Kotex, Kleenex, Huggies: Kimberley-Clark and the consumer revolution in American business.* Columbus, OH: Ohio State University Press.

Holtzhausen, D. R. (2000). Postmodern values in public relations. *Journal of Public Relations Research, 12*(1), 93–114.

Holtzhausen, D. R. (2002). Towards a postmodern research agenda for public relations. *Public Relations Review, 28*(3), 251–264.

Holtzhausen, D. R. (2005). Public relations practice and political change in South Africa. *Public Relations Review, 31*(3), 407–416.

Holtzhausen, D. R. (2007, May). *The postmodern turn in organizational theory.* Paper presented at the 57th Annual Conference of the International Communication Association, San Francisco, CA.

Holtzhausen, D. R., Petersen, B. K., & Tindall, N. T. J. (2003). Exploding the myth of the symmetrical/asymmetrical dichotomy: Public relations models in the new South Africa. *Journal of Public Relations Research, 15*(4), 305–341.

Holtzhausen, D. R., & Tindall, N. T. J. (2009, August). *Toward a roles theory for strategic communication: The case of South Africa.* Paper presented at the 92nd Annual Convention of the Association for Education in Journalism and Mass Communication, Boston, MA.

Holtzhausen, D. R., & Voto, R. (2002). Resistance from the margins: The postmodern public relations practitioner as organizational activist. *Journal of Public Relations Research, 14*(1), 57–84.

Holtzhausen, D. R., & Werder, K. G. P. (2008, October). *The emergence of new organizational structures and their relationship with public relations practice.* Paper presented at the Annual Congress of EUPRERA, Milan, Italy.

Ihlen, Ø., van Ruler, B., & Fredriksson, M. (Eds.). (2009). *Public relations and social theory: Key figures and concepts.* New York: Routledge.

Kearney, M. (1984). *Worldview.* Novato, CA: Chandler & Sharp.

Kincheloe, J. L., & McLaren, P. L. (1994). Rethinking critical theory and qualitative research. In N. K. Denzin & Y. S. Lincoln (Eds.), *Handbook of qualitative research* (pp. 138–157). Thousand Oaks, CA: Sage.

Kraidy, M. (2009). Reality television, gender, and authenticity in Saudi Arabia. *Journal of Communication, 59*(2), 345–366.

Laudan, L. (1977). *Progress and its problems: Towards a theory of scientific growth.* Berkeley, CA: University of California Press.

L'Etang, J. (2004). *Public relations in Britain: A history of professional practice in the 20th century.* London: Erlbaum.

Littlejohn, S. (1989). *Theories of human communication* (3rd ed.). Belmont, CA: Wadsworth.

Lyotard, J.-F. (1984). *The postmodern condition: A report on knowledge.* (G. Bennington & B. Massumi, Trans.). Minneapolis, MN: University of Minnesota Press.

Lyotard, J.-F. (1988). *The differend: Phrases in dispute: Theory and history of literature* (Vol. 46). Minneapolis, MN: University of Minnesota Press.

Lyotard, J.-F. (1992). Answering the question: What is postmodernism? In C. Jencks (Ed.), *The postmodern reader* (pp. 138–150). London: Academy Editions.

Lyotard, J.-F. (1993). *Libidinal economy*. Bloomington, IN: University of Indiana Press.

Macdonnell, D. (1986). *Theories of discourse. An introduction*. New York: Blackwell.

Morozov, E. (2009, June 20). The repercussions of a "Twitter revolution." *The Boston Globe*, p. A11.

Pal, M., & Dutta, M. J. (2008). Public relations in the global context: The relevance to critical modernism as a theoretical lens. *Journal of Public Relations Research, 20*(2), 159–179.

Pfeffer, J. (1997). *New directions for organization theory: Problems and prospects*. New York: Oxford University Press.

Potter, W. (2009). GOP fear tactic from health insurance companies. Retrieved from http://www.ireport.com/docs/DOC-315401

Roper, J. (2005). Symmetrical communication: Excellent public relations or a strategy for hegemony? *Journal of Public Relations Research, 17*(1), 69–86.

Sandhu, S. (2009). Strategic communication: An institutional perspective. *International Journal of Strategic Communication, 3*(2), 72–93.

Seidman, S. (1997). The end of sociological theory. In S. Seidman (Ed.), *The postmodern turn: New perspectives on social theory* (4th ed., pp. 119–139). Cambridge, UK: Cambridge University Press.

Sriramesh, K., & Verčič, D. (Eds.). (2003). *The global public relations handbook*. Mahwah, NJ: Erlbaum.

Sriramesh, K., & White, J. (1992). Societal culture and public relations. In J. E. Grunig (Ed.), *Excellence in public relations and communication management* (pp. 597–614). Hillsdale, NJ: Erlbaum.

Suppe, F. (1979). *The structure of scientific theories* (2nd ed.). Urbana, IL: Illinois University Press.

Sylvie, G., Wicks, J. L., Hollifield, A., Lacy, S., & Broadrick Sohn, A. (2008). *Media management: A case book approach*. New York: Erlbaum.

Verčič, D., Grunig, L. A., & Grunig, J. E. (1996). Global and specific principles of public relations: Evidence from Slovenia. In H. M. Culbertson & N. Chen (Eds.), *International public relations: A comparative analysis* (pp. 31–65). Mahwah, NJ: Erlbaum.

West, C. (1997). The new cultural politics of difference. In S. Seidman (Ed.), *The postmodern turn: A new perspective on social theory* (pp. 65–81). Cambridge, UK: Cambridge University Press.

Wright, P., Mukherjib, A., & Kroll, M. (2001). A reexamination of agency theory assumptions: Extensions and extrapolations. *The Journal of Socio-Economics, 30*(5), 413–417.

Zaharna, R. S. (2001). "In-awareness" approach to international public relations. *Public Relations Review, 27*(2), 135–148.

Suggested Readings

Appignanesi, R., & Garratt, C. (1999). *Introducing postmodernism*. Cambridge, UK: Icon Books.

Crome, K., & Williams, J. (Eds.). (2006). *The Lyotard reader and guide*. New York: Columbia University Press.

Foucault, M. (1980). *Power/knowledge: Selected interviews and other writings 1972–1977*. New York: Pantheon Books.

Jencks, C. (Ed.). (1992). *The post-modern reader*. London: Academy Editions.

Lyotard, J-F., & Thébaud, J-L. (1985). *Just gaming*. Minneapolis, MN: University of Minnesota Press.

Rabinow, P. (Ed.). (1984). *The Foucault reader*. New York: Random House.

Chapter 7

Critiquing the Generic/Specific Public Relations Theory

The Need to Close the Transnational Knowledge Gap

Robert Wakefield

The generic/specific theory of public relations offers a framework for guiding effective public relations practice in transnational organizations. This chapter examines how certain transnational entities, and particularly transnational corporations (TNCs), preserve equilibrium between globally coordinated generic principles and the specific factors of local markets that impact the entity. Culture is one element of generic/specific theory, and, as Sriramesh (2007) has argued, culture provides an essential foundation of public relations practice. In this chapter, therefore, I pay specific attention to how the generic/specific theory can encourage a better appreciation of the importance of culture in how public relations is practiced in the context of globalization.

The discussion addresses two presuppositions related to the generic/specific theory. The first is that public relations in many TNCs has degenerated into mechanistic support for a "megamarketing model" (Hutton, 2001) where a global emphasis overwhelms the local. This reconstitution of public relations provides legitimate fodder for questioning its value for the organizations it serves and for society (Verčič, 2009; Wakefield, 2000). The generic/specific theory was developed in part to help critically examine this problematic. The second presupposition, however, is that research on the generic/specific theory has not yet satisfied its original intent; rather than serving as a guide for examining communication practices of TNCs and, most importantly, the varying cultural environments and factors that affect these practices, research has so far focused mostly on what Molleda and Laskin (2005) argued are descriptive studies of public relations in various countries. As a result, there needs to be more examination of the current status of the generic/specific theory and alterations made to it if it is to have real utility for public relations practitioners. This is especially true where global dynamics have changed specific cultural and sociopolitical/economic factors which practitioners must necessarily address if they are to effectively carry out their functions. Such a condition broaches the question of whether the dynamics of globalization have melded these specific variables into the generic realm of the theory instead of the specific. This chapter, therefore, analyzes the operations and effects of TNCs and their public relations activities. However, it is insufficient to examine these TNCs in isolation; because they exist within a broader societal context, their operations and effects are fully understood only in that broader context.

Holtzhausen (2000) argued that "as a discipline that has far-reaching effects on society, public relations needs to be understood and examined in a broader social, cultural, and political context rather than in a narrowly defined organizational function" (p. 95). Ihlen and van Ruler (2007) made a similar point:

> Most public relations theorists are concerned with relationships of an organization with its publics and not so much with the problem of how an organization relates itself to the public arena and society at large.... Lauzen and Dozier (1992) claimed that public relations should not so much function as obedient to management but take a more distant stand. Their basic point was that scholarship should not be too tightly linked to the social institution it studies, as this leads to a loss of perspective or a preoccupation with only one perspective. The instrumental and administrative approaches that prevail must be supplemented with societal approaches that also expose what public relations *is* [emphasis in original] in society today, and not only what it *should* be at an organizational level. (p. 245)

In accordance with Lauzen and Dozier's (1992) suggestion, while scrutinizing public relations in TNCs, this chapter also outlines the public relations practices that interplay between TNCs and society. It seems difficult to fully understand the formation of relationships between organizations and various stakeholders in the broader society if one ignores the impact of the organization on those stakeholders and vice versa. Obviously, the great majority of public relations practitioners functions within some type of organization and often maintains a delicate balance between supporting the organization to achieve its profit-making goals and ensuring that the needs of the broader society are also met. On the one hand, they are subject to the worldviews and procedures of that entity; in fact, practitioners who are *disobedient* to management will likely not last long in their jobs. On the other hand, if practitioners harm society through actions taken on behalf of organizations, they should be held accountable. If organizational constraints prevent practitioners from maintaining this necessary balance between the goals of revenue enhancement and an organization's obligations to society, then practitioners can find themselves dealing with situations that, as Holtzhausen

(2000) stated, become "difficult, if not impossible" (p. 93) to negotiate. These problems will not be addressed if theorists ignore responsibilities to the broader society; nor will they be resolved without investigating the responsibilities of practitioners in organizations. Both perspectives are necessary.

Ironically, while research in the international arena has been criticized for focusing too much on the structuring of public relations within organizations (Culbertson & Chen, 1996), others have noted that there is not nearly enough research that examines the processes and effects of public relations specifically in transnational organizations (Molleda & Laskin, 2005). Indeed, Verčič (2009) stated that "because all companies affect or are affected by the world that lies beyond their borders, it is amazing that we have only a few quality publications on the public relations practices of transnational corporations" (p. 795). Gower (2006) also asserted, "The process of self-examination must include an understanding of how public relations really is practiced today on a global scale" (p. 185); such an investigation should not only help guide effective practice around the world but also determine what impacts practice has on the various societies where it occurs.

From here, then, this chapter looks into public relations in transnational organizations, its positioning within those entities, and the roles it plays in negotiating between the organizations and their broader societal contexts. It begins with the context in which most public relations practitioners now function in TNCs. This leads to a discussion about the generic/specific theory of public relations, and how it has attempted to examine relationship building between TNCs and their various stakeholders.

The Triumph of the Market Model and Megamarketing

Globalization has introduced a complex and very broad social context in which institutions and people operate and a context which has major impacts on those institutions and people. Friedman (2002, p. 3) and former World Bank chief economist Joseph Stiglitz (2002, p. 222) have argued, respectively, that the forces of globalization—the convergence of communication technologies, financial spectrums, the increased movement and interactions of people, the globalization of business, and the like (Robertson, 1996)—are "inexorable" and "here to stay." Other authors, like Micklethwait and Wooldridge (2000) and Panzner (2009), assert that these global forces are anything but inevitable. Nevertheless, it would defy reason to deny the widespread influences of globalization, for good or bad; and, no matter what happens, these influences will remain in one form or another for decades to come.

With the convergence of these global forces, society has witnessed what Artz (2007) called the "triumph of the market model" (p. 149). He explained this as follows:

> In the new millennium, with globalization, capitalism has become the first truly *world* [emphasis in original] system: capitalism has not only finally displaced all precapitalist formations, it has also completed the commodification of every meaningful instance of social life, including replacing nation-state public institutions and responsibilities with privatized, for-profit operations across the board— from natural resources such as land and water to social necessities such as education and health care. (p. 149)

Evidence of this market triumph is abundant worldwide. Governments devote enormous resources to attracting business through tax breaks and other incentives (Vogl & Sinclair, 1996). Nations also are caught up in the competitive world of transnational stock exchanges and the influences of global traders, to where they either play along or are left behind (Friedman, 2000). In community after community around the globe, entrenched native businesses have been replaced by the ever-present brands and buildings of TNCs, with McDonalds and Starbucks proving very immediate and obvious examples. Even small huts in poor villages are turned into billboards selling the wares and services of major TNCs. This all follows the U.S. capitalist tradition of making profits for shareholders, a tradition that is becoming increasingly global (Sirkin, Hemerling, & Bhattacharya, 2008).

Because of its overwhelming focus on revenues, the market model is emotionally charged in public discourse. Some authors have claimed that this model has generally increased standards of living and enabled arrangements between governments and businesses wherein society as a whole is improved (Vogl & Sinclair, 1996; Micklethwait & Wooldridge, 2000). Many other scholars see this market model as problematic (e.g., Hutton, 2001). They view it as bankrolling an elite society while creating even greater chasms between the wealthy and the increasing numbers of poor of the world. As Stark and Kruckeberg (2001) asserted, today's corporate mindset "pays more attention to immediate [financial] interests than to the future well-being of the corporations themselves and the environment in which they operate..." (p. 55). As a result, greater instabilities and hostilities are generated around the world (Micklethwait & Wooldridge, 2000; Panzner, 2009).

Where the market model triumphs, the marketing function rises to the core of organizational strategy because marketing is the essential function which, combined with its sales counterparts, directly fuels consumption and financial gain. As immediate revenue generation becomes the main imperative for corporations and as competition increases for consumer dollars, marketing grows even larger in organizational power and scope. Hutton (2001) has characterized this expansion as "megamarketing"—the all-encompassing marketing *and* communication role that strengthens, extends, and protects the brand.

Over the past 20 years or so, Hutton (2001) argued, marketing has "repackaged" and incorporated into itself the concepts of internal marketing (once seen as employee relations), crisis marketing (formerly crisis communications), cause marketing (issues management), and now relationship marketing (the former essence of public relations). Eschewing the essential contributions of public relations like environmental scanning, boundary spanning, and relationship building, megamarketing assumes proprietary responsibility over public relations in many organizations. Rather than seeing a purposeful "turf-grabbing" ploy, Hutton observed these expanded marketing roles as natural evolutions into a void left by a public relations industry that remains on the fringes of business strategy and scholarship. He warned that "marketing is essentially redefining itself as public relations ... [and] many public relations practitioners and scholars are not even aware of the trend" (p. 211).

Because of the public relations industry's traditional focus on relationships with all stakeholder groups, not just consumers, its practitioners are perhaps in the best position to help reduce the hostilities generated by the market model—particularly those hostilities aimed at TNCs that are seen as distant and insensitive flag bearers of this revenue enhancement emphasis. Yet, ironically, practitioners seem to be abandoning these strategic problem resolution roles in favor of those functions that support marketing and that simply disseminate messages to stakeholders. For instance, industry literature contains marketing-type phrases such as "getting to the brand marketing table" (Bush, 2007, p. 30). Additionally, practitioners often place a priority on fostering "the image or reputation of an organization relevant to product or service publicity or promotion" (Heath, 2001, pp. 1–2). Indeed, it has been argued that many public relations firms "see as their concern that of providing clients with a cheap mode of advertising [and therefore] have eroded ... any idea that the public relations concern should be anything other than getting media coverage" (Ehling, White, & J. Grunig, 1992, p. 366). Such claims are substantiated by way of industry associations that focus on providing tactical training, and university public relations courses that emphasize tactical communication skills over strategic thinking. As a result, "students are graduating [with] little or no understanding of what effects if any their work might produce within the groups that they target" (Macnamara, 2006, p. 9).

Because of the public relations industry's slide into megamarketing support, its traditional strategic roles are often being assumed by experts from other fields. Harold Burson (2004) noted that chief executives want at their side individuals with problem solving expertise. Increasingly, public relations practitioners are not among those who are there. He explained:

> In matters affecting employees, human resources departments and HR consultants are muscling in on what we public relations professionals always believed to be "our turf." Investor relations ... have been the purview of the chief financial officer in many companies for many years. Management consultants and Big Four audit firms are now into social responsibility and branding. General counsel and outside law firms are into public affairs. (Burson, 2004, p. 12)

If the public relations industry is to continue in its traditional strategic roles that benefit both organizations and society, moving into megamarketing support functions on behalf of their entities probably is not the best long-term approach. As more organizations are affected by a more complex world, practitioners need a much broader range of interaction and facilitation expertise, rather than retrenching into mastery of the glamorized technological communication tools (Starck & Kruckeberg, 2001). Furthermore, when public relations people abdicate their relationship building roles and move away from problem solving expertise, not only is the public relations industry harmed but, in the international arena, the ability to reduce hostilities against TNCs and to negotiate mutually beneficial relationships between these entities and their stakeholders is also diminished.

Changing the Formula to Meet Societal Imperatives

The triumph of the market model has facilitated expansion of TNCs into bigger, more powerful entities, where megamarketing is the turbocharged engine that helps them to reach consumers in unprecedented ways. Because of this concentration, the megamarketing worldview, even with its new relationship marketing function, is ill-equipped to address the obligations of transnational organizations to the societies in which they operate. Most organizations suffer from an inside-out mentality, centered on inputs, throughputs, and outputs; thus, any thought given to society would naturally focus on how to control stakeholders to help the organization thrive. Marketing extends this thinking into how far products can be pushed around the world with the most possible efficiencies and the least possible disruption. Any "relationship building" is intended to only maximize that marketing push to build a larger customer base (Wakefield, 2000).

However, as Heath (2001) explained, public relations scholars have been more interested in how public relations can help "to reduce the cost of conflict" rather than "generate market share and income" (p. 2). In these terms, the role of public relations is a problem solving one incorporating the need to nurture societal obligations in a way that can benefit both society and the transnational organization. This is a complex process that demands mutually reinforcing responsibilities for cultivating relationships as well as environmental scanning to understand the diffuse elements in society which monitor the organization and can be affected by or affect its behaviors (J. Grunig, 1992). The question here is, are these responsibilities best fulfilled through centralized global cooperation of public relations professionals, through local interactions, or both?

Some scholars and business executives champion the idea of *glocalization*, which Maynard (2003) saw as a tailoring of products and marketing to meet local variations in consumer demand. "Glocalization," he wrote, "suggests some sort of accommodation ... with the specific rules and conditions of each country in which they operate. Glocalization represents the need for multinationals to be global and local at the same time" (p. 57). Robertson (1996), on the other hand, described glocalization as "the simultaneous promotion of what is, in one sense, a standardized product, for particular markets, in particular flavors" (p. 224). Transnationals with a glocalization mindset often decentralize to serve specific market niches, either in given industries or in various geographic locations. Either way, the process still emphasizes products and services dispersed around the world by an organizational umbrella that values efficiencies and revenues.

Many TNCs have reached out to host communities and done much to build infrastructure and provide essential goods and services; yet, they often create hostilities in these same communities. Sometimes hostilities arise for no other reason than that the corporations are outsiders—and, in many cases, outsiders that embody Western dominance (see Bardhan & Patwardhan, 2004). Morley (1998) noted that "the relentless rise of the multinational corporation [has] posed a series of threats, or, at least, perceived threats, to local communities" (pp. 30–31). These threats have fostered the rise of "counter-corporate activism" around the world. Through this activism, "dozens of brand-based campaigns have succeeded in rattling their corporate targets, in several cases pushing them to substantially alter their policies" (Klein, 2000, p. 366).

Usually when corporations expand transnationally, they seek autonomy from government and activist interventions to operate as they wish (J. Grunig, 2006; Mintzberg, 1983). From a public relations perspective, Holtzhausen (2007) has rightly pointed out that organizations "are less autonomous than they desire or perceive, and it is therefore inevitable for organizations to deal with elements in their environment" (p. 359). As she outlines, the autonomy worldview "promotes the interests of organizations over those of activists and other members of society" (p. 359), and requires organizations to only begrudgingly interact with society. In these circumstances, organizations ignore at their peril the fact that they are obligated, just like any other citizen, to be responsible to the communities and societies in which they exist and operate (Starck & Kruckeberg, 2001). This is particularly the case for TNCs; their existence in any given nation is a privilege rather than a right.

Public relations practitioners should be filling the inevitable gap between organizations' global imperatives of brand promotion and the expectations of their stakeholders and communities, wherever they are located. Such gaps can only be filled through the careful *cultivation* of long-term relationships (Hung, 2007). Any farmer does everything possible to prepare for a successful harvest, but then he or she must petition nature to ensure that the harvest bears fruit. Such is the nature of relationships that are cultivated by a practitioner who understands the dynamic nature of people and the proper give-and-take that is necessary for genuine mutual benefits. As Heath (2001) noted, genuine community exists only through the cocultivation of "agreement and disagreement of many complementary and competing perspectives" (p. 7)—just one of which is the transnational organization housed in that community. But it takes senior public relations practitioners (not marketing staff) to undertake these processes of negotiation and relationship building—exactly the type of practitioner roles that are being lost to other fields. The roles require even greater expertise and understanding in the global realm due to the increased complexities of this multicultural, international, sociopolitical environment.

Theoretical Foundations for International/ Transnational Public Relations

One of the theoretical propositions for filling these gaps between organization and community needs was the proposition of Excellence in public relations and communication management (J. Grunig, 1992), which was founded on the two-way symmetrical model of public relations (J. Grunig & Hunt, 1984), the need for public relations to serve in the organization's dominant coalition, among other theories (J. Grunig, 1992). The theoretical proposition of Excellence in public relations was an attempt to mitigate the power that large and wealthy organizations seem to inherently have over the communities they serve. Developers of the proposition criticized typical public relations practices as asymmetrical and as primarily seeking to enhance and communicate the organization's power. The asymmetrical worldview suggested "that organizations can achieve powerful effects with communication"—effects such as behavioral changes among stakeholders toward organizational desires—but J. Grunig (1992) argued that "these effects seldom occur" (p. 10). By contrast, the two-way symmetrical model was seen as using "dialogue to manage conflict, improve understanding, and build relationships with publics. With the symmetrical model, both the organization and publics can be persuaded; both also may change their behavior" (J. Grunig, 1992, p. 39). In other words, *relationships* were the key to this theoretical proposition, and public relations practitioners, according to J. Grunig (1992), participated in the dominant coalition in order to ensure that organizations sought mutually beneficial relationships with their stakeholders.

The two-way symmetrical model and its positioning of public relations within the dominant coalition has been scrutinized more than any other theoretical proposition in the field (Curtin & Gaither, 2005; Holtzhausen & Voto, 2002; Murphy, 1991; Pieczka, 1996). Many have criticized the model, particularly in the context of globalization, suggesting that it is unrealistic for TNCs to give up immense power to create equal relationships with their publics (Holtzhausen, Petersen, & Tindall, 2003). This being the case, the management of relationships is seen as containing elements of insincerity and manipulation (Stoker & Tusinski, 2006). Murphy (1991) argued that it is difficult to make relationships endure when at least one side is focused on its own needs with little desire to concede anything to the other side. J. Grunig (1992) sees such manipulation as the essence of asymmetrical public relations, but critics have expressed similar concerns with the symmetrical concept (see Roper, 2005).

But what if we consider that new global communication technologies are helping to tilt the power pendulum away from corporate interests? While Starck and Kruckeberg (2001) argued that TNCs are becoming more powerful, Friedman (2000) asserted that issue groups are now better able to exert pressures on larger organizations. Holtzhausen (2007) suggested that activism offers democratic resistance that can, in some ways, be more important to pluralistic societies than the long-term survival of target organizations. Either way, social media have empowered individuals and groups in ways never thought possible just a decade ago (Friedman, 2002). These social media offer the means to monitor behaviors of transnational organizations and a forum for rallying together to exert direct pressure on what these groups see as wrong. As a result, transnationals can be held accountable and be made to prove legitimacy to society. As Metzler (2001) explained, "legitimacy is based on the actions of an organization and responsible communication about them; it is not a mere perception or façade created and manipulated to weather the latest storm (or to launch products or services). As issue-oriented publics ... intensify their scrutiny of organizations ... direct disputes of organizational legitimacy will become more prevalent" (p. 321).

This discussion highlights tension between large corporations and increasingly enabled communities for what each considers its right to flourish. A related point of tension in transnational organizations is the need to balance central control versus recognizing and interacting with various communities that affect the organization's ability to operate and that demand accountability at the same time. Rather than wrapping themselves up in marketing support roles, public relations practitioners who possess what Starck and Kruckeberg (2001) called "intercultural literacy" (p. 58) should be capable of handling these tensions through highly interactive, horizontal units—worldwide public relations units that are not controlled through any "top-down" approach, but wherein each practitioner throughout the world has equal opportunity to influence public relations decisions (Wakefield, 2001).

The Generic/Specific Theory

The generic/specific theory becomes relevant here because it provides a route through which to both explore and address these tensions. It is important to understand the intent of the theory, how the research around it so far has fallen short of that intent, and how the theory needs to be reexamined and perhaps reinvigorated—not to help transnationals become more effective at disseminating one-way messages, but to protect them from their own mistakes.

The generic/specific theory was conceived as a framework for observing variables or factors in local environments that might ideally guide public relations in the transnational organization—specifically in corporations (Wakefield, 1997). When research began in the early 1990s, Culbertson and Chen (1996) had noted that there are two research tracks in the global public relations environment: *comparative*, or studies of the practice from country to country, and *international*, or studies of public relations practices specifically *within* international organizations. Research with the latter focus, they noted, was virtually nonexistent at the time. Given the increasing number of transnational firms, there was a need to launch this type of research to guide public relations efforts. The generic/specific theory was intended to serve as a departing point for such research.

The generic/specific theory was, to some degree, an extension of the study on Excellence in public relations, the foundations of which included the two-way symmetrical concept (J. Grunig, 1992). As a result, the theory was based on a definitive presupposition that Excellent public relations assists organizations in preserving reputation through dialogic relationships with stakeholders throughout the world. Because so little had been written on international public relations at the time, this theoretical formulation borrowed from other domains, such as international development management, comparative businesses, and marketing. What was known from those domains was that when organizations extended operations into different parts of the world, they had to understand what to coordinate at headquarters and what was important to know and do in each market away from headquarters in order to be successful (Brinkerhoff & Ingle, 1991). The debate was one of standardization vs. customization, and often these concepts were couched as polar opposites. Some scholars claimed that to maintain the entity's mission, its efficiencies, and its consistencies in services, products, or messages, everything had to be handled centrally; others argued that cultural values, political systems, and other factors were so dissimilar as to preclude any desire for central control (Adler & Doktor, 1986).

In launching research on this theory, then, two things seemed apparent: first, that the concepts from other domains could apply to public relations, and second, the solution to effective international organization would be not at the extremes but somewhere in the middle; *both* central mission and consistencies *and* local relationship building were needed. Tim Traverse-Healy (1991), a veteran of public relations in Europe, had broached this possibility, and U.S. scholar Carl Botan (1992) had already suggested various local factors that might affect a sound international program. With this foundation, the generic/specific theory of public relations was proposed—the generic being those things to organize centrally and the specific being the local factors that affect transnational organizations and their public relations activities. Initial research consisted of two projects: a Delphi study conducted for a dissertation at the University of Maryland (Wakefield, 1997), and a study of the generic/specific principles in Slovenia to assess the extent to which the principles may apply outside of the Western context (Verčič, L. Grunig, & J. Grunig, 1996).

It is important to highlight a distinction in the initial intent of the research. Because the Excellence study had already occurred in the United States, Canada, and the United Kingdom, the generic part of this research project was partially an attempt to test the Excellence principles in other nations. Such research uses *deductive* reasoning, where certain "truths" are tested in new conditions for further validation (Severin & Tankard, 2001). In this case, where the Excellence principles suggested that a senior practitioner should be in the dominant coalition, the generic theory proposed that in an Excellent transnational organization a practitioner in *every* market office should sit in that local dominant coalition; where the Excellence principles suggested that the function should be separate from marketing, the same was proposed as a generic variable; and so on. It was assumed that if the variables of Excellence had already been supported in three nations, they might also apply elsewhere. As it turned out, the Delphi study of senior practitioners in more than 20 nations indicated agreement with all of the variables except diversity (defined in the study as inclusion of women and any other minority group that was not part of the mainstream of any given society), where too much distinction from market to market made it impossible to reach concurrence (Wakefield, 1997).

Research on the specific variables, on the other hand, was much more of an exploration. Because there was a lack of theories on international public relations at that point, this part of the research used *inductive* reasoning, where exploration leads to theory. For the purposes of gathering the data around the specific variables, the researchers proposed Botan's (1992) suggestions of what factors could affect public relations in various markets: culture, political system, economy (*level of development* was the term used), potential for activism, and media structure.[1] But the developers of this theory have never discounted the possibility of "other variables, or local variations of the previously cited variables, that need to be identified and integrated into the … literature" (Sriramesh, 2007, p. 508).

To some extent, the distinction between the deductive logic of the generic and the inductive reasoning of the specific allowed for *both* the study of TNCs *and* the societies in which they operate. In other words, the generic focus looked at organizational philosophy and structuring of public relations; in contrast, the emphasis on the specific side of the theory was on what factors in the various local environments affected the organization. Therefore, paradigmatic prescription would not be a completely accurate description of how the specific realm was intended to be studied. Particularly in the 1997 Delphi study (Wakefield, 1997), the goal, as with most Delphi studies, was to share philosophies and ideas of these public relations veterans around the world as to different effects on the practice and how public relations units should respond to these effects.

Early Delphi research was not without its flaws; for one thing, its propositions contained Western biases which may have been alien to some respondents. The very idea of proposing these concepts to respondents in 20 nations represented an attempt to expose and reduce these biases. But this process also had its problems. For example, the snowball sample used to identify experts is legitimate in a Delphi study (Delbecq, Van de Ven, & Gustafson, 1975; Verčič, van Ruler, Butschi, & Flodin, 2001); but when there are only one or two respondents from each nation, these participants can hardly be taken as representative of public relations practices of their countries. Further, the Delphi was conducted in English, which may have precluded some of the "real" experts. Also, because English was used, misunderstandings of the questions or inability to express oneself in a non-native language could have caused problems. Finally, since the respondents had been recruited by U.S. scholars who knew them, there could have been a built-in "group think" bias of people whose opinions swayed closer together because of past professional or academic associations (people, for example, who were already predisposed to the idea of two-way symmetrical public relations). It was assumed that the Delphi and Slovenia studies would be just a beginning of the exploration into public relations in transnational organizations.

Sadly, subsequent research has not provided much additional insight into the generic/specific theory. Most investigations on the topic so far are contained in only two editions of the same book: *The Global Public Relations Handbook* (Sriramesh & Verčič, 2003, 2009). Using the generic/specific theory as the framework, the two editions contain more than two dozen examinations of public relations in various countries. These chapters are beneficial in building the body of knowledge, but most do not delve into what these descriptions might mean for transnational organizations operating in each country.[2] The two editions also contain a section which examines public relations issues in governments, the United Nations, and public relations firms that service corporations, in addition to two chapters that specifically examined TNCs. In one of these chapters, Verčič (2009) outlined the challenges and opportunities faced by practitioners who are trying to organize and carry out public relations in transnational firms. He viewed this outline as important to the field (as I do) because "corporate public relations on the world stage is the forerunner of the best in public relations. It demands more work in a more complex environment. Therefore, to study the best in public relations we need to focus on transnational corporate public relations" (p. 804). This chapter serves as one of the few and most thoughtful treatises on the actual original intent of the generic/specific theory. The entire book, meanwhile, serves as a significant beginning for research into the theory, but much more is needed to offer guidance to those whose public relations work carries them across sociopolitical and cultural lines.

The Influences of Culture

One of the most crucial elements of the generic/specific theory is culture. Other specific variables exist, but culture tends to serve as the societal foundation that fosters these elements. For example, political and economic systems often arise from cultural moorings, and media systems and activism also are strongly affected by culture. In Japan, for example, media access is uniquely granted through a system of highly interconnected press clubs, and activism is discouraged because it disrupts the intricate nature of harmony in the society. Cultural literacy is crucial to effective public relations practice because "culture affects communication and is affected by it" and, "[b]ecause public relations is fundamentally a communication activity, it is logical to conclude that culture affects public relations" (Sriramesh, 2007, p. 509). Therefore, during the conception of the generic/specific theory, when it came time to identify specific influences on a global entity, culture, naturally, was the first that surfaced (Verčič et al., 1996; Wakefield, 2000).

Since the conception of the generic/specific theory, however, the global environment has changed dramatically. For example, the Internet has surfaced, expanded, been commercialized, and ushered in social media, where a person's thoughts, threats, videos, or tweets, often delivered anonymously, can have dramatic global impact. But the Internet, like all technology before it, is still a tool; a mechanism people use to communicate with others and to connect with the world around them. The values from which these desires to communicate arise can be as diverse as they are similar—and most are strongly embedded in cultural roots that are slow to change (Newsom, Turk, & Kruckeberg, 2001). Many authors have noted that as the world appears to converge through technologies and other means, different cultural societies react to these changes by retrenching and protecting their own traditions (Friedman, 2000; Panzner, 2009; Robertson, 1990). As globalization ushers in radically different communication and expands the influence of transnational organizations, public relations scholarship and practice are equally shifting to understand and accommodate these global forces. This is particularly the case in relation to issues of how culture affects organizations and what organizations must do to interact competently with cultural communities.

There should be little argument that the impact of culture on public relations practice is as strong today as it was at the conception of the generic/specific theory. For the project on Excellence in public relations, Sriramesh and White (1992) wrote that "public relations practitioners will have to sensitize themselves to the cultural heterogeneity of their audiences.... The result will be the growth of a culturally richer profession" (p. 611). Recently, however, Sriramesh (2007) lamented, "Unfortunately, well into the 21st century, our hope has not yet materialized" (p. 507). He added, "The 21st century has exploded as the century of globalization. In such an environment, where peoples of various cultures are becoming ever more interdependent, it is sad and alarming that the concept of culture is being treated almost as an afterthought in many disciplines, including public relations" (2007, pp. 521–522).

Yet Sriramesh certainly can find others who concur that culture still influences public relations practice. Doorley and Garcia (2006) asserted that "global communication practitioners need a comprehensive understanding of the many different cultures they will encounter" (p. 243). Newsom et al. (2001) added, "Today's global environment demands a greater sensitivity to cultural nuances, especially considering that public relations efforts for even a local market can have an international impact" (p. 650). They explained that "culture and tradition impose a style of communication and result in certain types of behavior. Traditions are rooted in values. These traditions have a strong impact on ethical issues, which figure significantly in communication and other aspects of business" (p. 652).

While culture should be a critical element influencing the public relations practices of transnationals, an important question is where in the entity should responses to the influences of culture come from? Should processes be in place centrally so as to globally monitor and nurture cultural influences? Or should these influences continue to be dealt with at the local level? Or is it some combination of the two levels?

Sriramesh (2009) has brought forth an interesting dialectic in his writings related to these questions of organizational balance and cultural tensions. On the one hand he mused, "I wonder whether one should talk any longer about 'international public relations' or 'global public relations' as being a specialty because even 'domestic' publics are becoming multinational and multicultural due to globalization" (p. xxxv). Yet, in seeming contrast to his own statement, Sriramesh (2007) emphasized a need for a *culture-specific* stance, where the cultural variations an organization encounters in different countries or regions is seen as one of the overriding influences on effective decision making. He wrote that in our "rapidly globalizing world, our field will [still] ignore culture at its own peril" (p. 507). These claims may seem contradictory, but they reflect the enormous dialectical complexities of our changing world, and the impacts these changes have on public relations and its theory building processes—including the generic/specific theory.[3]

Tensions between Global Forces and Cultural Roots

When the generic/specific theory was conceived, the influences of culture were thought to apply mostly at a national level, along the lines of Hofstede's (1980) landmark studies which equated nation and culture (see also the chapters in this volume by Courtright, Wolfe, and Baldwin, and by Kent and Taylor). Critics of Hofstede's work recognized that varying cultures also exist within nations (Adler & Doktor, 1986). Little was written then about ethnic groups moving across national boundaries. Since then, however, much has surfaced. One of the more intriguing publications in this regard was the book *Tribes*, written by Kotkin (1993).

Kotkin (1993) contended that large populations of ethnic groups have dispersed around the world, combining shared origins, values, and traditions with common beliefs of progress. Appadurai (1990) also observed these *diaspora*, referring to the movement of any ethnic population from their homelands to other locations either by force or voluntary migration. These cultural communities, Kotkin (1993) suggested, thrive in their new lands because they continue to retain strong bonds and to support each other wherever they settle. At the same time they adapt well to their new communities by assimilating many of the newly encountered cultural mores and behaviors. In the United States, many see this as the old "melting pot" concept, in which "in exchange for giving up some of their cultural distinctiveness and assimilating into the dominant culture," immigrants receive "promise of a better life" (Ogan, 2007, p. 312).

Other scholars are skeptical of the seeming ease of ethnic transitions (Kramer & Ikeda, 2000), and refer instead to a "salad bowl" environment of Canada and other nations. It seems apparent that much of what ethnic groups adopt in their new homes are the more superficial trappings of culture—a taste for at least some of the new food, clothing, and entertainment, and enjoyment of other aspects of the culture. However, as Ogan (2007) stated, "none of these groups ever really [become] totally assimilated" (p. 312). They often hold fast to the values and mores of "home," and some even retain a native language over a few generations. Only with succeeding generations does any real melding of cultures— referred to by some scholars as *cultural hybridity* (Ogan, 2007)—really begin to occur.

Nevertheless, these cultural dispersions have by now wrought significant economic, political, and sociocultural impacts on many societies. For one thing, ethnic dispersions have fostered more diversity, bringing both positive and negative consequences. Many immigrant groups have sought out their own media content, resulting in more multicultural media content in many nations. In the United States, some 10% of total media viewing time is occupied by Spanish-language media. Korean and Chinese soap operas have become popular in Japan (a former enemy and current cultural and economic competitor) and elsewhere in the region, and Middle Eastern media have spread into Europe and the United States, just to name a few examples (Tunstall, 2008). One of the negative influences is greater strife within nations and internationally as well. A recent example was the 2009 elections in Iran, when Iranian descendants in as many as 100 cities around the world held protests, sent and received *Twitter* and *Facebook* feeds from relatives or friends in Tehran, and encouraged their governments to pressure Iranian leaders to reexamine the election results and their internal human rights record (cnn. com, 2009). Martin and Nakayama (1999) noted, "Culture is seen not as stable and orderly, but as a site of struggle for various meanings by competing groups" (p. 7).

Transnationals are affected by the increasing complexity of the multicultural environments in which they operate. No longer, for example, can they plan to build relationships with any one ethnic community in simple geographic terms (Pal & Dutta, 2008). Culture also exhibits itself in other ways, such as through class distinctions. Kanter (1995) distinguished between people who rarely travel far from their own homes and who cling to local roots, versus "cosmopolitans"—people who embrace a global society and are comfortable moving between cultures and countries. These cosmopolitans have subsequently been categorized as an "international business class" (Artz, 2007; L'Etang, 2005, p. 524).

Transnationals also must consider the impact of activist movements that collaborate globally to pressure for change at both local and central levels. Although culture has been defined in hundreds of ways, most incorporate the notion of values, attitudes, and mores shared by all members of the community (Adler & Doktor, 1986). Such a description encompasses activist groups who share concerns over varying societal issues. Pal and Dutta (2008) outlined processes wherein "activist groups have emerged that mobilize locally, as well as globally, to shape global HIV/AIDS policies" (p. 165). Similar groups rally against corporations, even when those entities believe that they have accounted for local sensitivities. For example, when Hong Kong Disney opened, the park accommodated traditional weddings, complete with a menu including shark fin soup. This Chinese delicacy is controversial among animal activists because fishing units often cut off the fins and throw the sharks back into the ocean to die. When activists outside of Hong Kong heard that Disney had placed shark fin on its menus, they pressured the corporation into eliminating this delicacy from the wedding feast (Swann, 2008).

With these cultural influences spanning national borders, it would seem wise for a corporation to mandate a centralized global approach to dealing with these influences. As the Disney experience, Iranian elections, and many other occurrences indicate, the speed and reach of social media can spread any issue around the world within minutes (Gower, 2006; Newsom et at., 2001). Consequently, as Verčič et al. (2001) explained, "A global approach to the definition, dimensions and domain of public relations is needed because wherever one lives his [sic] home base is globalizing and for that reason 'localized' (even if U.S.-based) approaches to public relations are simply inadequate and out-of-synch with the times we live in" (p. 377).

The need for a global approach to public relations has been stressed (Wakefield, 2000, 2001). However, because culture changes slowly (Kramer & Ikeda, 2000), the impacts of local communities have not evaporated and most likely never will go away despite the impetus of globalization. For example, Newsom et al. (2001) state, "Internationally educated practitioners have to understand the ways in which governments control what happens within their borders" (p. 654). Governments have a great impact on media, both mainstream and specialized; they formulate and enforce laws related to ownership and uses of communication tools like telephones, computers, and the Internet; they carve out or deny social benefits to citizens; and they sometimes impose their will against citizens and organizations through their own military and police forces. Artz (2007) also suggested that even those who work for transnational organizations can harbor viewpoints that align more closely with their own cultures than with their distant employer. "This transnational working class still lives primarily on a national level, politically constrained by national borders, laws, and state-enforced coercion, and socially susceptible to nationalism, patriotism, and localism" (p. 152). When even the employees favor all of these familiar confines, certainly others within these same societies would have no predilection to accept "outsider" transnational entities over their own cultural values and mores (see Bardhan & Patwardhan, 2004). At best, they may accommodate transnationals hosted there for the employment they offer and income they bring to the local economy (although it is easy to raise criticism that much of that income goes back to the home country). Local citizens certainly deserve and will demand understanding, respect, and societal participation from these TNCS, but often this respect and understanding is not given by the transnationals that are concentrating solely on profitability. At worst, the local citizens will express outright hostility and anger toward these transnationals that are seen as failing to fulfill their citizenship obligations to the society.

Organizational Response

As is very apparent, the forces of both globalization and of traditional cultural roots significantly impact TNCs. Anything that happens anywhere can create instant public relations issues that must have centralized coordination and communication—between the international public relations staff or service firms, with other employees of the corporation, and with the great diffusion of multicultural and international stakeholders—or the issues will not be adequately resolved. At the same time, solid, long-term relationship building programs in all of the organization's geographic offices or markets, nurtured by practitioners who fully understand those cultures and societies, will both *reduce the chance* of a problem arising in that location and help *reduce the effects* of *any* problem that does arise—either in that market or any other. Therefore, to ensure the best possible environment for global relationship building and support for the organization, public relations programs throughout the world must be globally *coordinated* but not globally *mandated*, and globally *and* locally implemented. While global oversight is crucial, public relations programs which ignore stakeholders in specific geographic locations place their companies at great risk. Scholars such as Sriramesh (2007, 2009) regard this view as ethnocentric and inadequate because, as Verčič et al. (2001) have stated, the local is now globalized. But that, exactly, is my point: precisely because the local is globalized, so is the global localized. The global–local dialectic suggests that one cannot be neatly separated from the other. While it is true that an exclusively localized approach is inadequate, so is an exclusively globalized approach that does not sufficiently account for environmental scanning and relationship building needs wherever a transnational operates.

Most issues do not just appear from nowhere; they have roots that fester somewhere or with someone, and the issues are then orchestrated from those places or by those people. An organization should have sensors in place *everywhere*—not just at headquarters, or in regional offices, or just in given geographic units—in order to reduce the risks of issues arising to surprise the entity. An entity should seek and nurture long-term dialogic relationships and be responsible to their societal obligations, *everywhere*. The megamarketing approach that sees the local as another place to send messages would promote efficiencies by streamlining staff; a corporate mindset that sees public relations as a good insurance policy would have qualified scanners and relationship builders in every unit. Such cross-fertilization provides the best possible opportunity for long-term organizational success in the global society.

Are public relations practitioners fully prepared to understand this globalized world and to successfully implement programs of readiness and response? Has public relations theory assisted this goal? As both Foster (1998) and Verčič (2009) have observed, one of the major public relations challenges in TNCs today is insufficient staffing of qualified practitioners. One of the major skills required of qualified practitioners is intercultural understanding and communication competence. Starck and Kruckeberg (2001) proposed, "The sine qua non of this ... global community is intercultural communication. One of our major goals should be to promote intercultural literacy among present and future practitioners" (p. 58). Doorley and Garcia (2006) added that knowledge beyond the field is imperative: "In order to fully understand the practice of global corporate communication, one must not only understand the basic principles of public relations and corporate communications, but also draw upon a broad range of global society theories, cultural theories, management theories, and communication theories" (p. 243). Foster (1998) also explained that "Skilled international practitioners require a breadth of knowledge and a curiosity about the world.... Often they are proficient in several languages. But the one quality that marks the best of the international public relations professionals is the ability to recognize certain cross-cultural differences and be able to adjust to them" (p. 1).

Conclusion: Transnational Public Relations and Alternative Perspectives

This chapter has attempted to examine public relations as practiced in transnational organizations, with a focus on transnational corporations. It has looked at a theory of international public relations—the generic/specific theory—as one scholarly attempt to guide practitioners in this complex and mostly uncharted arena of public relations. In accordance with Culbertson and Chen's (1996) call for more research that emphasizes public relations practice within transnationals, the generic/specific theory was intended to maintain an organizational perspective. However, it is insufficient to examine organizational behaviors without acknowledging and investigating their concomitant effects on the societies around them, as well as the impacts of the values and behaviors of those societies on the organizations. Because these impacts are interconnected, it is important to have facilitators of mutual satisfaction between organizations and societies. Unfortunately, in the global arena, too often the balance of power between TNCs and the various societies in which they operate is tilted toward the large, powerful organizations, with their enormous resources and influence. This imbalance creates resentments, and it becomes even more imperative for the transnationals to provide these facilitators of mutual satisfaction.

Public relations practitioners who are experienced in the traditional public relations activities of relationship building are perhaps best equipped to perform these facilitation roles. Yet, as stated, the public relations industry seems to be moving away from traditional strategic facilitation roles and into support (figuratively and literally) of megamarketing, where one-way messaging prevails over the necessary activities of interacting with and listening to constituents in society, and helping to reduce fears and concerns about the encroachment of powerful transnationals into local markets around the world. As a result, the hostilities that can arise from these fears are increased when no one in the organization is available to interact with and respond to stakeholders in satisfactory ways.

This book is about differing perspectives in the global public relations environment, and an attempt to bring in suitable alternatives to current thinking and research. In that vein, it must again be noted that the formulation of the generic/specific theory began as an attempt to provide alternative viewpoints in the practice of public relations. Although it does not always turn out this way, exploration should, by its very nature, provide means for alternative ideas, new concepts, and differing viewpoints. Developers of the generic/specific theory attempted to bring these broad-based, international perspectives into the equation by pushing their studies, as best possible, outside of the United States. For example, the Delphi study mentioned previously sought to involve scholars and veteran practitioners from more than 20 nations in the exploration (Wakefield, 1997). Early developers also have carried out case studies related to the theory, first in Slovenia (Verčič et al., 1996), and then in other nations (Sriramesh & Verčič, 2009). In fact, perhaps the best evidence that the generic/specific theory is not altogether steeped in U.S. perspectives is that subsequent investigations founded on the theory have been framed mostly outside of the United States (Sriramesh & Verčič, 2009).

Nevertheless, alternative perspectives on the functioning and effects of public relations in TNCs are still much needed (Molleda & Laskin, 2005). Certainly, for example, much more is needed on the previously mentioned impact of culture on international and transnational public relations practice. Such research particularly must include more perspectives. To some extent, the many descriptive studies of the state of public relations in various nations are helpful; but more of these studies and others must begin to incorporate more in-depth examinations of public relations practices of TNCs operating in the various host nations. As Verčič (2003) mentioned, the public relations practices within transnationals often represent the most innovative and strategic elements of the public relations industry, requiring tremendous coordination and analytical thinking within and across national and cultural boundaries. This being the case, additional studies of both global interaction and of the specific relationship building practices in various parts of the world should be extremely beneficial.

Additional alternative insights would benefit the generic/specific theory, as well. One critical perspective, for example, would be that of host-nation practitioners in TNCs. The generic/specific theory was created largely within a globalized mindset; in other words, understanding was sought on questions such as what are the proper structures, processes, and factors that would influence public relations within a transnational organization? The specific half of the theory was intended to examine the impact of various "local" factors on organizations, and it ultimately has recognized the benefit of involving practitioners from every unit around the world in organizational decision making. However, the unstated notion still was that understanding of these specific variables would make for more effective practice throughout the global entity.

While holistic frameworks are important for guiding effective public relations performance on a global scale, they still represent what could be called an *inside-out* (or from headquarters out) perspective. What should be recognized and studied are the very real impacts of these inside-out frameworks on practitioners in host nations, and in turn the very real effects of the more localized activities and decisions of host-nation practitioners on the global entity. For example, what happens when decisions are handed down that local practitioners not only disagree with but see as particularly problematic within their own cultural settings? Even when host-nation practitioners are supposedly allowed rein to modify and adapt global messages and practices in their own environments, it is entirely possible that they can feel constrained by, and therefore resentful of, global decisions and procedures. How do these constraints and resentments affect their own decisions and activities? Therefore, to create more comprehensive understanding of effective practices of public relations throughout a TNC, more studies are needed from the perspective of host-nation practitioners—an *outside-in* perspective, as it were. Such additional perspectives would help extend understanding of the generic/specific theory.

Discussion Questions

1. In what ways might the generic/specific theory relate to other theories proposed in this book? In what ways is it different?
2. Should public relations that is practiced across political and cultural borders be referred to as *global public relations, transnational public relations, international public relations*, or *intercultural public relations*? What are the similarities and differences between these terms, and what philosophical implications does each term carry into the practice of public relations?
3. This book contains significant discussion on the need for critical examination of public relations theories. Has the author of this chapter offered sufficient critique of the generic/specific theory, or should it be dissected even more? If so, in what ways?
4. In noting Culbertson and Chen's distinction between international and comparative public relations research, the author then points out the argument from Molleda and Laskin that comparative public relations research really has not been conducted yet. Do you agree with this or not? If this is the case, how might scholars proceed with research that will build comparisons of public relations from nation to nation or culture to culture?
5. The author suggests that increasing devotion to the "megamarketing" model in society has made it increasingly easy for TNC public relations staff to ignore cultural imperatives when making and implementing global decisions. Do you agree or disagree with this assertion. Why?
6. The author suggests that TNC public relations programs which ignore either the local or the global in their public relations activities "put their companies at great risk." Do you agree or disagree with this statement. If you disagree, why? If you agree, what would this

suggest for how a TNC should organize and implement its public relations program to reduce the risk?

7. In TNCs, is relationship building with stakeholders the most important public relations activity, or is it most important to ensure that the TNC concentrate most on disseminating its messages in culturally appropriate ways? Are they equally important? In any case, justify your answer.

8. Is the generic/specific theory still relevant today as a model for public relations in a rapidly globalizing world, or have the Internet and other factors of globalization made it so that the original distinctions or separations between the global and the local are no longer needed?

Notes

1. In the Delphi study, language was proposed as another variable because in actual practice in transnational companies it always seems to be a challenge related to, but also distinct from, culture. Others in the development team felt there was too little difference to keep language as a separate variable (see, e.g., Verčič et al., 1996).

2. Interestingly, after conducting an exhaustive content analysis of international public relations research to date, Molleda and Laskin (2005) described these types of studies as attempts to fill the comparative research domain mentioned by Culbertson and Chen (1996). However, the authors then contended that while many of these studies have been conducted in various countries, the studies actually cannot be classified as comparative because no one has yet accumulated them to compare or contrast the various national environments and relate their effect on public relations practice.

3. Sriramesh actually is the greatest advocate in the public relations field for its practitioners all over the world to understand and appropriately respond to the effects of culture on the practice. His book chapters (Sriramesh, 2007; Sriramesh & White, 1992) that I have liberally cited here, among many others are well worth reading to understand his feelings on this important subject. Careful reading of them would show that his statements are not contradictory at all, but reflect the multicultural complexities of publics in a transnational world.

References

Adler, N., & Doktor, R. (1986). From the Atlantic to the Pacific century: Cross-cultural management reviewed. *Journal of Management, 12*(2), 295–318.

Appadurai, A. (1990). Disjuncture and difference in the global cultural economy. In M. Featherstone (Ed.), *Global culture: Nationalism, globalization, and modernity* (pp. 295–310). London: Sage.

Artz, L. (2007). The corporate model from national to transnational. In L. Artz & Y. R. Kamalipour (Eds.), *The media globe: Trends in international mass media* (pp. 141–162). Lanham, MD: Rowan & Littlefield.

Bardhan, N., & Patwardhan, P. (2004). Multinational corporations and public relations in a traditionally resistant host culture. *Journal of Communication Management, 8*(3), 246–263.

Botan, C. (1992). International public relations: Critique and reformulation. *Public Relations Review, 18*(2), 149–159.

Brinkerhoff, D. W., & Ingle, M. (1991). *Improving development program performance: Guidelines for managers.* Boulder, CO: Lynne Rienner.

Burson, H. (2004, October). *Is public relations now too important to be left to public relations professionals?* Annual distinguished lecture of the Institute for Public Relations, London.

Bush, L. (2007). Focusing on strategy: Moving beyond media relations and getting to the new brand marketing table. *The Public Relations Strategist, 13*(2), 30–32.

cnn.com (2009, July 25). Global protests staged over post-election crackdown in Iran. Retrieved from http://www.cnn.com/2009/WORLD/meast/07/25/iran. world.protests/index.html

Culbertson, H. M., & Chen, N. (1996). *International public relations: A comparative analysis.* Mahwah, NJ: Erlbaum.

Curtin, P. A., & Gaither, T. K. (2005). Privileging identity, difference, and power: The circuit of culture as a basis for public relations theory. *Journal of Public Relations Research, 17*(2), 91–115.

Delbecq, A. L., Van de Ven, A. H., & Gustafson, D. H. (1975). *Group techniques for program planning: A guide to nominal group and Delphi processes.* Glenview, IL: Scott-Foresman.

Doorley, J., & Garcia, H. F. (2006). *Reputation management: The key to successful public relations and corporate communications.* New York: Routledge.

Duncan, T., & Moriarty, S. (1998). A communications-based marketing model for managing relationships. *Journal of Marketing, 62*(2), 1–13.

Ehling, W. P., White, J., & Grunig, J. E. (1992). Public relations and marketing practices. In J. E. Grunig (Ed.), *Excellence in public relations and communication management* (pp. 357–394). Hillsdale, NJ: Erlbaum.

Foster, L. (1998). Atlas award lecture on international public relations. *International Section Monograph* (Vol. 2). New York: Public Relations Society of America.

Friedman, T. L. (2000). *The Lexus and the olive tree.* New York: Anchor Books.

Friedman, T. L. (2002). *Longitudes and attitudes: Exploring the world after September 11.* New York: Farrar, Straus, & Giroux.

Gower, K. K. (2006). Public relations research at the crossroads. *Public Relations Research Journal, 18*(2), 177–190.

Grunig, J. E. (Ed.). (1992). *Excellence in public relations and communication management.* Hillsdale, NJ: Erlbaum.

Grunig, J. E. (2006). Furnishing the edifice: Research on public relations as a strategic management function. *Journal of Public Relations Research, 18*(2), 151–176.

Grunig, J. E., & Hunt, T. (1984). *Managing public relations.* New York: Holt, Rinehart, & Winston.

Harris, T. L. (1995). IMC: A concept for today. *The Public Relations Strategist*, *1*(4), 28–31.

Heath. R. L. (2001). Shifting foundations: Public relations as relationship building. In R. L. Heath (Ed.), *Handbook of public relations* (pp. 1–9). Thousand Oaks, CA: Sage.

Hofstede, G. (1980). *Culture's consequences*. Beverly Hills, CA: Sage.

Holtzhausen, D. R. (2000). Postmodern values in public relations. *Journal of Public Relations Research, 12* (1), 93–114.

Holtzhausen, D. R. (2007). Activism. In E. L. Toth (Ed.), *The future of excellence in public relations and communication management* (pp. 357–379). Mahwah, NJ: Erlbaum.

Holtzhausen, D. R., Petersen, B. K., & Tindall, N. T. J. (2003). Exploding the myth of the symmetrical/asymmetrical dichotomy: Public relations models in the new South Africa. *Journal of Public Relations Research, 15*(4), 305–341.

Holtzhausen, D. R., & Voto, R. (2002). Resistance from the margins: The postmodern public relations practitioner as organizational activist. *Journal of Public Relations Research, 14*(1), 57–84.

Hung, C. J. F. (2007). Toward the theory of relationship management in public relations: How to cultivate quality relationships? In E. L. Toth (Ed.), *The future of excellence in public relations and communication management* (pp. 443–476). Mahwah, NJ: Erlbaum.

Hutton, J. G. (2001). Defining the relationship between public relations and marketing. In R. L. Heath (Ed.), *Handbook of public relations* (pp. 205–214). Thousand Oaks, CA: Sage.

Ihlen, Ø., & van Ruler, B. (2007). How public relations works: Theoretical roots and public relations perspectives. *Public Relations Review, 33*(3), 243–248.

Kanter, R. M. (1995). *World class*. New York: Simon & Schuster.

Klein, N. (2000). *No logo: Taking aim at the brand bullies*. London: Flamingo.

Kotkin, J. (1993). *Tribes: How race, religion, and identity determine success in the new global economy*. New York: Random House.

Kramer, E. M., & Ikeda, R. (2000). The changing faces of reality. *Keio Communication Review, 22*, 79–109.

Lauzen, M. M., & Dozier, D. M. (1992). The missing link: The public relations manager role as mediator of organizational environments and power consequences for the function. *Journal of Public Relations Research, 4*(4), 205–220.

L'Etang, J. (2005). Critical public relations: Some reflections. *Public Relations Review, 31*(4), 521–526.

Macnamara, J. (2006, September). *The fork in the road of media communication practice and theory*. Paper presented at the 4th Annual Summit on Measurement, Portsmouth, NH.

Martin, J. N., & Nakayama, T. K. (1999). Thinking dialectically about culture and communication. *Communication Theory, 9*(1), 1–25.

Maynard, M. L. (2003). From global to glocal: How Gillette's SensorExcel accommodates to Japan. *Keio Communication Review, 25*, 57–75.

Metzler, M. S. (2001). The centrality of organizational legitimacy to public relations practice. In R. L. Heath (Ed.), *Handbook of public relations* (pp. 205–214). Thousand Oaks, CA: Sage.

Micklethwait, J., & Wooldridge, A. (2000). *A future perfect: The challenge and hidden promise of globalization.* New York: Crown Business.

Mintzberg, H. (1983). *Power in and around organizations.* Englewood Cliffs, NJ: Prentice-Hall.

Moffitt, M. A. (2005). Comments on special issue public relations from the margins. *Journal of Public Relations Research, 17*(1), 3–4.

Molleda, J. C., & Laskin, A. V. (2005). *Global, international, comparative, and regional public relations knowledge from 1990 to 2005: A quantitative content analysis of academic and trade publications.* Retrieved from www. instituteforpr.org/files/uploads/Falconi_Nov06.pdf

Morley, M. (1998). *How to manage your global reputation: A guide to the dynamics of international public relations.* London: Macmillan.

Murphy, P. (1991). The limits of symmetry: A game theory approach to symmetric and asymmetric public relations. In J. E. Grunig & L. A. Grunig (Eds.), *Public Relations Research Annual, 3,* 115–132.

Newsom, D., Turk, J. V., & Kruckeberg, D. (2001). International public relations: Focus on pedagogy. In R. L. Heath (Ed.), *Handbook of public relations* (pp. 649–658). Thousand Oaks, CA: Sage.

Ogan, C. L. (2007). Communication and culture. In Y. R. Kamalipour (Ed.), *Global communication* (2nd ed., pp. 293–318). Belmont, CA: Thomson-Wadsworth.

Pal, M., & Dutta, M. J. (2008). Public relations in a global context: The relevance of critical modernism as a theoretical lens. *Journal of Public Relations Research, 20*(2), 159–179.

Panzner, M. J. (2009). *When giants fall: An economic roadmap for the end of the American era.* Hoboken, NJ: Wiley.

Pieczka, M. (1996). Paradigms, systems theory and public relations. In J. L'Etang & M. Pieczka (Eds.), *Critical perspectives in public relations* (pp. 124–156). London: International Thomson Business Press.

Robertson, R. (1990). Mapping the global condition: Globalization as the central concept. In M. Featherstone (Ed.), *Global culture: Nationalism, globalization and modernity* (pp. 15–30). London: Sage.

Robertson, R. (1996). Comments on the "global triad" and "glocalization." In N. Inoue (Ed.), *Globalization and indigenous culture* (pp. 217–225). Tokyo, Japan: Kokugakuin University.

Roper, J. (2005). Symmetrical communication: Excellent public relations or a strategy for hegemony? *Journal of Public Relations Research, 17*(1), 69–86.

Severin, W. J., & Tankard, J. W., Jr. (2001). *Communication theories: Origins, methods and uses in the mass media* (5th ed.). New York: Longman.

Sirkin, H. L., Hemerling, J. W., & Bhattacharya, A. K. (2008). *Globality: Competing with everyone from everywhere for everything.* London: Headline.

Sriramesh, K. (2007). The relationship between culture and public relations. In E. L. Toth (Ed.), *The future of excellence in public relations and communication management* (pp. 507–526). Mahwah, NJ: Erlbaum.

Sriramesh, K. (2009). Introduction. In K. Sriramesh & D. Verčič (Eds.), *The global public relations handbook: Theory, research, and practice* (rev. ed., pp. xxxiii–xl). New York: Routledge.

Sriramesh, K., & Verčič, D. (Eds.). (2003). *The global public relations handbook*. Mahwah, NJ: Erlbaum.

Sriramesh, K., & Verčič, D. (Eds.). (2009). *The global public relations handbook* (rev. ed.). New York: Routledge.

Sriramesh, K., & White, J. (1992). Societal culture and public relations: In J. E. Grunig (Ed.), *Excellence in public relations and communication management* (pp. 597–616). Hillsdale, NJ: Erlbaum.

Starck, K., & Kruckeberg, D. (2001). Public relations and community: A reconstructed theory revisited. In R. L. Heath (Ed.), *Handbook of public relations* (pp. 51–60). Thousand Oaks, CA: Sage.

Stiglitz, J. (2002). *Globalization and its discontents*. London: Penguin Books.

Stoker, K. L., & Tusinski, K. A. (2006). Reconsidering public relations' infatuation with dialogue: Why engagement and reconciliation can be more ethical than symmetry and reciprocity. *Journal of Mass Media Ethics, 21*(2&3), 156–176.

Swann, P. (2008). *Cases in public relations management*. Boston, MA: McGraw-Hill.

Traverse-Healy, T. (1991). The corporate aspect. In M. Nally (Ed.), *International public relations in practice* (pp. 31–39). London: Kogan Page.

Tunstall, J. (2008). *The media were American: U.S. mass media in decline*. New York: Oxford University Press.

Verčič, D. (2003). Public relations of movers and shakers: Transnational corporations. In K. Sriramesh & D. Verčič (Eds.), *The global public relations handbook: Theory, research, and practice* (pp. 478–489). Mahwah, NJ: Erlbaum.

Verčič, D. (2009). Public relations of movers and shakers: Transnational corporations. In K. Sriramesh & D. Verčič (Eds.), *The global public relations handbook* (rev. ed., pp. 795–806). New York: Routledge.

Verčič, D., Grunig, L. A., & Grunig, J. E. (1996). Global and specific principles of public relations: Evidence from Slovenia. In H. Culbertson & N. Chen (Eds.), *International public relations: A comparative analysis* (pp. 31–66). Mahwah, NJ: Erlbaum.

Verčič, D., van Ruler, B., Butschi, G., & Flodin, B. (2001). On the definition of public relations: A European view. *Public Relations Review, 27*(4), 373–387.

Vogl, F., & Sinclair, J. (1996). *Boom: Visions and insights for creating wealth in the 21st century*. Chicago: Irwin Professional.

Wakefield, R. (1997). *International public relations: A theoretical approach to excellence based on a worldwide Delphi study* (Unpublished doctoral dissertation). University of Maryland, College Park.

Wakefield, R. (2000). World-class public relations: A model for effective public relations in the multinational. *Journal of Communication Management, 5*(1), 59–71.

Wakefield, R. (2001). Public relations in the multinational organization. In R. L. Heath, (Ed.), *Handbook of public relations* (pp. 639–648). Thousand Oaks, CA: Sage.

Suggested Readings

Banks, S. P. (1995). *Multicultural public relations: A social-interpretive approach.* Thousand Oaks, CA: Sage.

Ellingsworth, H. W. (1977). Conceptualizing intercultural communication. *Communication Yearbook 1,* 99–106.

Freitag, A. R., & Stokes, A. Q. (2009). *Global public relations: Spanning borders, spanning cultures.* New York: Routledge.

Grunig, L. A., Grunig, J. E., & Dozier, D. M. (2002). *Excellent public relations and effective organizations: A study of communication management in three countries.* Mahwah, NJ: Erlbaum.

Inglehart, R., & Baker, W. E. (2000). Modernization, cultural change, and the persistence of traditional values. *American Sociological Review, 65* (1), 19–51.

Nigh, D., & Cochran, P. (1987). Issues management and the multinational enterprise. *Management International Review, 27*(1), 4–12.

Rhee, Y. (2002). Global public relations: A cross-cultural study of the excellence theory in South Korea. *Journal of Public Relations Research, 14*(3), 159–184.

Sahlins, M. (1999). Two or three things that I know about culture. *Journal of the Royal Anthropological Institute, 5*(33), 399–421.

Chapter 8

Public Relations and Marginalization in a Global Context

A Postcolonial Critique

Mohan Jyoti Dutta and Mahuya Pal

Contemporary globalization processes are marked by the increasing flow of goods and labor across national borders, accompanied by the increasing control of global economies in the hands of a few transnational corporations (TNCs). Simultaneously, the global landscape has witnessed increasing inequalities between haves and have-nots across various sectors, the failure of global economies that demonstrate the limits of the free market logic, the continuous reinvention of symbolic representations that seek to reproduce the agendas of this free market logic, and increasing opportunities for resistance across the various sectors of the globe that seek to rupture the hegemony of free market logic (Pal & Dutta, 2008a, 2008b). At the heart of globalization is the neoliberal logic, a theoretical and pragmatic lens that primarily vouches for political and economic configurations on the basis of free markets with minimum state involvement, manifested through privatization, deregulation, withdrawal of the state from many areas of social provision, and opening up of nation-states to foreign investment and foreign capital (Harvey, 2005).

Globalization, played out through the neoliberal logic that has been propagated over the last three decades by powerful political, economic, and social actors at the center, has been marked by the growth and rapid spread of TNCs, thereby consolidating power and control in the hands of a few dominant economic structures (Pal & Dutta, 2008a, 2008b). The interests, reach, and control of these TNCs have been supported by dominant nation-states at the center and by their institutions (treasury departments, the central banks), international organizations that regulate global trade and finance (such as the International Monetary Fund, World Trade Organization), civil society organizations, and local elites that stand to benefit from the economic and political control afforded by neoliberalism (Dutta, 2009; Harvey, 2003, 2005). This configuration of TNCs, nation-states, international institutions, civil society, and local elites is referred to as *transnational hegemony*. In the face of the globalization of power and control in the hands of transnational hegemony and the increasing inequalities between the haves and have-nots, forms of resistance have been organized locally as well as globally in order to bring about structural transformations (Pal & Dutta, 2008b). Central to these global systems of power and control and the processes of organizing that resist such control are public relations practices that manufacture, reproduce, and circulate symbolic representations and interpretive frames that carry out the agendas of globalization, as well as open up opportunities for resistance. The intersections of TNCs, nation-states, and globally situated pockets of resistance, and the central role of public relations practices in the realm of the materiality of the contemporary economic landscape, bring about opportunities for theorizing about the ways in which postcolonial theory informs how we understand and practice public relations.

Postcolonial theory examines the symbolic representations and material relationships that underlie processes of colonization, offering openings for emancipatory politics that challenge the systematic erasures of the narratives of oppression and exploitation embedded in colonial and contemporary neocolonial configurations, and creating spaces for listening to the voices of the subaltern sectors of the globe that have hitherto been treated as subjects to be scripted, coded, and worked over within dominant knowledge structures. Central to the articulations of postcolonial theory, then, are the possibilities of transforming those very epistemic structures that sustain and reproduce the agendas of colonialism/neocolonialism in the realm of modernity, rendering knowledge as an inherently political entity embedded within the politics, history, and geography of modern knowledge structures and their colonial agendas. A postcolonial lens lends itself particularly well to public relations theorizing because it explores the ways in which: (a) public relations practices serve the interests of TNCs and the free market logic that upholds their dominance; (b) public relations theories maintain the hegemony of West-centric articulations of modernity and development, thus contributing to the hegemony of Western configurations in the global landscape; and (c) resistive politics among the subaltern sectors seek to transform the global inequities in knowledge production, participation, and resource distribution, even as these opportunities for transformative politics are continually threatened by the cooptive politics of transnational hegemony.

Given the fluidity of the global processes we are experiencing today even as global structures are continually seeking to consolidate their powers, multiple dialectical tensions play out in the theorization of public relations in the realm of globalization (Pal & Dutta, 2008a, 2008b). For instance, the postcolonial context of public relations practice is rife with tensions between the local and the global. Globally situated policies and practices of TNCs continually negotiate with the local cultural contexts of dispersed yet interconnected global spaces. Similarly, tensions emerge in the centralization of power/control and the opening up of resistive possibilities that seek to transform the structures of inequality and injustice.

Throughout this chapter, we engage with the various dialectical tensions that emerge as we discuss postcolonial theory in the realm of public relations. Specifically, we examine the geopolitics of global public relations practices that continue to serve the agendas of neocolonialism, and the ways in which geopolitical institutions are resisted by activist politics. We begin by offering an overview of postcolonial theory, situating the discussion of the theory within the disciplinary moves in communication, and wrap up with a discussion of the theory in the realm of recent critiques in the public relations literature. This is followed by an overview of recent discussions of globalization in the public relations literature. Finally, a postcolonial lens is offered to critically interrogate the interplay of power and control in the geopolitics of contemporary public relations practices in the global landscape, offering the foundation for a discussion of the possibilities of resistive politics that promises to disrupt the hegemonic configurations of the status quo.

Power, Control, Postcoloniality, and Globalization

Postcolonial theory primarily engages with the dominant power of the West that imperializes developing nations by advancing the modernist logic of progress and development to justify global capitalism. It questions the idea of linear progress by drawing attention to the differences that have emerged economically and politically in the global situation. Identifying capitalism as West-centric, postcolonial theory interrogates issues related to inequality and exploitation in the capitalist world order (Dirlik, 2000; Shome & Hegde, 2002). Fundamental to the new form of global capitalism is the "transnationalization of production" (Dirlik, 2000, p. 224), where technologies provide a new temporal and spatial dimension to production with the goal of seeking maximum benefits for capital against labor. This new phase of global capitalism is driven by TNCs that are at the center of economic activities (Dirlik, 2000; Miller & Dinan, 2003, 2007; Miyoshi, 1993).

Postcolonial theory is committed to developing a critique of colonialism and imperialism. While colonialism typically is defined as overt coercion in the form of territorial occupation, imperialism is an act of economic and political domination. Generally speaking, postcolonial theory argues that under global capitalism Western power seeks to establish its hegemony not only politically, militarily, and economically, but also culturally and ideologically (Prasad, 2003). Postcolonial theory is thus rooted in decolonizing the mind at political, economic, and cultural levels with the goal of achieving a more equitable global system.

Some of the foundational concepts in postcolonial theory can be attributed to several influential theorists. Said's (1979) notion of "Orientalism" deconstructs Western discourses or cultural representations of the Orient. Said argued that the Orient is not Oriental in the commonplace sense, but that it was made to be Oriental, which dislocates the "familiar" concept of the Orient to expose how the Other helps define the West via contrasting languages, experiences, and images in "a relationship of power, of domination, of varying degrees of a complex hegemony" (p. 5). Bhabha (1994) points out that the idea of Otherness is an ambivalent simultaneous production of "an object of desire and derision" (p. 67). On one hand, colonial discourse suggests that the non-West is a category that is radically situated as the Other, outside of the West. On the other hand, it draws the non-West into the West by way of Western epistemologies. Hence, Bhabha forwards the concept of ambivalence in defining postcolonial subject positions. Articulating the division between the West and the non-West as the fundamental epistemological and ontological basis of the relational space within which the West and the Orient are projected, Said (1979) wrote:

> Orientalism depends for its strategy on this flexible positional superiority, which puts the Westerner in a whole series of possible relationships with the Orient without ever losing him the relative upper hand. And why should it have been otherwise, especially during the period of extraordinary European ascendancy from the late Renaissance to the present? (pp. 7–8)

Essential to the political economy of Western epistemology is the creation of the dichotomy between the West and the non-West that serves as the ontological basis of Western knowledge, which in turn is mobilized as the rationale for Western interventions.

Gayatri Spivak (1999, 2003) interrogates the colonial histories and geographies of disciplinary structures and institutional knowledge that constitutes the Anglo-European academy and reinforces the transformative impulse of postcolonial studies. Her scholarship has charted an intellectual trajectory that covers feminist deconstruction, Marxist critiques of international divisions of labor and the global flow of capital, critiques of imperial and colonial discourses, and critiques of race in the context of the intersections among nationality, ethnicity, and the politics of representation in a neocolonial world (Landry & MacLean, 1996). These provocative works provide rich theoretical linkages between colonialism and knowledge. The engagement of postcolonial studies with issues of race, class, gender, and sexuality in relation to geopolitical arrangements of nations and international histories sets it apart from other forms of critical scholarship.

It is also this demonstration of the structure of world power relations as a legacy of Western imperialism that makes postcolonial studies relevant in the context of globalization. Globalization has led to a number of situations—migration of people, blurring of national and economic boundaries, simultaneous homogenization and fragmentation within and across societies, and the interpenetration of global and local among other phenomena (Appadurai, 1995; Dirlik, 1995). A postcolonial lens critically explores these phenomena and argues that global capitalism manipulates the local for the interest of the global. Dirlik (1995) writes:

> What is ironic is that the managers of this world situation themselves concede the concentration of power in their (or their organizations') hands; as well as their manipulation of peoples, boundaries and cultures to appropriate the local for the global, to admit different cultures in the realm of capital only to break them down and to remake them in accordance with the requirements of production and consumption, and even to reconstitute subjectivities across national boundaries to create producers and consumers more responsive to the operations of capital. (p. 466)

The local has emerged not only as a site of manipulation for operations of capital that needs to be assimilated with global culture, but also as a site of resistance. In other words, the local becomes a site of complex forces. Postcolonial theory powerfully reminds us that such complexities need to be situated within the context of imperial centers, and the present and historical moments. Hence, as Shome and Hegde (2002) suggest, a postcolonial intervention enables more "socially responsible problematizations of communication" (p. 261) with the goal of eventually producing "a more just and equitable knowledge base about the third world, the other, and the 'rest' of the world" (p. 261).

Postcolonial theory urges us to disrupt the neocolonial interests of transnational hegemony by taking an activist stance in our articulations of knowledge. Given the spatiality of power and control in the ways in which resources are distributed and exploited, it is essential to explore the symbolic representations of the categories of the "West" and the "Third" that sustain colonial/neocolonial processes.

West-Centric Knowledge Structures

Central to the circulation of colonial/neocolonial practices is the symbolic representation of the necessity for colonization, justifying the violence of occupation, control, and exploitation. Any colonizing mission is justified rhetorically by the mantra of lifting the "burden of the soul," of delivering the "primitive" people of a "primitive" space from their savagery through the messages of enlightenment. The existence of colonialism is predicated upon dominance of the epistemology of colonialism that sets up the dichotomy of primitive/modern. Modernity is juxtaposed against the backdrop of the primitive spaces of the "Third World" that need enlightenment. Structures of knowledge (universities, research centers, grants, think tanks, etc.) are created and supported for the purposes of carrying out the interests of colonialism/neocolonialism. Therefore, an entire industry of academic, development, and marketing practices are manufactured to ensure the production and perpetuation of symbolic resources and practices that are at the core of colonialism/neocolonialism. These practices circulate the dichotomies of developed/underdeveloped to justify colonialism and the exploitation of the "Third" under the guise of offering aid and bringing about progress.

The hegemony of West-centric ways of knowing was often accomplished through the languages of rationality, science and medicine, positioned as the antithesis of the irrationalities of the natives (Dutta-Bergman, 2005a, 2005b). In contemporary discursive spaces, the interests of knowledge structures are weaved in with the interests of modernity. Knowledge, therefore, is intrinsically linked to the mercenary interests of the dominant institutions of capitalism (Dutta, 2008, 2009), and validates, privileges, and foregrounds certain forms of knowing that continue to celebrate the dominance of the West and Western institutions over other forms of knowledge from the "Third."

Capitalism, Modernity, and Colonial Agendas

One of the core elements of colonialism is the economic gain attached to the occupation of the space of the "Third." Occupied colonies offer cheap resources and labor for the production of commodities of modernity that then are sold to the markets created in the colonies, thus generating systems of profit for colonial institutions. Configurations of colonialism developed hand-in-hand with the interests of capitalist institutions to make profit, offering cheap sources of labor and ready-made markets for the commodities manufactured in the Empire. This linkage between colonialism and capitalism is aptly noted by Hegel:

> Through a dialectical impulse to transcend itself that is proper to it, such a society [capitalist market society] is, in the first place, driven to seek outside itself new consumers. For this reason it seeks to find ways to move about among other peoples that are inferior to it with respect to the resources it has in abundance, or in general its industry.... The development of relations offers also the means of coloni-

zation towards which, in either an accidental or systematic way, a completed civil society is impelled. (as quoted in Beverly, 1999, p. 121)

At the heart of colonialism, then, is its attachment with the market and its consensual relationship with the flow of capital; it offers the basis for the operation of capitalism (Marx, 1867/1965). Colonialism supplies the raw materials, labor, and market for the operation of capitalism. In the contemporary global configuration, the modernist tropes of capitalism are circulated through mainstream mediated and other communication channels, through knowledge structures, and through development-based public relations campaigns that often mask the hegemonic interests of TNCs.

It is in this realm of the flow of capital, then, that colonial agendas enjoy a two-way relationship with modernity and modernist institutions. On the one hand, the economic base of modernity is served by colonial agendas; on the other hand, the symbolic representation of modernity serves colonialism by making colonial interventions appear necessary and normal. Modernity is carried out through the consumption of goods and services produced by modernist institutions (e.g., TNCs); therefore, in order to perpetuate this logic, subjects in colonies are turned into mass consumers of products and services manufactured by the modernist institutions. Articulations of development/underdevelopment are continuously mobilized in order to serve the interests of neoimperial powers and transnational hegemonies. Profit making gets tied to notions of development; whereas development offers the rationale for neocolonial interventions, and profit making remains the ultimate objective. This consensual relationship between development and profit making is well articulated in the following policy report of the United States Agency for International Development (USAID, 2002):

> Successful development abroad generates diffuse benefits. It opens new, more dynamic markets for US goods and services. It generates more secure, promising environments for US investment. It creates zones of order and peace where Americans can travel, study, exchange, and do business safely. And it produces allies—countries that share US commitments to economic openness, political freedom, and the rule of law. (p. 2)

Development here serves as a strategic tool for opening up the markets of the "underdeveloped" economies to TNCs. Through the language of development, the United States finds a way to intervene, colonize, and ultimately create markets for U.S. investments, goods, and services. Most importantly, development offers the mechanism for spreading the mantras of neoliberalism through educational initiatives, public outreach, government lobbying, funding of favorable civil society organizations, development campaigns, and a wide variety of media relations activities.

In the contemporary global configuration, neocolonialism takes up various faces ranging from direct occupation of land that is similar to past forms of colonialism, to indirect occupation through the manipulation of nation-states to buy into the economic agendas of neocolonialism. Contemporary forms of neocolonialism transcend the historic location of power and control in the hands of a nation-state and locate power and control in the hands of clusters of TNCs and nation-states (thereby aiding transnational hegemony). Although transnational hegemony enacts its power beyond the traditional boundaries of nation-states, nation-states continue to be relevant as they serve as key players in carrying out, globally, the agendas of transnational hegemony.

Transnational Corporations, Nation-States, and Civil Society

Postcolonial theory is particularly relevant in the context of contemporary globalization processes as it offers a theoretical lens for examining the ways in which the intersections of TNCs, nation-states, global policy organizations, civil society, and local elites work hand-in-hand to perpetuate their neoliberal interests.

Inherent in the neoliberal configuration is the protection of the interests of private property owners, TNCs, and financial capital. Accordingly, the impetus is on channeling the influences of local, national, and global policies to facilitate the operation of free markets and free trade, with minimal state intervention. The role of the state, then, is to ensure the operation of the free market, at the same time intervening minimally once the market has been created in order to ensure that this market operates smoothly under its so-called free market logic. The paradox of neoliberalism lies in the very role of the state in enacting structural violence to ensure the smooth running of the TNCs. This is well articulated by Harvey (2005):

> The role of the state is to create and preserve an institutional framework appropriate to such practices. The state has to guarantee, for example, the quality and integrity of money. It must also set up those military, defense, police, and legal structures and functions required to secure private property rights and to guarantee, by force if need be, the proper functioning of markets. Furthermore, if markets do not exist (in such areas as land, water, education, health care, social security, or environmental pollution) then they must be created, by state action if necessary. (p. 2)

Against the backdrop of these state-sponsored systems and mechanisms of power and control that lie at the base of neoliberalism, the core of the neoliberal logic perpetuates the idea of minimal state intervention, deregulation, privatization, and the withdrawal of the state from many areas of social provision that were previously considered the responsibilities of the state. Harvey (2005) goes on to note:

> But beyond these tasks the state should not venture. State interventions in markets (once created) must be kept to a bare minimum because, according to the theory, the state cannot possibly possess enough information to second-guess market signals (prices) and because powerful interest groups will inevitably distort and bias state interventions (particularly in democracies) for their own benefit. (p. 2)

Worth noting here is the irony implicit in the conceptualization of the state in its relationship to multinational and transnational corporations. While on the one hand, the state serves as a mechanism for exerting power and control in order to ensure the creation and maintenance of markets, the role of the state is simultaneously omitted in the realm of regulating the profit-making ventures of private corporations. As a result, the state becomes a colonizing tool that continually serves the interests of the dominant social classes to enjoy profit and to maintain class power (Harvey, 2005).

Intrinsic in the processes of globalization is the formation of a social class that enjoys maximum power and control over social, economic, and political processes across the various sectors of the globe, and the simultaneous disenfranchisement of the lower classes from social, economic, and political processes where policies are made, debated, and implemented (Dutta, 2009; Pal & Dutta, 2008a, 2008b). As a result, globalization is marked by increasing inequalities at both the local and global levels, with a limited number of people having access to the majority of the resources of the globe, as a large majority of others struggle to barely make a living. A postcolonial lens applied to these increasing disparities between the haves and have-nots brings to the fore the necessity for looking beyond nation-states to examining the ways in which processes of exploitation and control play out globally; simultaneously, a postcolonial stance also calls for a reading of the global processes of power and control in terms of the agendas carried out by dominant nation-states at the center to continue to oppress and control nation-states at the periphery, utilizing the same colonial logics of development and enlightenment that have been historically used in the context of territorial colonization. Worth noting here is the clustering of TNCs within a certain configuration of nation-states at the center, and the continual utilization of national agendas and resources in the international arena to secure the interests of TNCs.

In the most recent example of Iraq, its penetration, and the subsequent occupation by the United States under the pretext of bringing freedom to the people of Iraq (through the unjust occupation of their land) served as the perfect set-up for establishing a neoliberal dream project in that country, a kind of state apparatus that Harvey (2005) calls a *neoliberal state* (p. 7), embodying the interests of private property owners, businesses, TNCs, and financial capital. Paul Bremmer, head of the Coalition Provisional Authority that was set up to run the newly occupied state spelled out four orders, including "the full privatization of public enterprises, full ownership rights by foreign firms of Iraqi businesses, full repatriation of foreign profits ... the opening of Iraq's banks to foreign control, national treatment for foreign countries and ... the elimination of nearly all trade barriers" (p. 6) to be applied to all areas of the economy including public services, the media, manufacturing, services, transportation, finance, and construction. This mandate was accompanied by strict regulation of labor, forbidding strikes and the right to unionize. The rhetoric of freedom and freeing the Iraqi people served as the façade for the neoimperial interests of the United States and the political-economic interests of TNCs. This is a prime example of how conglomeration of terms such as *democracy* and *freedom* can ultimately serve as justifications for the penetration and occupation of "Third World" spaces.

Furthermore, in the global politics of neoliberalism, those nation-states that receive aid agree to adjust their economic structures along the lines of the dictates laid out by the International Monetary Fund (IMF), the World Bank, and the World Trade Organization (WTO) (Harvey, 2005). The WTO and the World Bank serve as the primary channels for securing global markets for TNCs, dictating national policies, and exerting power and control over these policies to align them along the agendas of the TNCs. Monopolistic control over international policies held by private corporations becomes evident in the shaping of the Uruguay Round of General Agreement on Trade and Tariffs (GATT), which later led to the formation of the WTO, by agricultural giants such as Cargill and Monsanto.

Also critical to the global penetration of transnational hegemony is the role of civil society organizations in carrying out the agendas of TNCs, in opening up markets to foreign investments, liberalizing local economies, privatizing the public sectors, and in creating public opinion that is supportive of the broader goals of TNCs. Veiled under the chador of development aid, public relations tactics are put into place in Third World spaces in order to bring about support for the objectives of transnational hegemony. In Chile for example, between 1963 and 1973, U.S. corporations, the Central Intelligence Agency (CIA), and the U.S. Secretary of State worked hand-in-hand with domestic business elites to promote their agenda. And from 1970, they worked to undermine the democratically elected government of Salvador Allende, to violently repress all social movements and political organizations of the left, and to sponsor multiple civil society organizations run by the local elite that would carry out the agendas of neoliberalization, opening up the domestic market to foreign (read U.S.) capital and businesses (Dutta-Bergman, 2005a).

Resistive Politics

Historically, the forces of colonialism have also given rise to forms of resistance that operate across micro, meso, and macro levels locally as well as globally, seeking to challenge the oppressive forces of colonialism, working within them in new ways, and working to transform the oppressive structures of capitalism that limit the opportunities for listening to subaltern voices across the globe (Pal & Dutta, 2008b). These forms of resistance are situated locally; they also connect globally across national boundaries in order to influence global policies. Narratives of colonialism coexist with narratives of resistance that seek to rupture the dominant narratives of power and control through which the colonial forces created their systems of oppression.

Take for instance the protest organized by the residents of the Bolivian city of Cochabamba in 2000 against the high cost of privatized water sold by Aguas del Tunari, a subsidiary of Bechtel (Olivera, 2004). Even in the face of state sponsored violence that sought to thwart the protest and unleashed terror on the citizens, the protests continued, ultimately forcing the government to cancel the contract. Similarly, in Dabhol, India, women led the protests against the construction of the Dabhol Power Plant in 1997, a collaborative venture among three U.S.-based multinational corporations (Enron, General Electric, and Bechtel) (Bhavnani, Foran, & Kurian, 2003). It is in these spaces of resistive practices that alternative imaginations of public relations as a field of engagement that imagines the possibilities of structural transformation and the ways in which such transformation might be brought about through communication become possible (see also Edwards's chapter in this volume).

Public Relations in a Global Context

One of the key tools of globalization is public relations; simultaneously, one of the causes underlying the political economy of the public relations industry is globalization. Contemporary public relations in the global arena serves the interests of TNCs across global markets. It also serves the agendas of the development industry and the neocolonial configurations of dominant nation-states that continue to circulate the colonial logic of enlightenment in order to conquer resources, sources of labor as well as markets for goods. Public diplomacy initiatives further serve the task of consolidating power in the hands of a neoliberal hegemony by operating through the face of dominant nation-states in order to create spaces of support for privatization and economic liberalization. The voices of the subaltern sectors are systematically ignored. It is against the backdrop of this concentration of power in the hands of a few TNCs that possibilities of resistance and transformation in unequal global policies are imagined.

Transnational Corporations and International Public Relations

Transnational corporations exert their power and control globally through the development of a wide variety of public relations practices (media relations, community relations, government relations, etc.) that control the agendas of policy makers and publics locally, nationally, and globally (Harvey, 2005). With their top-down managerial agenda, these practices function to carry out the interests of TNCs to make profits. In addition, public relations practitioners seek to maintain the dominance of neoliberal hegemony through the deployment of a variety of strategies and tactics that seek to minimize global and local processes of evaluation that might hold TNCs accountable in terms of ethical practice and commitments and responsibilities to local communities (Pal & Dutta, 2008a).

A significant proportion of public relations monies are spent by TNCs on global lobbying, shaping the policies of global organizations such as the IMF and the World Bank (Dutta, 2008, 2009). Simultaneously, these TNCs spend large proportions of monies across nation-states globally to shape national policies, to influence the ways in which these policies are implemented, and to ensure that the power and control of the dominant structure are continually reproduced at the national level. A range of public relations activities such as community relations, lobbying, support of front organizations, and media relations operate hand-in-hand to influence the local policy climate, and align the local climate with the global demands of the organizations. In the following section, we demonstrate the linkage between corporate agendas and policy articulations in neoliberal hegemony through the case of Exxon Mobil—the world's largest publicly traded corporation, and also one of the world's largest producers of global warming pollution (Union of Concerned Scientists, 2007).

Public Relations Tactics as Strategic Manipulation

The public relations tactics used by Exxon Mobil in manipulating public opinion around global warming pollution reflect the transnational hegemony of public relations practices in a global context, constituted on the basis of omissions, erasures, foregrounding, and backgrounding. In this section, we review the wide array of public relations practices used by Exxon to channel and shape public opinion around the issue of climate control, and ultimately influence policy and regulation that would require significant investments in clean energy technologies or reductions in global warming emissions (Union of Concerned Scientists, 2007). In spite of the strong scientific consensus around the existence of global warming and the human generated causes of global warming, Exxon Mobil pumped money into front organizations, political campaigns, and lobbies in order to create and sustain uncertainty in the public mind about global warming. A "blunt speech" by then Exxon chairman Lawrence Rawl, on March 5, 1991, expressed "doubt that theories on global warming would eventually prove accurate" (Rawl, 1991). Creating such uncertainty around climate change is essential to the creation of barriers to regulations that would influence the business practices of Exxon.

In the face of growing evidence on global warming and the role of human activity in causing climate change, Exxon joined with other energy, automotive, and industrial companies in 1989 to form the Global Climate Coalition (GCC), the goal of which was to oppose the scientific consensus in the climate research community and prevent government action directed at solving the problem. Subsequently, in 1996, Exxon Mobil formed the Global Climate Science Team (GCST) to generate uncertainty around climate control, and thus influence policies that might negatively affect the business practices of Exxon. The GCST issued a memo in 1998, stating that "Victory will be achieved when average citizens understand (recognize) uncertainties in climate science" and when public "recognition of uncertainty becomes part of the 'conventional wisdom'" (Union of Concerned Scientists, 2007, p. 10).

The GCST set up a national media relations campaign to inform the media and the public about uncertainties around climate science, and recruited scientists to serve as spokespersons and offer the mark of credibility to its information laundering campaign. Part of GCST's strategy was to "identify, recruit and train a team of five independent scientists to participate in media outreach. These will be individuals who do not have a long history of visibility and/or participation in the climate change debate. Rather, this team will consist of new faces who will add their voices to those recognized scientists who already are vocal" (Union of Concerned Scientists, 2007, p. 14). Based on non-peer reviewed pieces that were published by GCST-sponsored scientists, Exxon created uncertainty around the issue of climate control on the basis of its claim of supporting "sound science," thus shifting the debate away from the role of Exxon in contributing to global warming, and stalling government action that would regulate its activities.

In addition to recruiting scientists who would serve as spokespersons, Exxon Mobil desseminated its message about global warming through seemingly independent non-profit organizations such as the American Enterprise Institute, the Competitive Enterprise Institute, the Cato Institute, the American Council for Capital Formation Center for Policy Research, the American Legislative Exchange Council, the Committee for a Constructive Tomorrow, and the International Policy Network, to name just a few, pouring in approximately U.S. $16 million between 1998 and 2005 to promote disinformation on global warming. Almost all of these institutions published and publicized the writings of a narrow subset of spokespeople, including scientists, who "misrepresent peer reviewed climate findings and confuse the public's understanding of global warming" (Union of Concerned Scientists, 2007, p. 11). Most of these institutions share the same set of individuals on their boards and as scientific advisers. Exxon quietly and effectively continues to promote its anti-regulation agenda by funding a wide array of organizations with redundant personnel, advisers, and spokespersons, offering the veneer of a broad platform for a narrow set of vocal climate science contrarians.

Exxon also backed Web sites such as Tech Central Station, which positions itself as an independent media outlet carrying objective journalistic pieces, although it is in fact part of a corporate strategy that helps corporations like Exxon get their messages out. Published by a firm called DCI Group, which is a registered lobbying firm that works for Exxon Mobil, Tech Central Station dresses up public relations articles as news articles, allowing global corporations like Exxon to communicate their agendas directly to the public, manipulating public opinion under the garb of objective journalism. Worth noting here is the redundancy of the same spokespeople sponsored by Exxon that write on global warming issues on Tech Central Station. Between 1998 and 2005, the TNC spent approximately U.S. $61 million on lobbyists to gain access to key decision makers (Union of Concerned Scientists, 2007).

What the example of Exxon demonstrates is the central role of public relations activities in carrying out the agendas of transnational hegemony. Public relations activities offer the core functions of creating and sustaining relationships with powerful actors at the center, thus continuing to create an environment of support for TNCs, minimizing resistance to the operations of these corporations, and offering maximum opportunities to them for making a profit. The nexus between policy makers and TNCs is essential to the functioning of the TNCs, carrying out their profit-making agendas, and centralizing power and control in the hands of transnational hegemony. The central role of public relations in developing and building relationships with governmental agencies, transnational agencies, and policy organizations at several levels is also visible in the agriculture, pharmaceutical, health, and other industries. What is also evident in the function of public relations here is the interplay of the local and the global. While the reach of transnational hegemony is global in carrying out the agendas of TNCs, nation-states offer entry points for carrying out the policy agendas at the global level, and it is through the funnel of the nation-states that TNCs wield their power on the global stage.

Public Relations, Public Diplomacy, and Neoimperial Agendas

One of the primary public relations functions through which neocolonial interests are carried out by nation-states is public diplomacy; that is, using the government's ability to enact power and control in the international arena to create spaces for neoliberal hegemony in foreign spaces. Public diplomacy is defined as a "government's process of communicating with foreign publics in an attempt to bring about understanding for its nation's ideas and ideals, its institutions and cultures, as well as its national goals and current policies" (Tuch, 1990, p. 3). In serving the agendas of the national government in the international arena, public diplomacy is typically carried out through a plethora of activities such as media programs, cultural programs, and educational exchange programs that are ultimately directed at shaping the policies of targeted nation-states.

According to Wang and Chang (2004), public diplomacy is a form of international public relations; in the international arena, public diplomacy often works as a strategic tool for carrying out the neoimperial interests of dominant nations and of transnational hegemony in creating spaces for support for the free market logic, bringing about more resources for the neoimperial powers, and creating additional markets for TNCs (Dutta-Bergman, 2006). Wang and Chang (2004) argue that both public diplomacy and public relations seek to reach out to target publics with the goal of maintaining and managing image, and share a great deal of strategic and tactical commonalities. For Signitzer and Coombs (1992), these two areas of communication overlap with respect to their objectives, processes, concepts, and tools. Public diplomacy involves the communication of a government to the people of another nation with the goal of influencing their image of the sender nation; in other words, public diplomacy is government-to-public communication in an international context where the target public is situated in another national context. Wang and Chang (2004) point out that the two-pronged goals of public diplomacy efforts are to create support for foreign policies and to generate "better" cultural understanding. Modern nation-states such as the United States "find themselves more and more in the area of public relations as they attempt to influence the opinion of foreign publics" (Signitzer & Coombs, 1992, p. 146).

As demonstrated by Dutta-Bergman (2006), instead of fostering cultural understanding, in reality, public diplomacy has often served the neocolonial interests of dominant nation-states in the West. For instance, in the context of the Middle East, U.S. public diplomacy efforts in the region have been dictated by U.S. economic interests in the petroleum produced in the Middle East and the centrality of oil to the U.S. economy, the geostrategic relevance of the region to the United States, and the role of the region as a market for U.S. capital. In articulating the relevance of public diplomacy in the region, one of the early National Security Council documents published in 1954 explicitly states:

> The near East is of great strategic, political, and economic importance to the free world. The area contains the greatest petroleum resources in the world; essential locations for strategic military bases in any world conflict against Communism; the Suez Canal; and natural defensive barriers. It also contains Holy Places of the Christian, Jewish, and Moslem worlds, and thereby exerts religious and cultural influences affecting people everywhere. The security interests of the United States would be critically endangered if the Near East should fall under Soviet influence or control. (National Security Council, 1954, p. 1)

What gets foregrounded in this document is the interplay of military and economic interests in the Middle East as the cornerstone for U.S. public diplomacy efforts in the region. This thread of economic and geostrategic interest in the region continues to play out in contemporary public diplomacy efforts, although many such efforts have now taken on an outward stance of seemingly being more directed toward utilizing public diplomacy to generate cultural understanding (Dutta-Bergman, 2006).

As demonstrated in the example of Iraq cited earlier, U.S. occupation of Iraq served as the primary tool for the neoliberalization of the country, for the privatization of public resources/sectors, and for the opening up of the country to foreign (primarily U.S.) investments; public diplomacy efforts were launched toward this end although these efforts were often portrayed as being directed toward bringing about greater understanding between the United States and Iraq. The commercial interests of the United States in Iraq is aptly captured in a U.S. Commercial Service, Department of Commerce (2009), document that sketches out the Iraqi space as a potential market for U.S. corporations, facilitated by the Office of Bilateral Trade Affairs of the U.S. government. The economic interests in Iraq were played out through public diplomacy efforts targeted at the Iraqi elite, members of the Iraqi leadership who were recruited and whose careers were fostered by the United States, and non-governmental organizations (NGOs) that received funding from the U.S. government as a part of U.S. public diplomacy efforts in Iraq. The document states:

> US firms looking to take advantage of the business opportunities in Iraq will need to develop thoughtful strategies in order to penetrate this uniquely challenging but rewarding market. Through its International Partner Search (IPS), CS Iraq can assist US companies to find a qualified partner in this dynamic market. (p. 4)

Captured in this document is the goal of public diplomacy to create and penetrate markets for U.S. corporations, and to serve the interests of neoliberal hegemony. The war in Iraq, accompanied by the use of public diplomacy efforts, served to diffuse the economic and military interests of the United States, lending credence to the relevance of postcolonial theorizing in the realm of public diplomacy.

With the increasing critique of public diplomacy as government propaganda and in order to tackle the resistance to overt initiatives of control, public diplomacy programs have started reinventing themselves with the language of participation, cultural exchange, and mutual understanding between disparate cultural spaces, national agendas, and political–economic interests. In spite of their seeming portrayal as vehicles for mutual understanding, international public diplomacy efforts are often driven by attempts to convert through the creation, management, and dissemination of persuasive communicative materials. This one-way penetration of communication to achieve goals is aptly captured in the recommendation of the advisory group (to the U.S. House of Representatives) on public diplomacy for the Arab and Muslim world (see Djerejian, 2003).

The advisory group states that its goal is to communicate to the Arab and Muslim world about the policies of the United States, not to influence U.S. policy making. In fact, the group reiterates that the United States should not modify its policy to suit the publics of the Middle East. Inherent in this suggestion is the one-way flow of communication, the articulation of monologue, and a top-down communication process rather than listening to the publics of the Arab and Muslim world (Dutta, 2006; Dutta-Bergman, 2006). In other words, any real inputs from the publics of the Middle East that suggest that U.S. policy in the Middle East be modified are undesirable; instead, diplomacy in its current form is used as a platform for using audience data to craft persuasive messages targeted to shift the underlying values and beliefs in the Middle East.

Inherent in the above conceptualization is the oppressive force of public diplomacy that seeks to alter one culture in order to suit the preferences of another (dominant) culture, based on differences in access to power. This reflects the politics of colonialism. Although communication here is created to assess the effectiveness of the policies being pushed, it does not create a sense of understanding between the involved stakeholders because of the coercive and unequal framework within which it is conceptualized. Cultural diplomacy becomes a way of engaging with surface level characteristics of a culture without a genuine commitment for listening to the voices of local publics in dispersed global spaces.

Essential to the justification of neocolonialism is the articulation of a need for the penetration of a foreign space. This, once again, is carried out in the form of public relations activities, executed simultaneously in local as well as global spaces. In the most recent example of Iraq, such public relations activities ranged from the manipulation of public opinion about Saddam Hussein's weapons of mass destruction (WMD) program to the articulation of a need to bring democracy to Iraq, to the construction of freeing the Iraqi people, and liberating Iraqi women. Public relations here served the manipulative agenda of drumming up support for the war, often on the basis of concocted evidence that was politicized, working hand-in-hand with mainstream media to create panic around Iraq's supposed WMDs (Dutta-Bergman, 2005b).

Of further relevance is the overt involvement and influence of businesses in contemporary public diplomacy initiatives (see for instance, Business for Diplomatic Action (BDA) at www.businessfordiplomaticaction.org). Essential to the smooth functioning of TNCs is the image of the United States as the space through which these TNCs operate.

Public Relations, Development, and Modernity

As a strategic communication tool utilized by modern-day bureaucracies to communicate and maintain relationships with their key publics, public relations is squarely located within the modernist project. With its primary bias toward serving corporate interests and managing relationships on behalf of corporate players, public relations is fundamentally a capitalist tool. Furthermore, the articulation of democratic processes as being interconnected with the ability of organizational actors to maintain and manage relationships suggests the modernist roots of the discipline. Inherent in the exercise of public relations practices are taken-for-granted assumptions about property, ownership, and the role of governance. It is on the foundations of this modernist logic that public relations has often been deployed for the purposes of "civilizing" the targeted territories of "Third World" nations. In this section, we specifically explore the role of public relations in the realm of development campaigns, nation building, media relations, government, and community relations.

Development Campaigns   Historically,   development   campaigns have served as the linchpin of communicative initiatives that define the relationships between the First and the Third Worlds. At the core of these development campaigns is the construction of the term "development" and what it means to be "developed." The altruistic motive of development has been framed in terms of a need in a primitive society for the intervention, often hiding the economic and geostrategic interests of the dominant actors underlying the development initiatives. Development campaigns have been carried out in a wide variety of sectors ranging from agriculture to population control to nation building and to health promotion.

Nation Building, Media Relations, Community Building, and Democracy Promotion   Recent years have seen substantive growth in public relations theorizing and empirically-based scholarship that celebrates the role of public relations scholars and practitioners in building nation-states and promoting democracy in various sectors of the globe (Pratt, 1985, 1986; Taylor, 2000a, 2000b). These projects of democracy promotion, as demonstrated by Dutta-Bergman (2005b), are often built around the interests of the dominant nation-states engaging in the nation building exercise, serving the political and economic interests of the senders/funders of these initiatives. Although the language of democracy promotion infuses these campaigns and their external positioning, inherent in them is a desire to impose West-centric values through non-participatory mechanisms, often through the use of symbolic violence and coercion. Most recently, the examples of Iraq and Afghanistan demonstrate the irony in the initiatives of democracy promotion that are fundamentally rooted in undemocratic occupation of Third World spaces. What is even more paradoxical is the profit motive attached to the democracy promotion and nation building efforts. As demonstrated in the examples of Chile and Iraq cited earlier, USAID utilizes the language of development in order to serve the global public relations interests of the United States. It ultimately utilizes these development initiatives to create spaces of geostrategic and military support for the United States, and open up new markets for U.S.-based corporations.

Public relations scholars and practitioners working on nation building initiatives often work on media relations in order to create and sustain U.S.-operated and U.S.-friendly media in the target spaces. Journalists are trained, media materials are created, content and process issues are taught, all under a West-centric framework based on a certain set of West-centric assumptions, and driven by a set of predetermined agendas (mostly of economic nature). The civil society and community relations initiatives that are put into place under the umbrella of democracy promotion are fundamentally driven by the objective of aligning Third World spaces along the agendas of the United States and TNCs. Those versions of civil society are supported that carry out the free market logic and diffuse this logic in the target spaces. Simultaneously, popular movements and local participatory processes that threaten the neoliberal hegemony are either vehemently attacked or are co-opted under neoliberal agendas (see Dutta-Bergman, 2005a, for a detailed discussion). Of utmost relevance here is the paradox inherent in the fundamental closure of democratic possibilities through subaltern participation by those very avenues of public relations that claim to be promoting democracy.

Corporate Social Responsibility

Over the last decade, corporate social responsibility (CSR) has taken center stage in public relations in the international arena (Munshi & Kurian, 2005, 2007). Corporate social responsibility embodies the public relations programs carried out by a corporation as a member of society, contributing to the so-called social good, and making the organization accountable to its publics. However, a postcolonial interrogation of CSR locates the practice under its primarily corporate-centered focus, as a rhetorical device for the organization that often draws attention away from the core issues on which the organization ought to be held responsible (Dutta, 2007, 2008; Munshi & Kurian, 2005). In the example of Exxon outlined above, CSR often becomes a veneer for drawing attention away from the unethical practices of the organization. The paradox of public relations here is the promotion of irresponsible practices even as organizations make claims of responsibility.

The neoliberal logic underlying CSR operates under the notion that corporate actors will hold themselves accountable in their various functions; however, a critical analysis suggests that organizations typically utilize CSR to engage with relevant publics that would feed into the organization's profit-making agendas; those marginalized sectors of society that don't matter to these agendas are left out of the discursive space. Drawing upon the omission of this marginalized sector, Munshi and Kurian (2005) point out that "it is this logic of capitalics—a politics fueled by global capital" (p. 439)—that also allows corporations to seduce or coerce Third World states to loosen or ignore their environmental and social regulations either through the allure of big bucks for foreign direct investment or "through their structural power and threat of relocation" (Clapp, 2005, p. 24). Corporate social responsibility, then, becomes a public relations practice that not only maintains the status quo, but also carries out the unequal and oppressive relationship between the Third World and TNCs.

Sites of Knowledge Production

As sites of knowledge production, Western educational institutions are key players in the dissemination of the neoliberal logic across the globe, playing out their roles as developers and evaluators of development campaigns, strategic partners in media relations and public diplomacy initiatives, consultants to TNCs, and machineries of propaganda for nation-states. Historically, for instance, much of the early communication research and more specifically, the scholarship on public relations developed in the realm of U.S. propaganda efforts, have worked to support and maintain the penetration of U.S. corporations into global markets. In this section, we examine the multiple linkages and nodal points through which academic knowledge production and universities, as sites of such knowledge production, carry out the agendas of neoliberalism.

In the last decade or so, educational institutions have demonstrated greater moves toward internationalization, and this has broadly been accepted as a good thing, particularly in terms of the opportunities it has brought for connecting the world. Worth noting here, however, is the directionality of flow in international education and the collaborative opportunities that have been created by this one-way logic, and the broader agendas within which these international initiatives have been constituted. The widespread diffusion of Western epistemological structures that perpetuate neoliberal agendas has created opportunities for widening the markets for the products and services of TNCs. Inherent in the production of education is the dichotomy of the primitive and the modern, which, as demonstrated earlier, has been at the core of the logics of development and modernization. From a public relations standpoint, educational initiatives have been targeted at creating spaces of support for U.S. geostrategic, political, and economic interests. For instance, in the realm of Operation Iraqi Freedom, educational institutions and universities served as some of the primary mechanisms for funneling grants and for playing out the neoliberal agendas of the United States through media relations, development, and community relations activities.

As outlined by USAID, education has historically served as a key public relations tool for the United States in creating public opinion globally that supported U.S. agendas. Through initiatives such as exchange programs, school programs, and Fulbright scholarships, the U.S. government developed mechanisms for training students and scholars from other nation-states, and for molding public opinion abroad through these opinion leaders. Education served as a mechanism for diffusing U.S. interests elsewhere, diffusing U.S. values and culture in the process, often achieved further through the diffusion of English into these spaces as a language that serves the interests of neoliberal hegemony. Language education, for instance, became a business and a tool for U.S. businesses to manage and control their interests in these global spaces.

Finally, when we consider the roots of theorizing in public relations, it becomes evident that much of this theorizing happens in the realm of West-centric understandings of epistemology and ontology, constituted within the realm of serving corporate and managerial interests. As a field, public relations is rooted in the tenets of capitalism and West-centric constructions of ownership of property (Miller & Dinan, 2007). Furthermore, the field is marked by the absence of much scholarship from elsewhere that offers alternative entry points into conceptualizing and talking about public relations. This is markedly noted in the dominance of scholars from the Western hemisphere in constructions of the body of knowledge in public relations. In instances where voices from elsewhere are heard, these are immersed within the context of the West-centric centers of knowledge production. Additionally, much of the public relations knowledge in the literature is created in the realm of private corporations, and the ways in which the profit-making goals of these corporations might be served by public relations knowledge. Worth noting here are the salient roles played by some of the central figures in the field of public relations in corporate consulting and in carrying out the public relations agendas of transnational hegemony. In other instances, scholars in the discipline have worked with USAID and other such agencies to carry out public diplomacy, and tasks of nation building. And of course, historically, much of the persuasion and development communication literature is built upon the role of academics carrying out development campaigns in the Third World, disseminating the epistemology and ontology of colonialism created and sustained by academic discourse. Ultimately, then, as Said (1979) argued in *Orientalism*, colonialism continues to operate on the basis of fundamental knowledge structures that are created and sustained by academia. However, it is also in the realm of these knowledge structures that possibilities of resistance are discursively constituted and imagined, and opportunities for transformative politics are opened up. Critical scholarship in public relations would be an example of such politics.

Resistive Practices, Organizing, and Global Activism

As noted earlier, globalization processes embody the dialectical tension between control and resistance. The global control in the hands of transnational hegemony (i.e., globalization-from-above—see Introduction chapter) works in tandem with globalized processes of local resistance that mobilize and foreground the voices of the subaltern sectors, and interrogate the basic assumptions of neoliberal hegemony which otherwise go unchallenged in much of the mainstream public relations theorizing and scholarship. The maintenance of relationships across multiple local actors that are globally dispersed is central to the mobilization of a mass scale movement against globalization and its neoliberal logic (i.e., globalization-from-below). The protests against the WTO meetings at Seattle in 1999 demonstrated the interplay of the local and the global in grassroots activism as resistive publics from the various dispersed sectors of the globe came together to protest global policies that would have negative impacts locally. The locally situated interests of these dispersed publics were interconnected through their experiences of marginalization in the face of global policies, and this offered an entry point for identity building, mobilization, and communication.

A Culture-Centered Approach

Based on the postcolonial examination of globalization processes and the public relations practices in the realm of these processes outlined in this chapter, we offer the culture-centered approach as an alternative theoretical lens for entering into the discussion of culture in relation to global public relations. As a critique of the dominant models of public relations and building upon the fundamental argument that the dominant epistemic structures have generally failed to listen to the voices of the marginalized sectors of the globe, the culture-centered approach is both deconstructive as well as coconstructive. The deconstructive turn begins with the examination of the erasures in the dominant epistemic structures that contribute to the circulation of the status quo. In this sense, the deconstructive move uncovers the taken-for-granted assumptions in mainstream approaches to public relations, bringing to fore the hidden agendas of development and modernization efforts, the discrepancies between the rhetoric and practice of public relations practices that are deployed to serve the agendas of transnational hegemony, and continually questioning the taken-for-granted assumptions that continue to guide much of the public relations activities in the contemporary global landscape. Simultaneously, the culture-centered approach outlines strategies of participatory development, solidarity building, and community-based organizing that seek to disrupt the status quo by listening to the voices of the subaltern sectors that have continually been omitted from dominant discursive spaces through a variety of public relations and material practices that have marginalized these sectors. The culture-centered approach outlines the importance of continuous reflexivity and vigilance in order to maintain the co-optive stance, and in order to resist the counter co-optive possibilities opened up by the status quo as it seeks to increase its power and control by reinventing itself using the language of participation, democracy, corporate social responsibility, and sustainability.

Culture-Structure-Agency

In opposition to the dominant articulations of the field that exhume agency from subaltern positions by circulating dominant narratives that construct the subaltern as passive recipients of the mantras of development and modernity, the culture-centered approach begins with the emphasis on the relevance of listening to subaltern voices, and foregrounding subaltern agency in the construction of narratives that are meaningful in the realm of subaltern experiences (Dutta, 2008). Agency here is conceptualized as the ability of individuals to make sense of their environment and choose a course of action that is meaningful to them. Furthermore, this agency is constructed at the intersections of culture and structure, and negotiated through a range of contextual experiences embedded in social structures.

The culture-centered approach conceptualizes culture as dynamic, as continuously constructed in local contexts, and realized in the realm of values, meanings, and human interactions. Structure refers to the systems of organizing that both constrain and enable the enactment of choices. By foregrounding the relevance of structure to public relations theorizing, the culture-centered approach attends to the inequities, the power structures, and the systems of organizing that limit possibilities at the margins. Further, by foregrounding the role of structures, the approach draws attention to the various elements of transnational hegemony that create and sustain these inequities; it is also in the realm of structures that theoretical entry points are created for transforming policies and existing practices that marginalize the subaltern sectors.

Much of the dominant framework in public relations takes a universal and etic approach to the field. In instances where culture has been taken into account, culture is thought of as a static entity, often scripted through the lens of the academic observer from the outside (see Bardhan's chapter in this volume). Cultures are measured in terms of their scores on scales such as individualism-collectivism, uncertainty avoidance, or power distance (Hofstede, 1997; also see chapters by Kent & Taylor, and Courtright, Wolfe, & Baldwin in this volume). In contrast, the culture-centered approach notes the malleability of culture. Culture is at once transmissive in terms of passing along values and meaning frameworks and offering constitutive spaces, and at the same time, transformative in terms of offering new opportunities in the realm of negotiation of meanings, rearticulation of values, and enactment of agency. It is this transformative possibility in culture that opens up spaces for resistance.

Communicative practices are constituted at the intersections of culture, structure, and agency. Structures are made meaningful within cultural contexts, and it is in the realm of these contexts that pathways of action are enacted. This interplay of culture, structure, and agency offers a theoretical and empirical opening for public relations scholars to study the ways in which global inequalities brought about by neoliberal logic are experienced by the people who have been pushed to the margins of policy debates and articulations. Listening to the voices of the marginalized through dialogic processes also foregrounds the voices of the dispossessed, the underserved, and the ignored. It offers to bring about change through the presence of those voices that have historically been written over, written about, stripped of agency, and targeted through interventions.

Resistance and Participation

Even as centers of power in neoliberal hegemony have sought to centralize power and control by penetrating globally dispersed local spaces, globally connected local movements of resistance have emerged to challenge the agendas of neoliberal hegemony. Beginning with a commitment to social justice and to structural transformation, the theorization of public relations-as-resistance opens up the possibilities of social change by theorizing about and engaging in the role of communicative practices, practices of mobilization, organization, networking, and relationship building garnered by activist groups that fundamentally seek to change the structures of inequity and oppression that create and sustain the margins.

For instance, Pal's (2008) study of resistance among farmers in Singur, West Bengal, located in Eastern India, theorized about the communication strategies, relational articulations, and renegotiation of meanings among the farmers to challenge their displacement brought about by the building of a car manufacturing factory on their agricultural lands. The farmers fundamentally challenged the meanings of development and work as constituted by the discourses of modernization and development in the dominant framework by making salient the value of agriculture and land in their lives. In listening to the voices of farmers rather than privileging the voices of TNCs and policy makers, Pal demonstrated the ways in which the farmers constituted new meanings of work and land against the backdrop of the neoliberal project, thus offering an alternative epistemological and ontological framework that resisted the neoliberal notions of development. Similarly, Kim's (2008) examination of resistive practices among activist farmers in South Korea foregrounded the communication processes, strategies, and tactics through which the farmers resisted the privatization, commodification, and liberalization logics imposed by the government. Both of these projects articulate the ways in which alternative conceptualizations of public relations resist the epistemological and ontological frameworks of dominant structures in public relations theory and practice. It is with this goal of politicizing the study and practice of public relations that the culture-centered approach offers entry points for scholars to engage in possibilities of resisting the dominant epistemological, ontological, and axiological frameworks of the field.

Furthermore, the culture-centered approach notes the importance of subaltern participation in the development, application, and evaluation of local, national, and global policies. A culture-centered interpretation of public relations calls for a continuous exploration of participatory mechanisms, processes, and strategies that would create new opportunities for listening to subaltern narratives, and incorporate these voices into policy platforms and campaigns.

Solidarity and Reflexivity

For public relations scholars engaging the field from a postcolonial stance, the culture-centered approach opens up possibilities of coconstructing knowledge through dialogue with the subaltern sectors. Therefore, the role of the public relations scholar/practitioner transforms from one of a distanced observer maintaining an objective stance to a highly politicized sojourner, listening to subaltern voices with respect, and engaging in possibilities of dialogue. Ultimately, much like the nation building, public diplomacy, CSR, and democracy promotion initiatives that we see inundate our discipline and directly in opposition to such neoliberal agendas, postcolonial public relations scholarship seeks to re-present the voices of the subaltern sectors in global policy articulations, attending to the inequities and the need for structural transformation. Epistemologically, the culture-centered approach calls for an enactment of solidarity as the researcher/scholar/practitioner enters the spaces of meaning coconstruction with subaltern participants, acknowledging the politics of scholarship and practice that has historically erased the subaltern, and seeking to enter into relationships of solidarity with members of the subaltern. It is in solidarity with the subaltern sector that problems are articulated and solutions are coconstructed.

On Reflexivity   Even as the postcolonial stance in public relations theorizing and praxis seeks to represent the voices of the subaltern sectors in the global arena, Spivak (1999) warns us of the problematics inherent in the act of representing. As we seek to represent the subaltern through our scholarship and through our politics of such scholarship, we come face-to-face with the understanding that one can never fully represent the subaltern, particularly in terms of "walking in his or her shoes." The voice that speaks for the subaltern is always a voice of privilege, one that has access to the dominant modalities of communication and to the dominant structures, and therefore, is continuously open to possibilities of co-optation by the dominant structure. Concepts such as democracy, participation, and dialogue are continuously co-opted by the dominant structure in order to minimize the possibilities of resistance and structural transformation (Dutta, 2008; Pal & Dutta, 2008b). In this context, reflexivity serves as an inwardly turned lens, a lens that continuously questions one's privilege and the ways in which this privilege could close off possibilities for meaningful dialogue and structural transformation. It is through this continuous reflexivity that postcolonial public relations scholars can start engaging with the possibilities of activist politics that can change global policies, neoliberal structures, and communicative structures that silence the subaltern.

Postcolonial Notes for Public Relations Practitioners, Students, and Scholars

In an increasingly complex global terrain where the role of public relations practice has been constituted in the realm of serving the political and economic interests of powerful social actors at the center, opting for a postcolonial lens to public relations interrupts the praxis of dominant public relations institutions by questioning their taken-for-granted assumptions. In this sense, this perspective participates in consciousness raising through the critique of global injustices and systems of oppression carried out by TNCs and the global social actors at the center. The application of such a perspective lies fundamentally in its resistance to the hegemony of public relations practices as agents of the status quo in perpetuating global inequities. Furthermore, bringing a postcolonial lens to public relations theory, research, teaching, and practice reconceptualizes the practices of public relations in the realm of activist politics that works in solidarity with the poor and the marginalized to create spaces of structural transformation. In essence, therefore, the postcolonial approach is fundamentally practical in its commitment to social justice, change, and structural transformation for a more just world.

Discussion Questions

1. Identify a public relations campaign that you believe utilizes a particular cultural logic. How does the campaign conceptualize culture? What role does culture serve in the realm of the campaign? What are the political goals served by the campaign, and what are the economic goals? How are these political and economic goals carried out by the campaign's conceptualization of culture?
2. What, according to the postcolonial perspective, is the role of public relations scholars and practitioners in the realm of development? How would a postcolonial scholar/practitioner respond to the global

terrain of public relations practices? What practical solutions would she or he offer?

3. One of the arguments made by the postcolonial approach highlights the ways in which terms such as *democracy, freedom,* and *participation* get utilized by dominant social institutions to treat cultures as pathologies and offer justifications for neoliberal interventions. The approach simultaneously discusses the possibilities of listening to the voices that are positioned at the margins through participatory means. How, then, is this tension negotiated in a postcolonial reading of public relations?

4. Think about a theory that you have often read about in your public relations textbooks. Now utilize the postcolonial lens to critique the theory, and to develop an intervention in response to the circulation of the theory.

5. What role does public relations play in marginalizing certain sectors in the global landscape? Discuss some of the alternatives you envision in opposition to the marginalizing practices of public relations. Develop a strategic plan for how you would put any one of these alternatives into practice.

References

Appadurai, A. (1995). Disjuncture and difference. In B. Ashcroft, G. Griffiths, & H. Tiffin (Eds.), *The post-colonial studies reader* (2nd ed., pp. 468–472). New York: Routledge.

Beverly, J. (1999). *Subalternity and representation: Arguments in critical theory.* Durham, NC: Duke University Press.

Bhabha, H. K. (1994). *The location of culture.* New York: Routledge.

Bhavnani, K., Foran, J., & Kurian, P. (2003). *Feminist futures: Re-imagining women, culture, development.* London: Zed Press.

Clapp, J. (2005). Global environmental governance for corporate responsibility and accountability. *Global Environmental Politics, 5*(3), 23–34.

Dirlik, A. (1995). The global in the local. In B. Ashcroft, G. Griffiths, & H. Tiffin (Eds.), *The post-colonial studies reader* (2nd ed., pp. 463–467). New York: Routledge.

Dirlik, A. (2000). The postcolonial aura: Third World criticism in the age of global capitalism. In D. Brydon (Ed.), *Postoclonialism. Critical concepts in literary and cultural studies* (pp. 207–236). New York: Routledge.

Djerejian, E. P. (2003). *Changing minds, winning peace: A new strategic direction for US public diplomacy in the Aram and Muslim world.* Washington, DC: The Advisory Group on Public Diplomacy for the Arab and Muslim World.

Dutta, M. (2006). Theoretical approaches to entertainment-education campaigns: A subaltern critique. *Health Communication, 20*(3), 221–231.

Dutta, M. (2007). Communicating about culture and health: Theorizing culture-centered and cultural-sensitivity approaches. *Communication Theory, 17*(3), 304–328.

Dutta, M. (2008). *Communicating health: A culture-centered approach.* London, UK: Polity Press.

Dutta, M. (2009). Theorizing resistance: Applying Gayatri Chakravorty Spivak in public relations. In Ø. Ihlen, B. van Ruler, & M. Fredrikson, (Eds.), *Social theory on public relations* (pp. 278–300). New York: Routledge.

Dutta-Bergman, M. (2005a). Civil society and communication: Not so civil after all. *Journal of Public Relations Research, 17*(3), 267–289.

Dutta-Bergman, M. (2005b). Operation Iraqi Freedom: Mediated public sphere as a public relations tool. *Atlantic Journal of Communication, 13*(4), 220–241.

Dutta-Bergman, M. (2006). US public diplomacy in the Middle East. *Journal of Communication Inquiry, 30*(2), 102–124.

Harvey, D. (2003). The right to the city. *International Journal of Urban & Regional Research, 27*(4), 939–941.

Harvey, D. (2005). *The new imperialism.* New York: Oxford University Press.

Hofstede, G. (1997). *Cultures and organizations: Software of the mind.* New York: McGraw-Hill.

Kim, I. (2008). *Voices from the margin: A culture-centered look at public relations of resistance.* (Unpublished doctoral dissertation). Purdue University, West Lafayette, IN.

Landry, D., & MacLean, G. (1996). *The Spivak reader.* New York: Routledge.

Marx, K. (1965). *Das Kapital* (F. Engels, Ed.). Chicago, IL: Regnery. (Original work published 1867)

Miller, D., & Dinan, W. (2003). Global public relations and global capitalism. In D. Demers (Ed.), *Terrorism, globalisation, and mass communication* (pp. 193–214). Spokane, WA: Marquette Books.

Miller, D., & Dinan, W. (2007). *A century of spin: How public relations became the cutting edge of corporate power.* London: Pluto.

Miyoshi, M. (1993). A borderless world? From colonialism to transnationalism and the decline of the nation-state. *Critical Inquiry, 19*(4), 726–751.

Munshi, D., & Kurian, P. (2005). Imperializing spin cycles: A postcolonial look at public relations, greenwashing, and the separation of publics. *Public Relations Review, 31*(4), 513–520.

Munshi, D., & Kurian, P. (2007). The case of the subaltern public: A postcolonial investigation of corporation social responsibility's (o)missions. In S. May, G. Cheney, & J. Roper (Eds.), *The debate over corporate social responsibility* (pp. 438–447). New York: Oxford University Press.

National Security Council. (1952). *United States objectives and policies with respect to the Arab states and Israel.* Washington, DC: Author.

National Security Council. (1954). *United States objectives and policies with respect to the Near East.* Washington, DC: Office of the President.

Olivera, O. (2004). War. In O. Olivera & T. Lewis (Eds.), *¡Cochabamba!: Water war in Bolivia,* (pp. 33–49). Cambridge, MA: South End Press.

Pal, M. (2008). *Fighting from and for the margin: Local activism in the realm of global politics* (Unpublished doctoral dissertation). Purdue University, West Lafayette, IN.

Pal, M., & Dutta, M. (2008a). Public relations in a global context: The relevance of critical modernism as a theoretical lens. *Journal of Public Relations Research, 20*(2), 159–179.

Pal, M., & Dutta, M. (2008b). Theorizing resistance in a global context: Processes, strategies and tactics in communication scholarship. *Communication Yearbook, 32,* 41–87.

Prasad, A. (2003). The gaze of the other: Postcolonial theory and organizational analysis. In A. Prasad (Ed.), *Postcolonial theory and organizational analysis: A critical engagement* (pp. 3–43). New York: Palgrave Macmillan.

Pratt, C. (1985). The African context. *Public Relations Journal, 41*(February), 11–16.

Pratt, C. (1986). Professionalism in Nigerian public relations. *Public Relations Review, 12*(4), 27–40.

Rawl, L. (1991, March 6). Speech by Exxon chairman. *New York Times.* Retrieved from Lexis Nexis Academic.

Said, E. W. (1979). *Orientalism.* Harmondsworth, UK: Penguin. (Original work published 1978)

Shome, R., & Hegde, R. (2002). Postcolonial approaches to communication: Charting the terrain, engaging the intersections. *Communication Theory, 12*(3), 249–270.

Signitzer, B., & Coombs, T. (1992). Public relations and public diplomacy: Conceptual convergence. *Public Relations Review, 18*(2), 137–147.

Spivak, G. C. (1999). *A critique of postcolonial reason: Toward a history of the vanishing present.* Cambridge, MA: Harvard University Press.

Spivak, G. C. (2003). *Death of a discipline.* New York: Columbia University Press.

Taylor, M. (2000a). Toward a public relations approach to nation building. *Journal of Public Relations Research, 12*(2), 179–210.

Taylor, M. (2000b). Media relations in Bosnia: A role for public relations in building civil society. *Journal of Public Relations Research, 26*(1), 1–14.

Tuch, H. N. (1990). *Communicating with the world: US public diplomacy overseas.* New York: St. Martin's Press.

Union of Concerned Scientists. (2007). *Smoke, mirrors, and hot air: How Exxon Mobil uses Big Tobacco's tactics to manufacture uncertainty on climate science.* Cambridge, MA: Author.

U.S. Agency for International Development (USAID). (2002). *Foreign aid in the national interest.* Washington, DC: Author.

U.S. Commercial Service. (2009). *Doing business in Iraq.* Washington, DC: U.S. Department of Commerce.

Wang, J., & Chang, T. K. (2004). Strategic public diplomacy and local press: How a high-profile "head-of-state" visit was covered in America's heartland. *Public Relations Review, 30*(1), 11–24.

Suggested Readings

Chaturvedi, V. (2000). *Mapping subaltern studies and the postcolonial*. New York: Verso.

Harding, S. (1985). A role for postcolonial histories of science in theories of knowledge? Conceptual shifts. In S. Harding (Ed.), *Is science multicultural? Postcolonialisms, feminisms, and epistemologies* (pp. 1–22). Bloomington: Indiana University Press.

Shiva, V. (1988). Reductionist science as epistemological violence. In A. Nandy (Ed.), *Science, hegemony, and violence: A requiem for modernity* (pp. 232–256). Calcutta, India: Oxford University Press.

Spivak, G. C. (1987). *In other worlds: Essays in cultural politics*. London: Methuen.

Spivak, G. C. (1993). *Outside in the teaching machine*. London: Routledge.

Spivak, G. C. (1990a). The post-colonial critic. In S. Harasym (Ed.), *The postcolonial critic: Interviews, strategies, dialogues* (pp. 67–74). New York: Routledge.

Spivak, G. C. (1990b). Questions of multi-culturalism. In S. Harasym (Ed.), *The postcolonial critic: Interviews, strategies, dialogues* (pp. 59–66). New York: Routledge.

Spivak, G. C. (1996). Bonding in difference: Interview with Alfred Arteaga. In D. Landry & G. MacLean (Eds.), The *Spivak reader: Selected works of Gayatri Chakravorty Spivak* (pp. 15–28). New York: Routledge.

Chapter 9

Chi-Based Strategies for Public Relations in a Globalizing World

Jensen Chung

Harmony, long-term human relationships, and unity of the universe are some of the major principles within *I-Ching* (which translates into English as "The Book of Change"), a cornerstone of the Eastern philosophies. This chapter explains how these principles, complemented by *chi* (energy flow)-*shih* strategies (suck, duck, buck, and construct), can strategically address some of the complex and sometimes contradictory issues faced by public relations practitioners operating in the context of globalization. Although the *chi-shih* strategies can be used both at the strategic and tactical levels of communication, this chapter focuses on the strategic plane of public relations.

In this chapter, I first outline interconnectedness and instantaneousness as two basic elements which lie at the heart of globalization. This is followed by an examination of the dialectics of familiarity-novelty and globalization-localization. Drawing on the Eastern philosophy of *I-Ching* and its offspring concept, *chi* or energy flow, I then discuss how *shih*, or strategic advantage, the sibling concept of *chi*, can be applied to public relations issues in the context of globalization. A number of cases are used to illustrate these concepts all of which, with one exception, are drawn from my own public relations consulting experience in the United States and two Asian countries. In drawing on these cases, some facts and situations have been modified to protect the privacy of individuals, organizations, or public relations firms.

Globalization

Globalization has been defined as "the compression of the world and the intensification of consciousness of the world as a whole" (Robertson, 1992, p. 8). Although market globalization dates back to the transnational expansion of capitalism (Wallerstein, 1974), globalization became a focus of academic attention only in the latter half of the 20th century, and especially in the 1990s. Two defining features of globalization have emerged and are of significant importance to public relations: first, interconnectedness among nations and organizations around the world; and second, instantaneity of communication.

Interconnectedness

Advanced technologies and computer-mediated communication (CMC) have virtually shrunk the world through compression of time and space. These technologies have also integrated production relations and the organizations, peoples, and nations of the world to a very large extent. For example, when a U.S. customer orders an H-P Pavilion laptop online, the validated order is transmitted to Taiwanese-owned Quanta plant in Shanghai, China. The laptop is assembled from parts from all over the world. Hard disk drives are put together in Japan, China, Singapore, and the United States; power supplies and magnesium casings come from Taiwan and China; memory chips from South Korea, the United States, and Germany; liquid-crystal display from Taiwan, South Korea, Japan, and China; microprocessors from the United States; and graphic processors are designed in the United States and Canada but made in Taiwan. The merchandise is then shipped to the United States by air ("The Laptop Trail," 2005). This process illustrates only a part of interdependence at the global level. For globalized public relations practice, understanding the ramifications of interdependence is crucial because it implies the possibility of cultural conflict and the need to identify ways to resolve that conflict. The relationship between two parties that are motivated to interact and interconnect, and experience conflict in the process, cannot be furthered unless both parties are willing to engage in cultural negotiations and integration. For organizations to meet the challenges of increasing global interconnectedness, public relations practitioners play an important role in this integration. Economic incentives and motives often drive how people/organizations interact and depend on each other, and communication and relationship building skills are vital to the success of their effective interactions. This is especially true in the context of globalization, the intertwined nature of relationships, and the high speed of CMCs that are so central to that context.

Instantaneousness

Computer-mediated technologies such as e-mail, the Internet, social network sites, teleconferences, and blogs have vastly increased the pace of public relations practice. Synchronous communication can involve huge publics, general or specific, across the globe. New features of social media networks such as *YouTube, Facebook,* or *Twitter,* make it difficult for public relations practitioners to cope with information overload and knowledge explosion, especially during crises. A simple rumor related to the client organization, for instance, may force practitioners to race desperately against time and compete for public attention with bloggers or Tweeters, to quell misinformation or tame anger. Hence, the challenge of building intercultural relations is further compounded by the fast pace of communication and information flow across national and cultural borders.

Dialectical Challenges of Globalization

In addition to the challenges of interdependence and instantaneousness, public relations practice faces some dialectical tensions in the global context. These are first, the dialectics of novelty-similarity, and second, the dialectics of globalization-localization. In the context of intercultural communication, Martin and Nakayama (1999) state "that the most challenging part of the dialectical perspective is that it requires holding two contradictory ideas simultaneously..." (p. 14). They note that in a culturally complex world, it is necessary to transcend binaristic thinking (e.g., good vs. bad, local vs. global) and move toward a model of thinking that "recognizes and accepts as ordinary, the interdependent and complementary aspects of the seeming opposites" (p. 14).

The first dialectic, familiarity-novelty, stems from the very process of intercultural communication. When cultures intersect, new ideas and practices interface with culturally familiar ones. Because globalization has ushered in increased cultural diversity and contact, the appearance of new ideas or practices is a constant phenomenon. Globalized public relations may involve new ideas, practices, or products, the novelty of which may attract attention, appeal to publics, and lead to adoption. On the other hand, when a new concept, practice, or product is introduced, it may be clouded with uncertainty and difficult to understand. This could lead to cultural roadblocks on the path of adoption. When the newness takes the public out of their comfort zone of familiarity, resistance may be encountered and the novel idea or product attacked or rejected. This intercultural dialectic of familiarity-novelty is especially common in public relations practice when a newly adopted idea results in the redistribution of resources such as finances or prestige.

The second dialectic for globalized public relations results from the continuous tension between the local and the global (Hall, 1991, pp. 19–40). The simultaneous resistance and acceptance of globalization on the local level has created environments of contradiction and uncertainty. Some of the contradictions are related to issues of identity and diversity (Juan, 1994) that belong largely in the realm of culture. Robertson (1992) notes that individuals, movements, and institutions that have participated in actions that advanced the globalization process, have simultaneously been resistant to the process. Globalization itself contains homogenizing (Barker, 1999; Hall, 1991) and heterogeneous processes (Hamilton, 1994; Inglehart & Baker, 2000). Some theorists point out that the emergence of global culture or globalization will inevitably lead to a unified world culture or world culture system in which the economically strong will dominate (Chuang, 2000). Tenbruck (1990) notes that multicultural conjunctures will affect and perhaps threaten the very survival of local cultures. Others, meanwhile, have theorized in favor of the rise of cultural pluralism and transformation which leads us to the concept of *glocalization*—a notion that attempts to transcend the global–local dialectic (Robertson, 1995). However, glocalization, a word commonly used to express this dialectic, cannot be achieved by simply combining globalization and localization, nor can it be about scratching the surface of cultures at the symbolic level. Glocalization is meaningful only if it is forged at the deep-structure level of cultures. As Robertson (1995) has argued, glocalization is a state that is neither global nor local, but a third state that arises from deep interconnections and interactions between global and local forces over time.

Public relations practitioners have an important role to play in the achievement of this third state. Yet, in the global cultural context, public relations appears to be beset by the types of dialectical tensions outlined above. In this chapter, therefore, I pose the question: "How can practitioners accomplish the grand mission of achieving harmony?" I use *I-Ching* philosophy and its offspring, *chi* theory, which are dialectics-based and harmony-centered, to provide an answer to this question.

Chi Theory of Communication

Chi (pronounced "chee" in Chinese and spelled and pronounced "ki" in Japanese and Korean) is commonly translated as "energy flow" in English. It generally refers to perceived energy that appears to have the potential of doing work or exercising physical or psychological power. Risking oversimplification of its heuristic richness, this concept may be explained with examples of *chi* in communication or public relations contexts before a more detailed explication is offered. Two opposite natures of *chi* can represent *chi* as it is commonly used in social and professional contexts. One is the *chi* of atmosphere, which is close to the concept of "climate." The other is the *chi* of "spirit," similar to the concept of "morale." Both are an emotional state that can facilitate communication and public relations. A cordial *chi* (atmosphere) may smooth communication (e.g., alleviate hostility), and an intense spirit kind of *chi* (morale) may excite communication (e.g., motivating a target public to take action on the cause spearheaded by a public relations campaign). While both kinds of *chi* (atmosphere and morale) can facilitate public relations campaigns, public relations activities can also create both (atmosphere and morale) kinds of *chi*. For instance, social conversations may create a cordial energy flow or *chi* between organizational leaders and local community leaders; and a fiery motivational speech by a CEO may boost the morale (*chi*) of the internal public or employees.

The concept of *chi* originated from ancient Chinese philosophies of Taoism and Confucianism. It is omnipresent in the languages of East Asian countries. In the past 2,000 years, its applications in daily lives, including communication practices, have been ubiquitous in China and have subsequently permeated into the cultures of Korea, Japan, Vietnam, and Taiwan. This philosophical and practical concept has been formerly adopted as a communication construct in recent years. It is generally understood as a quality and quantity of vitality and dynamism in human bodies, art works, natural environments, dwelling designs, furniture arrangements, and a range of locations. In its evolution, the concept has taken on various denotations in different applications and contexts. *Chi* is thus an umbrella term for a wealth of concepts, especially communication concepts.

I-Ching

Chi is considered to have generated from the dual qualities of *yin* and *yang*, which is delineated in the *I-Ching* (also spelled as "Yi-jing" in some English translations to be closer to its Mandarin pronunciation). The *I-Ching* ("*I*" is pronounced as "ee" or "yi") is a major wellspring from which ancient Chinese philosophies—Taoism, Confucianism, and Far Eastern Buddhism—drew inspiration. An assumption of *I-Ching* is that the universe is an interconnected whole united by opposites. Within parts, between parts, and between parts and the whole are a myriad of things (objects or concepts) which can be categorized as *yin* and *yang*. *Yin* means shade, while *yang* means sunshine. The two opposite qualities, or natures, interact to create and re-create, or produce and reproduce. The movement of Mother Nature best illustrates this principle: cold winter and hot summer, the two opposite natures rotate, making a change, and facilitate giving birth to a myriad phenomena. Here the cold winter, like all other things relatively supple in nature, is represented by the word *yin*; and hot summer, like all other relatively strong phenomena in nature, is represented by the word *yang*. The production and reproduction are a harmonious and constantly changing rotating cyclical process. Karcher (1997) points out that "the modern functionalistic thinking considers change as objective and predictable as described by statistics and norms. The worldview in *I-Ching*, on the other hand, sees changes as chances with a pattern depending on certain situations and changing principles" (p. 6). Siu

(1968) summarizes *I-Ching* thoughts into three words: *opposition, rotation,* and *transformation*. Yu (2005) synthesizes philosophers' discussions into an essence of *I-Ching*: creativity and unceasing generations. The essence includes four principles: (1) temporality and process, (2) creativity and novelty, (3) human participation, and (4) interdependence and harmony. Chen (2009) identifies five characteristics of human communication derived from *I-Ching*: holistic, creative, interconnected, hierarchical, and harmonious. Chung and Ho (2009) also employ *I-Ching* principles to develop a public relations practice model, describing the relationships between the client/organization, the public relations practitioners, and the public. How can public relations practices utilize *I-Ching* principles? Understanding the functioning of *chi* provides some directions.

Yin *and* Yang *Interact to Generate* Chi

Chinese thinker Lao Tzu, born presumably in 571 BCE, and a contemporary of Confucius (Lin, 2009), was inspired by *I-Ching* philosophy and made a classical philosophical statement that set a cornerstone for *chi* concepts, principles, and philosophies. In *Tao Te Ching*, a text that was a compilation of his thoughts, Lao Tzu states that a myriad things carry *yin* and embrace *yang*, interplaying *chi* to achieve harmony. The interaction of *yin* and *yang* is the primary principle of *chi*. Most interpretations of this statement suggest that everything in the world—person, object, phenomenon, behavior, or issue—has the dualistic characteristics of *yin* and *yang* in itself, and the two properties can interact or be interplayed to generate *chi*. Public relations practitioners can utilize the *yin chi* and *yang chi* to reach harmony. For example, when a company announces a furlough policy of vacation without pay, it is normally demoralizing to employees, the internal public of the company. The atmosphere would be gloomy, and the spirits low, but a *yin-yang* interplay may make a difference. The president may give a "soft" speech, explaining the company's financial situation given the Wall Street meltdown and the country's economic slump, praise the hard work of the employees of the company, and express her appreciation of the sacrifices of her "colleagues." Such a soft speech would generate a *yin chi*. Then, she can deliver a motivational message that brings hope and excites the employees, thereby creating a *yang chi*. The sagging morale may thus be uplifted. The *yin* and *yang* interplay by the president may boost employee morale more effectively than simply giving either a soft (*yin*) pep talk or a motivational (*yang*) speech.

However, if there is a strong union waging a battle, the communication strategy may be switched to another kind of *yin-yang* interplay, such as carrot (*yin*) and stick (*yang*). The company could reveal a plan of either laying off junior employees or slashing the pay of senior employees. This threatening proposal would be a "hard" message, displaying the management's *yang* kind of power. The message would contain energy with *yang chi*. The organization could then propose a furlough. Preceded by the threatening message (*yang*), the furlough policy would appear to be a relatively "soft" part of the power wielded by the management. Thus, the energy in the furlough message would appear weaker (*yin*), and the impact of the furlough would be lightened. Through such a maneuver, the management may not only foil strike attempts, but also reap a public relations benefit of winning a reputation of "taking care of all employees because no one was laid off." With this example, it is easier to understand the process of *yin-yang* interplay: when an audience receives a message containing the *yin* and *yang* elements, the perception moves from one to the other, triggering a comparison process. Like cold air flowing to hot air, a *yang* message moving to a *yin* message (or vice versa) can trigger a comparison. If the *yin-yang* difference is large, a radical *chi* (e.g., excitement) is generated. If the difference is small, a mild or cordial *chi* (e.g., affability) may arise. Although the comparison is in the communicator's mind, members of the *chi* culture would call messages or message senders that have the potential of influencing message receivers as possessing *chi*.

Based on Lao Tzu's statement that all things contain *yin* and *yang*, the new generation of *chi* can, in turn, further generate *chi*. There exists normally more than one generation of *chi*. Interplay (e.g., the process of coordinating or communicating) can generate *chi*, which, in turn, contains a second generation of *yin* or *yang* dialectics. For example, an organization from a dominant culture can tone down its public relations activity's theme or rhetoric from a usually forceful tone (*yang*) to a gentler one (*yin*) to the public of a less privileged cultural group, which may change from being intimidated (negative, *yin*) into becoming more empowered (positive, *yang*). Through such an accommodation process (moving the dominant one from *yang* toward *yin* and the less privileged one from *yin* toward *yang*), it is possible to produce a second generation of *chi* which is a more harmonious atmosphere. On the other hand, a different kind of interplay may generate the *yang* kind of *chi*. For instance, if the organization from the dominant culture wields its power in its public relations communication, displaying a tone of superiority and intimidating members of the weaker culture, the strong culture may silence the weaker one and thus become even more aggressive in its tone or rhetoric. In this case, the *chi* or atmosphere between the two will be characterized by an aggressive tone (even stronger *yang*). In either case, the new *chi* is the third *chi*, different from the original ones.

Chi *of Communication*

Some principles relevant to *chi* in public relations and globalization can be drawn from *I-Ching* and Taoist philosophy. First, there is the *yin-yang* rotation. Since, as explained, all phenomena possess the properties of *yin* and *yang*, every substance, issue, reality, including *chi*, contains its own opposite, and the two kinds of *chi* rotate. Second, there is the issue of temporality. *I-Ching* suggests that everything is in a state of constant change. The status of *yin chi* and *yang chi* thus will not stay in its status quo permanently; there is a tentative balance but no permanent stability (i.e., the principle of temporality as noted in the early part of the *I-Ching* section). The ultimate point of one state, issue, or phenomenon elicits the rise of its opposite. One of the key tenets in *I-Ching* philosophy is that when *yin* reaches its maximum state, the *yang* will rise, and vice versa. For example, in the context of globalization, when the stronger culture acts or appears extremely strong (displaying *yang chi*), it already contains in itself the seed of being weak, showing a *yin* energy (e.g., budding corrupt elements). Meanwhile, the weaker culture approaching the extremely weak state already contains in itself the seed of being strong and the determination to resist and counter-attack which propels the rise to power. Third, there is the issue of long-term relationships and harmony. The change, evolution, or rotation of the opposing forces of *yin chi* and *yang chi* is a long process that depends on the maintenance of the *yin-yang* relationship. Coordinated or adjusted well, the status quo between the two kinds of *chi* may be maintained longer (i.e., the *I-Ching* principle of harmony). Otherwise, the rotation may occur sooner. A good example would be the constant power struggle that leads to cyclical power change between the conservative and the liberal political forces in the United States. The fourth *chi* principle of communication that is drawn from *I-Ching* and is related to public relations is creativity. *Yin* and *yang* interaction brings change as well as creativity. In fact, change and creativity are the same concept (Yu, 2005). Therefore, communicating to bring forth the *yin chi* and *yang chi* interaction in public relations can foster creativity.

Shih *(Strategic Advantage) to* Chi *in Communication*

Chi is not only a concept stemming from the philosophy delineated in *I-Ching*, but also a means to facilitate the implementation of the philosophical principles stated in *I-Ching*. Yet an appreciation of the concept of *shih* is also needed to understand how to generate *chi*. The concept of *shih* is a little younger than that of *chi*. In contemporary East Asian languages, *shih* and *chi* are even used interchangeably (and thus incorrectly). Like *chi*, *shih* has gathered various denotations along the course of its evolution as a concept. Ames (1994) ingeniously translated this word into English as "strategic advantage." Both ancient and modern scientific examples can help explain this concept.

Around 2,250 years ago in China, Sen Dao, presumably a Confucianist (Lu, 2004), introduced five metaphors to elucidate the concept of *shih*. One of these describes how a 1-inch tall sapling on a cliff appears taller than a 10-foot tall tree at the bottom of the valley. Here, the relative height of the cliff is a strategic position, and the 1-inch sapling has the relatively more favorable strategic advantage, or *shih*, over the 10-foot tree. Another metaphor Sen Dao used depicted how a child, who cannot normally move a bulky water buffalo, can maneuver it at will by holding a rope that is pierced through the soft cartilage in the buffalo's nose. The soft spot is a strategic position, somewhat similar to Achilles' heel in Greek mythology. The child holds the strategic advantage or *shih* over others who try to move the animal simply by using their hands. An example from modern physics further illustrates the concept of *shih*. In archery, the bow, when drawn, holds potential energy because, when released, the arrow can shoot or even kill something. The position value of the arrow connected to the bow is like the position value in human interactions. The bow in the front (*yin*) and the arrow in the back (*yang*) constitute a *yin-yang* strategic structure, just like the less privileged culture (holding a *yin* position) and the dominant culture (possessing a *yang* position) in the context of globalized intercultural communication constitute a *yin-yang* structure. Just as the arrow drawn into position has the strategic advantage of doing work (transforming into energy), the privileged culture has the strategic advantage of persuading or influencing the weaker culture. The *appearance* of the ability to do work because of holding a strategic position or gaining a strategic advantage is *shih*.

In communication, *shih* can be a mega trend, general context, or an overarching sociocultural value. Setting up a *shih* can influence or facilitate the *chi* of communication. *Shih*, in the context of public relations, is discussed further in the latter part of this chapter.

Communication Assumptions

While *chi* is generated by the interplay of *yin* and *yang*, the *yin-yang* interplay is carried out through communication (Chung, 2008). From the communication point of view, the *I-Ching* principles can lead to the following assumptions (Chung, 2008).

First, communication itself and its elements such as communicators, messages, and environments, are part of "all things," and thus have the properties of *yin* and *yang*. Second, *chi* can multiply in terms of generations. The interplay of *yin* and *yang* can create certain kinds of energy flow or *chi* that has the apparent potential to do work. This first generation of energy, in turn, may be classified as *yin* or *yang* depending on its quality. For example, a humble attitude or behavior is conventionally labeled as *yin*, while a superiority complex, attitude, or behavior is labeled as *yang*. Third, the communication process may be seen as a coordination process of interplaying *yin* and *yang*. For example, communicators' or interactors' attitudes and behaviors may shape a certain kind of atmosphere or climate, which is a kind of *chi*. Modifying one's attitude or adjusting one's behavior may change the *chi* between two actors involved in a confrontation. Fourth, the communication process can be a means of interplay to reach harmony.

In communication, *shih* is a strategic leverage point. Setting up a *shih* with the *yin* and *yang* contrast can influence or facilitate the *chi* of communication.

Chi-Shih *Strategies*

I have discussed some key principles in *I-Ching*, such as harmony (playing opposites to reach harmony), cyclicity (the opposites eventually change places), creativity (with vitality, things multiply), and unity (viewing the world in terms of oneness). In putting these principles into practice, *shih* strategies can help to generate the desired *chi*.

To implement the *chi* method, exploiting *shih* is necessary and this involves some common and useful strategies, which are called *shih* strategies. These *shih* strategies include "suck," "duck," "buck," and "construct." Chung and Busby (2002) identify four kinds of set-ups: suck *shih* (taking advantage of existing strategic advantage), duck *shih* (avoiding a disadvantageous situation or *shih*, including an overwhelming trend or force in order to reserve energy), buck *shih* (going against the big *shih* to produce the "David vs. Goliath" effect), and construct *shih* (creating strategic advantage). Depending on the situation, the appropriate *shih* strategy could help generate the desired *chi*.

Isaacson and Chung (2004) applied these four strategies to analyze the rhetoric of the Bush vs. Gore confrontation during the 2000 U.S. presidential election recount. When Bush and Gore both spoke in front of the American flag, they used the suck *shih* strategy in an attempt to evoke the American root values of patriotism and democracy. Bush employed the strategy of constructing *shih* when he projected an image of a presumptive president. He invited the house speaker and the senate majority leader for a meeting at the Bush ranch in Crawford, Texas, and his aides invited photographers and reporters to record those symbolic moments. The *chi* of Bush's speech was buttressed by the constructed *shih*, which enacted the presumptive official position (the higher, thus the *yang*) as opposed to Gore's apparent underdog position (the lower, thus the *yin*). Based on this explanation of *chi-shih* strategies, we can better understand how *chi* theory can offer a heuristic perspective on public relations in global cultural contexts.

Implementing *I-Ching* and *Chi* Principles through *Chi-Shih* Strategies in Globalized Public Relations

Public relations requires strategic thinking, which involves going above the tactical plane. As Austin and Pinkleton (2001) point out, "When public relations practitioners respond to problems and challenges strategically instead of tactically, they have a much greater likelihood of helping organizations meet their challenges, solve or avoid protracted problems, and adjust to the expectations of key stakeholders in mutually beneficial ways" (p. 4). As already outlined in this chapter, public relations in global cultural contexts is much more complicated and urgent because of the issues of interrelatedness and instantaneousness that characterize communication and information flow in a world marked by time-space compression. This context makes strategic thinking much more crucial and necessary than in traditional public relations practice.

The *I-Ching* principles of harmony, cyclicity, creativity, and unity are relevant to globalized public relations. Understanding these principles and strategically applying them in public relations communication can help practitioners reach the goal of harmony when faced with intercultural conflict. *Chi-shih* strategies are presented next to demonstrate how they can serve each of these principles. Each of the four principles is illustrated below in examples which each demonstrate two of the four *chi-shih* strategies—suck, duck, buck, and construct. The principles and the strategies thus constitute a matrix or conceptual framework as shown in Table 9.1.

Harmony

Lao Tzu highlighted *I-Ching*'s nuances by stating that *yin* and *yang* can interplay to reach harmony. The ideal state in the *yin-yang* interplay and transformation is a harmonious state (Chen, 2009). Harmony is one of the most prized values in East Asian cultures. In the West, attaining harmony is considered the essence of the public relations process. Seitel (2001) cites public relations educator Malvin Sharpe as stating that public relations should boil down to a process that "harmonizes" long-term relationships among individuals (publics) and organizations in society. Since globalized public relations is fraught with dialectical tensions and possibilities of intercultural conflict, the driving need is to search for ways to reach harmony. Two *chi-shih* strategies suck and duck can serve this purpose.

Table 9.1 Examples for *Chi-Shih* Strategies in the Matrix of *I-Ching* Principles

	I-Ching implication	*Cases & examples used*
Harmony principle		
Suck strategy	networking	Japanese satellite firms
Duck strategy	letting go of the trivial	journalistic gaffe
Cyclicity principle		
Suck strategy	grasp large context	Normura & Lehman Bros.
Duck strategy	give and take rotate	community reciprocity
Creativity principle		
Buck strategy	defying rule	encouraging spending
Construct strategy	third alternative	non-uniform
Unity principle		
Buck strategy	exciting the base external network	union vs. predator
Construct strategy	external network	women's network power

Suck   The suck strategy involves absorbing the energy flow generated by taking advantage of the existing *shih* (set-up). The universe and a myriad things within it are interrelated. It is not difficult to identify commonalities in goals between, for example, the host culture and the guest culture. Going along with the goals together could save a great deal of energy and promote a harmonious atmosphere (*chi*). Some common goals, however, could be hidden in different cultural vocabularies, idioms, and stories. Unearthing the common meanings and usages and surfing on them should smooth the energy flow and cultivate an amiable atmosphere in communication. Another suck strategy involves utilizing networks in the public relations environment. Networks can be professional organizations, social clubs, or other connections or units that are pertinent to the client organization. In a melon field, covered with leaves, an effective way to find and pick the melons is to trace the vine. In some cultures, such as Japanese culture, employees who leave the company often form a company to become a satellite of the previous employer. Thus, numerous networks are formed centering around certain corporations. These offshoot or spin-off networks are like the lotus root (rhizome), popular in East Asian cuisine: even after the root is broken, the strings (fibers) of the cut-off parts stay attached to the root. This attachment phenomenon is in stark contrast with what we commonly see in many other cultures where employees leave the company with zero sentiment, if not resentment. The inability to understand this kind of a network partly explains the difficulties some companies experience in penetrating the market and social networks in East Asian cultures. It is necessary to identify and cultivate such networks. Sucking the advantages of social networks is required for strategic thinking and planning in globalized public relations, especially in East Asian cultures (as my personal and professional experience has taught me).

In addition to networks operating at the organizational level, there is a variation of the notion of network, which is called *guanxi* (Huang, 1997) or particularistic ties (Chung, 1996; Jacobs, 1984). Classmates, alumni, clan folks, and social club members are all considered sources of connections. These connections form the basis of a strong *shih* in several East Asian cultures.

In globalized public relations, CMC channels constitute the most powerful networks which public relations practitioners cannot afford to neglect. After all, globalization, to a large extent, is fueled by computerized communication. In the technologically privileged parts of the world, the speed of transmission, the quantity of dispensation, and the convenience of access to people and information are revolutionizing public relations practice. Traditional networks have become more powerful than before because of CMC networks. Like a tiger with added wings, human networks coupled with computer networks are more ferocious than we could have imagined in the era of pre-market globalization. This is the current strongest *shih*, or strategic position, in public relations.

In sum, a harmonious climate enhances either traditional networking such as that in the Japanese example or the recently emerging online social networking. Networking, when operated properly, can, in turn, enhance harmony. Taking advantage of networks is the most powerful and necessary suck strategy for public relations practice nowadays.

Duck Taoism, one of the philosophies stemming from *I-Ching* philosophy, is characterized by its "non-action" philosophy. Lao Tzu, the founding father of the philosophical Taoism, argued for dodging strict and complicated laws or strenuous efforts. At the strategy level, a second *chi-shih* strategy, ducking *shih*, is to dodge an unfavorable opposing strategic position such as cultural values, forces, or trends. There are at least two circumstances under which public relations practitioners would be wise to avoid confrontations. The first is when the *shih*, strategic position, of the opposing values, forces, or trends are overwhelmingly strong, and battling against them is thus destined to lead to failure. The other is when the opposing *shih* is insignificant; fighting would not only boost the opponents' morale but also bring them increased public support. In this situation, the fight is not worth the trouble. The following is a brief account of a successful public relations effort adopting the duck strategy to reach harmony that serves the public relations purpose.

An overseas regional president of a global firm was shocked to hear that his picture had appeared in a local television station's special report about international tourists shopping for sex. He filed a libel suit. The director of public relations, however, saw it as trivial, because the picture in the tape, shot with other regular travelers at an airport, was a hardly recognizable profile. It was shot by a reporter merely in order to represent Europeans (tourists) in her feature story. The public relations director suggested converting this into a public relations opportunity. With the permission of the regional president, he visited the president of the local media association and asked him to discuss the case. The association president then mediated the dispute. When the television company agreed to clarify the journalistic gaffe and apologize, the regional president withdrew the case. The media association leader was proud of successfully resolving the conflict, and consequently the regional president and his company developed friendships with journalists and top media management both at the television station and within other media outlets. The president and the company developed good relations with press circles and enjoyed positive treatment in the media by implementing a series of activities designed by the public relations department. Nine months later, when an ex-aide of the regional president was allegedly involved in organized crime, the president and the company's reputation remained intact due to the earlier, proactive public relations efforts. The public relations profit came from the non-investment—ducking ugly legal confrontation and instead winning a good communication climate (amiable *chi*) with a critical public: the press.

Cyclicity

According to *I-Ching*, the universe and all things in it change constantly, and the change revolves in a *yin-yang* rotating pattern. The two eventually will change place and the strong power will become weak, and the weak power strong. The privileged (*yang*) has the prospect of becoming the underprivileged (*yin*), and vice versa. The tentativeness of this process has some implications. The first is the sensitivity to crisis; those with the upper hand need to be alert to their likelihood of downfall. For public relations practitioners, the *yin-yang* rotation implies that it is critical to discern the public's perception of the non-domestic corporation's pecking order among other cultures compared with that of the host culture. In addition, it is important to assume that members in the less privileged culture may one day gain the upper hand be it, for example, economic or, in the more extreme cases, through military intervention.

Therefore, practitioners need to restrain their own display of any sense of cultural superiority. These issues can be addressed by employing the suck strategy in the *chi* approach.

Suck Before initiating a change in practice methods or advocating a novel cause, public relations practitioners working in the global realm need to identify and understand the cultural values and norms of local publics. Knowing the local practices and values, the public relations activities could ride the existing energy flow (*chi*). The following case can serve as an example of the suck *shih* strategy.

Before the U.S. brokerage firm Lehman Brothers collapsed in 2008, the Japanese brokerage firm, Normura, acquired Lehman's Japanese branches. In a push to further the globalization of the firm, which has branches in Europe, Africa, and the Middle East, Normura set up a transition team to help with the integration effort, apparently due to the requisite of interconnectedness. But cultural clashes presented a stumbling block in this process. For example, according to a *Wall Street Journal* report, when more than one investment-banking client appeared at the same auction of securities (such as bonds, notes, or stocks), the former Lehman brokers chose to serve the ones who paid the higher fees. Normura, in contrast, places more emphasis on other factors, such as length of the relationship. They considered their new colleagues, the former Lehman brokers, "too willing to dump loyal clients for a quick profit" (Tudor, 2009, p. A12).

In view of cyclicity, organizational integration and differentiation are rotating *yin* and *yang*. To expedite or impede the cycling process, one would need to identify the *shih* (strategic advantage) such as societal factors and cultural values so that one can adopt the right *shih* strategy to generate *chi* for that purpose. In this Normura/Lehman Brothers example, the driving *shih* includes high or low social mobility, materialism/rationalism, or relationship/*guanxi*. For example, to smooth the integration process, Normura could adopt two different strategies. In a society of low social mobility or a culture that values relationship/connection, Normura would prefer long-term ("loyal") clients over higher-fee clients. On the other hand, in more materially driven cultures such as that of the United States, Normura could choose to serve ones who paid the greater fees.

If different sets of practice guidelines are allowed to coexist in a globalized corporation it could ride the cultural values—suck *shih*—to generate the amiable spirit (*chi*) among employees with different cultural backgrounds and between brokers and clients. In the course of integration, especially after sufficient internal communication, members of the two corporate cultures may negotiate to adopt one or the other practice or even create a third alternative practice. This "peaceful coexistence" strategy would make public relations practitioners mindful of the importance of holding an open attitude toward cyclic differentiation-integration transformation. Allowing the nature of the organization to take its (cyclic) course could diminish unnecessary conflicts and thus enhance morale.

Duck   Once people internalize the concept of cyclicity, they may better understand the impermanent nature of human relationships and be better able to endure frustrations in relationships, anticipating a *yin-yang* rotation. In the context of public relations, practitioners may look beyond the current organization/client–public relationship for the prospect of a better relationship. For example, two newly arrived expatriates of a global company based in the United States were separately involved in verbal and then physical scuffles with local residents in an East Asian country within a month. The media saw the potential for some dramatic news coverage and flocked into the community to unearth conflict stories. To the dismay of the media, the community almost unanimously threw its support (*yang* role) behind the company (*yin* role) by counting the generous support they had received (*yin* role) from the company (*yang* role). The give (*yang*)-take (*yin*) roles reversed. The public relations personnel held a news conference to explain how the conflicts had resulted from language barriers, cultural differences, and misunderstanding. The aggressive press then tried to elicit the company's position on the issues of injury settlement for its employees. A hostile journalist even plumbed the vice-president's personal views on local politics. Instead of displaying the assertiveness often associated with Western values, the company personnel at the conference humbly apologized and tactfully shunned highly charged topics. Reading the media reports, the community approved of the conciliatory tone of the vice-president at the news conference. The conflict was quickly resolved, and the resentments of both conflicting parties gradually evaporated. In a fascinating about-turn the press actively sought out more stories about how the company supported the community through, for example, local hires inviting expatriates to join the local festivals and celebrations, and how the company CEO routinely gave talks at local schools speaking in both English and the local languages.

As the above example demonstrates, realizing the revolving roles of *yin* (e.g., take) and *yang* (e.g., give), public relations practitioners should be more mindful of the value of long-term relationships between the organization and its publics. The duck strategy and the ensuing tactics may prevent self-inflicted wounds, a common by-product of heated confrontation with specific constituents such as the press or large publics. The effort to create peace may prove to be wise when the give (*yang*) and take (*yin*) relationship shifts.

Creativity

I-Ching is concerned with the principle of change. The "change" process in *I-Ching* is characterized by vitality and creativity. The ability to create indicates vitality. Creativity results from the interactions between the two qualities of *yin* and *yang* of all things. In public relations, for example, a relatively small organization (*yin*) may advocate a cause, rallying the public behind it, to fight a larger organization or power (*yang*). A wealth of novel strategies, new information, fresh ideas, or emergent policies may result from the communication (criticism, defense, counter-attack, or compromises) between the two camps. Depending on the *yin* or *yang* an organizational public relations team views itself to be, it can adopt certain *chi-shih* strategies. The following section explicates the buck strategy.

Buck   As opposed to the suck strategy, which involves going along with the strong (*yang*) organization, cause, trend, social concerns, or public opinion, the buck strategy involves the smaller organization (*yin*) going against the *yang*. The public relations campaign of a global firm in an East Asian country illustrates the buck strategy. At the early stage of the 2008 to 2009 global economic recession, the firm launched a campaign to encourage the local public to "spend money." The ostensible theme went against the value of frugality, which is not only a core value in the local culture but also an age-old value of many cultures. The campaign, as expected by the public relations team, encountered furious attacks from local religious and educational groups. The fact that the firm was from a foreign country further clouded the motive of the advertisements in the eyes of the local public. A local leader contemptuously mocked the idea as more difficult to understand than a foreign language. Without confronting the groups, the firm further reinforced its theme with a simple and intentionally puzzling slogan: "spend money." Simple illustrations and copy (advertising texts) also served to reinforce the slogan. Two weeks after the campaign started, the team changed the slogan in its advocacy advertisements, so that it read: "Spend money on training!" The firm even used the expertise of its employees to offer a series of free training workshops on computer programming, which was unrelated to its business. Two months later, the national government started its own "spend money" programs and campaigns as an economic stimulus package. High tech related job-skill training was among the spending items. The knowledge base and foresight of the firm thus boosted its image among the local community. Behind the success of the firm was the buck strategy of obstensibly challenging the strong local cultural value of prudence. The public relations team's withholding its arguments fueled criticisms and helped to widen the gap between the *yin* (the lone voice of the corporation's advocacy theme) and the *yang* (the force of the strong local cultural value). The *shih* thus boosted the *chi* in the campaign messages. Before pin-pointing an issue to take on, and before programming and forging actions, it could be fruitful for the public relations practitioner to survey situations to identify *yin* and *yang* aspects of the issues, contradictions, or paradoxes involved. In other words, employing a buck strategy, the public relations practitioner may find the fulcrum or the high leverage point from which to operate strategically.

Construct   If employees are allowed to participate in decision making, contribute ideas, and implement policies this reduces the difference and distance between *yin* (employees) and *yang* (management). An amiable *chi* is thus produced. The story of a successful public relations operation in a global firm in the United States well exemplifies this strategy.

The firm, headquartered in Taiwan, has a dress code which is implemented by its branches around the world. However, a couple of years after its U.S. arm began operations, tensions developed in it over wearing uniforms. Younger employees, including Taiwanese expatriates, defied the code in favor of no uniform. The public relations office spent half a year conducting research on this matter, and convinced the top management to substitute the dress code with a standing committee for a wardrobe design contest. Employees were rewarded for submitting ideas or designs for the most attractive and appropriate wardrobe. The company also subsidized the design and manufactured the wardrobe designed by the annual award winner. Employees adopted the "non-uniform" on a voluntary basis—80% of its 261 employees chose to wear the "non-uniform." The committee was later expanded to a program of comprehensive suggestion solicitation. Incorporated into the company's Total Quality Control (TQC) program were brainstorming sessions. This public relations innovation, which evolved from the tension between the management and the employees, created a strong, positive *chi* of morale. The director of the public relations department was rewarded with a promotion to the position of vice-president, a structural change that the department had been fighting for over the years. The reduction of the gap between *yin* (employees) and *yang* (the management), therefore, constructed an amiable *chi* that fostered morale.

Unity

Like their Indian neighbors, the Chinese believe there is "an ultimate reality which underlies the multiple things and events we observe" (Capra, 2000, p. 104). The whole is also composed of multi-levels and multi-facets of *yin-yang* opposites, interacting with each other. For example, at the organizational level, a corporation and the media may have a *yin-yang* (organization/public) relationship, but at lower levels, there may be other *yin-yang* (e.g., advertiser/media or buyer/seller) relationships. Therefore, the larger universe is conceived to include countless small universes. Because of such intertwined relationships and interdependences, the universe is composed of complicated dynamic interactions. Public relations practitioners play an indispensable role in navigating this dynamism to form interconnections and relationships. As Wilcox, Cameron, Ault, and Agee (2003) note:

> Diffusion-of-knowledge theorists call public relations people "linking agents." Sociologists refer to them as "boundary spanners" that act to transfer information between two systems. As the last lines of the official statement on public relations by the Public Relations Society of America note: "The public relations practitioner utilizes a variety of professional communication skills and plays an integrative role both within and between the organization and the external environment." (p. 8)

From the perspective of *chi*, because of the intricate *yin-yang* interplays, there are highly active and multi-directional energy flows in public relations in the context of globalization. It is the practitioner's responsibility to map these flows and act as a bridge builder between cultures through strategic action. The following two *chi-shih* strategies, buck and construct, help demonstrate how practitioners can work with the principle of unity to build harmonious relationships.

Buck   As discussed above, the buck strategy is particularly crucial when one is in a relatively weak, disadvantageous, or underprivileged (*yin*) position. By battling the strong (*yang*), the weak could win public acclaim and thus gain the *chi* in communication. *I-Ching* provides some guiding principles for the weak to build unity: forging friendships and alliances, setting the purpose, and remaining steadfast in one's virtues to dissipate uncertainties (Siu, 1968). In public relations, practitioners, especially those with relatively small organizations, may coordinate, network, and build relations with certain cause bases (such as social or advocacy groups) to compete with larger organizations. They can forge alliances by identifying common purposes and focus on mutually beneficial mission and rally the spirited bases behind the organization or client. Common purposes with allies facilitate networking to wage a war against the strong foe. Some examples illustrate the buck strategy amid and subsequent to the discussion on the construct strategy in the next section.

Construct   As discussed in the *chi* theory section, there are two categories of *chi*, the radical or vigorous *chi* and the amiable *chi*. To create a vigorous kind of *chi*, one could create a set-up (*shih*) to maximize the difference between *yin* and *yang* (e.g., the evilness of the attackers vs. the righteousness of the organization). For example, to fend off a global firm which was trying to acquire a local company, the union of the local company issued a press release highlighting the compensation gap between executives and the rank-and-file employees of the predator firm. The union claimed that, compared with the value of equality preferred in the local company, the predator's large pay gap showed its desire for greedy exploitation and plunder. This construct strategy could boost the union members' morale because the argument set up a contrast between the *yin*, the local company's equality, and the *yang*, the large global firm's greed. The set-up has the greater potential of firing up the fighting spirit than a message without opposites (the *yin* and *yang* symbols here are subjectively and arbitrarily assigned). The two strategies of buck and construct need not be separated. In addition to the case of union vs. business predator cited above, the following example also demonstrates their mixed implementation.

A relatively new and small multinational air freight company started its operations in several countries. Taxed by inconveniences and barriers and, in some countries, being "bullied" as the new kid on the block, the freighter hired a public relations firm to craft a strategy to build up its power in inter-organizational relations. Under the objective of maximizing networks of relationships with minimum cost, the public relations strategy started with a pilot project in this East Asian country's operation center. Numerous brainstorming sessions churned out an unexpected strategy: using employees' female spouses to establish a social organization for the air cargo firm. A tabloid newspaper just happened to have exposed a series of extramarital scandals involving celebrities, and one paper reported a rising trend among the high brass of corporate executives of having mistresses. The spouse team took advantage of these current events to spearhead an "anti-mistress campaign." Their approaches to developing a huge network were as creative as their campaign theme: they sponsored a series of social activities across organizations and even trades while involving their male spouses in the activities. The activities included events such as speeches, workshops, and hiking (but not golfing or feasting, which are traditionally privileged to high ranking executives). The internally used slogan was: "Find partner life for your life partner," meaning that, without a mistress, the domestic partners can regain the life with their life-long partner. Within less than a year, the organization grew and boasted of having recruited over 1,600 members from all walks of life including among the freight company's competitors. The employees of the freight company joined their spouses to participate in the campaigns and activities, with social networking placed on the top of their agenda. As the employees and their spouses played the leadership roles in the organization, the freighter's social relations power was quickly built up. The immediate result was indicated by a significant privilege granted to the company when the airport authority opened a new terminal: the once-bullied "new kid" freight company was allocated the parking bay closest to its airport office.

The *chi-shih* strategies in these cases involve both the buck and the construct. The public relations team of the small freighter (*yin*) motivated the employees by appealing to their psychological need to wrestle with large competitors (*yang*). This buck strategy was put into operation by building an intricate network to develop social relationships, a construct strategy.

Conclusion

Based on *I-Ching* philosophy, the *chi* theory of communication, and the *chi-shih* strategies, I illustrate a flexible and dynamic model of communication for globalized public relations in this chapter. The selection of the strategy depends on the degree of *yin-yang* contrast, which has to be assessed by practitioners. Overall, the *chi* approach is more human than task oriented. It also carries the potential for reducing the cost of remedial communication in an organization because of its emphasis on prevention of conflict (Chen & Chung, 1994, 1997). Finally, *chi* is flexible, changeable, emergent, and maneuverable, and, as an emotion-related substance, is subject to cocreation.

The symmetrical model of public relations (Grunig & Hunt, 1984) emphasizes the balance of attitude and practice in the relations between an organization and its publics. The *chi* model of public relations, however, aims at discerning the differences and even polarities in the selection of strategies. Its focus is on the power differences between two cultural values or two degrees of cultural dominance. This focus on differences is a necessary step toward figuring out strategies for building and maintaining harmonious client-public relationships.

A word of caution, however, is necessary. When put into practice, the *chi* approach could involve potential ethical risks. The values of harmony and unity may be exploited or even abused by some dominant cultures in the process of homogenizing economically weaker cultures. Worded differently, this model, the suck strategy in particular, may be adopted for maintaining the status quo. Second, the emphasis on relationships and networking might legitimize the power-motivated in-group and out-group dichotomy, paving the way for nepotism and unfairness, if not corruption, in public relations practices. These are caveats to be kept in mind.

Drawing on an ancient philosophy, the *I-Ching* approach offers new ways of studying, teaching, and practicing public relations in the context of globalization. *I-Ching* is well-known for being difficult to comprehend, but its principles are practical and heuristic. Employed to develop *chi-shih* strategies, these principles are applicable, memorable, and recyclable (*I-Ching* principles have been repeatedly adopted for prediction and analysis for 2,000 years).

Discussion Questions

1. What do you think are the strengths and weakness of the *chi*-based public relations strategies in addition to what is argued in the conclusion?
2. The four *chi-shih* strategies (suck, duck, buck, and construct) operate at the strategic level. Can they be applied to the tactical (such as verbal and non-verbal messaging) level in global or local public relations practices? Illustrate with an example.
3. Among the cases illustrating the various strategies, which ones would likely not have happened in a local public relations context? Which ones could likely not be solved without employing the *chi-shih* strategies?
4. How would you formulate hypotheses or research questions in public relations studies based on the *chi* principles of communication? Think of a specific study as an example.

References

Ames, T. (1994). *The art of rulership*. Albany, NY: SUNY Press.

Austin, E., & Pinkleton, B. (2001). *Strategic public relations management*. Mahwah, NJ: Erlbaum.

Barker, C. (1999). *Television, globalisation and cultural identities*. Buckingham, UK: Open University Press.

Capra, F. (2000). *The Tao of physics*. Boston, MA: Shambhala.

Chen, G. (2009). Toward an *I-Ching* model of communication. *China Media Research, 5*(3), 72–81.

Chen, G., & Chung, J. (1994). The impact of Confucianism on organizational communication. *Communication Quarterly, 42*(2), 93–105.

Chen, G., & Chung, J. (1997). The "five Asian dragons": Management behaviors and organizational communication. In L. A. Samovar, & R. E. Porter (Eds.), *Intercultural communication: A reader* (8th ed., pp. 317–328). Belmont, CA: Wadsworth.

Chuang, R. (2000). Dialectics of globalization and localization. In G. Chen & W. Starosta (Eds.), *Communication and global society* (pp. 19–33). New York: Lang.

Chung, J. (1996). Avoiding a "Bull Moose" rebellion: Particularistic ties, seniority and third-party mediation. *International and Intercultural Communication Annual, 20,* 166–185.

Chung, J. (2008). The *chi/qi/ki* of organizational communication: The process of generating energy flow with dialectics. *China Media Research, 4*(3), 92–100.

Chung, J., & Busby, R. (2002). Organizational communication with naming strategies: The *chi-shih* approach. *Intercultural Communication Studies, 11*(1), 77-96.

Chung, J., & Ho, M. (2009). Public relations, *I-Ching*, and *Chi (Qi/Ki)* theory: A new model from an old philosophy. *China Media Research, 5*(3), 94–101.

Grunig, J., & Hunt, T. (1984). *Managing public relations.* New York: Holt, Rinehart, & Winston.

Hall, S. (1991). The local and global: Globalization and ethnicity. In A. King (Ed.), *Culture, globalization and the world-system* (pp. 19–40). Binghamton, NY: SUNY at Binghamton Press.

Hamilton, G. (1994). Civilizations and organization of economics. In N. Smelser & R. Swedberg (Eds.), *The handbook of economic sociology* (pp.153–205). Princeton, NJ: Princeton University Press.

Huang, K. (1997). Guanxi and mientze: Conflict resolution in Chinese society. *Intercultural Communication Studies, 7*(1), 17–42.

Inglehart, R., & Baker, W. (2000). Modernization, cultural change, and the persistence of traditional values. *American Sociological Review, 65*(1), 19–51.

Isaacson, F., & Chung, J. (2004). The Bush vs. Gore rhetoric after the 2000 election impasse: A *ch'i-shih* analysis. *SIMILE, 4*(2), 1–12.

Jacobs, B. (1979). A preliminary model of particularistic ties in Chinese political alliances: Kan-ching and guan-shi in a rural Taiwanese township. *China Quarterly, 78*(June), 237–273.

Juan, K. (1994). Linking the issues: From identity to activism. In K. Juan, D. Huang, & M. Jaimes (Eds.), *The state of Asian America: Activism and resistance in the 1990s* (pp. 1–15). Boston, MA: South End Press.

Karcher, S. (1997). *The I-Ching plain and simple.* London: Element.

Lin, Y. (2009). *The wisdom of Laotse.* Beijing, China: Foreign Language Teaching & Research Press.

Lu, R. (2004). *Zhong guo gu dai xiang dui guanxi si wei tan tao* [Investigation of the ancient Chinese relativistic relations]. Taipei, Taiwan: Shiang Ding Culture.

Martin, J., & Nakayama, T. (1999). Thinking dialectically about culture and communication. *Communication Theory, 9*(1), 1–25.

Robertson, R. (1992). *Globalization: Social theory and global culture.* Newbury Park, CA: Sage.

Robertson, R. (1995). Glocalization. In M. Featherstone, S. Lash, & R. Robertson (Eds.), *Global modernities* (pp. 25–44). London: Sage.

Seitel, P. (2001). *The practice of public relations* (8th ed.). Upper Saddle River, NJ: Prentice-Hall.

Siu, R. G. H. (1968). *The man of many qualities: A legacy of the I-Ching.* Cambridge, MA: MIT Press.

Tenbruck, F. (1990). The dream of a secular ecumene: The meaning and limits of policies of development. In M. Featherstone (Ed.), *Global culture: Nationalism, globalization and modernity* (pp. 193–206). Newbury Park, CA: Sage.

The laptop trail. (2005, June 9). *Wall Street Journal,* p. B1.

Tudor, A. (2009, July 29). Nomura stumbles in new global push. *Wall Street Journal,* pp. A1, A12.

Wallerstein, I. (1974). *The modern world system: Capitalist agriculture and the origins of the European world economy in the sixteenth century.* New York: Academic Press.

Wilcox, D., Cameron, G., Ault, P., & Agee, W. (2003). *Public relations: Strategies and tactics* (7th ed.). San Francisco, CA: Allyn & Bacon.

Yu, Y. (2005). Creativity in the *I-Ching* and in Whitehead's philosophy. *Jiao Yu Zi Liao Ji Kan [Journal of Educational Materials],* 30, 21–46.

Suggested Readings

Asante, M., Miike, Y., & Yin, J. (2008). *The global intercultural reader.* New York: Routledge.

Bardhan, N., & Patwardhan, P. (2004). Multinational corporations and public relations in a traditionally resistant host culture. *Journal of Communication Management, 8*(3), 246–263.

Baxter, L., & Montomery, B. (1996). *Relating: Dialogues and dialectics.* New York: Guilford.

Botan. C., & Hazleton, V. (2006). *Public relations theory* (Vol. 2). Mahwah, NJ: Erlbaum.

Bridges, J., & Nelson, R. (2000). Issues management: A relational approach. In J. Ledingham & S. Bruning (Eds.), *Public relations as relationship management* (pp. 95–115). Mahwah, NJ: Erlbaum.

Chang, C. Y. (1963). *Creativity and Taoism: A study of Chinese philosophy, art, and poetry.* New York: Harper & Row.

Huang, Y. (2000). The personal influence model and *gao guanxi* in Taiwan Chinese public relations. *Public Relations Review, 26*(2), 219–236.

Kruckeberg, D. (2000). Public relations: Toward a global professionalism. In J. Ledingham & S. Bruning (Eds.), *Public relations as relationship management* (pp. 145–157). Mahwah, NJ: Erlbaum.

May, R. (1975). *The courage to create.* New York: Bantam Books.

Chapter 10

Public Relations, Globalization, and Culture

Framing Methodological Debates and Future Directions

C. Kay Weaver

Globalization brings significant challenges for public relations scholarship. Public relations was once an *apparently* relatively contained phenomenon, comprised of practitioners operating for organizations in definable localities—regions, nations, or internationally. It could be identified through its genres of practice (e.g., media relations, crisis and issues management, employee relations, investor relations, community relations, government relations, and so on), its strategic intentions, and its engagement of specific publics. However, as the public sphere has been taken over by a "Niagara of PR" (Moloney, 2006, pp. 1–14), as the boundaries between public relations and other forms of communication have become increasingly blurred, as its methods have been adopted by activists, governments, "spin doctors," politicians, celebrities, unions, royalty, and even guerrilla revolutionaries (see Grimshaw, 2007; Knudson, 1998), as its communication objects and subjects have become increasingly deterritorialized, and its research and theorizing has been conducted from a variety of paradigmatic perspectives by scholars in different parts of the world, exactly what public relations is, or what it should be, has become highly contested and progressively more difficult to define.

With globalization also being a notoriously difficult construct to define, there is little wonder that there is no precision in, and little sense of consensus about how "global public relations" should be researched and theorized. There has been a plethora of calls to better understand public relations in the global context (e.g., Bardhan, 2003; Creedon & Al-Khaja, 2005; Curtin & Gaither, 2007; Gower, 2006; Yannas, 2006), but a dearth of actual empirical investigation of the phenomenon. There is a sense that from our various perspectives we all want to understand the role that public relations plays in globalization and how it is utilized and practiced differently according to varying cultural contexts, and how the profession is responding to deterritorialization, but few scholars have been able to develop tangible and manageable investigations to explore this. Good examples to date of attempts to do so are Curtin and Gaither's cultural-economic model (2006, 2007; Gaither & Curtin, 2008) and Molleda, Connolly-Ahern, and Quinn's (2005) content analysis of campaigns conducted across cultural borders. However, a much greater range of research than this is needed.

The past decade has witnessed the academic study of public relations become much broader than it was in the field's "first generation" of research (Gower, 2006, p. 177), which focused primarily on the production of instrumental knowledge. As calls continue for the discipline to draw from social, cultural, and political theories (e.g., Ihlen & van Ruler, 2009; Wehmeier, 2006; Yannas, 2006), there is a growing appreciation of the need to understand the "place" of public relations in, and its contributions to, the shape of this globalizing world. Yet, in the act of bringing public relations into a "second generation" of inquiry—where a range of paradigmatic approaches to its research investigation and theorizing coexist in some kind of plurality (McKie & Munshi, 2007)—we have staked out our own different "cultural tribes" (Leichty, 2003) within public relations research.

My aim in this chapter is to reflect on two of these tribal groupings—systems Excellence theorists and critical theorists—in relation to paradigmatic methodologies underpinning their scholarly investigations of public relations, and how these represent particular sets of knowledge, beliefs, and value systems. These methodologies, as cultures themselves, provide insight into how and why public relations theorists hold the profession in the regard that they do, and also, importantly, how they articulate its ethics.

I focus specifically on "Excellence" and critical theory perspectives in this chapter because of the vociferous debate enacted between them; a debate which involves some misunderstandings and misrepresentations of each perspective's intentions and relationship to public relations practice. Both perspectives have limitations and blind spots and, in the context of globalization, we need to move beyond these and bring more insightful ways of knowing to researching and theorizing public relations.

In examining the direction that public relations research might take in future consideration of globalization and culture, the latter part of the chapter introduces the *kaupapa* Maori methodological framework—a participatory approach developed in New Zealand which calls for research practice that benefits its communities of inquiry. This is introduced for two reasons. First, as we to strive to investigate and theorize public relations in a globalizing context, *kaupapa* Maori perspectives alert us to more carefully consider how our research constructs peoples and cultures, on whose behalf we claim to speak, for whose rights, and how well we imagine theories represent the needs of "others." Second, *kaupapa* Maori positions constructively challenge universalizing

Western understandings of professional ethics in emphasizing "ways of being" rather than "acts of doing," and focus attention on the ethics of methodology, methods, research analysis, and dissemination. There are lessons to be taken from this perspective for both systems Excellence and critical theorists.

The "Science" of Excellence Research

As is well documented, the first wave of major theory building in public relations scholarship began in 1985 with the U.S.-based Excellence project led by James Grunig at the University of Maryland, which was funded by the International Association of Business Communicators (IABC). In terms of the social and cultural positioning of public relations and especially within academia, this project brought considerable legitimacy to the profession following decades of a troubling association with propaganda (Pieczka, 2006; Weaver, Motion, & Roper, 2006). Further, both external and internal credibility was brought to the research itself through its "scientific" methodological approach.

The scientific method has dominated how "reality" has been investigated and constructed in the Western world since the 17th century Enlightenment turn, and is "identified with the highest standards of intellectual rigor and the most reliable procedures for gaining and accessing knowledge" (Schuster & Yeo, 1986). Ontologically, the method posits that reality and knowledge exist independently from the research act. In order to discover the "facts" of this reality, rigorous and systematic empirical observations or experiments are used to test hypotheses or propositions. The aim in this research enterprise is to discover causal relationships between phenomena, and to be able to predict the outcomes of future actions. Since the Enlightenment, the scientific path has become entrenched as the best path to discovering "truth."

In keeping with the expectations of scientific research, the Excellence project comprised (1) an extensive literature review of theories from a range of disciplines which informed the development of propositions about public relations best practice; and (2) the survey and analysis of data gathered from 225 organizations which tested these propositions. From this the theory of Excellence was developed that described "14 characteristics of excellent communication departments and three effects of their communication programs" (Excellence in Public Relations and Communication Management, 1991). The theory was then further empirically tested through the surveying of over 200 organizations in Canada, the United States, and the United Kingdom including corporations, non-profits, and government agencies. The countries selected for involvement in this research are indicative of a Western cultural focus and bias in the project. Implicitly, and very likely unconsciously, these countries were judged the most suitable or representative cultural sites for providing insight into the public relations profession.

Systems theory, in which the Excellence theory of public relations is embedded, has its own cultural biases. The theory has its roots in biology and seeks to explain the relationships between elements in terms of how effectively they adapt to the environmental system of which they are a part. Yet, while this theory originated out of Western scientific thought (its founder, Ludwig von Bertalanffy, was German), forms of systems thinking are also found in non-Western philosophies such as Buddhism, Chinese *I-Ching* philosophy, and in indigenous cultures such as the New Zealand Maori and Australian Aborigines where the notion of interconnectedness comprises a fundamental value through which actions and their effects are judged (e.g., Bishop, 2008; Chung, in this volume; Khisty, 2006; Smith, 1999). However, in these non-Western philosophies, the totality of the system is not perceived in rationalist machine-like terms. Instead, an appreciation of interconnectedness among all living things brings in a spiritual and non-scientific dimension to the quality of humanity.

From a positivist rationalist perspective, systems theory represents the organization as a complex social system made up of interdependent parts, and as linked to and dependent on the environment in which it operates. Closed organizations do not recognize their dependence on the system, and are unlikely to survive in the long term. Open systems, on the other hand, recognize the nature of their interdependence. Thus, the importance of public relations to the organization is stressed: "Public relations is one of the primary links in sustaining this interdependence, both internally and externally, to an organization" (Plowman, 2005, p. 840). Consequently, public relations theorists were especially concerned to investigate the significance of the public relations "function" to the effective organizational achievement of goals—both as part of the organizational system and as a means by which the organization intersects with its external environments. As Witmer (2006) explains:

> From a systems perspective, public relations functions as both systems component and boundary spanner.... Environmental scanning brings information into the organization, and external communications send information into the organizational environment.... Therefore, public relations activities serve a feedback function that helps the client systems interpret the environments in order to maintain homeostasis. (pp. 363–364)

It was from within systems theory framing of organizations and their need to effectively intersect with their operating environment that the four models of public relations were developed: press agentry, public information, one-way asymmetrical, and two-way symmetrical. It was concluded that those organizations that practiced two-way symmetrical communication were more likely to succeed in adapting to the needs of the environment in which they operated because "public relations serves the public interest, develops mutual understanding between organizations and their publics, contributes to informed debate about issues in society, and facilitates a dialogue between organizations and their publics" (J. Grunig & White, 1992, p. 53).

The ideals underpinning the two-way symmetrical model are laudable. But these ideals are also rested within the context of the political and economic system under which it was assumed they could be achieved—laissez-faire capitalist pluralism. In this context a definition of the "public interest" is worked out through "democratic" debate and negotiation in the "marketplace of ideas." Though a competitive environment, this context *ideally* allows "equal access to and equal power in the policy making process" (Coombs, 1993, p. 112). In these terms, "The public interest is best served when the voices of diverse special interests are heard. Marketplace theory rests on the premise that 'truth' will emerge from robust public debate and be determined by the people who evaluate competing ideas and messages" (Fitzpatrick, 2006, p. 4).

Within the Excellence model, public relations practitioners play an important role in representing organizations, facilitating two-way dialogue with publics, and negotiating "win-win" situations by bringing the public interest to bear on organizational decision making. Systems theory claims that for public relations to effectively achieve this it needs to be part of the "dominant coalition"—and thereby involved in management decision making (Sriramesh, J. Grunig, & Buffington, 1992), rather than being merely a technical function within the organization. Advocates of the model remain firm in this view. For example, J. Grunig, and L. Grunig (2009) reiterate this by stating:

> Amplifying the voice of publics in the process of organizational decision making demands more of a communicator than a technician's skills. It requires someone at the management level who can function as a peer professional among other members of the organization's dominant coalition. Inclusion in that power elite, or at least direct reporting to the C-suite (with the other chief executives) is a major premise of the Excellence study. (p. 638)

Systems theory is, then, both managerialist (in that it emphasizes the causal value of efficient management to organizational success), and "scientific" (in presenting a universal law of causality between how public relations is practiced and organizational effectiveness), in cultural orientation. Indeed proponents of systems based public relations theory clearly align themselves with the culturally "progressive" imperatives of Western scientific thought stating, for example, that:

> the scientific method has changed the world and the way people think about the world. In general, the scientific method *has improved people's lives and has forced them to think logically and systematically* [emphasis added] about the things they observe and experience. As a result, many professions—including public relations—have looked to science to ground the practice of their profession. (J. Grunig & White, 1992, p. 31)

It would be inaccurate, however, to describe systems theorists as strictly positivist. J. Grunig and White (1992), for example, do not claim that science can be totally objective, value neutral, or able to discover "truths." This is an important distinction as these theorists do acknowledge that human subjectivity (and with that we can include culture) influences how public relations is perceived, practiced, and taught.

Yet, what also needs to be understood is how "organizational effectiveness" is judged under systems theory, and how this is intrinsically embedded in a sympathy of, and support for the Western neoliberal capitalist economy. Indeed, Excellence researchers acknowledged that ultimately the approach judged organizational effectiveness in financial terms. For example, in exploring "What is an effective organization?" L. Grunig, J. Grunig, and Ehling (1992) stated that "the contribution of public relations to the bottom line requires a logical, theoretical argument to connect communication objectives to broader organizational goals" (p. 65). Ehling (1992) additionally argued for a cost-benefit analysis of public relations, asserting that "the economic component of public relations management should loom large in determining the worth (specified in monetary terms) of not only a specific public relations program but also of the public relations department and its function in an organization" (p. 617). While these financial imperatives provided the baseline from which successful public relations work was judged, absent in the original Excellence project was any clear articulation of the intersection between public relations and culture. Unquestionably, however, the imperatives of 20th century U.S. modernist capitalist *culture* played a pivotal role in determining how "Excellent" practice was defined, though this was never explicitly expressed within the Excellence project itself.

Excellence, Systems Theory, and Culture

Excellence theorists acknowledged early on that "systems theories disregard the impact of culture, a key element of the environment, on organizational processes" (Sriramesh et al., 1992, p. 578). Consequently, propositions based on existing literature about the likely relationship between *corporate culture* and public relations (Sriramesh et al., 1992, p. 578), and between *social culture* and public relations (Sriramesh & White, 1992) were developed. But it was Geert Hofstede's theory of how management styles varied across different national cultures that proved especially appealing to first generation inter-national public relations researchers.

Developed from the study of 100,000 IBM employees situated in different parts of the world, Hofstede identified five different indices of cultural values: power distance, uncertainty avoidance, individualism vs. collectivism, masculinity vs. femininity, and long- vs. short-term orientation (1984, 1997). Sriramesh (2009a) tellingly comments that "Scholars who have tried to link societal culture with public relations have almost exclusively relied on Hofstede's dimensions. This is partly because of the lucidity with which he described and operationalized these constructs. But it is also because of the *ease of replicating his reliable and valid survey instrument* [emphasis added]" (p. 55). It seems it was not so much the perceived accuracy of Hofstede's model that was attractive to early international public relations researchers, but its commensurability with a managerial organizational focus and scientific predictive agendas.

As outlined earlier in this book, there are significant problems with Hofstede's dimensions of culture and their application to public relations. These dimensions treat culture as static and essentialize different cultures. They also present nation-state and culture as synonymous, nations as containing homogenous cultures, and fail to reflect the shear diversity and complexity of culture and cultures. For example, in New Zealand, my own country of residence, the majority of the population is White European in descent and individualistic in orientation. The indigenous Maori, who were in the majority up until the latter half of the 1800s (King, 2004) and who have maintained significant levels of political and cultural influence, are more familial collectivist in orientation. But then not all Maori are collectivist, and there are significant cultural differences between urban and rural Maori and within and across these groups. Furthermore, New Zealand now has a sizable Asian population with a range of cultural values that are different again from those of the Europeans and Maori. In this context, to say that Hofstede's cultural dimensions "tend to act as an essentializing discourse, neglecting the nuances of bicultural and multicultural policies" (Motion, Leitch, & Cliffe, 2009, p. 116) is a generous treatment of the theory. Sadly, as is the case in many complex cultural contexts in increasingly multicultural societies, no substantial research has been conducted on how public relations practitioners negotiate the many and varied cultural dynamics present in New Zealand.

This is not to say that research that applies Hofstede's dimensions to the examination of the relationships between public relations and culture has no value. Vasquez and Taylor's (1999) application interestingly found, for example, that "American practitioners continue to practice one-way models of public relations even when their organizations may not dictate one-way communication with publics.... [P]ublic relations practitioners who have collectivist values tend to practice two-way models of public relations" (p. 433). There have also been a number of country specific studies which extended Hofstede's dimensions of culture in identifying other cultural factors that impacted on how public relations was conducted in different nation-states (see Sriramesh, 2009b, for a discussion of these). Researchers continue to draw on Hofstede's cultural dimensions in explaining public relations practice in different national contexts, and position it as a "valuable tool for developing public relations strategies conducive to building and maintaining relationships with multicultural audiences" (Kang & Mastin, 2008, p. 54). Indeed, Kent and Taylor, and Courtright, Wolfe, and Baldwin's contributions to this volume support Hofstede's dimensions as continuing to have at least some relevance to the study of public relations in a globalizing world, though they do encourage movement into theories and methods that can more adequately address public relations practice within the context of cultural diversity and complexity.

Criticisms of Systems/Excellence Theory

Systems theory has been hugely influential in public relations scholarship and comprises the discipline's most extensive "body of knowledge." But it has also been heavily criticized, and has in many ways constrained theoretical developments within the discipline because of its dominance (McKie, 1997). A significant amount of criticism has been directed at how the Excellence framework became the normative model for public relations not just in the United States, but also in contexts which do not share U.S. political, economic, and cultural values. A further issue of concern relates to how Excellence theory positions two-way symmetrical public relations as "ethical" practice. Critics have decried the naivety of the failure to recognize that organizations which are in a position to afford and utilize public relations expertise will likely have far greater resources at their disposal than the publics they "dialogue" with (e.g., Coombs, 1993; Creedon, 1993; Duffy, 2000; Leitch & Neilson, 1997; Weaver, 2001). When these power differentials are taken into account, the two-way model is in fact far from symmetrical.

Critiques of the models of public relations aside, other challenges to systems based theory concern how organizational effectiveness is defined primarily in terms of profit, and how groups are only identified as publics if they have the capacity to impact on the bottom line. McKie and Munshi (2007) critically illustrate this by using the world's worst industrial disaster—the gas leak at the Union Carbide plant in Bhopal, India—as their case in point. This "accident," caused by Union Carbide's lack of safety maintenance at the factory, killed thousands, left many thousands injured, and continues to have devastating effects on people and the environment. Yet, the primary concern of the company's crisis management campaign was focused on maintaining corporate reputation and stock value in the United States. At no time were the people of Bhopal ever deemed to be an organizational "public." The case indicates how little corporations and public relations efforts are inclined to value peoples and cultures unless there is an economic advantage in doing so—and how Excellence theory indirectly supports this kind of practice through its stated support of the bottom line. As McKie and Munshi (2007) detail, extraordinarily, the Bhopal case is frequently cited as an example of successful crisis management in public relations text books (see Patwardhan & Bardhan, 2006, for a critique of the case). One is left wondering how such an organizational response to a disaster even warrants categorization as "public relations." But then, as Higginbottom (2007) has argued, for transnational corporations those living in the Southern Hemisphere are "the often ignored 'unpeople'" (p. 278).

This returns us to the vexed question of who defines public relations, how are they defining it, and according to whose cultural imperatives and interests? Bardhan (2003) has posed these questions in relation to non-Western contexts. She asks:

> What does public relations mean in a country where public opinion is not incorporated into the political fabric? What is public relations in an environment where consumer activism is not a popular or viable concept...? What is public relations in a system where the mass media are mostly or completely government controlled? What is public relations in a culture where the word *public* does not exist ... in the language? (p. 228)

In these terms, culture becomes a very troubling concept for systems theory, and the Excellence theory in particular. Other methodological "ways of knowing" have, however, had more success in incorporating culture into public relations scholarship.

The Critical Project

Culture has been a concept at the very heart of critical theory since its 1925 birthing in the German Frankfurt School. Following the writings of Marx and Engels, Frankfurt theorists identified what they believed to be the effects of capitalism on culture and cultural production (e.g.,

Adorno, 1991; Adorno & Horkheimer, 1944/1998; Marcus, 1991). In public relations scholarship, critical theorists have made significant strides in theorizing the relationship between the industry and culture and, in doing so, have engaged in a paradigmatic battle (Pieczka, 2006) with Excellence theorists. This is largely because, especially in the context of globalization, critical researchers theorize public relations as part of, and embedded in, the material and symbolic practices of imperialist capitalism. But just as systems Excellence theorists have their own paradigmatic cultural biases, so do critical theorists.

Deetz (2005) has explained that "Critical theory is as much a way of living as a 'theory' in the more traditional, everyday sense" (p. 90). It is an openly politicized approach to inquiry through which "researchers often regard their work as a first step toward forms of political action that can redress the injustices found in the field site or constructed in the very action itself" (Kincheloe & McLaren, 2008, p. 406). They further state:

> Research in the critical tradition takes the form of self-conscious criticism—self-conscious in the sense that researchers try to become aware of the ideological imperatives and epistemological presuppositions that inform their research as well as their own subjective, intersubjective, and normative reference claims. Thus, critical researchers enter into an investigation with their assumptions on the table, so no one is confused concerning the epistemological and political baggage they bring with them to the research site. (p. 406)

Additionally, critical theory, as originally conceived, has a transformative agenda where the aim is to "expose and, ideally, alleviate oppression" (Shugart, 2003, p. 275). It would be essentializing to say though that all critical theorists exactly follow such an agenda. L'Etang, for example, who has played a significant role in the development of critical public relations research, explains her scholarly motivation as being more focused on seeking "to understand better the nature of public relations as a social practice" (L'Etang, 2005, p. 524).

For positivists and post-positivists, the intentionally subjective and activist agenda of critical theory can be both perplexing and nonsensical. For example, in response to Dutta's (2009) postcolonial analysis of public relations, Bentele and Wehmeier (2009) contested:

> We are not totally convinced that the postcolonial scholar should work with activist movements in creating openings for emancipation through continual reflections and critique.... The main role of the scholar should be: observing, describing, analyzing, criticizing, but not being part of a movement. That would only diminish his or her trustworthiness. (p. 356)

Interestingly, in advocating a "scientific" position, Bentele and Wehmeier demonstrate little recognition of how they too are part of a cultural worldview, and one which prevents and paralyzes action because
it views such action as a "form of contamination of research results and
processes" (Guba & Lincoln, 2008, p. 266). This may be contrasted
to Foley and Valenzuela's (2008) argument that "Researchers who are
involved directly in the political process are in a better position to understand and theorize about social change" (p. 306).

Communication was not a specific focus of early critical theorists,
though they did identify the mass media as playing a central role in
the spread of capitalist ideology and culture. Burkart (2009) explains:
"Their point was that mass media, controlled by advertising and commercial imperatives, serve the needs of dominant corporate interests and
play a major role in ideological reproduction in creating subservience
to the system of consumer capitalism" (p. 141). Much critical theory
analysis of public relations reaches similar conclusions with statements
such as "the PR consultancy sector has an elective affinity with market
ideology" (Miller & Dinan, 2000, p. 20), and "public relations practitioners seek to maintain the dominance of neoliberal hegemony" (Dutta
and Pal, in this volume). For critical theorists, because of its historical
evolutionary association with the spread of capitalism, the support that
it provides to corporate and, more recently, transnational organizations
as well as the transnational organizing of public relations itself, public
relations is very often regarded as a tool of oppression.

All critical public relations researchers concentrate on issues of power
and ideology in one way or another, whether at the level of the social,
cultural, political, economic, organizational, textual, or the level of language. A wide variety of theoretical tools and perspectives informed by a
range of social, political, and cultural theories are brought to this project.
Detailing these is well beyond the scope of this chapter, but, crudely, they
range from those examining the political and economic forces behind
public relations activity (e.g., Miller & Dinan, 2000; Sklair, 2007), close
textual readings of public relations communication campaigns or texts
(e.g., Henderson, 2005; Motion & Weaver, 2005; Weaver & Motion,
2002), and those that bring cultural theories such as postmodernism
(Duffy, 2000; Holtzhausen, 2000) and subaltern studies (e.g., Dutta
and Pal, and Edwards, in this volume; Munshi & Kurian, 2005; Pal
& Dutta, 2008) to bear on the analysis. Some studies combine two or
more of these approaches (e.g., Curtin & Gaither, 2007). Irrespective of
the methodological framing of the research, there is a general consensus
among critical public relations researchers that the global growth and
reach of the public relations industry is driven by the interests of Western
capitalism, corporatization, and the deregulation of markets which only

facilitates transnational corporations' (TNCs) further access to new territories or "emerging markets" (Millar & Dinan, 2000).

While economic interests are the driving force behind public relations "going global," critical theory also attempts to explain how the industry creates a climate of acceptance for the political and cultural privileging of these interests. For example, discourse theory has identified public relations practice as constructing and promoting symbolic meanings that serve organizational needs. From this perspective, Motion and Leitch (1996) theorize practitioners "as discourse technologists [who are] actively involved in ... discursive struggles to maintain or transform sociocultural practices" (p. 301). In the global context, critical research has explored how TNCs participate in transforming sociocultural practices and meanings to align with their ideological needs and imperatives and the cultural symbolic meanings of their product and brands (Dutta and Pal, in this volume). For example, companies such as Coca-Cola and McDonald's promote discourses of the American Dream and the attainment of happiness through consumption (Curtin & Gaither, 2007). A range of postcolonial theories have been brought to this kind of analysis in an effort to "expose ... attempts by PR theory and practice to communicate corporate goals that coincide with a dominant, largely Western, model of economic growth and development" (Munshi & Kurian, 2005, p. 515).

Much of this postcolonial work is conducted at a purely theoretical level, as indeed is a significant amount of critical writing in public relations. This is a matter of concern because, as Pal and Dutta (2008) have argued, "it does not really create and sustain a discursive space for engaging with the voices of stakeholders who are typically marginalized through the dominant practice of public relations" (p. 173). There is a need for research that investigates how the public relations communication of TNCs is interpreted by the diversity of publics and audiences that come into contact with it. Media theory has a long history of such audience reception research, and offers a range of methodological perspectives that could be applied to public relations study (e.g., Alasuutari, 1999; Kitzinger, 2008; Press & Livingstone, 2006). Creating space for the voices of publics and stakeholders in research, can also, as has happened in media studies, provide a much richer and complex understanding of power in the circuit of communication and culture (Miller, Kitzinger, Williams, & Beharell, 1998). Digital and mobile media have added to the complexity of these processes bringing increased postmodern potential for audiences to take on multiple, fluid, and fragmented identities as both media producers and consumers/users.

Critical theorists have also investigated the potential for resistance to public relations campaigns and globalization (Curtin & Gaither,

2007), as well as activists' development of their own campaigns protesting against Western cultural imperialism, its policies, products, or brands (e.g., Henderson, 2005; Knudson, 1998; Weaver, 2010). Studies of such campaigns illustrate that public relations is not the exclusive domain of corporations, governments, and non-government organizations. Protestors can equally use its strategies if they have access to sufficient resources (Weaver, 2010). Yet, as Edwards (in this volume) argues in a powerful and intricate exposition of Appadurai's conceptualizing of globalization as a "work of the imagination," power is multifaceted and public relations practice should not be only assessed through studies of resistance, but also in terms of how it participates in the production of "new imaginaries" and material changes.

Critiquing Critical Approaches

While critical perspectives introduced new ways of researching and theorizing public relations, the critical project also has its failings. One concern is its identification and theoretical construction of groups or peoples as "oppressed" by political, socioeconomic, or cultural power structures, and its general failure to deliver any form of emancipation for these groups (Smith, 1999). Furthermore, as Shugart (2003) has explained:

> Because critical scholars are engaged in describing oppression—its conditions, its subjects, and its purveyors ... [there is the] significant potential to lock "characters" in their respective roles, thus essentializing them and undermining the ostensible purpose of the cultural critic—to explicate and offer redress to oppressive conditions or to examine resistance and thus contribute to social change. (pp. 290–291)

The lack of an explicit transformative and emancipatory practice in much critical work is partly attributable to academic systems, which prioritize research and publication above and even to the exclusion of community participation and activism. Critical theorists have been especially vocal in charging their own tribal members with pursuing an exclusively academic endeavor detached from a commitment to change (e.g., McChesney, 1999). In this endeavor, academic "specialists" in positions of privilege (almost exclusively seated in Western universities) narrate the experience of "others" as disenfranchised, marginalized, and dominated. Such theorizing fails to credit these "others" with any form of agency, and instead constructs them as "victims" (Cobb, 1994). Consequently, critical work has been accused of paternalism and elitism, and, in the context of public relations scholarship, L'Etang (2005) warns:

"One danger that critically focused academics do have to be aware of, is that of egocentric thinking which might lead to intellectual arrogance, closed mindedness, unfairness (to those who hold other views) or of intellectual conformity to a new set of conventions" (p. 524).

Postmodernist approaches might be regarded as less problematic in these terms as they are less essentializing than other critical perspectives in theorizing the potential for multiple fragmented identities, the complexity of multiple experiences of both freedom and possibility, but also domination and manipulation. However, there is also the need to be careful of celebrating the postmodernist concepts of multiple, fluid and "free-floating" identities in a globalizing world. From the indigenous Maori worldview, Smith (1999) has written:

> While the West might be experiencing fragmentation, the process of fragmentation known under its older guise as colonization is well known to indigenous peoples. We talk about fragmentation of lands and cultures. We know what it is like to have our identities regulated by laws and our languages and customs to be removed from our lives. Fragmentation is not an indigenous project, it is something we are recovering from. While shifts are occurring in the ways in which indigenous peoples put ourselves back together again, the greater project is about recentring indigenous identities on a larger scale. (p. 97)

From such an indigenous perspective, postmodernism represents yet another form of colonization where the West, having rejected its own metanarratives, rallies to "maintain the status quo ... by undermining all criteria of reality and truth" (Sardar, 1998, p. 15).

From another perspective, Excellence theorists have decried critical public relations scholarship for making no contribution to professional practice (e.g., J. Grunig, 2001; Tyma, 2008). As argued in the introductory chapter to this book, this reflects a misunderstanding of the critical theory project which developed as a call to action against the material and symbolic practices of capitalism. For most critical public relations theorists, the public relations industry is part of the problem, not the solution. Yet there certainly are critical researchers who actively work to bring about change in public relations and associated industry practices, and who attempt to politicize and involve others in these campaigns through Web sites such a the U.K.-based Spinwatch(n.d.)and the U.S. sites PR watch (n.d.) and CorpWatch (n.d.).

Critiques of critical theory are also voiced by scholars from "marginalized" groups who support emancipatory research agendas, but for whom critical theory has failed as a transformative project. Some such criticisms have come from *kaupapa* Maori researchers who advocate a participatory research paradigm which removes the locus of power from the individual researcher and places it in the hands of research participants as coresearchers (Bishop, 2008).

Kaupapa Maori and Future Methodological Directions

Kaupapa Maori research represents a response to the hand-in-hand European colonization of New Zealand and the dominance of Western positivist research (Cram, 2001; Smith, 1999, 2008). As Smith (2008) states, "the history of research for many indigenous perspectives is so deeply embedded in colonization that it has been regarded as a tool of colonization.... Research is a site of contestation not simply at the level of epistemology or methodology but also in its broadest sense as an organized scholarly activity that is deeply connected to power" (p. 116). For indigenous peoples, Western research has "Othered" their cultures and experiences through methodologies that objectify and scrutinize them through Western eyes, cultural imperatives, and values.

This is not merely a problem of history and how things were done before researchers "knew any better." These practices continue today. For example, in 2006, at the 11th International Congress on Human Genetics, two scientists presented a paper (Lea & Chamber, 2007) identifying Maori as having an overrepresentation of monoamine oxidase—a "warrior gene"—which predisposes them to violent and criminal behavior. By association this was offered as an explanation for proportionally higher rates of domestic violence, alcoholism, and incarceration among Maori. The research was later discredited (Hook, 2009), but in the meantime the media publicity that it attracted, with headlines such as "Violence Is Blamed on 'Warrior Gene' in the Maoris" (Chapman, 2006) only served to reinforce racial stereotypes of Maori as "uncivilized." Hook (2009) expounded: "The implications that follow from the 'warrior' gene hypothesis should it become fact in the minds of the general public are horrendous" (p. 5). He went on to say:

> Maori are not the only indigenous people to find themselves accused of violence by their mainstream colonizers.... The only common factor amongst all these indigenes appears to lie in the perceptions of their colonizers, their dispossession from their lands, their impoverishment, deprivation and assimilation. Somewhere in there might lie the real reason for indigenous violence. (p. 7)

Other scientists also contested the "warrior gene" research and distanced themselves from Lea and Chamber's "scientific" claims. Crampton and Parkin (2007), for example, took issue with it, emphasizing that "Ethical principles governing research involving human subjects bear largely on empowering individual participants and protecting them from risk." However, from a *kaupapa* Maori perspective, institutionalized ethics have done nothing to protect or empower the interests of Maori (Smith, 1999; Walker, Eketone, & Gibbs, 2006).

A few sentences is insufficient to explain what *kaupapa* Maori research is, and interested readers should consult "key explanatory" texts (e.g., Bishop, 2008; Cram, 2001; Smith, 1999, 2008). *Kaupapa* is a Maori term which loosely translates as "purpose" or "theme" and Walker et al. (2006) explain that:

> As a research strategy it is related to Maori ownership of knowledge, and acknowledging the validity of a Maori way of doing. Some commentators suggest it is unwise to try to define kaupapa Maori research because it is both more and less than a paradigm, a form of resistance and agency and a methodological strategy. (p. 333)

Epistemologically, *kaupapa* Maori research is positioned within the Maori worldview. This defines what knowledge is, how it should be used, and who has access to it. Genealogical and familial relationships are also central to this worldview, as are cultural protocols, and *te reo* (language) as it is only in *te reo* that Maori concepts are fully encapsulated.

Methodologically, *kaupapa* Maori research is governed by the principles of *tino rangatiratanga*—"sovereignty, self determination, governance, autonomy, and independence" (Walker et al., 2006, p. 333). This requires that:

> The research itself is driven by the participants in terms of setting the research questions, ascertaining the likely benefits, outlining the design of the work, undertaking the work that had to be done, distributing rewards, providing access to research findings, controlling the distribution of knowledge, and deciding to whom the researcher is accountable. (Bishop, 2008, p. 159)

Working within this methodology requires considerable time and dialogue with coresearcher participants and the ceding of power and control over the research, a factor which "mainstream" researchers might find too risky for their liking.

As a research methodology, *kaupapa* Maori offers considerable food for thought for both Excellence and critical public relations scholars, not because it provides anything that can easily be incorporated into these perspectives, but because, as a participatory paradigm, it challenges the dominant conceptions of the role of the researcher in the production of knowledge, worldviews, and how we understand what constitutes ethical practice. In professional and academic practices, what "ethical" means revolves around institutional codes of conduct, and in the "Excellence" project, around critiqued notions of symmetry. However, *kaupapa* Maori researchers stress the need to imagine ethics in much more extensive ways.

Smith (2008) writes that:

> For indigenous and other marginalized communities, research ethics is at a very basic level about establishing, maintaining, and nurturing reciprocal and respectful relationships, not just among people as individuals but also with people as individuals, as collectives, and as members of communities, and with humans who live in and with other entities in the environment. The abilities to enter preexisting relationships; to build, maintain, and nurture relationships; and to strengthen connectivity are important research skills in the indigenous arena. They require critical sensitivity and reciprocity of spirit by a researcher. (p. 128–129)

In several respects, this articulation of research ethics is similar to the dialogical communication approach to public relations ethics advocated by Kent and Taylor (2002). Smith's statement additionally advances an appreciation of how public relations might think about an *ethics of relationship building*. However, as an immense array of public relations research literature attests, not only that produced by critical theorists, but also those with extensive experience in the profession (e.g., Moloney, 2006), public relations is rarely practiced in either a dialogic or symmetrical way. Instead, it is strategically persuasive in intent, designed to benefit the (primarily economic) needs of the organization, and at the lowest cost.

There is also a further problem with the normative theory of public relations in terms of participatory ethics in its positioning the public relations executive within the organization's dominant coalition. While, as outlined above, this has been critiqued as managerialist, the conceptual intention was to provide the public relations function with the power to be heard and to "favorably influence organizational choices, ideology and practices" (Berger, 2005, p. 8). In this way, the public relations manager could encourage the organization to be morally and socially responsible. Pieczka (2006) has questioned this suggesting that "the manager appears to be in a position to *decide* what is in the public interest and what is ethically acceptable" (p. 352, emphasis added). Further, Berger's interviews with public relations executives identified how "a number of organizational constraints and a gendered dialectic in dominant coalitions curb their abilities to advocate effectively and do the right thing" (2005, p. 18). But he also encourages practitioners to take on activist roles in pushing organizations to be more socially accountable and transparent. Holtzhausen and Voto (2002), Holtzhausen, and Butta and Pal (in this volume) make a similar argument from a postmodern perspective. It may be through such "activism" that practitioners can steer organizations to better recognize the importance of participatory methodologies in how they dialogue with publics—not just indigenous or marginalized publics, but *all* publics. It might be contested that this empowers publics to the disadvantage of organizations, and there is no doubting that working from a participatory approach, such as *kaupapa* Maori, is expensive, complex, and time consuming (Comrie, Gilles, & Day, 2002). However, I would argue that we need to change our worldviews and with them the notion that organizations are accountable to shareholders, to one in which organizations and their shareholders are accountable to society at large. Furthermore, we need to value investments in deep and long-term relationship building rather than in short-term monetary gain.

There has been minimal research into how practitioners intersect with Maori in the development of public relations initiatives in New Zealand. What limited research is available suggests that practitioners are very aware of the need to construct culturally sensitive communications (Comrie et al., 2002; Comrie & Kupa, 1998/1999; Tipene-Leach, Abel, Haretuku, & Everard, 2000). However, there is little evidence that a full *kaupapa* Maori approach has been used in the development of campaigns. Rather, a culturally sensitive approach that recognizes the importance of face-to-face communication, the use of Maori media, and the involvement of Maori publics in the development and design of projects has been utilized. This represents good practice, but to empower publics requires much more than this.

Conclusion

Public relations practice and scholarship has increased exponentially in its complexity in the last two decades, and academic research has developed an extensive body of knowledge about this highly influential profession. The debates and tensions between Excellence theory and the critical paradigm have not always been constructive, but they have provoked greater depth of discussion about the discipline, its professional practice, research directions, and ethics. There is no doubt that we are better equipped to understand the contribution that public relations makes to supporting and shaping material and symbolic practices, what its cultural consequences are, and how culture in turn impacts on how public relations is conducted and theorized.

It is vital that we also understand the cultural worldviews that public relations theorists promote through their methodologies and research agendas. Too infrequently do theorists articulate these agendas in their research projects and resulting publications. As scholars we seek to understand the role that public relations plays in this globalizing world or encourage certain professional practices in that world, and equally, we also need to understand our scholarly contributions to globalization and its impacts. The articulation of *kaupapa* Maori perspectives is important here. They allow none of us to claim the intellectual high ground: Excellence and critical theorists alike are capable of contributing to the continuing colonization of cultures while they, ironically, celebrate new advances in theory and practice.

As globalization advances relentlessly onward, we need to put continuing thought into reimagining and articulating what the aims of public relations scholarship are in its many guises, whose purposes it serves, and to what extent it can enter a participatory paradigm. Through such endeavors, academic resources, and the methods we use can be put to work for, and empower those voices outside of academic institutions which are too infrequently heard.

To this end, the words of Abraham Lincoln's 1863 Gettysburg Address, which are a mantra for many indigenous groups, may resonate across all of our worldviews: "Of the people, by the people, for the people."

Discussion Questions

1. Why would researchers want to identify the contributions that public relations makes to the process of globalization?
2. Identify a global public relations campaign (for example, a petroleum company's promotion of its global corporate social responsibility program; or a fast food company's international promotion of healthy eating). Explain how the campaign could be researched (a) from an Excellence theory perspective, and (b) from a critical theory perspective.
3. From a critical theory perspective, is two-way symmetrical public relations achievable? If so how, and if not, why not?
4. Explain how a participatory framework, such as *kaupapa* Maori, could be used in the development of a public relations campaign.
5. Identify your own ontological worldview and how it informs your understanding and evaluation of public relations practice in a globalizing world.

References

Alasuutari, P. (Ed.). (1999). *Rethinking the media audience*. London: Sage.
Adorno, T. W. (1991). *The culture industry*. London: Routledge.
Adorno, T. W., & Horkheimer, M. (1998). *Dialectic of enlightenment*. G. S. Noerr (Ed.), E. Jephcott (Trans.). Stanford, CA: Stanford University Press. (Original work published 1944)

Bardhan, N. (2003). Rupturing public relations metanarratives: The example of India. *Journal of Public Relations Research, 15*(3), 225–248.

Bentele, G., & Wehmeier, S. (2009). Commentary: Linking sociology with public relations—Some critical thoughts in reflexive times. In Ø. Ihlen, B. van Ruler, & M. Fredriksson (Eds.), *Public relations and social theory: Key figures and concepts* (pp. 341–362). New York: Routledge.

Berger, B. K. (2005). Power over, power with, and power to relations: Critical reflections on public relations, the dominant coalition, and activism. *Journal of Public Relations Research, 17*(1), 5–28.

Bishop, R. (2008). Freeing ourselves from neocolonial domination in research: A kaupapa Maori approach to creating knowledge. In N. K. Denzin & Y. S. Lincoln (Eds.), *The landscapes of qualitative research* (3rd ed., pp. 145–183). Thousand Oaks, CA: Sage.

Burkart, R. (2009). On Habermas: Understanding and public relations. In Ø. Ihlen, B. van Ruler, & M. Fredriksson (Eds.), *Public relations and social theory: Key figures and concepts* (pp. 141–165). New York: Routledge.

Chapman, P. (2006, August 10). Violence is blamed on "warrior gene" in the Maoris. *The Daily Telegraph.* Retrieved from http://www.telegraph.co.uk/news/1526042/Violence-is-blamed-on-warrior-gene-in-the-Maoris.html

Cobb, S. (1994). A critique of critical discourse analysis: Deconstructing and reconstructing the role of intention. *Communication Theory, 4*(2), 132–152.

Comrie, M., Gillies, A., & Day, M. (2002). The Maori electoral option campaign: Problems of measuring "success." *Political Science, 54*(2), 45–57.

Comrie, M., & Kupa, R. (1998–1999). Communicating with Maori: Can public relations become bicultural? *Public Relations Quarterly, 43*(4), 42–46.

Coombs, W. T. (1993). Philosophical underpinnings: Ramifications of a pluralist paradigm. *Public Relations Review, 19*(2), 111–119.

Corp Watch. (n.d.). www.corpwatch.org

Cram, F. (2001). Rangahau Maori: Tona tika, tona pono—The validity and integrity of Maori research. In M. Tolich (Ed.), *Research ethics in Aotearoa New Zealand* (pp. 35–52). Auckland, New Zealand: Pearson Education.

Crampton, P., & Parkin, C. (2007). Warrior genes and risk taking. *The New Zealand Medical Journal.* Retrieved from http://www.nzma.org.nz/journal/120-1250/2439

Creedon, P. (1993). Acknowledging the infrasystem: A critical feminist analysis of systems theory. *Public Relations Review, 19*(2), 157–166.

Creedon, P., & Al-Khaja, M. (2005). Public relations and globalization: Building a case for cultural competency in public relations education. *Public Relations Review, 31*(3), 344–354.

Curtin, P., & Gaither, T. K. (2006). Contested notions of issue identity in international public relations: A case study. *Journal of Public Relations Research, 18*(1), 67–89.

Curtin, P. A., & Gaither, T. K. (2007). *International public relations: Negotiating culture, identity, and power.* Thousand Oaks, CA: Sage.

Deetz, S. (2005). Critical theory. In S. May & D. Mumby (Eds.), *Engaging organizational communication: Theory and research* (pp. 85–111). Thousand Oaks, CA: Sage.

Duffy, M. E. (2000). There's no two-way symmetric about it: A postmodern examination of public relations textbooks. *Critical Studies in Media Communication, 17*(3), 294–315.

Dutta, M. J. (2009). On Spivak: Theorizing resistance—Applying Gayatri Chakravorty in public relations. In Ø. Ihlen, B. van Ruler, & M. Fredriksson (Eds.), *Public relations and social theory* (pp. 278–300). New York: Routledge.

Ehling, W. P. (1992). Estimating the value of public relations and communication to an organization. In J. E. Grunig (Ed.), *Excellence in public relations and communication management* (pp. 617–638). Hillsdale, NJ: Erlbaum.

Excellence in public relations and communication management. (1991, September). *Executive summary/initial data report.* Retrieved from http://www.iabc.com/rf/pdf/Excellence.pdf

Fitzpatrick, K. R. (2006). Baselines for ethical advocacy in the "marketplace of ideas." In K. R. Fitzpatrick & C. Bronstein (Eds.), *Ethics in public relations: Responsible advocacy* (pp. 1–18). Thousand Oaks, CA: Sage.

Foley, D., & Valenzuela, A. (2008). Critical ethnography: The politics of collaboration. In N. K. Denzin & Y. S. Lincoln (Eds.), *The landscape of qualitative research* (3rd ed. pp. 287–310.). Thousand Oaks, CA: Sage.

Gaither, T. K., & Curtin, P. A. (2008). Examining the heuristic value of models of international public relations practice: A case study of the Arla Foods crisis. *Journal of Public Relations Research, 20*(1), 115–137.

Gower, K. K. (2006). Public relations research at the crossroads. *Journal of Public Relations Research, 18*(2), 177–190.

Grimshaw, C. (2007). A tour of the united Kingdom's public relations industry. In W. Dinan & D. Miller (Eds.), *Thinker, faker, spinner, spy* (pp. 33–50). London: Pluto Press.

Grunig, J. E. (2001). Two-way symmetrical public relations: Past, present, and future. In R. L. Heath (Ed.), *Handbook of public relations* (pp. 11–30). Thousand Oaks, CA: Sage.

Grunig J. E. (Ed.). (1992). *Excellence in public relations and communication management.* Hillsdale, NJ: Erlbaum.

Grunig, J. E., & Grunig, L. (2009). Public relations in the United States: A generation of maturation. In K. Sriramesh (Ed.), *The global public relations handbook: Theory, research and practice* (rev. ed., pp. 621–653). New York: Routledge.

Grunig, L. A., Grunig, J. E., & Ehling, W. P. (1992). What is an effective organization? In J. E. Grunig (Ed.), *Excellence in public relations and communication management* (pp. 65–90). Hillsdale, NJ: Erlbaum.

Guba, E. G., & Lincoln, Y. S. (2008). Paradigmatic controversies, contradictions, and emerging confluences. In N. K. Denzin & Y. S. Lincoln (Eds.), *The landscapes of qualitative research* (3rd ed., pp. 255–286). Thousand Oaks, CA: Sage.

Henderson, A. (2005). Activism in "Paradise": Identity management in a public relations campaign against genetic engineering. *Journal of Public Relations Research, 17*(1), 117–137.

Higginbottom, A. (2007). Killer coke. In W. Dinan & D. Miller (Eds.), *Thinker, faker, spinner, spy* (pp. 278–294). London: Pluto Press.

Hofstede, G. H. (1984). *Culture's consequences: International differences in work-related values* (abridged ed.). Beverly Hills, CA: Sage.

Hofstede, G. H. (1997). *Cultures and organizations, software of the mind: Intercultural cooperation and its importance for survival.* New York: McGraw-Hill.

Holtzhausen, D. R. (2000). Postmodern values in public relations. *Journal of Public Relations Research, 12*(1), 93–114.

Holtzhausen, D. R., & Voto, R. (2002). Resistance from the margins: The postmodern public relations practitioner as organizational activist. *Journal of Public Relations Research, 14*(1), 57–84.

Hook, G. R. (2009). "Warrior genes" and the disease of being Maori. *MAI Review, 2.* Retrieved from http://www.review.mai.ac.nz

Ihlen, Ø., & van Ruler, B. (2009). Introduction: Applying social theory to public relations. In Ø. Ihlen, B. van Ruler, & M. Fredriksson (Eds.), *Public relations and social theory: Key figures and concepts* (pp. 1–20). New York: Routledge.

Kang, D. S., & Mastin, T. (2008). How cultural difference affects international tourism public relations websites: A comparative analysis using Hofstede's cultural dimensions. *Public Relations Review, 34*(1), 54–56.

Kent, M. L., & Taylor, M. (2002). Toward a dialogic theory of public relations. *Public Relations Review, 28*(1), 21–37.

Khisty, C. J. (2006). Meditations on systems thinking, spiritual systems and deep ecology. *Systemic Practice and Action Research, 19*(4), 295–307.

Kincheloe, J. L., & McLaren, P. (2008). Rethinking critical theory and qualitative research. In N. K. Denzin & Y. S. Lincoln (Eds.), *The landscapes of qualitative research* (3rd ed., pp. 403–455). Thousand Oaks, CA: Sage.

King, M. (2004). *The Penguin history of New Zealand.* Auckland, New Zealand: Penguin.

Kitzinger, J. (2008). Audience understandings of AIDS media messages: A discussion of methods. *Sociology of Health and Illness, 12*(3), 319–335.

Knudson, J. W. (1998). Rebellion in Chiapas: Insurrection by Internet and public relations. *Media, Culture & Society, 20*(3), 507–518.

Lea, R., & Chambers, G. (2007). Monoamine oxidase, addiction and the "warrior" gene hypothesis. *Journal of the New Zealand Medical Association, 120,* 1250. Retrieved from http://www.nzma.org.nz/journal/120-1250/2441/

Leichty, G. (2003). The cultural tribes of public relations. *Journal of Public Relations Research, 15*(4), 277–304.

Leitch, S., & Neilson, D. (1997). Reframing public relations: New directions for theory and practice. *Australian Journal of Communication, 24*(2), 17–32.

L'Etang, J. (2005). Critical public relations: Some reflections. *Public Relations Review, 31*(4), 521–526.

Marcus, H. (1964/1991). *One dimensional man.* Boston, MA: Beacon Press.

McChesney, R. W. (1999). *Rich media, poor democracy: Communication politics in dubious times.* Urban, IL: University of Illinois Press.

McKie, D. (1997). Shifting paradigms: Public relations beyond rats, stats, and 1950s science. *Australian Journal of Communication, 24*(2), 81–96.

McKie, D., & Munshi, D. (2007). *Reconfiguring public relations: Ecology, equity, and enterprise.* London: Routledge.

Miller, D., & Dinan, W. (2000). The rise of the PR industry in Britain, 1979–1998. *European Journal of Communication, 15*(1), 5–35.

Miller, D., Kitzinger, J., Williams, K., & Beharell, P. (1998). *The circuit of mass communication.* Thousand Oaks, CA: Sage.

Molleda, J-C., Connolly-Ahern, C., & Quinn, C. (2005). Cross-national conflict shifting: Expanding a theory of global public relations management through quantitative content analysis. *Journalism Studies, 6*(1), 87–102.

Moloney, K. (2006). *Rethinking public relations* (2nd ed.). Abingdon, UK: Routledge.

Motion, J., & Leitch, S. (1996). A discursive perspective from New Zealand: Another world view. *Public Relations Review, 22*(3), 297–309.

Motion, J., Leitch, S., & Cliffe, S. (2009). Public relations in Australasia: Friendly rivalry, cultural diversity, and global focus. In K. Sriramesh (Ed.), *The global public relations handbook: Theory, research and practice* (rev. ed., pp. 101–121). New York: Routledge.

Motion, J., & Weaver, C. K. (2005). A discourse model for critical public relations research: The Life Sciences Network and the battle for truth. *Journal of Public Relations Research, 17*(1), 49–67.

Munshi, D., & Kurian, P. (2005). Imperializing spin cycles: A postcolonial look at public relations, greenwashing, and the separation of publics. *Public Relations Review, 31*(4), 513–520.

Pal, M., & Dutta, M. J. (2008). Public relations in a global context: The relevance of critical modernism as a theoretical lens. *Journal of Public Relations Research, 20*(2), 159–179.

Patwardhan, P., & Bardhan, N. (2006). The Bhopal Carbide disaster: A lesson in international crisis communication. In M. Parkinson & D. Ekachai (Eds.), *International and intercultural public relations: A campaign case approach* (pp. 220–238). Boston, MA: Pearson Education/Allyn & Bacon.

Pieczka, M. (2006). Paradigms, systems theory, and public relations. In J. L'Etang & M. Pieczka (Eds.), *Public relations: Critical debates and contemporary practice* (pp. 333–357). London: Erlbaum.

Plowman, K. D. (2005). Systems theory. In R. L. Heath (Ed.), *Encyclopedia of public relations* (Vol. 2, pp. 839–842). Thousand Oaks, CA: Sage.

Press, A., & Livingstone, S. (2006). Taking audience research into the age of new media: Old problems and new challenges. In M. White & J. Schwoch (Eds.), *Questions of method in cultural studies* (pp. 175–200). Malden, MA. Blackwell.

PR Watch. (n.d.). Http://www.prwatch.org

Sardar, Z. (1998). *Postmodernism and the other: The new imperialism of western culture.* London: Pluto Press.

Schuster, J. A., & Yeo, R. R. (1986). Introduction. In J. A. Schuster & R. R. Yeo (Eds.), *The politics and rhetoric of scientific method* (pp. ix–xxxvii). Dordrecht, Holland: D. Reidel.

Shugart, H. A. (2003). An appropriating aesthetic: Reproducing power in the discourse of critical scholarship. *Communication Theory, 13*(3), 275–303.

Sklair, L. (2007). Achilles has two heels: Crises of capitalist globalization. In W. Dinan & D. Miller (Eds.), *Thinker, faker, spinner, spy* (pp. 21–32). London: Pluto Press.

Smith, L. T. (1999). *Decolonizing methodologies: Research and indigenous peoples*. London: Zed Books.

Smith, L. T. (2008). On tricky ground: Researching the native in the age of uncertainty. In N. K. Denzin & Y. S. Lincoln (Eds.), *The landscapes of qualitative research* (3rd ed., pp. 113–143). Thousand Oaks, CA: Sage.

Spinwatch. (n.d.). www.spinwatch.org

Sriramesh, K. (2009a). The relationship between culture and public relations. In K. Sriramesh (Ed.), *The global public relations handbook: Theory, research and practice* (rev. ed., pp. 47–61). New York: Routledge.

Sriramesh, K. (2009b). Introduction. In K. Sriramesh (Ed.), *The global public relations handbook: Theory, research and practice* (rev. ed., pp. xxxiii–xl). New York: Routledge.

Sriramesh, K., Grunig, J. E., & Buffington, J. (1992). Corporate culture and public relations. In J. E. Grunig (Ed.), *Excellence in public relations and communication management* (pp. 577–595). Hillsdale, NJ: Erlbaum.

Sriramesh, K., & White, J. (1992). Social culture and public relations. In J. E. Grunig (Ed.), *Excellence in public relations and communication management* (pp. 597–614). Hillsdale, NJ: Erlbaum.

Tipene-Leach, D. C., Abel, S., Haretuku, R., & Everard, C. (2000) The Maori SIDS prevention programme: Challenges and implications for Maori health service developments. *Social Policy Journal of New Zealand, 14*, 65–77.

Tyma, A. (2008). Public relations through a new lens: Critical praxis via the "Excellence Theory." *International Journal of Communication, 2*, 193–205.

Vasquez, G. M., & Taylor, M. (1999). What cultural values influence American public relations practitioners? *Public Relations Review, 25*(4), 433–449.

Walker, S., Eketone, E., & Gibbs, A. (2006). An exploration of kaupapa Maori research, its principles, processes and applications. *International Journal of Social Research Methodology, 9*(4), 331–344.

Weaver, C. K. (2001). Dressing for battle in the new global economy: Putting power, identity, and discourse into public relations theory. *Management Communication Quarterly, 15*(2), 279–288.

Weaver, C. K. (2010). Carnivalesque activism as a public relations genre: A case study of the New Zealand group Mothers Against Genetic Engineering. *Public Relations Review, 36*(1), 35–41.

Weaver, C. K., & Motion, J. (2002). Sabotage and subterfuge: Public relations, democracy and genetic engineering in New Zealand. *Media, Culture & Society, 24*(3), 325–343.

Weaver, C. K., Motion, J., & Roper, J. (2006). From propaganda to discourse (and back again): Truth, power, the public interest and public relations. In J. L'Etang & M. Pieczka (Eds.), *Public relations: Critical debates and contemporary practice* (pp. 7–21). London: Erlbaum.

Wehmeier, S. (2006). Dancers in the dark: The myth of rationality in public relations. *Public Relations Review, 32*(3), 213–220.

Witmer, D. F. (2006). Overcoming system and culture boundaries: Public relations from a structuration perspective. In C. Botan & V. Hazleton (Eds.), *Public relations theory* (Vol. 2, pp. 361–374). Mahwah, NJ: Erlbaum.

Yannas, P. (2006, May). *PR theory in the age of globalization.* Paper presented at the annual meeting of the International Communication Association,

Dresden International Congress Centre, Dresden, Germany. Retrieved from http://www.allacademic.com/meta/p91462_index.html.

Suggested Readings

Cottle, S. (Ed.). (2003). *News, public relations and power.* London: Sage.

Hager, N., & Burton, B. (1999). *Secrets and lies: The anatomy of an anti-environmental PR campaign.* Nelson, New Zealand: Craig Potton.

Stauber, J., & Rampton, S. (1995). *Toxic sludge is good for you—Lies, damn lies and the public relations industry.* New York: Common Courage Press.

Stauber, J., & Rampton, S. (2002). *Trust us, we're the experts: How industry manipulates science and gambles with your future.* New York: Tarcher/Penguin.

Sussman, G. (2007). Globalizing politics: Spinning US "democracy assistance" programmes. In W. Dinan & D. Miller (Eds.), *Thinker, faker, spinner, spy* (pp. 175–195). London: Pluto Press.

Author Index

Subject Index